*YOU HAVE LIVED BEFORE —AND WILL LIVE AGAIN

This is just one of the messages from Michael, an ancient entity that can unlock the wisdom of the ages. You will not fail to be amazed—or moved. Dispelling our fear and satisfying our curiosity, Michael's messages fortify our hope that there is a meaning to life.

* **TRUTH IS THE GREATEST GOOD, AND LOVE IS THE HIGHEST TRUTH.**

* **ALMOST ALL PHOBIAS ARE TRAUMAS REMEMBERED FROM A FORMER LIFE.**

* **BELIEF IS NOT REQUIRED: YOU WILL REINCARNATE, ANYWAY. A LEAF DOES NOT HAVE TO BELIEVE IN PHOTOSYNTHESIS TO TURN GREEN.**

* **PLEASE BELIEVE US WHEN WE TELL YOU THAT THERE IS NO ONE "OUT THERE" WHEN YOU EXIT WHO WILL ASK YOU IF YOU WERE AN EPISCOPALIAN.**

Michael speaks, we listen—but tomorrow we may be the speakers ourselves. Life is without end, and to read MESSAGES FROM MICHAEL is to have access to all eternity.

"An astonishing account."—FORECAST

MESSAGES FROM MICHAEL

CHELSEA QUINN YARBRO

BERKLEY BOOKS, NEW YORK

MESSAGES FROM MICHAEL

A Berkley Book / published by arrangement with
the author

PRINTING HISTORY
PBJ Books edition / October 1980
Berkley edition / April 1983
Fourth printing / January 1986

ISBN: 0-425-09349-2

*For all those who have had
messages from Michael*

Author's Note

The following material has been compiled from the transcripts of literally thousands of hours of mediumistic dictation beginning almost a decade ago. For the sake of the privacy of the medium, her family, and her many associates, all names have been changed, except the name of the entity with whom the medium has been in contact. The opinions and comments given by the entity Michael appear in caps and small caps and are entirely those of the entity. They do not necessarily agree with the attitudes, opinions, convictions, or beliefs of anyone else connected with this book.

Contents

9

Preface

Occult studies have always fascinated me: for more than twenty years I've been actively interested in the field, and for the last eighteen, I have practiced certain of the less strenuous disciplines, such as tarot card reading and palmistry. For a little more than four years I read cards at the Magic Cellar, a San Francisco nightclub devoted mainly to stage magic, now unfortunately closed. I've also experimented with alchemy in conjunction with writing a series of historical horror novels, published by St. Martin's Press and New American Library.

For the most part I avoid other occultists, particularly those who put the emphasis on the window-dressing aspect of their studies. I also dislike the generally manipulative attitude and dogmatic approach of occult groups.

My introduction to the woman I call Jessica Lansing in this book had nothing to do with the occult, and nothing to do with my writing. She and I share an intense interest in music, and it was through musical activities that we met. I did not know about her occult interests and she did not know about mine until we had been acquainted for almost a year. At that time I gave her passes to the Magic Cellar, and during the evening, read her cards. It was roughly two months later that I attended my first session at her home.

At first I was dubious about what she was doing. It seemed so easy and so pat. She had, of course, a great deal of practice and familiarity with her technique as well as the inner discipline of concentration that enabled her to work for hours without any visible sign of fatigue. Her group was also interesting because the members were neither the credulous acolytes that mark a great many such groups, nor upper middle-class dabblers after an extra thrill. The people were professionals, calm, sensible, and questioning. They checked out Michael's facts and challenged them. I liked that. There was no religious devotion to the teaching, only a careful exploration. I liked that. The emphasis was on understanding and clarity. I liked that. And Michael has an acerbic wit, which delighted me.

Inevitably the question arises: do I believe it? The only answer I can give is: sometimes. Certainly Michael has an uncanny ability to pick out significant moments in my life and has identified the times in the historical past to which I am most drawn. It could be that Jessica is a very skillful telepath. It could be that she is creating this, after exhaustive study, out of whole cloth. But I don't think that's the case. Whatever it is she does, she does it legitimately. She has got information about people that she doesn't know and that I don't know and the response has been positive. For example, one of my friends, knowing that I was attending these sessions, told me that her cousin Sunny had written to her: Sunny had a new male friend she couldn't make up her mind about, and was seeking advice. I did not know Sunny or the man involved. However, I took the question to the session and was given the following answer by Michael:

THE MAN IN QUESTION HAS AN AGREEMENT WITH THE LADY LENORE. THE AGREEMENT INVOLVES THE FURTHERING OF AN INTELLECTUAL PROJECT. WE WOULD DOUBT THAT ANYTHING OF AN INTIMATE NATURE WOULD COME OF THIS ASSOCIATION; HOWEVER IT WILL GREATLY HELP BOTH OF THEM IN THE COMPLETION OF THEIR LIFE TASKS.

I relayed this answer to my friend. As it turns out, she did not pass it on to her cousin because, she said, she was chicken to admit she had asked a Ouija board about it. Six months later, the cousin and the man opened an art gallery in San Diego, and their partnership has been financially and professionally successful. Incidentally, the cousin *is* named Lenore, but usually goes by her nickname, Sunny, because the aunt for whom she is named is still alive.

No, I can't explain it.

There have been psychic researchers who have investigated these sessions, and they, too, vouch for Jessica's legitimacy. Whatever she is doing, and whoever she has contact with, there is no fakery involved.

This book came out of ten special sessions and the transcripts of eight years of general sessions. Those transcripts cover three thousand typed pages and the number is increasing. I have made every attempt to present the material as directly and as uncomplicatedly as possible. I have not changed anything Michael has said, although I have often reduced several of the group's questions to one question in order to avoid confusion. When that occurs in the text, there are no quotations around the question, indicating that it is a simplification of a number of related questions.

At this time I would like to give special thanks to the fourteen members of the Michael group who gave generously of their time and allowed me to use their material as well as themselves (with changed names) in the text. Gratitude is also due Sharon Jarvis, my editor at Playboy Press, who has been unstinting in her encouragement; to Terry Garey, who helped me organize the material; to Lyndall MacCowan, who prepared the manuscript and found her way through more than a thousand file cards; and most particularly, a great deal of thanks to Jessica Lansing for making all her records and her special gift available to Michael and to this book.

CHELSEA QUINN YARBRO
Albany, California
October 1978

Chapter 1

THE FIRST SESSION:
INTRODUCTION TO MICHAEL

WE ARE HERE WITH YOU TONIGHT.

With that phrase the entity known as Michael introduced himself to Jessica Lansing on a pleasant night in October of 1970. Jessica, then thirty-two, is a publicist by profession, a well-educated woman with an extensive background in the arts, religion, psychology, and history. Her husband, Walter, is a building contractor; a pleasant-faced man with an abiding interest in all aspects of engineering. On that particular evening, they were entertaining a number of dinner guests including Craig and Emily Wright. There were four other guests, but they were not to participate in the extraordinary event that would occur.

Jessica and Walter Lansing had long been interested in parapsychology and psychic studies and occasionally tried their hands at different techniques, but with no significant results. On that October night they had decided to try the Ouija board that Jessica had been given as a gift. The dinner party was not going well; the mixture of guests had not "clicked."

The Wrights were interested in the Ouija board. Walter thought it might be fun, and it was easier to try that than to dream up conversation. Besides, Jessica had been curious about the board for some time.

"I had my doubts about the board, of course," Jessica says now very matter-of-factly. "Sometimes I still do. What startled me at first was that it was so *unexpected*."

They did not really expect anything to happen as they sat at the dining room table with the board between Jessica and Walter, their fingers placed lightly on the planchette, waiting for something to happen. There were a few random movements of the planchette, and what might have been letters indicated were faithfully read off and written down by Emily Wright. All in all, it did not seem very exciting, and they began to relax, and as Jessica herself says now, "We decided that it didn't matter; nothing had happened and nothing was going to happen. I was beginning to wonder if we ought to put away the board and play cards. Two other guests, Leah and Arnold Harris, were good at canasta."

This letting go of expectations, although Jessica did not realize it then, was crucial to opening up that part of her mind through which the entity Michael operates. That night she had ceased to want the board to work, her mind was open and, though alert, it was wandering somewhat. Walter, too, was becoming restless and their other guests were talking quietly over coffee in the living room while Craig and Emily sat with Jessica and Walter in the dining room. They were comfortable and very much at ease, not upset or hostile.

It was then that the planchette began to move, slowly at first, and then briskly. The words were spelled out, and the message read: WE ARE HERE WITH YOU TONIGHT.

Reaction ranged from derision to confusion to curiosity. Walter was quite disturbed, insisting that he had had no part in that comment, that the planchette had just "moved." He thought that Jessica might have done it, but she insisted that if anyone had, it was Walter. Emily was the one who thought to ask who "WE" might be.

Jessica was reluctant to try the board again after so unexpected a response. Walter was unsure that it was a good idea to ask any more questions as they might be tampering with persons or forces they had no desire to deal with. This sentiment was echoed by Craig, who was immediately suspicious of the message. "Besides," he recalls, "all I could

think of at the time was what it might say. There might be
someone there with hidden anger or malice who would want
this kind of outlet—a safe way to express what they would
not say in words." Did Craig have anyone in particular in
mind? "No. I knew Jessica and Walter fairly well, but the
other two couples I'd met only once or twice before." Then
why did he have this reaction? "Well, if there's one thing
I've learned in my practice as a surgeon," he says, "it's
that people *will* find a way to express what's frightening
them or angering them. Often it comes out in illness. jit's
one of the most difficult problems doctors have to deal with.
Michael has warned us about this tendency many times.
Many illnesses have psychosomatic origins, and with something as chancy as a Ouija board, well, I was suspicio.is—
let's put it that way."

Jessica chuckles. "What Craig means is that he didn't
believe a word of it. He was certain that Walter or I had
done something."

"Not consciously," Craig protests.

"That doesn't make it any better," Jessica retorts. "The
funny thing is," she continues reflectively, "that Craig was
the one who was most anxious to go on. I was scared and
Walter was reluctant and Emily was alarmed, but that skeptic over there"—she nods toward Craig—"he was all for
it."

Finally curiosity overcame their reluctance and Jessica
took her place at the table again, opposite her husband, her
hands on one side of the planchette and Walter's on the
other. Very hesitantly they asked who or what was speaking
through the board.

You MAY CALL US ANYTHING YOU WISH.

"We were nonplussed," Walter says. "None of us knew
what to say to that, but even though I felt damned silly, I
asked the board what we would call it if we wanted to make
contact with it again. Was there some name that whatever-
it-was would accept?"

THE LAST NAME A FRAGMENT OF THIS ENTITY USED WAS
MICHAEL.

"Entity? Fragment?" Jessica said, somewhat puzzled.
"What does that mean?"

Craig and Emily, who were sitting at the head of the table,
had no answer.

"Do you think this Michael-thing will explain?" Emily asked, looking up from her notebook where she had been writing down the responses as Jessica read the letters off the board.

"I hope so," Walter said.

The other two couples had retreated to the living room and were enjoying an after-dinner drink, rather pointedly ignoring what was happening in the dining room.

"I realized that we weren't being very sociable," Jessica recalls, "but I really wanted to hear the explanation."

The explanation took some time, and Jessica began to get a headache as she followed the movement of the planchette around the board. Walter said little, only calling out the letters as the little plastic device hovered over one after another.

EACH SOUL IS A PART OF A LARGER BODY, AN ENTITY. EACH ENTITY IS MADE UP OF ABOUT ONE THOUSAND SOULS, EACH OF WHICH ENTERS THE PHYSICAL PLANE AS MANY TIMES AS IS NECESSARY TO EXPERIENCE ALL ASPECTS OF LIFE AND ACHIEVE HUMAN UNDERSTANDING. AT THE END OF THE CYCLES ON THE PHYSICAL PLANE, THE FRAGMENTS ONCE AGAIN REUNITE AS WE HAVE REUNITED.

"It's a kind of astral guru," Emily said, not quite sure she believed it.

WE ARE OF THE MID-CAUSAL PLANE, was the prompt correction. THE ASTRAL PLANE IS ACCESSIBLE TO THE PHYSICAL PLANE. WE ARE NOT.

"I guess that tells us," Jessica said, thinking that this would be the end of it. "Then," she recalls, "I had a strange sensation at the back of my head. It seemed to go down my shoulders and into my arms. My hands felt prickly, as if I were about to break out in hives. I must have turned pale, too, because Walter was alarmed and suggested that we stop."

"But this was just getting interesting," Emily had said, beginning to enjoy herself.

"I was somewhat upset," Jessica says now, remembering that evening, "and probably rather frightened." Just probably? "Well," she says reasonably, "that was some time ago, and I've had a lot of time to get used to Michael. He certainly doesn't frighten me now. But that first evening, I was probably scared. It *was* alarming, sitting there with this board and planchette, getting words that made sense that I didn't have any control over."

Jessica decided to continue working with the board a little longer. Emily and Craig had paper and pens now, and were writing as the information came. After some misgivings, Walter agreed to keep at it a little longer.

"OK, then, if you aren't an astral plane guru, what are you?" Walter demanded.

WE ARE NOT THE PATH TO SPIRITUAL ENLIGHTENMENT. WE OFFER A WAY TO HUMAN UNDERSTANDING BASED ON OUR OWN EXPERIENCE, FIRST AS HUMANS OURSELVES IN BOTH TROUBLED AND TRANQUIL TIMES AND NOW AS THE REINTEGRATED FRAGMENTS OF A CAUSAL BODY NO LONGER ALIVE AS YOU KNOW IT BUT STILL WITH KEEN AWARENESS OF WHAT BEING HUMAN ENTAILS.

"Does that mean that you have the answer to enlightenment? That seems kind of farfetched," Craig remarked as he finished writing down the dictated letters.

The answer came promptly: WE ARE NOT THE PATH. WE ARE AN ANCIENT ENTITY THAT COMES TO ALL WHO ASK. OUR PURPOSE IS TO TEACH SOME UNDERSTANDING OF THE EVOLUTION ON THE PHYSICAL PLANE SO THAT THE STUDENT CAN REACH SOME INSIGHT INTO HUMAN BEHAVIOR WHICH WILL ENABLE HIM THEN TO STOP BROODING OVER INTERPERSONAL RELATIONSHIPS OR THE LACK THEREOF AND CONCENTRATE ON PERSONAL LIFE PLANS.

"Sounds like merit badges," one of the other guests said sarcastically. He had come back into the dining room and had been listening. "Are you going to keep at this nonsense much longer? Doris and I were hoping you'd have time to talk about the room addition, Walter."

This very definite disapproval made the four at the dining table suddenly uncomfortable. Walter hesitated, because, as he admits now, "What the board was saying was fascinating. I wasn't sure I liked it, but I knew damn well that I had a lot more questions I wanted to ask." Nevertheless, being a good host, he left the dining room and went to talk with the two couples in the living room.

"I wish he didn't act like that," Jessica sighed, meaning their guest. "He's always putting down anything psychic. He insists there's nothing to it, and then refuses to examine any information that might prove him wrong."

Emily looked at the Ouija board. "I wonder what Michael has to say about that?" She was not more than half serious, but Jessica said, "Walter's not here."

Craig said he'd work the other half of the board; after an initial hesitancy, Jessica agreed. Craig took Walter's chair and Emily waited with her pen poised.

HUMAN BEHAVIOR AT TIMES DEFIES UNDERSTANDING UNTIL A TEACHER CAN BRING THIS UNDERSTANDING ABOUT; THEN THE STUDENT MUST AGREE THAT THE TEACHER'S WORDS ARE RIGHT AND TRUE. IN OTHER WORDS, THE STUDENT MUST REALIZE WITHIN HIMSELF THAT THE TEACHING IS TRUE. UNDERSTANDING OCCURS WHEN THE STUDENT CAN GO ON TO AGAPE [the Greek concept of selfless and nonsexually expressed unconditional love], WHICH IS THE GOAL.

"Are you saying you are that kind of teacher?" Jessica asked. She says now that she was both enthusiastic and frightened at what Michael's response might be.

YES. The next part of the message came slowly, and with many long pauses. "It happens sometimes," Jessica says philosophically. "There are many things that Michael has trouble expressing in words, and when that happens, the letters come with difficulty."

IF ONE IS TO SEEK THE PATH TO SPIRITUAL ENLIGHTENMENT ONE MUST FIRST BECOME AWARE OF ONE'S OWN INNER HUMANNESS AND EXPLOIT THIS TO ITS FULLEST. IF ONE IS TO SEEK THE HIGHEST TRUTH OF ALL, ONE MUST FIRST BE ABLE TO RECOGNIZE WHAT IS FALSE—IN OTHER WORDS, THE LIES MUST BE TOLD BEFORE THE TRUTH CAN BE SOUGHT. IN ORDER TO UNDERSTAND, THERE MUST BE AGREEMENT ON ALL LEVELS. LOVE IS THE TRUTH TOWARD WHICH WE ALL ASPIRE. IN THIS WE INCLUDE OURSELVES AND OTHER ENTITIES LIKE OURSELVES STILL SEEKING.

"But *why*?" Jessica asked helplessly when the message had been read back to her. Even at the time, she observed, "That's one of the big ones," with an uncertain laugh. She has said that she did not seriously expect an answer, but the planchette moved again.

THERE IS NO EXALTED PURPOSE BEHIND HUMAN LIFE. THE LIFE ITSELF IS THE PURPOSE AND IS ONLY ONE STAGE OF EVOLUTION, WHICH PROCEEDS IN AN AWESOMELY ORDERED, UNALTERABLE LINE UNTIL THE CREATED IN EFFECT

EVOLVES TO BECOME THE CREATOR. WE PREFER NOT TO USE THE WORD GOD IN SPEAKING OF THE ULTIMATE CREATIVE FORCE OF THE UNIVERSE.

"You don't call it *God,*" Craig said. "I'm an agnostic, but I don't object to the word. Why don't you use it?"

PRIMARILY BECAUSE THE WORD GOD IN YOUR SOCIETY HAS BECOME MASCULINIZED AND REQUIRES THE USE OF THE MASCULINE PRONOUN, THUS PERPETUATING THE PERSONIFICATION OF THE UNIVERSAL CREATIVE FORCE, WHICH IS ETHEREAL AND NOT PHYSICAL. THIS CANNOT BE PERSONIFIED, EVEN FOR TEACHING PURPOSES WITH THIS CADRE [the groups of students in contact with the entity Michael]. IT WOULD BE TREADING ON THIN ICE FOR THIS ENTITY. FOR US, THIS TEACHING IS A FORM OF EVOLUTION. UNFORTUNATELY THE WORD GOD GIVES RISE TO ANTHROPOMORPHIC FANTASIES THAT HAVE NO PLACE IN THIS TEACHING. FOR OUR PURPOSES WE SHALL CALL THIS CONSTANT CREATIVE FORCE THE TAO, FOR IT IS IMPOSSIBLE FOR THE WESTERN MIND TO CONSTRUCT ANY VISUAL IMAGE AROUND THIS WORD.

"What on earth is he talking about?" Emily asked when she had read back the answer. "The Tao. That's Chinese, meaning the *way,* isn't it?" She looked toward Craig for help.

Michael was the one to answer her question, somewhat obliquely.

FROM THIS TAO COMES ALL THINGS PHYSICAL AND NONPHYSICAL; TO THIS TAO MUST ALL THINGS RETURN, EACH IN HIS TIME AND ONLY WHEN EACH HAS EVOLVED TO THAT POINT.

Jessica stopped and said that she wanted a cup of coffee. "I felt very spacey that night," she says now. "I thought I was in another world, and I suppose in a way I was. I kept thinking that none of it should be happening. And I wondered, 'why me?' I mean, look at me. I'm a sensible married woman. I'm forty. I've got a teen-aged daughter. I work in public relations. I'm not exactly the sort of woman usually exploring the occult."

It is easy to agree with Jessica Lansing. She sits in her high-ceilinged living room dressed in a neat suit. Her hair is light brown, a short pageboy cut. She is wearing a pair of jade earrings, but none of the bangles, bracelets, or shawls that one usually associates with many of those pursuing the occult. She is an attractive woman, not much different from those who live in the other houses on this woodsy hill. Her hazel eyes are direct and intelligent; she has a ready laugh and a subdued charm.

"You know, when Michael said that there was no way to end the cycles prematurely, I was shocked. I'd read some of the Hindu religious writings, and I remembered what had been said about that. The worship of Kali is supposed to extinguish the soul once and for all. Buddhism also teaches that the soul wants to return to Nirvana and be free of the burdens of rebirth. This seemed a direct contradiction of what I had read."

There were more contradictions to come, over the years. That night, Michael explained:

THERE IS NO PREMATURE RETURN TO THE TAO. EVOLUTION IS AN EXTREMELY SLOW AND PAINSTAKING PROCESS, FOR ONLY PERFECTION BECOMES THE STUFF OF WHICH UNIVERSES ARE MADE. WE ARE FAR FROM THAT PERFECTION, EVEN ON OUR EXALTED PLANE: WE CANNOT EVEN DEFINE PERFECTION WHICH IS THE END POINT OF EVOLUTION. WE CAN ONLY KNOW THAT IT EXISTS BECAUSE WE SENSE A HIGHER STATE IN THOSE ABOVE US, JUST AS YOU CAN ONLY SENSE HIGHER CENTERS IN EXALTED SOULS ON YOUR PLANET.

"But if that's the case," Craig objected, "then what are we doing here?"

HUMAN UNDERSTANDING IS THE LESSON OF THE PHYSICAL PLANE; WITHOUT IT, THERE CAN BE NO GROWTH OF THE SOUL. TO STRIVE FOR SPIRITUAL ENLIGHTENMENT WITHOUT GAINING HUMAN UNDERSTANDING IS TO DISREGARD THE REAL PURPOSE OF YOUR EXISTENCE ON THE PHYSICAL PLANE. WE CANNOT STRESS THIS ENOUGH. TO THIS END, WE MAKE THIS TEACHING AVAILABLE TO ALL WHO ASK.

Walter, who had just seen the other four guests out the door, came back into the dining room. "I think they're annoyed with us," he said mildly. "It probably wasn't very wise of us to get so caught up in this stuff while they were here."

The others had to agree. "One of those women hasn't spoken to me since," Jessica says, a trace of a frown between her brows. "I know it was rude of us to ignore them as we did, but this seemed so much more *important* than an evening of whist." She pauses a moment with the beginnings of a smile on her face. "Well, now that I think about it, this *was* much more important than whist. I wish they hadn't felt so . . . threatened by what we were doing. There's nothing to be afraid of in what Michael has to say. It doesn't always make you happy, but there's nothing to fear in it." She sounds a little defensive as she speaks and her well-manicured hands tighten on the arms of her bentwood rocking chair. "I wish more people were willing to accept this material. I never talk about this at work. It's unfortunate that this has to be so secretive. But my boss wouldn't know how to handle this, if he was aware of it. And it could be so *useful*."

That first night none of the four anticipated that these sessions would become a regular part of their lives, taking up many hours, and with transcriptions running over two thousand pages.

"It seemed like one glorious chance, and so I stayed at the board with Walter or Craig much longer than I should have. I've learned now that there's a time to stop. That night, I thought I'd never have another session, and that I'd have to get everything I could at once."

It was Craig who asked how Michael saw himself.

THIS ENTITY PERCEIVES ITSELF AS A PART OF THE GREATER WHOLE THAT IS THE ONENESS. THIS ENTITY ALSO PERCEIVES ALL OF ITS FRAGMENTS MAKING UP THE WHOLE, MUCH AS YOU PERCEIVE THE INDIVIDUAL PARTS OF THE ANATOMIC STRUCTURE. WE WOULD HAVE TO, AT THIS POINT IN OUR OWN EVOLUTION, AGREE THAT THERE IS A PERVASIVE COSMIC AWARENESS THAT IS CERTAINLY PRESENT AT THE TAO. IT IS EXTREMELY DOUBTFUL, HOWEVER, THAT THOSE LOFTY ENTITIES ON THE BUDDHIC PLANE REALLY LONG FOR THE PERSONALITIES THEY LEFT BEHIND AEONS AGO. WHAT IS LOST IS NOT THE PERCEPTION OF SELF—WHAT IS LOST IS THE PERSONALITY'S PERCEPTION OF THE APARTNESS, THE SEPARATENESS WHICH IS AN ILLUSION OF THE PHYSICAL PLANE.

THIS ENTITY DOES NOT PERCEIVE THE APARTNESS THAT YOU FEEL WHEN YOU ARE COMMUNICATING WITH OTHERS. YOU PERCEIVE IT BECAUSE YOU ARE CAUGHT IN THE ARTI-

FICIAL LIMITATIONS OF THE SOLID, RIGID, SPACE-TIME CON-
TINUATION OF THE PHYSICAL PLANE.

Jessica herself was the one who asked about that. "You make it sound as if reality isn't very dependable."

THE REALITIES, OF COURSE, DEPEND UPON THE PER-CEIVER. THIS SESSION ITSELF IS A GOOD EXAMPLE. SOME IN THIS ROOM PERCEIVE US AS REAL. OTHERS DO NOT. THE SAME COULD BE SAID OF UNIDENTIFIED FLYING OBJECTS AND OTHER UNEXPLAINED PHENOMENA. ANOTHER CON-CEPT OF REALITY BEGINS WITH THE WIDESPREAD AGREE-MENT THAT A CERTAIN OBJECT IS "REAL." WE THINK THAT BISHOP BERKELEY HAD A FEW WORDS ON THIS SUBJECT. THERE IS, OF COURSE, AN ULTIMATE REALITY THAT IS AB-SOLUTE. THIS CAN ONLY BE GLIMPSED WHEN THE LOGOS IS BROUGHT TO BEAR. PHYSICAL THINGS ARE VERY REAL ON THE PHYSICAL PLANE, AND SHOULD BE RESPECTED AS SUCH IN ORDER TO AVOID POSSIBLE SERIOUS COLLISIONS WITH DOORS THAT ARE REALLY AND TRULY THERE. ON THE AS-TRAL, THINGS ARE TRULY REAL ON THE ASTRAL PLANE. IN ANOTHER FRAME OF REFERENCE THE SAME ADMONITION HOLDS TRUE. WE ON THIS PLANE ALSO PERCEIVE CERTAIN CAUSAL PHENOMENA AS REAL, AND THERE IS AGREEMENT. WE BELIEVE THAT HOLDS TRUE FOR THE HIGH PLANES. THIS SAME SUBJECT HAS BEEN OCCUPYING PHILOSOPHERS HAP-PILY NOW FOR MANY THOUSANDS OF YEARS. THERE IS, ODDLY ENOUGH, ALWAYS AN OPPOSING OPINION THAT GOES SOMETHING LIKE—ACCEPT THAT NOTHING IS REAL. DOES THIS SUGGEST ANYTHING TO YOU?

"But we're reasoning beings," Walter protested. "We need a rational world. If any of this is valid, what does that do to reason?"

REASON. MAN HAS ALWAYS ENDEAVORED THROUGH THE CREATION OF CHAOS, OR OF A CHAOTIC SYSTEM (THEY'RE ONE AND THE SAME), TO CREATE THE ILLUSION OF COM-PLEXITY WHICH EXISTS ON THE PHYSICAL PLANE. THIS IL-LUSION OF COMPLEXITY, THAT WHICH WE CHOOSE TO CALL FALSE ORDER, BY ITS VERY CHAOTIC NATURE CREATES OR-DER OF A SORT EASILY INCORPORATED INTO THE BELIEF SYSTEMS OF THOSE WHO ARE LIMITED TO IT. THE CONCEPT OF A PHYSICAL GOD WAS CREATED OUT OF THIS VERY CHAOS—THE NECESSITY TO SOLIDIFY. THE SOLIDIFICATION OF THE COSMOS—IN AN IRONIC SENSE, IS TRUE, OF COURSE.

SINCE THERE IS NO SUCH THING AS NOTHING . . . NO-THING. BUT THE SOLIDIFICATION OF THE COSMOS IS MAN'S FIRST STEP TOWARD EXPLAINING AWAY THOSE UNEXPLAINABLE PHENOMENA WITH WHICH HE IS CONFRONTED WHEN HE FIRST CONFRONTS THE PHYSICAL UNIVERSE. HE MUST, OF COURSE, REDUCE IT TO THE SMALLEST POSSIBLE LIMITS.

Emily had said little during the session, but there was something disturbing her and finally she talked about it. "I'm a fairly religious person," she remarked, "and it sounds to me as if Michael is making antireligious statements. That troubles me. If there's only this Tao he talks about, where does that leave me?"

YOU, EMILY, HAVE ACCEPTED RESTRICTIONS THAT YOU DO NOT NEED. YOUR SOUL DOES NOT SEEK AN ANTHROPO-MORPHIC GOD. THE SOUL HAS SEARCHED THROUGH THE AGES FOR TRUTH. THE SCHOLAR HAS SOUGHT TO INTELLEC-TUALIZE ALL EXPERIENCES OF ECSTASY AND HAS THERE-FORE DENIED THE EXPERIENCE. BEING NOW IN TOUCH, HOWEVER TIMOROUSLY, WITH TRUTH, IS BOTH THREATEN-ING AND INCREDIBLY INVITING. TO ALLOW THE EXPERI-ENCE, RITUAL OR SOME FORM, THAT WILL ENABLE THE IN-TELLECT TO RECEDE COULD BE BENEFICIAL. MORE TALKING ABOUT IT IS NOT GOOD WORK, AND MERELY PROLONGS THE AGONY THAT MUST, OF COURSE, PRECEDE THE ECSTASY. WE PATIENTLY AWAIT YOUR TRYING ANOTHER DOORWAY.

It was after midnight and Jessica had an intense headache. "But I was determined to go on," she says, chuckling. "The next day I felt as if I'd fallen down a flight of stairs, but, well, *good* in spite of it all."

"But this sounds like you're preaching reincarnation," Craig had said as Jessica and Walter worked the board. "I just can't believe in that."

BELIEF IS NOT REQUIRED: YOU WILL REINCARNATE ANY-WAY. A LEAF DOES NOT HAVE TO BELIEVE IN PHOTOSYN-THESIS TO TURN GREEN.

"Michael," Craig said as he stared at the Ouija board, "is a smart-ass."

The others laughed then, a little embarrassed at Craig's statement.

"We agreed with him," Jessica says merrily. "That made it worse. It's true, though. Michael *is* a smart-ass."

That first night the session lasted almost five hours. "We

were all so groggy we could hardly speak," Jessica recalls. "There wasn't a coherent sentence between us. I kept thinking that I didn't want it to be over. Then Walter got up enough nerve to ask if Michael would still be around to communicate with us if we stopped the session for a while."

The answer came back quickly.

BY ALL MEANS. WE NOW HAVE ACCESS TO ETERNITY.

Chapter 2

THE FORMING OF THE MICHAEL GROUP...

"To tell you the truth," Jessica says ruefully, "we were all pretty scared. At first I was afraid that nothing would happen, and then I was afraid that there would be more material from Michael, and I don't know which feeling was worse."

Walter pauses in the buffing of his eyeglasses. "I was very bothered then, too. Here we were mucking about with something we didn't really know, didn't understand, and that might turn out to be pretty dreadful."

Emily adds to this, "I kept thinking about all the warnings in the Bible about various malicious spirits, and I didn't know what to think. The more I considered it, the more worried I got." Emily is a tall, slender woman with curly dark hair, steady hazel eyes, and a shy smile. She smiles now. "I can't imagine what I was afraid of. I didn't think I really wanted to deal with this Michael thing, but there were one or two questions I wanted answered . . ."

The others join in her laughter. "One or two questions," Jessica says in mock despair. "I remember how many pages of transcripts we've filled answering one or two questions."

"*I* know," Lucy North says. "I've typed most of them." Lucy joined the group early on the suggestion of a friend,

Craig. She became the typist for the Michael group in its first year. "When I first attended a session, my life was in a shambles. I'd tried shrinks and ministers and every other kind of therapy you can imagine. I did it all. I'd lost my religious faith, my sense of direction, my self-esteem, the whole works. I figured this couldn't be any worse than what I'd already been through, so when Craig suggested I come to a session, I did."

It's hard to imagine this attractive, self-possessed woman in the state she describes.

"This wasn't a presto-chango wonder cure, but it gave me answers. I've gone back to my church, and I feel comfortable about that decision, which I wouldn't have been at the beginning, you know?" Lucy glances at the others. "Michael isn't out to change anything or anybody, but if you pay attention to what he says, you can make changes in yourself, if you want to. After a while, I wanted to."

Jessica and Walter Lansing, Craig and Emily Wright, Lucy North, Leah and Arnold Harris—were these people the extent of the group?

"For about the first six months," Jessica sighs. "Then the group got a lot bigger. Most people come only for a few meetings and then leave. This is not easy information to deal with over a long period. It's very demanding. However, there are about thirty people who have been with the group for more than a year, and, of course, some of us have been at it for longer than that." She looks at her guests. There are ten other people in her living room. "Most of us here have been actively involved getting this information and attending sessions for more than six years. As you know, I've been at this about eight years. Lucy has been with us almost eight years. Leah and Arnold have been with us about seven years. Sam Chasen, over there, is a social worker and he's been with us off and on for about seven years. David Swan, the tall guy with the turquoise eyes, has been with us a little over six years. Corrine Lawton, the woman with the beautiful silver hair, has been in the group about five years. She's the most expert one in the group on Eastern philosophy, and she's been a great deal of help. The last one, over by the window, is Tracy Rowland. She and Craig and I are the ones who work the board for this group."

This is not the sort of group most people would expect to

find involved in this sort of work. They are not bohemians, dropouts, or thrill-seekers. Lucy North is a secretary, a woman in her early forties with close-cropped dark hair and bright blue eyes, dressed in a shirt and slacks. There are grass stains on the knees of her slacks because she has been gardening.

"It's my hobby," she explains without apology. "I like working with plants."

Leah Harris is a lean woman, strong featured, with deep-set intelligent eyes. She dresses with restrained good taste and has a beautiful speaking voice. Her husband, Arnold, looks very much like the banker he is: trim, loose-limbed, his hair badger gray, his face craggy, his brown eyes direct, his expression grave until he gives one of his rare smiles that lights up his face.

Sam Chasen is in his late thirties, a tall, sandy-haired man with deeply etched lines in his face. There are braces on his legs, the result of polio in his childhood. He has a gentle restraint to his manner that verges on shyness.

David Swan is a museum curator. At first it seems out of character, for David Swan is tall, heavy-limbed, and barrel-chested, his hands huge, his dark hair permanently tousled. His deep speaking voice booms out melodically and his laughter is hearty thunder.

Corrine Lawton is forty-six years old, a very well-educated woman from a distinguished academic family of mixed racial heritage. Her skin is the color of dark honey, her eyes are almost black. She is a widow with three children, all of whom are living away from her. She is presently working as a consulting mathematician for a major computer firm, though her real interests lie in the area of esoteric philosophy.

"I came to philosophy through math," Corrine says. "Mathematics, the further you get into it, is more and more like philosophy and art. I found that I couldn't confine myself to the academic side alone, that I had to be more involved in all aspects of it, and over the years, that's drawn me to various esoteric teachings. Most of the teachings, of course, don't hold up under this kind of scrutiny, but those that do continue to fascinate me. That's why I'm still in the Michael group."

Tracy Rowland, who has been with the Michael group a

little over two years, is in her mid-thirties, with a background in civil engineering. She is compact and occasionally intense. She had a fair amount of occult studies behind her when she came to the Michael group and began working the board when she had been with the group a little more than a year.

"At first it was scary, as Jessica says. The planchette really does move by itself. I tried at first to think of reasons for it: perhaps subterranean water or sunspots or earth tremors or something devious in the back of my brain. But I'm more used to it now, and I've stopped looking for 'rational' explanations and simply take it as it comes." She hesitates, then says, "I wish now I'd been here the night they had a more-or-less physical manifestation of Michael. The first time I was told about it, I was relieved that I wasn't in the group yet, but now, I think I missed something very important."

Then there was a manifestation in the physical sense?

"Oh, yes," Jessica says with a rather tense nod. "When the group had been going about a year it was starting to get large, and there were people coming to the sessions who were making a game out of the material. They were showing up with questions in sealed envelopes that they wanted Michael to answer."

And did he?

"The first few times, yes," Walter says. "The questions were predictably silly. 'How can I get my daughter to clean up her room?' 'Why does my husband insist on having his brother over every Sunday when he knows I can't stand him?' 'Will I take a vacation to Hawaii this year?' 'What horse will be the next triple crown winner?' That sort of nonsense."

"Michael took it pretty well," Jessica goes on. "He said that there was no way to force the daughter into cleaning her room, and that this woman would do better to understand why her daughter wanted to live in chaotic surroundings. He said that her husband and his brother had been comrades-at-arms in three earlier lives, and that those bonds are never broken. He flatly refused to predict."

"He occasionally mentions possibilities," Craig says quickly. "When he feels that there are choices to be made. But he will not predict anything."

What did Michael tell this person?

"At the third session this person attended, Michael's patience ran out." Jessica puts her hand to her head in a mock gesture of dismay. "The first question that this woman asked was: 'Has my husband committed adultery?' "

YOUR HUSBAND HAS FULFILLED CERTAIN AGREEMENTS THAT HE MADE BETWEEN LIVES. IT IS ONLY THE CULTURAL AND SOCIETAL DEFINITIONS OF THE PHYSICAL PLANE THAT DEFINE SUCH RELATIONSHIPS AS LEGITIMATE OR ADULTEROUS.

"Her second question was: 'Is there a way I can get my neighbor to stop dropping in so often?' "

YOUR NEIGHBOR COMES BECAUSE SHE FEELS SHE IS WELCOME. YOU MUST MAKE UP YOUR MIND IF YOU WANT HER THERE OR NOT, AND THEN TELL HER HOW YOU FEEL. WE REALIZE YOU FEAR TO GIVE OFFENSE, BUT YOU MUST MAKE UP YOUR MIND WHICH IS MORE IMPORTANT TO YOU—YOUR PRIVACY OR HER FEELINGS.

"Her third question was: 'How can I gain the confidence of my boss?' " Jessica laughs merrily. "Michael's answer was wonderful!"

WE ARE NOT THE ANN LANDERS OF THE COSMOS.

All eleven people in the room chuckle, except for David Swan, who guffaws.

Was that the same night as the manifestation?

"Yes," Walter says, and at once the others are serious.

"It was strange," Jessica says quitely. "Michael was getting . . . well, it's hard to describe, but I guess you'd call it *stronger*, and everything on the board was coming faster and more emphatically. Craig had asked if I was the only one who could transmit the messages. This was before Craig was working the board, of course."

WE CAN MANIFEST THROUGH ANY OF YOU IN THIS ROOM. IT WOULD REQUIRE A LIGHT TRANCE, WHICH ALL OF YOU ARE CAPABLE OF ACHIEVING AND MAINTAINING.

Was that how Michael manifested?

Jessica shakes her head and her voice drops a little. "No. He said that there were those who would consider that suspect, so he would use another method." She takes a deep breath and glances once at Walter. "We had moved into the house only eight months before. I mention that because I want you to understand that the house was brand new. Some of the windows hadn't been opened yet. The laundry hadn't been hooked up. We hadn't installed a pet door for the dog and cats yet. It was a foggy night, so everything was closed up."

Walter takes up the story. "It was a little after ten, and there were eight people at the session, not counting Jessica and me. The couch was against the far wall rather than where it is now. The Franklin stove hadn't been installed. We checked around the house afterward to see if there were any openings we had neglected, but we didn't find anything."

"Michael announced that he would do something to convince us that he was actually here and that he had force." Jessica sits very still as she says this.

WE ARE NOT OF THE PHYSICAL PLANE, Michael began, BUT OUR EXISTENCE IS VALID, NONETHELESS. FOR THAT REASON, WE WILL MANIFEST TO YOU IN A WAY THAT IS NOT PHYSICAL BY YOUR STANDARDS. WE ARE NOT DOING THIS TO FRIGHTEN YOU. WE ARE ONLY INTERESTED IN ASSISTING YOU TO VERIFY US SO THAT YOU WILL CONCENTRATE ON THE TEACHING.

"First," Jessica says, "the temperature in the room dropped. I mean just *dropped* about twenty degrees, like walking into a refrigerator. There was nothing gradual about it. Then a wind went around the room, blowing things over. The sheet music on the piano was scattered all over the room, the paperbacks on top of the bookcase were blown off, two pictures that were matted but not framed were blown off the walls, and anything that could rattle, did."

The others are silent. Finally Lucy speaks. "It was only the second session I had attended, and I was afraid something like that would happen often. I was scared to drive home that night. That wind was unreal!"

Has anything like that happened since?

"Only once," Walter says with an expression of relief. "That was a little over a year ago, when we had a very troubled person attending a few sessions. We all became more and more uncomfortable with him, because it was growing clear that he did not want to truly pay attention to Michael's teaching. He wanted to be given some sort of instant magic that would change him around. Instead, Michael kept telling him things about karma and agreements and soul development, and this guy just got madder and madder."

"I tell you, I was scared for a while," Jessica puts in. "This man would sit there just glaring at me while I worked the board, and it was harder and harder to open myself up to what Michael was saying. Finally I wanted to stop altogether, and that was when the manifestation occurred."

Was it the same as the first manifestation?

"No," Jessica says emphatically, and the others agree. "This time, the room seemed to get very dark, as if the lights were failing. It wasn't really any darker, but there was this shadow gathering in the room. I don't know how else to express it. The air itself was shadowed."

"It was worse than that," Lucy corrects her. "I don't like snakes, you know? I *really* don't like snakes. I felt as if there were this huge snake somewhere in the room."

"Come on, Lucy," Jessica admonishes her, "it wasn't that bad. It was eerie. There was also a sound that I can't begin to describe, as if a voice were talking in a foreign language on a telephone line that was full of static."

What was that manifestation? Was it Michael?

"According to Michael, it came from the members of that man's entity who were between lives and who were trying to reach him." Walter nods to the others as they agree with him. "Michael says that those of us on the physical plane do have access to these disembodied fragments, but that we tend to reach out to them only in moments of stress. Obviously, for this guy, he was going through some real stress."

"Yes," Jessica says. "Afterward, Michael gave us a warning about that kind of personality."

OF COURSE YOU MUST REALIZE THAT SPIRITUALLY ORIENTED GROUPS OF PERSONS WHERE ACCEPTANCE IS THE CARDINAL RULE WILL ATTRACT MANY LONELY, MALADJUSTED PERSONS SEARCHING FOR THE REAFFIRMATION OF THEIR HUMANNESS, AND THESE PERSONS WILL NOT BE HELPED TO GROW SPIRITUALLY BUT WILL BASK IN THE WARMTH OF ACCEPTANCE FOR A TIME. THOSE SPIRITUALLY ON THE TRUE PATH WILL STILL BE ABLE TO SEE THE SICKNESS. THIS PHENOMENON IS CERTAINLY NOT UNUSUAL. IT IS ONLY THAT THESE GROUPS ARE FOUNDED UPON THE PRINCIPLES OF LOVE AND ACCEPTANCE AND OFTEN THE MEM-

BERS FAIL TO CONFRONT EVEN THE MOST OBNOXIOUS BE-
HAVIOR IN THESE SPIRITUAL INTERLOPERS. WHAT IS APPAR-
ENT THERE IS THAT THESE PERSONS ARE NOT GOING FOR-
WARD IN GROWTH AT ALL AND ARE IN FACT ACTING AS
DEAD WEIGHT AND MAKING THE PATH MORE DIFFICULT FOR
OTHERS TO CLIMB.

"Well, it's true enough that the occult fields are full of
weirdos and kooks," David Swan says with a laugh, "but
we've really been lucky. Over the years there have been
more than a hundred people attending sessions at one time
or another, and no more than a dozen of them were real
whackos. Those that were we spotted very quickly, and
most of the time, we weren't offering what they wanted. No
Messiahs here, thanks very much."

Jessica agrees. "We have been lucky. Though Michael
has said that luck has very little to do with it."

"I think it's luck," Lucy says quietly.

"I kept hoping," Walter says, "that there would be a way
to reach this guy. I can see now that it probably wasn't
possible. But if we're trying to learn agape, it's not good
work to reject someone in trouble."

"Michael addressed himself to that," Corrine says from
her chair by the tall picture window.

IT IS TRUE, WALTER, THAT THIS PERSONALITY CANNOT
LOVE. ONLY THE ESSENCE, THE INTRINSIC CORE OF THE
SOUL, IS CAPABLE OF LOVING, AND ONLY WHEN ITS DE-
MANDS ARE MET WILL YOU, ANY OF YOU, TRULY LOVE. WE
HAVE SUGGESTED TO YOU THAT THE WAY TO ACHIEVE THIS
IS GIVING UP THE PERSONALITY'S EXPECTATIONS OF THE
EXPERIENCE. YOU ARE YET SCORNFUL OF THIS TRUTH.
PRIOR EXPECTATIONS POISON THE EXPERIENCE. YET, IT
GOES FAR DEEPER THAN THIS. YOU ARE, ALL OF YOU, PART
OF SOMETHING MUCH GREATER THAN YOU KNOW, AND MOST
OF YOU FEAR TO REALIZE THIS. ONLY WHEN YOU BECOME
WILLING TO PART WITH YOUR ULTRAPRECIOUS IDENTIFI-
CATION WILL YOU GLIMPSE THE VASTNESS BEYOND. MOST
OF YOU LOVE ON YOUR OWN TERMS ONLY, AND THIS IS NOT
THE GOAL. YOU MUST LEARN TO LOVE ON NO TERMS. WITH
THE TROUBLED YOUNG MAN YOU ASKED OF, YOU, WALTER,
INSISTED THAT HE ACCEPT YOUR AID IN ORDER TO EARN
YOUR LOVE. THIS IS NOT GOOD WORK. IF YOU WISH TO
LEARN TRUE AGAPE, YOU MUST BE ABLE TO LOVE HIM WITH-

OUT QUALIFICATION. BY LOVE, WE DO NOT MEAN THAT SENTIMENTAL OUTPOURING THAT MOST OFTEN PASSES FOR LOVE IN THIS SOCIETY, OR THE SEXUAL OBSESSION THAT IS LABELED LOVE TO MAKE THE LUST ACCEPTABLE. WE DO NOT MEAN TO IMPLY THAT AFFECTION AND SEXUALITY ARE, OF THEMSELVES, DETRIMENTAL, BUT WE DO MEAN THAT YOUR EXPECTATIONS IN THESE AREAS ARE MORE VULNERABLE THAN MOST.

"That took the wind out of my sails," Walter says philosophically. "I understand now what it was that Michael was telling me, but at the time, I was really indignant. After all, I was reaching out to this poor, troubled man, prepared to coax him into improvement. Talk about expectations!" He shakes his head.

"When Michael said that to Walter, I got upset," Emily recalls. "I thought it wasn't fair to talk to Walter like that, and I said so."

WE IMPART OUR KNOWLEDGE IMPARTIALLY. WE DO NOT REQUIRE THAT YOU AGREE. YOU MAY REJECT ANYTHING WE SAY. THE CHOICE IS YOURS.

"Michael has emphasized that over and over, that everything we do is by choice," Jessica says. "We have agreements that we can fulfill or not, as we choose. We are responsible for ourselves and to ourselves."

Not even to Michael?

The people in the living room laugh.

"I thought that Michael was sort of superparent for a while," Craig says. "Then I began to realize that he meant what he said—that he didn't really give a damn if we paid any attention to him or not."

"It was Corrine who asked why such reunited entities as Michael bother to teach at all, if everything is in the hands of us individually."

DURING THE ASTRAL INTERVAL, THE STUDY IS RETROSPECTIVE AND UNCHANGEABLE. ON THE PHYSICAL PLANE YOU HAVE THE OPPORTUNITY TO CHANGE RIGHT UP UNTIL THE MOMENT OF THE LAST BREATH.

"That sounds like death-bed repentance and forgiveness," Lucy observed when the words came through.

THERE MUST BE A PERCEPTION BEHIND THE WORDS. THE WORDS HAVE BEEN MUTTERED MANY TIMES IN MEANINGLESS CONTEXTS BECAUSE THEY WERE LITERALLY BLOWING

IN THE WIND AND ADDRESSED TO FORCES COMPLETELY DE-
TACHED AND UNABLE TO ANSWER. IN ORDER TO HAVE THIS
CONCEPT MADE VALID, THE SITUATION MUST BE APPRE-
HENDED AND THE PLEA ADDRESSED TO THE CORRECT
SOURCE.

"What is the correct source?" Craig asked, saying now
in retrospect, "I thought we had Michael that time. I was
sure he'd do the god number on us."

THE CORRECT SOURCE IS WITHIN YOU, IN THE SOUL THAT
IS ETERNAL. THAT IS YOUR ONLY SOURCE OF ASSISTANCE IN
THE PHYSICAL PLANE OR ANY OTHER.

"Then why do people make so many mistakes?" Corrine
asked.

THE SOUL, SANS BODY, TENDS TO FORGET THE INTENSITY
OF THE EXPERIENCE AND THE PAIN. DETACHED REVIEW IS
ALMOST IMPOSSIBLE ON THE PHYSICAL PLANE. THE SOUL
MAKES ITS CHOICE BETWEEN LIVES, SELECTING THE LO-
CALE, THE SOCIOECONOMIC STATUS, THE PARENTS, ALL AS
PART OF PROGRAMMING THE BIOCOMPUTER. THE CLOSER
THE SOUL COMES TO ITS TRUE ESSENCE IN LIFE, THE LESS
THE FRAGMENT WILL HAVE TO CHANGE TO MEET THE SIT-
UATION. THE ARTIFICIAL PERSONALITY IS A CHAMELEON.
THE FACE THAT YOU PRESENT TO THE WORLD IS DETER-
MINED BY THIS FALSE PERSONALITY. HOW OFTEN HAVE YOU
THOUGHT THAT IN ORDER TO BE WITH AUNT MINNIE, YOU
MUST NOT TALK ABOUT THE THINGS THAT INTEREST YOU
MOST. THIS DOES NOT TRULY HELP AUNT MINNIE, AND IT
IS DAMAGING TO YOUR SOUL.

"But," Emily objected at the time, "if we're to be loving
and compassionate, shouldn't we consider the feelings of
others?"

WE DID NOT SAY THAT YOU SHOULD NOT BE LOVING AND
COMPASSIONATE, BUT WHY SHOULD THAT REQUIRE YOU TO
CHANGE IN ORDER TO PLEASE OTHERS?

"We haven't finished fighting about that one yet," Emily
says.

"But it's true," Walter remarks in a more serious tone,
"that for a long time we all tried to react in 'appropriate'
ways. We were all eager to show the others how much of
this we were getting."

Did Michael have anything to say about that?

"It was more than a comment," Jessica answers. "He gave us a project."

WE WOULD PROPOSE AN EXERCISE IN PHOTOGRAPHY FOR ALL OF YOU AS FOLLOWS: BEGIN TO PHOTOGRAPH YOUR SELVES' REACTION TO SUGGESTION OF CHANGE WITH THE STATEMENT, "I CANNOT." THEN REALIZE THAT THIS IS NOT TRUE. SOMETIMES THE TRUTH WILL BE THAT YOU DO NOT POSSESS AT THE PRESENT MOMENT THE REQUIRED SKILLS OR KNOWLEDGE, BUT MORE OFTEN THAN NOT, THE TRUTH WILL BE, "I DO NOT WANT TO." THIS IS VITAL AND A POS-ITIVE STEP ON THE PATH. YOU CAN HELP BY PHOTOGRAPH-ING EACH OTHER AT CRUCIAL MOMENTS. ALL OF YOU ARE GUILTY NOW OF USING THE "I CANNOT" EXCUSE SEVERAL TIMES A DAY. IT ALLOWS YOU TO SHIFT BLAME AND RE-SPONSIBILITY VERY NEATLY. MOST OF YOU ARE STILL TER-RIFIED OF RESPONSIBILITY AND FREEDOM OF CHOICE. IT IS MUCH EASIER TO BE CONSTRAINED THAN TO CHOOSE. WHEN YOU ARE CONSTRAINED YOU PRESENT THE PICTURE OF THE HELPLESS STUDENT AT THE MERCY OF THE COSMOS, WHICH IS, OF COURSE, ABSURD.

YOU MUST REMEMBER THAT PERSONALITY SETS UP MANY BARRIERS ALONG THE PATH. THIS HABIT OF DENIAL IS ONLY ONE OF THEM AND CHIPPING AWAY AT THIS WILL ONLY RESULT IN THE UNCOVERING OF MANY MORE SIMILAR GUISES. THE GOAL OF THE ORGANISM IS, QUITE NATURALLY, SURVIVAL, AND ONE OF THE MAIN EXPRESSIONS OF SUR-VIVAL IS THROUGH SEXUALITY. SEXUALITY IS MADE MORE DIFFICULT BY CULTURALLY IMPOSED BARRIERS AND ARTI-FICIAL CONDITIONS AND SOCIETALLY IMPOSED EXPECTA-TIONS. THESE ARE OTHER BARRIERS. DENIAL OF THE PLEA-SURES OF EATING, SLEEPING, AND JUST BIDING TIME ON A PLEASANT DAY ARE MORE. THE PERSONALITY CAN COME UP WITH MANY SUCH EFFORTS TO RATIONALIZE WHY THESE PLEASURES SHOULD NOT BE EXPERIENCED: THEY ARE NOT GOOD FOR YOU, THEY COST TOO MUCH, THEY WASTE TOO MUCH TIME, THEY ARE NOT USEFUL, THEY WILL UPSET AND BEWILDER OTHERS, THEY DISTRACT YOU, THEY ARE NOT APPROVED BY GOD OR THE ARMY OR THE SCHOOL OR THE NEIGHBORS, THEY ARE EVIL, ET CETERA.

"But there are times when we must deny things we want to do," David Swan said in response to this. "There are many requirements on this physical plane, and I think it's important that we learn to honor our obligations."

WE DID NOT SAY THAT YOU SHOULD NOT DO SO. HOW-EVER, WE REMIND YOU THAT THOSE REQUIREMENTS AND OBLIGATIONS AND RESPONSIBILITIES ARE OFTEN EXCUSES TO AVOID DEALING WITH MORE PROFOUND AND DISTURBING FACTORS IN YOUR LIFE. THINK OF THE HUSBAND WHO WORKS LATE AND DILIGENTLY EVERY NIGHT SO THAT HE WILL NOT HAVE TO FACE HIS WIFE'S VERY LEGITIMATE DIS-APPOINTMENT AND ANGER.

WE REALIZE THAT YOU HAVE COMMITMENTS THAT ARE QUITE LEGITIMATE, BUT OFTEN YOU ALLOW YOUR PER-SONAL AGENDAS TO GET IN THE WAY OF YOUR SEARCH. BY PERSONAL AGENDAS WE REFER IN THIS INSTANCE TO THE IRRELEVANT THOUGHTS FLITTING THROUGH THE MIND THAT PREVENT A FOCUS ON INSIGHT AND THE TEACHING, THE PROJECTIONS INTO THE BUSINESS WORLD AND THE MOVIE YOU SAW THREE YEARS AGO, AN UNPAID BILL. THESE AND SIMILAR ITEMS ARE THE SORT TO WHICH WE REFER.

WE WOULD ASK YOU TO THINK ABOUT YOUR LIVES FOR A MOMENT. WHEN YOU ARE GARDENING, YOU THINK ABOUT PLANTS AND EARTH AND FERTILIZER AND SHADE AND ROOT CONDITIONS AS WELL AS THE WEATHER AND THE PLANT-NESS OF PLANTS. WHEN YOU ARE MAKING A MEAL YOU THINK ABOUT SMELL AND TASTE AND TEXTURE AND HUN-GER AND APPEARANCE AND TIME AND RESOURCES. WHEN YOU LISTEN TO MUSIC, YOU THINK ABOUT NOTES AND RHYTHMS AND DYNAMICS. THIS IS AN AUTOMATIC CONCEN-TRATION, A PATTERN OF CONCENTRATION THAT HAS BEEN LEARNED. MOST OF THE TIME, IF YOU ALLOW OTHER CON-SIDERATIONS TO INTRUDE, YOUR PLANTING OR COOKING OR LISTENING WILL NOT GO AS WELL, AND YOU WILL BE DIS-APPOINTED. YOU WILL BE AWARE OF IT AT THE TIME. SOMETHING WILL NOT SEEM RIGHT AND YOU WILL BE EAS-ILY IRRITATED OR FRUSTRATED. IT IS THE SAME WITH THIS TEACHING. AS YOU LEARN THE MOST WORKABLE PATTERN OF CONCENTRATION, IT WILL BE EASIER TO MAINTAIN THAT CONCENTRATION. AT THE MOMENT YOU ARE EASILY DIS-TRACTED AND FRUSTRATED, AND TOO MUCH OF WHAT YOU MIGHT CALL THE OUTSIDE WORLD INTRUDES. WE URGE YOU TO BE AWARE OF THIS, AND TO STRIVE TO OVERCOME THE TEMPTATIONS OF DISTRACTIONS.

WE WOULD LIKE TO POINT OUT TO YOU AT THIS TIME
THAT MANY OF YOU ARE DABBLERS. YOU DABBLE IN THIS
AND THAT, TASTING ALL OF THE FRUITS, BUT EATING NONE,
AND IN THIS SAME WAY, YOU DABBLE IN SPIRITUAL GROWTH
AS WELL. NOW THIS IS ALL RIGHT. THERE IS NOTHING
WRONG IN SUCH DABBLING. IT INCURS LITTLE KARMA, BUT
ON THE OTHER HAND, IT LEADS NOWHERE. THE CONCEPT
OF AGAPE REQUIRES THE ACTIONS OF A CLOSELY KNIT GROUP
OF SUPPORTIVE STUDENTS IN ORDER TO BE TRULY EX-
PRESSED. THE SUPPORT OF OTHER STUDENTS IS NECESSARY
TO OFFSET THE NEGATIVISM YOU OFTEN FIND AROUND YOU.
NO ONE CAN FEEL AGAPE IN AN IVORY TOWER OR A HER-
MIT'S CELL.

MOST OF YOU HAVE A GREAT FEAR OF INVASION OF YOUR
PRIVATE, INNER WORLDS. THIS IS DUE IN PART TO A LOW
LEVEL OF TRUST AS WELL AS CULTURALLY INDUCED GUILT.
MANY OF YOU ARE NOT CONVINCED THAT OTHERS ARE CA-
PABLE OF ACCEPTING YOUR PRIVATE LIFESTYLES, AND ARE
NOT WILLING TO RISK FINDING OUT. ALSO THERE IS A TE-
NACIOUS DESIRE TO RUN FROM ANY POSSIBLE TAMPERING
WITH YOUR LIVES BY OTHERS. MANY OF YOU NEED TO
WORK ON THIS FOR THIS IS THE FALSE PERSONALITY DIG-
GING IN FOR A LAST DITCH STAND AGAINST THE REAL NA-
TURE OF THE SOUL. ALL OF YOU HAVE A SET OF RIGID
SPECIFICATIONS, SET BY PERSONALITY, CONCERNING YOUR
NEEDS. NONE OF THESE SPECIFICATIONS HAVE TRUE VALID-
ITY; THEY ARE ONLY MORE BARRIERS. WE DO NOT INSIST
THAT YOU DISCARD THESE TRAITS OVERNIGHT. IN FACT,
SUCH DRASTIC MEASURES WOULD PROBABLY RESULT IN
EVEN MORE DIFFICULTIES. WE ONLY ENCOURAGE YOU TO
BE AWARE OF THESE PRESSURES IN YOUR LIVES AND TO REC-
OGNIZE THEM FOR WHAT THEY ARE.

"When that message came through," Jessica says remi-
niscently, "four people left the group in a huff."

"That's an antique car with wire wheels," Sam Chasen
murmurs, a wicked twinkle in his eye.

"We were very despondent about that," Craig remarks.
"It was another example of the way expectations can be a
barrier. We thought that because there were people who
rejected what Michael had to say, that we had all failed. It
wasn't the case, but it really shook our confidence at the
time."

"I stopped coming to sessions for a while," Lucy says with a quick nod.

"So did we," Leah Harris adds, putting her hand on her husband's. "Both Arnold and I were bitterly disappointed at the time. We thought we were being put down, when Michael said what he did about dabblers. I know that I'm not wholeheartedly committed to this teaching, but I want to follow it as long as it has answers."

Arnold agrees. "You may think it odd for a banker to be interested in this kind of thing. I know that our professional image isn't very metaphysical, but I know there's more to life than balance sheets, though I suppose you can think of karma as a kind of balance of payments."

Corrine smiles widely. "I didn't mind as much as the rest of you. I didn't leave, partly because I had some very specialized questions that I wanted answered and I didn't feel badly about taking up the time to have them answered."

Lucy sighs. "I remember transcribing those sessions. They were very tough going. I didn't know what half of it was all about. That stuff on the astral and higher planes still baffles me."

"It baffles me, too," Corrine says. "It goes along with a lot of metaphysical thinking, but it is still way beyond the kinds of concepts I think in easily, and I'm a mathematician."

THERE ARE, OF COURSE, SEVEN PLANES IN ALL, EACH WITH SEVEN LEVELS. FIRST IS THE PHYSICAL PLANE. BEYOND THE UPPER AND LOWER ASTRAL PLANES ARE THE CAUSAL PLANE WITH SEVEN LEVELS, THREE LOW, ONE MIDCAUSAL UPON WHICH WE EXIST, AND THREE HIGHER LEVELS UPON WHICH RESIDE THE HIGH CAUSAL BODIES, THE TRANSCENDENTAL SOULS CONTIGUOUS WITH THIS PLANE. WE REMIND YOU THAT OUR CYCLES CONSIST OF SEVEN LEVELS, JUST AS YOURS DO. THE MENTAL PLANE IS THE AKASHIC PLANE, WHICH IS A PHOTOGRAPHIC RECORD OF ALL HISTORY. SOME VERY HIGH ADEPTS HAVE ACCESS TO THIS PLANE. ON THE MENTAL PLANE RESIDE THE INFINITE SOUL AND THE LOW AND MIDMENTAL BODIES. BEYOND THIS ARE THE BUDDHIC PLANES, AND UPON THAT LEVEL ARE ALL THOSE SOULS WHO HAVE ACHIEVED PHYSICAL COMMUNICATION WITH THE TAO. BEYOND THIS, OF COURSE, IS THE TAO ITSELF.

SINCE THE SOUL, BETWEEN LIVES, IS WITHOUT A SUITABLE PHYSICAL VEHICLE, IT MUST RESIDE ON THE LOW ASTRAL PLANE, SINCE THAT IS THE LOWEST LEVEL WHERE A BODY OF THE ORGANIC SORT IS NOT REQUIRED. OCCASIONALLY SUCH ASTRAL SOULS MANIFEST IN VARIOUS PROJECTIONS, BUT NOT OF THE SORT THAT HAVE OCCURRED HERE.

"Can you tell me what the significance of the number seven is?" Corinne asked at one of these sparsely attended sessions.

SEVEN IS THE CLOSEST THING WE KNOW OF TO A "UNIVERSAL" NUMBER. IT EXPRESSES NOT ONLY THE THREE ASPECTS OF DUALITY, BUT THE RESOLUTION OF THE DUALITIES. IT IS THESIS, ANTITHESIS, AND SYNTHESIS. IN THE DUALITIES, OR POLARITIES, THERE ARE THOSE THAT ARE CONCERNED WITH EXPRESSION, ACTION, AND INSPIRATION, AND THE SEVENTH IS ASSIMILATION. CONSIDER EXPRESSION, WHICH MAKES THINGS ACCESSIBLE, EITHER THROUGH THE ACT OF CREATING THINGS, BUILDING THINGS, AND SHAPING THINGS WITH ITS HIGHER POLARITY, WHICH IS THE REALIZATION OF THE THING BUILT, CREATED, OR SHAPED. IN ACTION, THERE IS THE ACTION ITSELF, THE EXPLORATION, THE EXTENSION, AND THE COHESION OF THE RESULTS OF THE EXPLORATION AND EXTENSION. IN INSPIRATION THERE IS THE LIFTING UP, AND THE PURSUIT OF THAT BEYOND WHAT HAS BEEN LIFTED UP. AND THEN, THERE IS THE CONTEMPLATION AND UNDERSTANDING OF THE DUALITIES IN A SINGLE EXPERIENCE.

AS WE IMPART THE TEACHING, WE WOULD URGE YOU TO KEEP THIS IN MIND, FOR THERE ARE MANY ASPECTS OF YOURSELVES THAT ARE INFLUENCED BY THIS RULE OF SEVEN. REMEMBER THE INTERRELATIONS OF THE POLARITIES AS WELL AS THEIR SYNTHESIS.

"What does that have to do with the casting out of souls by the Tao?" Walter asked.

IT IS THE FIRST STEP TO UNDERSTANDING THE SEARCH. THE CASTING IS NOT CASTING OUT, BUT RATHER CASTING INTO. THE TAO IS NOT A COSMIC MOTHER, AS YOU HAVE REALIZED BY NOW. NOR IS IT A COSMIC FATHER. THE TAO IS NOT SUBJECT TO PERSONIFICATION. THE SOUL FIRST CAST FROM THE TAO IS AT ONCE CLOSEST AND FURTHEST FROM THE TAO. THE ANALOGY WITH A HUMAN INFANT IS APT BUT SOMEWHAT MISLEADING. THE SOUL THAT IS NEWLY

CAST FROM THE TAO RETAINS SOME OF THAT ESSENTIAL ALLIANCE WITH THE TAO NOT UNLIKE THE HUMAN INFANT'S CLOSENESS TO ITS MOTHER, BUT THE HUMAN INFANT IS NOT AWARE THAT IT IS FAR FROM THE GOAL AND THE NEWLY CAST SOUL IS. THE LADDER MUST BE CLIMBED AND THE INFANT SOUL IS AWARE OF THIS. ITS CLOSENESS TO THE TAO COMES FROM THIS KNOWLEDGE. BEYOND THIS, THE KNOWLEDGE IS NOT EXPANDED.

IN THE CASTING, THE TOTAL AWARENESS OF THE ETERNAL PLAY IS LOST, BUT NOT THE FEELING OF LOSS. THE INFANT SOUL THEN EXPERIENCES THE LOSS AND THE CLOSENESS SIMULTANEOUSLY. THE NEWLY CAST SOUL IS AGAIN UNIQUE IN THIS SENSE OF LOSS AND MUST START THE SORTING THAT LATER BECOMES THE SEEKING OF THE TAO.

"Does that mean that we are all newly cast souls?" Emily asked.

IF YOU WERE YOU WOULD NOT BE HERE. ONLY SOULS WHO HAVE BEGUN THE SEARCH COME TO THIS TEACHING. YOU HAVE ALL TAKEN MANY STEPS ON THE PATH. WE ARE HERE MERELY TO POINT THE WAY. HOW FAR YOU GO, WHAT YOU WILL DO WITH YOUR KNOWLEDGE, HOW YOU WILL USE IT, WHETHER YOU ACCEPT IT OR REJECT IT, IS UP TO YOU.

Apparently these eleven people have decided to accept the knowledge.

"Well, most of the time," David Swan says with uncharacteristic hesitation. "I don't always like what Michael tells me, and there are times I don't want to look any farther than the end of my nose. I'll tell you what really got to me." He leans forward, his strong face intent. "Michael did a full review of one of my lives; told me all about it. Now, the thing that made it difficult was that it sounded so familiar, like a childhood memory that had stayed just outside my attention and needed one little trigger to bring it into sharp relief. That was bad enough. But Michael told me about historical people who were involved, and mentioned documentation. So I thought I'd investigate. It took me about six months to get all the material, because some of it was in European libraries and could not be obtained over here. That was one time I was glad I work for a museum, let me tell you. Well, as the material came in, I found out that it all fit. There really had been a person that Michael had described. He wasn't famous, but he had known famous people."

Was it possible that Jessica knew about this person beforehand?

Jessica laughs outright at this suggestion. "If I had half the information on history that has come through the board, I would need three or four major degrees and be able to speak languages I don't know, including Arabic, Chinese, and one or two major African languages, as well as Mayan, Aztec, and the languages of the American Indian. I can tell you right now that I don't. I know English, German, some Dutch and Spanish, and a little, a very little, Russian. And that's it. I don't have access to the archives of foreign universities, and even if I had, and was inclined to take the time, trouble, and money to get the information, if I *could* get it, I probably wouldn't be able to read most of it."

"Occam's razor," Sam remarks. "It means that the simplest explanation is usually the correct one, among other things. Either Jessica is doing a tremendous job of research and preparation to keep all these things straight and consistent in her head for almost eight years, and is continuing to stay one step ahead of us while holding down a full-time job, running this house, and being actively involved in three or four community projects, and has done it so secretly and successfully that no one, not even her husband, has found out about it, *or* there is something that calls itself Michael that speaks to her through the Ouija board." He opens his hands helplessly. "I've seen her work the board a long time, and I've heard her in trance sessions, and I've come to accept that she is doing it through the board."

"Those first couple of years, though," Jessica says with some agitation, "they were something. When the sessions first caught on . . ." She rolls her eyes heavenward. "At first Walter and I would get together with Craig and Emily, oh, maybe once a month, and we'd ask a few questions, very timorously, and Michael would give answers, rather slowly, since I was still resisting it. Then Craig said that he had a couple of friends who might be interested in the sessions, and so they were invited, and we started getting together twice a month, usually on Saturday afternoon since that's when Craig was able to be with us. Then some more people, like David and Sam and Leah and Arnold and Lucy, started coming to sessions, and the meetings had to be longer, and eventually were happening on both Saturday and

Sunday every weekend. Thinking back on it now, it seems unreal. I think we were fortunate to have had so few real difficulties as we did have. With so many people involved, it was pretty chaotic."

"I put my foot down after a while," Walter adds. "I came home one Friday and found sixteen people camping out in the living room, and that was too much."

"And we could easily have had more," Jessica sighs. "People seemed to come out of the woodwork at these sessions. I remember one afternoon when two astronomers from the university were here asking questions about space and time and astrophysics. They said they were very pleased with what they learned. We've had many physicians, mostly friends of Craig's, wanting to know how to deal with certain patients. We've had a few psychologists and one dogmatic psychiatrist who were all looking for more information than they could find in their disciplines. In one case, Michael said that it was necessary for a certain patient to experience madness, which was why she had chosen this particular psychologist to treat her. That poor man!" She chuckles, not unkindly. "He went out of here in a rage."

"I can't blame him," Lucy interjects. "He was so certain that he would get all kinds of strokes from us, and that he would also show us that there was nothing to this kind of work."

"Finally, I stopped using the board for six months. There was too much happening that distracted us. There were personality problems developing, which in so large a group isn't surprising. Some of the members wanted to become overnight adepts. The trouble was that the people who really wanted to get information were the first to shut up and back out. It was good to stop for a while. And when we started again, there was a new feeling to the group."

Walter is somewhat less tolerant of the disruption. "We simply couldn't handle it, or I couldn't. I had to stop working the board with Jessica because it was too exhausting. Strangely enough, this was a good thing. The material comes faster when there is just one person working the board."

Jessica nods in agreement. "I didn't think it would work at first, but then, it just took off! I'd get this strange sensation in my neck and hands, and the letters would come very fast. We had to have several people taking down the letters because it was not always possible for Lucy to take it all down by herself.''

What was Michael's reaction to the change in the group, if there was one?

"Not bad, all things considered," Jessica says.

WE WOULD SPEAK TO YOU OF THE WISDOM WHICH COMES TO US FROM THE PLANE BEYOND AND YET INTERPENETRATING THIS ONE. IN GIVING YOU SOME DIRECTION TO YOUR PURPOSE, YOU HAVE, DURING THE INTERVAL BETWEEN PHYSICAL LIVES, CHOSEN TO LIVE A LIFE IN SERVICE TO THE SEARCH. THE MANNER IN WHICH YOU WILL DO THIS IS NOW BECOMING INCREASINGLY CLEAR TO MANY OF YOU, AND YOU ARE NO LONGER SAD TO SEE THE COMPLEXION OF THE GROUP CHANGING, THOUGH A FEW OF YOU THINK THAT YOU OUGHT TO BE SAD. IT SHOULD BE CLEAR TO YOU ALL AT THIS JUNCTURE THAT THOSE WHO HAVE DROPPED BY THE WAYSIDE WERE MOTIVATED BY OTHER FACTORS THAN THE SEARCH, MANY OF THEM HAVING KARMIC REASONS TO GO ON THEIR WAYS. SOME PARTED WITH SADNESS FOR THEY FELT INEXPLICABLY BOUND TO YOU, BUT COULD NOT CONTAIN A RESTLESS SPIRIT. NOW YOU FIND YOURSELVES AT THIS TURNING POINT TOGETHER WITH OTHERS WHO ARE DRIVEN BY THE SAME CHOSEN PURPOSE. YOU WILL FIND IT NOW EASIER TO PLAN, FOR THIS IS THE PLANNING OCTAVE, JUST AS THE ONE COMPLETED WAS THE INVESTIGATION OCTAVE, WHICH IS, OF COURSE, THE COMPLETION OF SEVEN LEVELS AND ATTAINING THE EIGHTH, WHICH IS THE FIRST STAGE IN THE NEXT OCTAVE. THINK OF THE STRENGTH IN MUSIC AS IT MOVES UP THE SCALE, WHICH IS ANOTHER SORT OF LADDER. SO YOU MOVE UP A SCALE. THOSE WHO HAVE CHOSEN TO GO ON THE SEARCH WILL ADD TO YOUR MELODY.

Chapter 3

JESSICA LANSING'S
OUIJA BOARD . . .

Jessica Lansing sits in her bentwood rocker tailor fashion,
her specially designed Ouija board balanced on her knees
and the arms of her chair. She holds the planchette negli-
gently in her right hand; there is a cup of coffee in her left.
There are two more people in the living room—Marjorie
Randall, a professor of biology, and Kate O'Brien, who is
working for her master's degree in literature. Both are young
women, intelligent, articulate, and practical. Lucy has gone
to the kitchen to make tea for those who don't like coffee.

"We went through I don't know how many of the commercial boards before I had sense enough to get one of my
own. A woman in the group made this for me. She's living
in Minneapolis now." She pats he glass surface of the
board. "Those commercial boards don't hold up at all. I'd
use one for a month, and then it would start to sag, or the
letters would fade. We tried plastic coating them, mounting
them on heavier backing, everything. They simply weren't
designed for this kind of use."

Most of the people in the living room have notebooks with
them. Leah's is a thick ring binder, David's is a clipboard,
Tracy's is a yellow legal-size pad. The rest are the usual
run-of-school-variety notebooks.

Does everyone write during a session?

"They better," Jessica says with an admonishing glance around the room. "It's too much to expect one person to get everything. When Michael gets going, he dictates very fast." Jessica pats the board with a kind of absent-minded affection. "When I got this board, he started going even faster."

The board is larger than the commercial Ouija boards, and heavily framed like a picture. The planchette rests on smooth glass, and under it is the alphabet, A through M on the top row, N through Z on the bottom. Both rows curve slightly to accommodate the swing of the planchette when it is in motion. The backing is mustard yellow, the letters are black. There are a yin-yang symbol, three Arabic letters, and two heads of Roman soldiers on the board.

"Because of my interest in things Roman," Jessica explains. "I've had this board for over five years, almost six. I've gotten used to it now."

"I've only used this board once or twice," Walter puts in. "Jessica is much better at this than I am. She has more energy and she takes care to get everything that Michael has to offer her."

Does that mean that others have worked the board? And if they have, do their results tally with what she has got?

"Sure," Jessica says, nodding emphatically. "Craig works his own board, at his own sessions, and Michael says the same things to him that he does to our group. The wording is the same, the attitude, the style, the feel . . . it's all Michael. We've also got another woman in the group now who works the board occasionally, and her results are like mine. I'm glad to have someone else to work the board here, because now," she goes on eagerly, "there is someone who can get answers to *my* questions for me. When I work the board, I don't trust the answers I get to my own questions."

Why is that?

"Because I'm too afraid that it would be easy for me to tap into my subconscious rather than to Michael."

Could Jessica tell the difference?

"Most of the time, yes. There's a sensation that goes with Michael. I find it hard to describe. It has something to do with that heat and tingling I mentioned, but there's another dimension, a *presence* that is Michael. When I want to know things for myself, I might be able to fool myself into thinking I had that sensation, when, in fact, all that was happening was that I wanted to believe it."

"That was what we were worried about the first time Jessica worked the board alone," Walter admits. "There's no question that she had the concentration and the ability to do this, but we were all worried that the messages she got might be, well, distorted."

"We were very quickly disabused of *that*." Jessica grins. "The first night I worked the board, Michael took over at the beginning."

WE ARE HERE WITH YOU TONIGHT. WE HAVE SEVERAL COMMENTS TO MAKE BEFORE WE BUCKLE DOWN TO BUSINESS. ONE CONCERNS FORMATORY SPEECH AND PERTAINS TO QUESTIONS ASKED IN EARLIER SESSIONS. WE HEAR MORE FORMATORY SPEECH IN RESPONSE TO VERBALIZED INSIGHTS THAN AT EARLIER SESSIONS, ESPECIALLY THOSE VOICED BY DAVID SWAN. WE DO NOT SAY THAT YOU SHOULD NOT COMMENT ON INSIGHTS, BUT GIVE SOME THOUGHT TO UNDERSTANDING BEFORE EXCLAIMING "WOW" OR "FAR OUT." EXERCISES IMPOSED ON TEACHINGS MUST BE INDIVIDUALIZED. WE ARE NOT HERE TO GIVE YOU A NEW DOGMA. REMEMBER THAT WHEN THE MEDIUM THROUGH WHOM WE ARE TRANSMITTING IS FATIGUED, CONTRADICTIONS OCCUR. IT IS MORE CONVENIENT FOR US TO OPERATE THROUGH ONE CHANNEL, BUT IT IS MORE DEMANDING FOR THE MEDIUM, AND YOU ALL MUST BE AWARE OF THAT. THIS CAN BE DIFFICULT, WE UNDERSTAND. HOWEVER, IN ORDER TO MAKE THE BEST USE OF ENERGY, WE WOULD SUGGEST THAT YOU PREPARE YOUR QUESTIONS IN ADVANCE. IT IS TOO EASY FOR YOU TO BE LURED BY YOUR EXPECTATIONS INTO MAKING THIS A NEW FAITH, WHICH IS IN COMPLETE OPPOSITION TO OUR INTENTION. BLIND FAITH ELIMINATES UNDERSTANDING, AND WITHOUT UNDERSTANDING THERE CAN BE NO GROWTH OR AGAPE, WHICH IS THE GOAL.

"Well," Jessica says as she reads off the first message she got operating the board by herself, "that certainly told us."

"It took awhile to get used to this new routine," Walter remembers. "Not just having Jessica at the board by herself, but Michael's determination to keep us from making a gospel of his messages. He gets quite adamant about it, even now."

"This business of wanting the Truth with a capital *T* was

a real problem," Jessica adds. "We had several people in the group who were determined to make this a new rule to live by. One woman, who did not stay with us long, kept mentioning religious doctrine and insisted that such teachings and the statements of various esoteric masters must be regarded as absolute and immutable. Michael did not agree."

ON THE CONTRARY, WHEN THE TEACHER DIES, THE TEACHING PASSES INTO LITERATURE AND SHOULD BE REGARDED AS SUCH.

"But what about real revelation?" the woman asked, challenging Michael's answer.

YOU ARE IMPOSING A COMPLEXITY WHERE NONE NEED EXIST. THESE MOMENTS ARE MOMENTS OF UTTER SIMPLICITY. OF COURSE, IT IS DIFFICULT TO MAINTAIN IN THIS STATE, IN THE FALSE ORDER, THE COMPLICATED CHAOS THAT THIS AND OTHER CULTURES LIKE IT HAVE CREATED. AS WE HAVE SAID BEFORE, TO EXPLAIN AWAY THE UNEXPLAINABLE, MAN MUST CREATE FOR HIMSELF THE ANSWER TO ALL THOSE QUESTIONS, THOSE IMPONDERABLES FOR WHICH THERE IS NO PROOF. MAN, IN ORDER TO BE SATISFIED, MUST DEFINE, WITHIN THE LIMITS OF HIS BELIEF SYSTEM, ALL THOSE PHENOMENA WHICH HE OBSERVES. IN MOMENTS WHEN THE ESSENCE BREAKS THROUGH THE BARRIERS, THE TRUE ORDER—THE NATURAL ORDER—BECOMES PERCEIVABLE. MAN TAKES THE SMALLEST ACTIVITY AND RENDERS IT COMPLEX BY ANALYZING, EXAMINING, GRANTING IT PRIORITY, GRANTING IT PRECEDENCE. WE SHOULD NOT LIMIT THIS SIMPLY TO MAN. THIS IS COMMON TO CREATURES OF REASON THROUGHOUT THE PHYSICAL PLANE. THIS IS NOT UNIQUE TO WHAT YOU CALL MAN. MAN TAKES THE SIMPLEST FUNCTION AND RENDERS IT COMPLEX IN ORDER TO GIVE AN ILLUSION OF IMPORTANCE TO HIS LIFE.

"Is the synthesis simpler than the systems that man erects?" one of the others asked.

IN ITS MOST EVOLVED FORM, YES. IN WORDS SUITABLE FOR COMMUNICATION WITH THE MEMBERS OF THIS ENCLAVE IT BECOMES COMPLEX. AGAIN, CREATURES OF REASON TAKE THE SIMPLEST ACTIVITY AND RENDER IT COMPLEX THROUGH SYMBOLS. THE SYNTHESIS IS NOT COMPLEX. THE SYNTHESIS SEEKS INTEGRATION, SIMPLICITY. CREATURES OF REASON SEEK TO JUSTIFY THEIR EXISTENCE THROUGH EXPRESSIONS OF INDIVIDUALITY, ISOLATION, ALIENATION.

CREATURES OF REASON SEEK TO JUSTIFY THEIR EXISTENCE BY ASSIGNING THEMSELVES A ROLE, EVEN A NEGATIVE ONE, IF THAT BE THE CASE. OF SUBROGATION, TAKING THE RESPONSIBILITY FROM THEMSELVES AND ASSIGNING THAT RESPONSIBILITY TO A HIGHER POWER, CONVENIENTLY BEYOND THE FIVE PHYSICAL SENSES, AND THEREFORE, UNARGUABLE, UNPROVABLE, UNASSAILABLE, SAFE, COMFORTABLE, COMPLEX. GO AWAY! . . . THIS SOUL GROWS RESTIVE!

"Michael can be quite autocratic," Jessica remarks, remembering the afternoon that those particular responses were given.

"We had a lot of that to contend with for about a year," Walter says. "It calmed down after a while, and Michael began to give information about the nature of the soul. There was an awful lot of it, and we still haven't gotten it all."

Does that mean that Michael lost much of his smart-ass ways, and began to talk with a more reverent attitude?

"Not at *all*." Jessica chuckles. "There are times Michael is absolutely *kittenish*."

Walter smiles, too. "He used to do all kinds of things to throw us off, particularly when we started taking this much too seriously. Oh," he hastens to add, "it's a serious matter, and learning from it can be a painful experience, but Michael doesn't want anyone to approach this teaching on all fours. We're supposed to use it, explore it."

One evening, Michael began the session with COME JOIN US TONIGHT.

"Who are you?" Craig asked.

WE ARE HERE WITH YOU TONIGHT.

"And who are you?" he insisted.

WE ARE CALLED BY YOU, MICHAEL. WHY THE CONCERN?

"I guess, because the greeting was different."

HOW RIGID.

"That's true. We wouldn't want to spend the time talking to Christmas Past," Lucy remarked with asperity.

THIS ENTITY WAS GUILTY OF THAT TYPE OF HUMOR AT ONE TIME, TOO.

"Well, we like to be certain it's you," Emily tried to explain.

YOU ARE RELYING TOO MUCH ON LABELS AND FORMS. THE NAME WE ARE CALLED IS MICHAEL. THAT IS A CONVENIENCE AND NOT A TRUTH. ONLY ONE SMALL FRAGMENT

OF THIS ENTITY HAD THAT NAME. WE ARE INTEGRATED FRAGMENTS OF A LARGER ENTITY AND WE COME TO YOU FROM THE CAUSAL BODY, NOT THE ASTRAL. MOST OF YOU ARE ACCUSTOMED TO DEALING WITH ASTRAL ENTITIES.

"OK, and how long has the Ouija been used, and what other means of communication are possible?" It was Jessica who asked, holding the planchette tightly.

WE HAVE COMMUNICATED THIS WAY FOR APPROXIMATELY ONE HUNDRED YEARS. WE COMMUNICATE DIRECTLY WITH ALL THOSE STUDENTS WHO HAVE MASTERED THE SKILL OF ASTRAL TRAVEL. WE ARE WILLING TO USE HYPNOSIS FOR INDUCTION OF TRANCES, BUT TRANCE MEDIUMS WHO CAN GO INTO TRANCES SPONTANEOUSLY ARE EASIER TO WORK WITH. THERE ARE DIFFERENT KINDS OF MEDIUMS.

"I wish," Lucy said quietly, "that I could develop Jessica's kind of gift. She's so good at this. But I'm afraid." Lucy was new to the group then, and quite uncertain about the sessions. She was faster and more accurate than any other in the group at taking down the rapidly dictated letters that Jessica gets from the board.

WISHES, LIKE EVERYTHING, HAVE POSITIVE AND NEGATIVE POLES. THERE MUST BE ATTRACTION AND REPULSION OR NOTHING EXISTS BECAUSE NO ENERGY IS BEING GENERATED. THE PRIMORDIAL FORCE WAS ENERGY, NOT MASS. THINK ABOUT THAT WHEN YOU ARE HUNG UP ON CAUSE AND EFFECT. THE MORE PRIMITIVE ONE IS ENERGY. DOES IT NOT SEEM THAT ALL SEEKING THE LEAST COMPLEX WILL RETURN TO THE ENERGY FROM WHENCE THEY CAME?

"But I really *want* to work the board," Lucy protested.

THE DESIRE IS POLAR, TOO. EVERYTHING IN THE UNIVERSE IS, OF COURSE. ALONG WITH THE DESIRE IS ALWAYS THE DREAD. THE CHOICE DOES NOT BECOME CLEAR TO YOU UNTIL YOU HAVE EXPERIENCED THE DESIRE FROM ANOTHER DIMENSION. YOU MUST STAND AND OBSERVE FROM THE SHADOWS OF DREAD.

Leah, a realtor, had come to the group fairly early on, and had begun to ask questions with strong personal importance. At this session she asked, "Sometimes a person may become stuck at the same point. Is he pulled or pushed by some force? It seems you are required to make some action to move."

YOU ARE MERELY GIVEN A SET OF PLANS AND TOOLS. THE REST IS UP TO YOU. THE PLAY GOES ON FOREVER.

"I've played the same game for forty-five years. It was unchanging. I could have spent my whole life in one spot. Is it my own volition or chance that will change my life?"

INTELLIGENCE IS NOT A DETERMINING FACTOR, AT LEAST NOT IN THE TERMS OF SCHOLASTIC PROWESS. IT IS MORE A SUBTLE DISCERNMENT STEMMING FROM MEMORY EXPERIENCE AND THE SHEER POWER OF AGE. THE YOUNG SOUL IS LOST TO THE SEARCH JUST AS A CHILD OF TEN WOULD BE LOST IN THE BUSINESS WORLD. THE MATURE SOUL HAS ALL OF THE CONFLICTS OF THE CELESTIAL ADOLESCENT OR YOUNG ADULT; ONLY THE OLD SOUL HAS THE EXPERIENCE TO SURRENDER TO THE DESIRE. YOU MUST REMEMBER THAT MAN IS A PECULIAR COMBINATION OF THE SACRED AND THE PROFANE: THERE IS THE ALERT, SOLITARY ANIMAL HUNTING ITS PREY AND THE IMMORTAL SOUL TRAPPED IN THIS HUNTER. THIS IS ANOTHER KIND OF POLARITY, AND IS ONE OF THE LESSONS OF THE PHYSICAL PLANE.

"That makes us sound like victims, and not thinking creatures," Craig objected.

HARDLY VICTIMS, UNLESS THAT IS YOUR CHOICE. YOU, CRAIG, AS A PHYSICIAN, MUST BE AWARE OF THE FRAILTY OF THE BODY AS MUCH AS YOU ARE AWARE OF ITS STRENGTH. IT IS THE SAME WITH THE SOUL. EXPLORATION HAS ALWAYS APPEALED TO CREATURES OF REASON AS SOON AS THEY HAVE LEARNED TO CONQUER THEIR NATIVE ENVIRONMENT AND SUBDUE IT SUFFICIENTLY TO INSURE LONG-RANGE SURVIVAL. THEIR THOUGHTS TURNED AUTOMATICALLY TO THE STARS. AS THEIR TECHNOLOGICAL MIGHT INCREASED, THEIR HORIZONS BROADENED. WE BELIEVE THAT THE MAN BERTRAND RUSSELL HIT UPON A BASIC TRUTH WHEN HE DESCRIBED THE "UTTER TERROR OF COSMIC LONELINESS" THAT MAN FEELS WHEN HE CONTEMPLATES THE COSMOS. MAN IS NOT ALONE IN THIS. ALL CREATURES OF REASON EXPERIENCE IT. IT IS PART OF THE EVOLUTIONARY PROCESS ON THE PHYSICAL PLANE AND CANNOT BE AVOIDED. OUR STUDENT FEELS THAT THIS, PERHAPS, WILL RESULT IN A CULTURAL, AS WELL AS SPIRITUAL, EXCHANGE LEADING TO MUCH SPIRITUAL GROWTH ON BOTH WORLDS. THIS REMAINS TO BE SEEN.

YOU CHOOSE TO CONTINUE TO LIVE WITH TERROR ONLY

BECAUSE THE INSTINCTS FOR SURVIVAL IN A TERRIFYING ENVIRONMENT ARE STILL SO STRONG. YOU RAISE YOUR OWN DRAGONS. THEY ARE CAREFULLY NURTURED IN THE BOSOM OF YOUR SOCIETY AND USUALLY AS CAREFULLY RELEASED WHEN THE NEED ARISES TO FAN THE FIRES. IF THIS CEASES, THEN AGAIN THE WAR IS WEAKENED AND ALL THOSE IN-STINCTS BEGIN TO SPIN WHEELS AND LEAK ENERGY. WITH-OUT A TEACHING YOU DO NOT KNOW THAT THERE IS ANY ALTERNATIVE TO THIS AND YOU DO NOT HAVE A CHANCE TO BREAK THE PATTERNS. THIS PERMEATES ALL FACETS OF YOUR LIVING; EVEN YOUR EATING AND SLEEPING RITUALS ARE STYLIZED AND SMACK OF EARLIER TIMES. FEW BREAK FROM THESE PATTERNS AND EVEN THOSE WHO DO FEEL PAIN WHEN THEY DO.

"Is Michael talking about instincts?" David Swan, an assistant curator at a local museum, asked. "Isn't the need for love instinctive?"

NURTURING, NOT LOVING, IS INSTINCTIVE.

FOOD GATHERING IS ALSO INSTINCTIVE: JUST WITNESS THE HOARDING THAT TAKES PLACE WHEN A FAVORITE FOODSTUFF MAY BE IN SHORT SUPPLY. RECENTLY THERE WAS SUPPOSEDLY A COPPER SHORTAGE, AND THERE IMME-DIATELY BEGAN A HOARDING OF COPPER COINS JUST AS THOUGH THEY WERE INTRINSICALLY VALUABLE. THEY ARE NOT, OF COURSE, AND THIS CULTURE WOULD CERTAINLY SURVIVE IF NOT A SINGLE PENNY WERE EVER MINTED AGAIN. THIS BEHAVIOR REMINDS US MUCH OF SQUIRRELS STORING UP FOR WINTER USE AND THERE IS NO REASON FOR IT.

PRIVATE STORES OF FOODSTUFFS IN THIS AFFLUENT CUL-TURE ARE ENORMOUS AND YET THERE IS AMPLE FOR EVERY-ONE. NO LONGER IS IT NECESSARY TO STOCK UP ON ANY-THING, ESPECIALLY IN THE URBAN AREAS, AND YET THE NEED FOR HOARDING IS PERPETUATED BY MANIPULATION OF THE ECONOMY. THIS IS SUBTLE INDEED, BUT NEVER-THELESS NECESSARY FOR THE PERSONALITY TO RETAIN CON-TROL AND TO BE ALLOWED TO PERPETUATE THE OLD SAFE HABITS SUCH AS FOOD GATHERING AND MAINTAINING ONE'S POSITION IN THE PECKING ORDER.

"But isn't instinct often really fear?" David Swan per-sisted.

WORDS CAN BE USED AS A MASK.

Lucy spoke up softly. "I realize that, in me, fear predominates over love no matter how strong the love is."

FEAR OF LOSS OF CONTROL BESETS ALL OF YOU. WITH YOU, IT IS A LOSS OF EMOTIONAL CONTROL. WITH ANOTHER STUDENT, IT IS FEAR OF BEING CONSIDERED INSANE. WITH MANY OF YOU IT IS FEAR OF LOSS OF REASONING. IF THE PERSONALITY WAS NOT LIVING IN FEAR, IT WOULD NOT GO TO SUCH ELABORATE MEANS TO AVOID THE PAIN-PRODUCING SITUATION.

"Is that what keeps holding us back?" Leah's banker husband, Arnold, asked. "I have been reluctant to get involved with the extraconsciousness, out-of-body phenomenon. Is this from fear?"

IT IS MERELY THE SAME OLD FEAR OF THE UNKNOWN. FOR ONE THING, ARNOLD, YOU ARE NOT TOO SURE THAT YOU EVEN BELIEVE IN ASTRAL PROJECTION. YOU DO NOT NEED THIS EXPERIENCE. IT WOULD BE INTERESTING, AND ALSO EXHILARATING, BUT WE REPEAT, IT IS NOT IMPERATIVE THAT YOU DO THIS.

Emily was still very much concerned about the religious implications of what Michael had been saying. "The Bible says that perfect love casts out all fear. Are you saying that it doesn't?"

DO YOU THINK YOU HAVE EXPERIENCED PERFECT LOVE, EMILY? LOVING THE CREATIVE FORCE ITSELF REQUIRES SEPARATION FROM ANY PERSONIFICATION.

Emily was quick to seize on this. "I found in the past that this high state of love made every moment overflowing—day and night I was turned on and that's the only way I know how to say it. Now I'm too old and it's too late for that kind of search. So I take this substitute search."

THE SOUL EXPERIENCES ALL EMOTIONS AT A DIFFERENT LEVEL THAN DOES THE MORE TEMPORAL ORGANISM. THE VISCERAL PLEASURES ARE TEMPORARY. WE DO NOT SUGGEST THAT YOU ESCHEW THEM. JUST DO NOT EXPECT THEM TO SUSTAIN THE ESSENCE.

The astute David Swan picked up on this. "There's physical love on this plane. What about that?"

ARE YOU ASKING ABOUT EROS OR AGAPE?

"Either one," David responded at once. "Or both."

EROS [the Greek concept of sexually expressed love] IS A PRODUCT OF FALSE PERSONALITY AND IS BASED ON THE

SIGNS AND SYMBOLS OF THE PHYSICAL PLANE. THERE IS
NOTHING SPIRITUAL ABOUT THIS AT ALL. IT IS BASED ON
PHYSICAL ATTRACTIVENESS AND DEPENDS UPON STABILITY
TO PERPETUATE ITSELF.

"Still," David persisted, "that doesn't answer my questions. Simply, in the past, love was always directed toward someone. Now what do we do—direct it toward God or Jesus? He said to direct it to yourself, but you can't do that—not a burning love inside yourself. Can you?"

A DEEP SENSE OF SPIRITUAL SATISFACTION IS THE ONLY
REWARD THAT WE KNOW OF. YOU MAY CALL IT ECSTASY
OR WHATEVER YOU WISH. STOP FOR A MOMENT AND ASK
YOURSELF WHY IT IS THAT YOU SEARCH AND FOR WHAT.

"I can think of one time that feeling overlapped into Eros," Lucy said with a slight blush. "It didn't turn out very well, but while it was going on it was heaven. Even when I'm angriest with him, I keep thinking about what it was like before. Sometimes I think I'd do anything to have that back. As it is . . . ." her voice trailed off sadly.

WHEN YOU TRULY WISH TO BE FREE OF THAT INFLUENCE,
TRY MAKING A MENTAL TALLY OF ALL POSITIVE EXPERIENCES THAT HAVE COME ABOUT AS A RESULT OF THE RELATIONSHIP. IN THAT RELATIONSHIP, YOU WERE ABLE TO
GIVE THE GIFT OF HIGHER EXPRESSION. IT WAS NOT RECIPROCAL BECAUSE HE WAS NOT IN TOUCH WITH HIGHER CENTERS, BUT HE ALSO HAS MEMORIES; THIS IS OFTEN THE CASE.
YOU COULD NOT RECAPTURE THAT EXPERIENCE, BUT YOU
COULD DUPLICATE THE HIGHER EMOTIONAL ENERGY OUTPUT, NOW ESPECIALLY. BUT FIRST YOU MUST STOP EQUATING THE EXPERIENCE YOU HAD WITH A SPECIFIC PARTNER.
IT WAS YOUR EXPERIENCE. YOU WERE READY TO HAVE IT.

"But I keep thinking that if he *knew* how important the relationship was to me, he might think about it again." Lucy looked to the others for support.

"Have you talked to him?" Craig asked.

"Of course not. What would I say? How could I do it?"

The others in the room made a few suggestions, and finally the question was directed to Michael.

YOU MUST COMMUNICATE YOUR NEEDS AND WANTS TO
THOSE AROUND YOU. UNLESS YOU ARE TELEPATHIC, YOU
MUST DO IT VERBALLY. THEN YOU MUST LEAVE THEM WITH
AN OPTION. YOU MUST MAKE THAT OPTION KNOWN TO

THEM. THE ALTERNATIVES, WITH ALL THE RAMIFICATIONS, MUST BE UNDERSTOOD, AS WELL AS THE MOTIVATION OF THEIR ACCEPTANCE OR REFUSAL. WHEN THERE IS COMPLETE UNDERSTANDING, THERE WILL BE NO DISAGREEMENT. YOU HAVE ALL HEARD THIS BEFORE, AND WE MUST EMPHASIZE IT BECAUSE IT IS THE SECRET TO EFFECTIVE COMMUNICATION, WHICH WILL BANISH THE SPECTER OF UNFULFILLED EXPECTATIONS.

"There's nothing like talking," Jessica says now, her hazel eyes twinkling. "Lucy did talk to the man—he was her ex-husband—but they couldn't find a way to work things out between them. Lucy admits that it was a good thing, now, but at the time it was very difficult."

Later that afternoon, Lucy agrees with Jessica. "At first I thought there wasn't anything left for me, but I kept thinking about what Michael said—that it was *my* experience and *my* energy. I didn't believe I could feel like that again without Dan, but I found out I could." Lucy smiles animatedly. "You betcha!"

Then what Michael told her helped.

"Not at first," she admits slowly. "It was pretty hard to accept some of those things, you know? Talking to Dan was really awful, but afterward, I thought, 'Well, I've done everything I can, and I tried to make him understand, and it didn't work.' That was painful, but I got rid of that icky 'if only' feeling. I did the 'if only' and that was that."

"The worst of it was really a question of expectations. Most of Lucy's family thought she should make allowances for him, whatever that means," Jessica says. "It was assumed that she should be willing to accept an intolerable situation."

"Well, I almost did," Lucy agrees. "There was a lot of pressure on me to go along with what Dan wanted. For a while I thought about it. I kept thinking I'd make a *marvelous* drudge."

If the pressure was so strong, why didn't Lucy give in?

"Good sense, for one thing," she says, "and another one of Michael's little lectures."

YOU SEE, THE INSTINCTIVE DRAMA IS SAFE AND EASILY LEARNED, FOR THE MEMORIES ARE STILL THERE. THE DOMINANT SPECIES FROM WHICH YOU ASCENDED LIVED IN TRIBES AND THERE WAS A DOMINANT LEADER. THIS HAS

CONTINUED, FOR IT ENABLES THE PERSONALITY TO ABDI-
CATE FROM SELF-RESPONSIBILITY. IN OTHER WORDS, THE
BOSS TOLD ME TO DO IT, HITLER TOLD ME TO DO IT, GOD
TOLD ME TO DO IT—WHATEVER YOUR PARTICULAR PERSUA-
SION HAPPENS TO BE. YOU CAN ALWAYS MANAGE TO DEL-
EGATE THE RESPONSIBILITY. EVEN IN EMOTIONAL BATTLES,
IT IS ALWAYS SOMEONE ELSE WHO IS ULTIMATELY BLAMED
OR CREDITED FOR THE ACTION. THIS IS ANIMAL BEHAVIOR
AND IT IS WIDESPREAD IN THE CULTURE. WE SEE EXAMPLES
OF THIS EVERY DAY, EVEN IN THIS CADRE, WHERE THE RE-
SPONSIBILITY IS GIVEN TO SOMEONE ELSE, WHILE THE
CHOICE AND RESULT WERE DISTINCTLY YOURS. ON SOME
PLANES, EVEN ON THIS WORLD, THE DISTINCTION HAS BEEN
MADE BY GOOD STUDENTS AND ADEPTS, AND THE INSTINC-
TIVE PATTERNS HAVE BEEN OVERRIDDEN. BUT IT IS NOT
EASY. ESPECIALLY SINCE SO MANY OF YOU HAVE CHOSEN
TO BE TOP BABOON AND THE PECKING ORDER IS WELL DE-
LINEATED. THIS TOP SPACE IS JUST AS HARD TO GIVE UP AS
THE BOTTOM RUNG. EVEN THOUGH THE LATTER DOES AF-
FORD MUCH MORE MAGNIFICENT SUFFERING: TO BE BOTTOM
BABOON IN THIS CULTURE IS AN ENVIABLE SPOT, AS EVERY-
ONE CAN FEEL SORRY FOR YOU AND OFFER SYMPATHY AND
COMFORT. TOP BABOON REQUIRES INDEPENDENCE AND IS
RATHER DIFFICULT IN THIS CULTURE, AS YOU ARE TOLD
FROM THE CRADLE THAT SOMEONE ELSE OR MANY SOME-
ONES ARE IN CHARGE OF YOUR LIVES: YOUR PARENTS, YOUR
TEACHERS, YOUR BOSSES, GOD, YOUR CLERGY . . . THOUGH
NO ONE IS IN CHARGE BUT YOU. YOU EVEN CHOOSE TO LIVE
WITH TERRIFYING ORGANIZATIONS WITHIN THE FABRIC OF
SOCIETY, JUST TO KEEP THE CONFLICT GOING. THIS IS THE
ONLY REASON. IF THESE ORGANIZATIONS WERE ELIMI-
NATED, THEN THE CONFLICT WOULD BE WEAKENED.

WHEN SOULS ARE FIRST CAST INTO A DOMINANT SPECIES,
SOME, OR RATHER MANY, OF THE INSTINCTIVE DRIVES OF
THE CREATURE OF NO REASON STILL REMAIN EMBEDDED
WITH THE BIOCOMPUTER. THE PERSONALITY MAKES NO AT-
TEMPT TO OVERRIDE THESE INSTINCTIVE BEHAVIOR PAT-
TERNS AND FIGHTS AGAINST THE INTRUSION OF ANY OUT-
SIDE SOURCE.

THIS SUGGESTS THAT THEY CAN BE OVERRIDDEN. ONE
WHO OBSERVES FROM THIS VANTAGE POINT IS STRUCK BY
THE COMMANDING, OVERRIDING TRAIT OF THIS CULTURE . . .

THAT OF LONELINESS. YOU ARE THE LONELIEST PEOPLE WE KNOW OF. THIS IN PART RELATES TO YOUR NOT ATTEMPTING IN ANY WAY TO OVERRIDE THE EMBEDDED INSTINCTS LEFT AS VESTIGES OF A MORE PRIMITIVE SELF. BEFORE SOULS WERE CAST, THE CREATURES OF NO REASON FROM WHICH YOU HAVE ASCENDED WERE LARGELY GOVERNED BY FEAR, AND THEIR LIVES WERE TAKEN UP IN MANY CEASELESS BATTLES FOR SURVIVAL. THIS IS NO LONGER NECESSARY ON THIS WORLD, AND YET IT GOES ON CEASELESSLY IN SPITE OF THIS.

THERE ARE FEW LARGE CARNIVORES ROAMING THE CITY STREETS AND YET MOST OF YOU BEHAVE AS THOUGH THERE WERE.

THE BATTLE FOR SURVIVAL IS BUT ANOTHER TAPE LOOP THAT PLAYS ON AND ON, EVEN TO THE POINT OF STARVING LARGE PORTIONS OF THE CULTURE, WHILE OTHERS WASTE AND HOARD. THIS ONLY PROVIDES FOR THE REALISM IN THE DRAMA, FOR THIS IS NO LONGER NECESSARY AT ALL. THERE ARE ABUNDANT RESOURCES ON THIS PLANET EVEN THOUGH IT HAS BEEN RATHER RUTHLESSLY PLUNDERED. THERE IS STILL MUCH TO SPARE. THE LONELINESS IS HEARTBREAKING, LITERALLY, AS IT IS SO UNNECESSARY AND SOMETHING THAT THE PERSONALITY EFFECTS AS A METHOD TO KEEP THE BATTLE GOING. IF THE PERSONALITY NO LONGER FELT THREATENED AND ALIENATED THERE WOULD BE NO INCENTIVE TO CONTINUE THE INSTINCTIVE DRAMA.

"So I decided to get off the bottom rung," Lucy declares, "and face up to loneliness."

Was it easy?

"Hell, no," she says. "I'm still working on it. It's hard to get along without all that lovely sympathy and justification."

Is it worth it?

"To be in charge of your own life? Are you kidding? *Of course* it's worth it."

But how does she manage it? Does Michael still give her good advice?

"Whether I like it or not," she affirms, glancing at Jessica.

"Oh, yeah," Jessica says with feeling. "He's told me a couple of things . . ." She stops, shaking her head.

When someone else was working the board?

"Sure. He's told me a little about the task I've set myself in this life, and, let me tell you, it's *scary*."

What does she mean, her task in this life?

"Michael has told us that in each life you choose one major task, and then work to accomplish it. The older a soul you are, the more . . . 'demanding' isn't really the right word. I guess you'd say it becomes more compelling. There are things you simply have to do."

Why is that?

"Well, it has to do with the nature of the soul," Jessica says carefully. "The way the soul ages, and the experiences it has, the karmic debts, the monads, the sequences agreed upon . . ." She makes a gesture of uncertainty. "It's what Michael has been trying to teach us—the nature of the soul."

Chapter 4

THE NATURE
OF THE SOUL . . .

The nature of the soul. That's a very big order. What precisely is the soul? Is what is known in the medical profession as the subconscious—is the subconscious the essence of the soul?

NO. MOST PSYCHIATRISTS, WHERE THEY SPEAK OF THE SUBCONSCIOUS, THEY MERELY SPEAK OF ALL THOSE EXPERIENCES WHICH THE BRAIN RECORDS BUT YOU CANNOT IMMEDIATELY RECALL. THE RECALL OF THIS MATERIAL IS OFTEN BLOCKED BY VERY EFFECTIVE BARRIERS. SOME FEW PSYCHIATRISTS, SUCH AS JUNG, BEGAN TO SEE MORE, BUT FEW HAVE KNOWN OF THE MYRIAD DATA ACTUALLY AT YOUR COMMAND, MUCH LESS THE SOURCE.

The soul is not the subconscious. You've already indicated that it isn't instinct. What is it?

ALL SOULS, OR FRAGMENTS, AS WE CHOOSE TO CALL THEM FOR NOW, ARE OF COURSE A PART OF THE UNIVERSAL CREATIVE FORCE, WHICH WE CALL THE TAO. HOWEVER, WHEN THIS FRAGMENTATION OCCURS AND THE PHYSICAL CYCLE BEGINS, THIS FRAGMENT IS MORE REMOTE FROM THE TAO AND FROM WHAT WE CALL THE INFINITE SOUL. WE THINK THAT WE HAVE A PROBLEM WITH THE SEMANTICS

HERE. LET US USE AN ANALOGY AND PERHAPS THIS WILL BECOME CRYSTAL CLEAR. IMAGINE THE ATLANTIC OCEAN AS THE WHOLE; IMAGINE FILLING TEN TEST TUBES, THEN SEALING THEM SO THAT THEY ARE BOTH AIRTIGHT AND WATERTIGHT, THEN IMAGINE DROPPING THEM BACK INTO THE OCEAN. THEY ARE A PART OF THE WHOLE, YES, BUT UNLESS SOME OUTSIDE FORCE LIBERATES THEM, THEY ARE REMOTE FROM THE SOURCE AND TRAPPED IN AN EFFECTIVE PRISON. THIS SAME WAY THE SOUL IS TRAPPED IN THE BODY. THE BODY IS VERY LIMITED IN WHAT IT CAN DO. THE SOUL IN ITS TRUE SPIRITUAL STATE HAS NO LIMITATIONS OR HANDICAPS.

You keep referring to the individual souls as fragments. What is the soul a part of?

WHEN THE SPIRIT ENTITY FIRST BECOMES EARTHBOUND THERE CAN BE AS MANY AS A THOUSAND FRAGMENTS. AS THE ENTITY PROGRESSES, THE FRAGMENTS UNITE. AS EACH LESSON IS LEARNED, THE MONADS [essential and complete experiences and relationships] ARE FORMED. THIS IS NOT TO SAY THAT THE SOUL IS ENTIRELY LIMITED BY THE PHYSICAL PLANE. YOU SEE, THE SOUL IS CAPABLE OF EXISTING IN ALL DIMENSIONS. TRAVEL IMPLIES PHYSICAL SPACE, PHYSICAL SPEED. THIS SOUL NOW EXISTS IN DIMENSIONS BEYOND THE THREE-DIMENSIONAL LIMITATIONS WHICH MECHANICAL MAN IMPOSES UPON HIMSELF. THE FREED ESSENCE HAS NO SUCH LIMITATIONS, AND IS FREE TO TRAVEL, OR FREE TO MOVE, OR FREE TO EXIST, IN A MULTIDIMENSIONAL UNIVERSE.

That spoils my concept . . . then the Schlitz Beer ads aren't correct? One time around . . . However, this also spoils the concept of the continuation of that consciousness. I would be united with my entity and would no longer be conscious of myself as I know it.

THAT IS INVALID. THE WHOLE IS THE SUM OF THE PARTS. WE HAVE NO DOMINANT FRAGMENTS. WE ARE AN ENTITY-INTEGRATED WHOLE. THERE IS NO SENSE OF LOSS, WIST-FULNESS, POIGNANCY, OR WHAT HAVE YOU. THE LOSS IS PERCEIVED ONLY ON THE PHYSICAL PLANE. NOW WE ARE WHOLE. BEFORE WE WERE SPLIT APART AND THEREFORE HAD LESS THAN TOTAL. THERE IS STILL EVOLUTION IN STORE FOR US. ALTHOUGH WE APPREHEND THIS, WE STILL DO NOT SEE IT AS IT WILL BE WHEN THIS OCCURS. RIGHT NOW YOU FEEL THAT THE LOSS OF THE INDIVIDUALITY

WILL BE FELT AS PAIN. THIS IS NOT TRUE. THE INDIVIDU-
ALITY IS PAINFUL, BUT NOT THE INTEGRATION.

What does this have to do with personality? The soul
seems very remote, if it exists in conditions of all-time and
no-time, part of a whole that seems to run by its own rules.
Where does the personality fit in?

IN ORDER TO FULLY COMPREHEND THIS CONCEPT OF THE
SOUL'S GROWTH, IT IS NECESSARY TO PERCEIVE THE TRUE
NATURE THAT EXISTS WITHIN THE "HUMAN" SOUL OR ES-
SENCE. IT IS A SEPARATE ENTITY FROM THE PERSONALITY,
WHICH IS FOR THE MOST PART A SURVIVAL MECHANISM FOR
THE BODY. THE SOUL'S GOAL IS DISTINCT FROM THOSE OF
PERSONALITY AND THEREFORE THE ELEMENTS ARE IN ETER-
NAL CONFLICT. THIS IS THE LESSON LEARNED ON THE PHYS-
ICAL PLANE. ONLY THE SOUL CAN ASK THE QUESTION "WHY
AM I HERE?" THE PERSONALITY DOES NOT REQUIRE SUCH
INFORMATION.

But what about all the other fragments? Do they enter the
body in sequence, while the rest of the entity hangs around
up there?

ENTIRE ENTITIES ARE CAST FROM THE TAO. THEY FRAG-
MENT INTO PHYSICALLY TRAPPED SOULS FOR AS LONG AS IT
IS NECESSARY FOR THEM TO EXPERIENCE ALL OF LIFE
THROUGH THE CYCLES. THIS MEANS THAT WHEN DAVID'S
ENTITY FIRST FRAGMENTED, OTHER ENTITIES FRAGMENTED
ALSO. THE ENTITY WHICH INCLUDES DAVID FRAGMENTED
AT THE SAME POINT IN HISTORY AS DID THE ENTITY WHICH
INCLUDES JESSICA AND LEONARD [Jessica's immediate boss].
THERE IS GROWTH ON THE HIGHER PLANES AS WELL, VERY
LIKE THOSE OF THE PHYSICAL PLANE, AND AS THE SOUL
GROWS OLDER ON THE PHYSICAL PLANE IT BECOMES MORE
AWARE OF THIS HIGHER EVOLUTION. THE HIGHER PLANES
EACH HAVE SEVEN LEVELS OF EVOLUTION, NOT JUST THE
PHYSICAL. THE CONTINUOUS CREATIVE FORCE THAT IS UNI-
VERSAL CASTS OUT ENTITIES INTO PHYSICAL LIFETIMES.
THESE ENTITIES FRAGMENT AND BECOME MANY DIFFERENT
PERSONALITIES. THEIR INTEGRATION IS THE EVOLUTIONARY
PATTERN FOR ALL SOULS. YOU DO NOT FEEL THE DESIRE TO
SEEK THE REMAINING FRAGMENTS OF YOUR ENTITY UNTIL
THE LAST PHYSICAL CYCLE. THEN, AT THAT TIME, THERE
IS ALMOST A COMPULSION. YOU DO NOT ALWAYS KNOW
WHY YOU DO, BUT YOU ALWAYS SEEK.

Is this a process of growth and evolution, and for what purpose, or just indigenous, and if so, why?

TO INSURE THE CONTINUOUS CREATIVE FORCE IS THE ONLY PURPOSE WE KNOW. THE ENTITIES, NO LONGER EARTHBOUND, EXPERIENCE LENGTHY PERIODS ON THE HIGH PLANES AND AT THE END, REUNITE WITH THE PRIMEVAL FORCE THAT IS CREATION. THUS, THE CREATED BECOMES THE CREATOR, AND THE CYCLE REPEATS ITSELF AD INFINITUM. <u>THIS IS INFINITY</u>.

Then what happens between lives? It sounds as if the soul goes to school.

SCHOOL IS A DECEPTIVE TERM. THERE IS MUCH TIME FOR REFLECTION AND MUCH GUIDANCE. MANY SOULS REMAIN SUSPENDED IN A LIMBO OF THEIR OWN MANIFESTATION FOR MANY OF YOUR YEARS. OLD SOULS WELCOME THE INTERVAL. THERE IS NORMALLY A VERY SHORT TRANSITION FROM THE PHYSICAL BODY TO THE LOW ASTRAL PLANES.

Can you be more specific? Where do people stay after death?

THIS DEPENDS A GREAT DEAL ON THE LEVEL OF THE SOUL AND THE BELIEF SYSTEM GOING ON AT THE TIME OF TRANSITION. FOR INSTANCE, THOSE WHO MAKE TRANSITION BELIEVING IN A LITERAL HEAVEN AND HELL WILL HAVE TO EXPERIENCE THIS BEFORE THEY CAN EXPERIENCE ANYTHING ELSE, AS UNFORTUNATELY, THEY CREATE THIS OUT OF ASTRAL MATERIAL WITH THE THOUGHTS OF TRANSITION. THEN THOSE SOULS LIKE JEAN-PAUL SARTRE MUST EXPERIENCE A LONG PERIOD OF NOTHING BEFORE THEY GO ON. THEN THE SOUL BECOMES A HABITUÉ OF THE LOW ASTRAL PLANE. THE ALTERNATIVE THREADS CAN BE PURSUED, THE ALTERNATIVE COURSES OUTLINED, AND THE CHOICES MADE.

Then why is the world in the state it's in, if all these souls are busy learning things between lives?

THIS IS VERY MUCH A PLANET OF YOUNG SOULS, AND IT IS NOT THE NATURE OF YOUNG SOULS TO SEEK SUCH SOLUTIONS. THIS PLANET HAS EVOLVED TO THE POINT WHERE IT COULD CERTAINLY HAVE A STABLE ECONOMY AND AN EFFECTIVE GLOBAL GOVERNMENT BASED UPON SOMETHING BESIDES WHIM. AND YET EVEN DISCUSSION OF THIS PRODUCES DELICIOUS FEAR ENOUGH TO KEEP IT FROM EVER GETTING PAST THE CONFERENCE TABLE. TRIBES ARE STILL NECESSARY, YOU SEE, IN ORDER TO KEEP THE CONFLICTS

GOING. IF THE TRIBES WERE ELIMINATED, THEN THERE WOULD BE NO MORE TERRITORIAL BATTLES, AND THEN WHERE WOULD ALL THAT LOVELY NEGATIVE ENERGY GO? IT WOULD NEVER OCCUR TO THE PERSONALITY TO YEARN FOR PEACE ON EARTH, AND YET IT FREQUENTLY PARROTS THIS IN SPEECHES AND EXHORTATIONS—BUT PIN IT DOWN AND PEACE ON EARTH IS THE LAST THING IT WANTS. IT HAS NOW SCARED ITSELF NIGH UNTO DEATH, THOUGH, WITH THE NUCLEAR WEAPONS IT HAS DEVISED. THIS HAS EFFECTIVELY PUT A MORATORIUM ON WAR ON ANY GRAND SCALE FOR A WHILE. THIS IS PRECISELY WHY THERE IS NOW A RESURGENCE OF EFFORT ON THE PART OF CAUSAL TEACHERS TO BRING CADRES SUCH AS YOURS TOGETHER IN THIS BRIEF RESPITE. IF ENOUGH ARE BROUGHT TOGETHER IT COULD TURN THE TIDE, BUT ONLY IF THE TEACHING IS LIVED.

That's a pretty dreary picture you paint. Do we have any choice in how things will turn out, or are we bound by negative energy?

WELL, YOU SEE, THERE ARE APPROXIMATELY TEN ALTERNATIVE COURSES OPEN TO THIS WORLD AT THIS TIME, EIGHT OF WHICH WE WOULD CONSIDER FAIRLY UNATTRACTIVE. THE OTHER TWO CONCERN WHAT WE ARE TERMING PSYCHIC REVOLUTION. THIS WOULD, OF COURSE, BE IN FACT THE OVERTHROW OF THE PREVALENT BELIEF SYSTEMS THAT NOW CONTROL THE GOVERNING FORCES OF THIS WORLD, AND WOULD RETURN LEADERSHIP TO THOSE BEST QUALIFIED TO LEAD ON THE BASIS OF INTUITIVE KNOWLEDGE, AND WHAT WE CALL TRUTH. WHETHER YOU LIKE THIS OR NOT, IT IS WHAT IS HAPPENING NOW, AND IT IS WHAT THE CADRE HAS BEEN ASKED TO BECOME A PART OF. THIS REVOLUTION, LIKE ALL OTHER REVOLUTIONS, WOULD RESULT IN WIDESPREAD ANXIETY, AND PERHAPS EVEN AN EXCHANGE OF HOSTILITY. WE CAN NO WAY GUARANTEE THAT THIS WILL NOT HAPPEN, BUT IT IS FAR LESS "BLOODY" THAN THE EIGHT ALTERNATIVES. THEY WILL BURN WITCHES AGAIN, AS THEY HAVE IN ALL AGES PAST. WE NEVER TOLD ANY OF YOU THAT IT WOULD BE A ROSE GARDEN. THE MAJOR LIFE-TASKS ARE SELDOM EASILY ACCOMPLISHED. THE REASON YOU HAVE ALL COME TOGETHER, UNDER FAIRLY UNUSUAL CIRCUMSTANCES, IS, AS WE HAVE PREVIOUSLY INFORMED YOU, BECAUSE OF THE STRONG DRIVE OF THE OLD SOUL TO REUNITE WITH ITS FRAGMENTS. FALSE PERSON-

ALITY IS UNAWARE OF THIS DRIVE, OF COURSE, AND OC-
CASIONALLY REJECTS SEEMINGLY UNSUITABLE RELATION-
SHIPS BECAUSE OF THIS LACK OF KNOWLEDGE. TWO OF THE
ENTITIES OF WHICH THIS GROUP IS A PART WERE FIRST BORN
AT THE SAME TIME. THE DRIVE THERE IS STRONGER.

You say that this is a young soul planet. What does that
mean? What effect does it have?

WITHIN THE CYCLES THERE IS A VAST DIFFERENCE IN
PERCEPTION. EACH PERCEIVES TO THE LIMITS IMPOSED BY
THE AGE OF THE SOUL. THE MATURE SOULS OFTEN VIEW
OTHERS IN ERROR FROM ONE POINT OF VIEW: THAT BEING
THAT OTHERS AROUND HIM WILL PERCEIVE ANOTHER SOUL
IN QUITE A DIFFERENT WAY. THERE IS, OF COURSE, AN UL-
TIMATE PERCEPTION THAT IS THE SYNTHESIS. THIS, OF
COURSE, IS "TRUTH." OLDER SOULS HAVE A TENDENCY TO
BE LESS HARSH IN THEIR PERCEPTIONS, AND AS GROWTH
OCCURS, THIS GENTLENESS GROWS TOO. IT IS VERY MUCH
A QUESTION OF PERCEPTION: THE APPROXIMATE AGE OF THE
SOUL CAN BE DETERMINED BY ITS PERCEPTION OF ITSELF
AND THE WORLD AROUND IT.

Then you mean there's hope?

AS CIVILIZATION AGES WITH THE SOUL AGE OF THIS
PLANET, SO SOLUTIONS TO THE HUMAN CONDITION WILL
EMERGE AS THE AVERAGE SOUL LEVEL RISES IN AGE. CIVI-
LIZATION WILL BECOME PRIMARILY PHILOSOPHICAL. RIGHT
NOW PERSONALITY, WHICH IS A CAMOUFLAGE FOR THE
BODY, HAS THE UPPER HAND.

Can anything be done to speed the process?

WHY DO YOU ASK THAT, WHEN YOU ALREADY SUFFER
FROM GROWING PAINS? THE SOUL, LIKE THE BODY, MUST
DEVELOP WITHIN CERTAIN SET LIMITS. THERE IS NO EX-
PRESS LANE TO THE HUMAN UNDERSTANDING. THERE IS
ONLY GROWTH, OFTEN DIFFICULT, MOSTLY PAINFUL BE-
CAUSE SO FEW OF YOU ARE WILLING TO LEARN THROUGH
JOY.

THERE ARE SEVEN LEVELS OF EVOLUTION OF THE SOUL,
FIVE OF WHICH MANIFEST IN THE PHYSICAL PLANE.

THE INFANT OR FIRSTBORN SOUL

THE MOTTO OF THE INFANT SOUL IS "LET'S NOT DO IT." THESE CYCLES, LIKE PHYSICAL INFANCY, HAVE A VERY LIMITED RANGE OF PERCEPTIONS AND ACTIVITIES. FOR THAT REASON, MANY INFANT SOULS ARE BORN INTO VERY SIMPLE STATIONS OF LIFE AND WILL FIND ANY DEMAND OR COMPLEXITY FRIGHTENING. NEW EXPERIENCES ARE MORE APT TO TERRIFY THAN EXCITE THE INFANT SOUL.

THE INFANT OR "FIRSTBORN" SOUL PERCEIVES ITSELF AND THE WORLD AROUND IT SIMPLY AS "ME" AND "NOT ME." IN THIS CYCLE THERE ARE NO RACIAL MEMORIES. IF "NOT ME" IS PERCEIVED AS HOSTILE AND UNKIND EARLY IN LIFE, WITHDRAWAL OCCURS, AND A CONDITION KNOWN AS AUTISM OFTEN DEVELOPS. IF THIS PERCEPTION OCCURS LATER, THE INFANT SOUL MAY REACT WITH UNCHECKED VIOLENCE: SADISM, MURDER WITHOUT VISIBLE CAUSE, ACTS OF UNBELIEVABLE CRUELTY. THE INFANT SOUL TRULY DOES NOT <u>KNOW</u> THE DIFFERENCE BETWEEN RIGHT AND WRONG ACTION, BUT IT CAN BE <u>TAUGHT</u> THE LAWS OF COMMON SENSE AND DECENCY.

INTELLECT IS A PRODUCT OF CULTURE, AND EVEN FIRSTBORNS AND INFANT SOULS CAN BE TAUGHT TO READ AND WRITE AND COMPUTE ARITHMETICALLY. INFANT SOULS RARELY SEEK HIGHER EDUCATION UNLESS FORCED. THEY ARE BEWILDERED AND HOSTILE IN STRANGE SITUATIONS.

INFANT SOULS DO NOT, IN GENERAL, SEEK EMPLOYMENT AS SUCH. THIS IS A CHARACTERISTIC THEY SHARE WITH VERY OLD SOULS. MANY INFANT SOULS ARE REGARDED BY COMPLEX AND TECHNOLOGICAL CULTURES AS MENTALLY LACKING AND MAY, ERRONEOUSLY, BE IDENTIFIED AS MENTALLY DEFICIENT.

THE INFANT SOUL ADOPTS THE RELIGION OF ITS PARENTS WITHOUT MODIFICATION, ALTHOUGH ITS INTEREST IS CURSORY AND ITS UNDERSTANDING POOR.

THE INFANT SOUL PERCEIVES LOVE ONLY IN THE FORM OF LUST. IT PERFORMS THE SEX ACT WITH ALL THE FRENZY OF A WILD ANIMAL, COMPLETELY DEPENDENT UPON SOME INNATE ESTRUS IN BOTH SEXES LOST TO HIGHER CYCLES. IT IS POWERLESS TO CHANGE THIS.

INFANT SOULS COOK AND EAT TO SURVIVE, AND THE FOOD IS USUALLY TASTELESS AND OVERCOOKED. THE SOULS ARE FEARFUL (OF ALMOST EVERYTHING) AND THEIR KITCHENS ARE USUALLY ANTISEPTICALLY CLEAN.

INFANT SOULS ARE OFTEN BITTEN BY DOGS WHO HAVE NO PREVIOUS HISTORY OF BITING, SIMPLY BECAUSE OF THEIR INORDINATE FEAR. MOST INFANT SOULS WOULD NOT BE CAUGHT DEAD ON HORSEBACK. ALLERGIES TO ANIMALS ARE DENIALS.

THE BABY SOUL

THE MOTTO OF THE BABY SOUL IS "DO IT RIGHT OR NOT AT ALL."

THESE CYCLES ARE MORE COMPLEX. THE SOUL, SO TO SPEAK, HAS LEARNED TO TODDLE AND IN THESE CYCLES WILL LEARN TO RUN AND CLIMB TREES.

THE BABY SOUL PERCEIVES ITSELF AND THE WORLD AROUND IT AS "ME" AND "MANY OTHER ME'S." THE BABY SOUL FORMS STRONG BELIEFS EARLY IN CHILDHOOD, BORROWED FROM THOSE AROUND IT, AND THESE ARE LITERALLY UNSHAKABLE. THE BABY SOUL IS NORMALLY AGREEABLE—A PILLAR OF THE COMMUNITY—UNTIL AN OPPOSING VIEWPOINT IS EXPRESSED. THEN, INWARDLY, THE BABY SOUL IS BEWILDERED AND BAFFLED BY THE DIFFERENCE. OUTWARDLY, IT WILL EXPRESS ANGER, HOSTILITY, NEGATIVE EMOTIONAL ENERGY, BELLIGERENCE.

THE BABY SOUL OCCASIONALLY SEEKS HIGHER EDUCATION AND DOES WELL IN SMALL CONSERVATIVE LIBERAL ARTS COLLEGES, TRADE SCHOOLS, ETC.; LEARNS "PROPER" SUBJECTS; AND IS OFTEN THE "GOOD STUDENT."

BABY SOULS SOMETIMES SEEK TO BECOME THE BIG FISH IN THE TINY PUDDLE RATHER THAN SEEKING NATIONAL ACCLAIM. NO MATTER WHAT AREA OF ENDEAVOR THEY ENTER, BABY SOULS SEEK TO FULFILL THEIR ROLES IN A DIFFERENT SENSE SINCE PRESERVING THE STATUS QUO IS THE GOAL OF THIS CYCLE.

THE BABY SOUL TENDS TO BE FUNDAMENTALISTIC IN ITS RELIGIOUS BELIEFS. PERSONIFICATION OF THE GODHEAD IS STRONGEST IN THIS CYCLE. THE BABY SOUL BELIEVES IN THE FORCES OF EVIL.

THE BABY SOUL VIEWS ITS OWN SEXUALITY WITH A VAGUE UNEASINESS, AND IF THE CULTURE FOSTERS SUCH, WILL THINK OF IT AS SOMEHOW SHAMEFUL. THE BABY SOUL WILL BE EMBARRASSED BY OVERT DISPLAYS OF HONEST SEXUALITY, AND IT WILL STRIVE TO KEEP THE OTHERS AROUND IT BOUND DOWN BY ITS OWN REPREHENSIBLE MORAL CODE. BEHIND CLOSED DOORS, THE BABY SOUL IS MORE OFTEN THAN NOT QUITE AS PRUDISH AS IT IS IN PUBLIC, AND SELDOM SUSTAINS ANY SORT OF SENSUAL PLEASURE. NOT HAVING EXPERIENCED SUCH, IT NATURALLY DOES NOT "BELIEVE" IN THE EXISTENCE OF THE EXPERIENCE.

JUST AS THE BABY SOUL'S KITCHEN IS ANTISEPTICALLY CLEAN, SO THE FOOD THE BABY SOUL COOKS IS APT TO BE TASTELESS AND UNINTERESTING. BABY SOULS KNOW WHAT KIND OF FOOD IS "GOOD" FOR YOU. THEY WILL RARELY VENTURE BEYOND THE MOST SIMPLE FARE.

<u>MOST BABY SOULS SOMATIZE</u>. ANY MEDICAL PATIENT WHO FIXATES ON A PARTICULAR ORGAN SYSTEM CAN USUALLY BE CATEGORIZED IMMEDIATELY. FOR INSTANCE, ALL ELDERLY LADIES WITH BOWEL FIXATIONS ARE BABY SOULS. BABY SOULS ARE ASHAMED OF THEIR SEXUALITY, WHETHER IT BE HOMOSEXUAL OR HETEROSEXUAL. <u>BABY SOULS ARE PRONE TO USE THE COURTS EXCESSIVELY WHEN THEIR SENSE OF JUSTICE HAS BEEN OUTRAGEOUSLY INSULTED</u>.

THE YOUNG SOUL

THE MOTTO OF THE YOUNG SOUL IS "DO IT MY WAY."

THIS IS AN ADVENTURESOME TIME, WITH THE SOUL RANGING INTO NEW TERRITORY. THIS IS WHERE THE MOVERS AND SHAKERS ARE FOUND; YOUNG SOULS ARE EAGER TO TAKE ON TASKS IN THE PHYSICAL PLANE AND OFTEN SET THEMSELVES IMPOSSIBLE GOALS IN THEIR LIVES. THEY ARE THE ARCHITECTS OF CIVILIZATION.

THE YOUNG SOUL PERCEIVES ITSELF AND THE WORLD AROUND IT IN QUITE A DIFFERENT MANNER THAN IN THE PRECEDING CYCLES. IT PERCEIVES ITSELF AS "ME" AND IT PERCEIVES YOU AS "YOU," BUT IT PERCEIVES "YOU" AS DIFFERENT FROM "ME," AND EXPERIENCES THE NEED TO CHANGE YOU—BRING YOU AROUND TO ITS POINT OF VIEW. YOUNG SOULS RARELY QUESTION THEIR MOTIVATION AS

THEY ARE LIMITED BY THEIR PERCEPTIONS IN A WAY THE MATURE SOUL IS NOT.

THE YOUNG SOUL ALMOST ALWAYS SEEKS HIGHER EDUCATION, USUALLY GRADUATE DEGREES. THE YOUNG SOUL IS A TIRELESS WORKER FOR ITS CAUSE, AND WILL GO THROUGH UNBELIEVABLE HARDSHIP TO BRING THIS CAUSE TO BEAR. EDUCATION CAN BE AN EXAMPLE OF THIS.

ACHIEVEMENT IS THE WATCHWORD OF THIS CYCLE. YOUNG SOULS SEEK THE LARGER OCEAN AS THE SPHERE OF THEIR ACTIVITIES.

THE YOUNG SOUL, IF RELIGIOUSLY INCLINED, TENDS TOWARD ORTHODOXY IN THE EXTREME. IT WILL CAMPAIGN TIRELESSLY AGAINST ALL RELIGIOUS REFORM. IF THE YOUNG SOUL IS ATHEISTIC, IT WILL BE EQUALLY TIRELESS IN ITS EFFORTS TO WIPE OUT THE ORTHODOXY OF OTHERS.

IF THE YOUNG SOUL'S OWN PERSONAL OPINION OF SEX IS RATHER LOW, IT WILL DO ITS BEST TO CONVINCE OTHERS AROUND IT THAT SEX IS EVIL AND SHOULD BE ESCHEWED. RENUNCIATE MONKS AND NUNS ARE QUITE OFTEN YOUNG SOULS. THEY RENOUNCE LOUDLY AND TAKE EVERY OPPORTUNITY TO REMIND THE WORLD AROUND THEM THAT THEY HAVE RENOUNCED. ON THE OTHER HAND, THE YOUNG SOUL CAN BE AN EQUALLY ZEALOUS PROPONENT OF TOTAL SEXUAL FREEDOM. THE YOUNG SOUL PERCEIVES LOVE AS EROS, SOLELY PREDICATED UPON THOSE EXPECTATIONS IT HAS OF THE OTHERS AROUND IT. IF THE OTHERS FAIL TO LIVE UP TO THOSE EXPECTATIONS, THE YOUNG SOUL CAN HATE WITH EQUAL ZEST. SEXUAL CONFLICTS CAN BE AGONIZING IN THIS CYCLE—EARLY TRAINING VERSUS INTERNAL URGE.

EARLY-CYCLE YOUNG SOULS TEND TO ADHERE TO THE FOOD PATTERNS LEARNED IN CHILDHOOD. IN THE MIDDLE OF THIS CYCLE EXPERIMENTATION IS RAMPANT, BUT THE APPETITE IS USUALLY POOR. LATE-CYCLE YOUNG SOULS CONTINUE TO EXPERIMENT WITH FOOD, AND FOREIGN FOOD FETISHES OFTEN DEVELOP. RACIAL MEMORIES ARE STRONGER NOW AND THE <u>DÉJÀ VU</u> DRAWS THEM TO CERTAIN TYPES OF FOOD.

YOUNG SOULS OFTEN OWN STATUS PETS, SUCH AS OCELOTS AND LHASA APSOS. YOUNG SOULS RIDE THE RODEO. ALLERGIES TO ANIMALS ARE DENIALS, WE REMIND YOU.

THE YOUNG SOUL IS MUCH ATTACHED TO THE PHYSICAL BODY AND LESSONS ARE OFTEN NOT LEARNED, EVEN IN THE

ASTRAL INTERVAL. THE YOUNG SOULS SEEK TO RETURN AS SOON AS POSSIBLE. BEING OUT OF THE BODY IS UNPLEASANT FOR THE YOUNG SOUL. IT IS TERRIFYING FOR THE BABY SOUL, INTERESTING TO THE MATURE SOUL, AND WELCOMED BY THE OLDER SOUL.

THE MATURE SOUL

THE MOTTO OF THE MATURE SOUL IS "DO IT ANYPLACE BUT HERE."

THESE ARE DIFFICULT CYCLES, DEMANDING MUCH INTROSPECTION AND OFTEN SEEMING TO GIVE LITTLE PEACE IN RETURN. THE HARD-WON LESSONS OF THE YOUNG CYCLES ARE BROUGHT TO BEAR ON THE MATURE SOUL.

THIS IS THE MOST DIFFICULT CYCLE OF ALL, FOR THE MATURE SOUL PERCEIVES OTHERS AS THEY PERCEIVE THEMSELVES. BECAUSE OF THESE PERCEPTIONS THE MATURE SOUL WILL OFTEN SEEK TO SEVER RELATIONSHIPS, SEEMINGLY FOR NO REASON, OR BY THE SAME TOKEN, SEEK TO PERPETUATE OUTWARDLY INAPPROPRIATE RELATIONSHIPS. IF YOU AND I ARE BOTH MATURE SOULS, WITHIN THIS FRAMEWORK ARE ALSO YOUR EXPERIENCES OF ME. IN OTHER WORDS, WHILE I AM EXPERIENCING YOU, YOU ARE EXPERIENCING ME, AND AT THE SAME TIME, YOU ARE AWARE OF MY EXPERIENCE, AND UPON THIS DEEPER AWARENESS, YOU AND I WILL BASE ANY FUTURE SOCIAL INTERCOURSE. AS YOU CAN IMAGINE, SOMETIMES THIS MAKES LIVING DIFFICULT. THE MATURE SOUL IS NOT AS OPEN TO THE OCCULT AS THE OLD SOUL. THE MATURE SOUL PERCEIVES BEAUTY WITH A CLARITY NOT FOUND IN THE EARLIER CYCLES.

AT THE END OF THE CYCLE, THE MATURE SOUL BEGINS TO PERCEIVE TRUTH. THIS PREPARES THE SOUL FOR THE SEARCH. THIS IS NOT TO SAY THAT THE MATURE SOUL IS ISOLATED FROM ITS FELLOWS; QUITE THE CONTRARY. WHEN THE MATURE SOULS PERCEIVE THE UNHAPPY ONES, THEY DESIRE TO SHIELD THEMSELVES FROM THE UNPLEASANT VIBRATIONS. YOU HAVE ALREADY EXPERIENCED THE BACKLASH FROM THIS. BUT KNOW THIS WELL: YOU CANNOT ALTER THEIR PLAY NO MATTER HOW MUCH YOU LOVE THEM. IT IS THE NATURE OF THE MATURE SOUL TO SEEK AND TO QUESTION THE MOTIVATION FOR ALL OF LIFE'S ACTIONS.

WHEN THIS OCCURS, THERE IS A GRADUAL OPENING UP OF THE SOUL, AND WHEN THIS HAPPENS, WE CAN MAKE LIMITED CONTACT. MORE OF THE UNUSED PORTION OF THE BRAIN COMES INTO PLAY DURING THIS CYCLE AND PSYCHIC PHENOMENA OCCUR WITH MORE FREQUENCY UNTIL THEY ARE FINALLY ACKNOWLEDGED AND THE SERIOUS WORK BEGINS. THIS IS MADE MORE DIFFICULT BECAUSE THIS CYCLE IS REALLY FRAUGHT WITH <u>MAYA</u> [artificial behavior], MORE SO THAN ANY OTHER CYCLE: THE PERCEPTION OF THE OLDER SOUL BEGINS TO EMERGE, BUT THE UNDERSTANDING DOES NOT. MATURE SOULS FEEL ALL OF THE HOSTILE VIBRATIONS AROUND THEM. THEY HAVE A NEED TO REMOVE THEMSELVES FROM THIS, BUT ARE TOO CAUGHT UP IN THE TRADITIONAL MORES TO REMOVE THEMSELVES ENTIRELY. THEY FEEL A CERTAIN SENSE OF DUTY WHICH DOES NOT DISSIPATE UNTIL THE TRANSITION IS MADE. THIS IS WHY A SKILLED THERAPIST WOULD BE OF HELP IN THIS CYCLE. BY THERAPIST WE DO NOT MEAN A YOUNG SOUL PRACTICING PSYCHIATRY EITHER.

IN THE MATURE CYCLE THERE IS ACUTE PERCEPTION OF THE VEIL THAT LIES BETWEEN THE REAL AND ARTIFICIAL SPACE, AND AS NEVER BEFORE, THE LONGING TO PENETRATE THIS VEIL AND GO BEYOND THE SENSES TO GLIMPSE THE PANDIMENSIONAL. TO KNOW THAT YOU ARE NOT ALONE IN THE VOID, YOU MUST WALK OUT ON THE THIN ICE AND THAT WAY TEST THE PHYSICAL UNIVERSE AND ITS RESPONSE TO YOUR PLEA. MOST MATURE SOULS FEEL THIS, AND IN SOME WAY TRANSLATE IT INTO DREAMS OF INCREDIBLE STRENGTH AND STRANGE BEAUTY. NOT MANY, UNFORTUNATELY, RETAIN THE MEMORY OF THESE DREAMS OR QUESTION THEIR MEANING. WHEN A SOUL NOT IN TEACHING ENCOUNTERS THE TRUE PERSONALITY IN ESSENCE FOR THE FIRST TIME, IT IS, OF COURSE, A DEVASTATING EXPERIENCE. THIS USUALLY COMES ABOUT IN MOMENTS OF EXTREME STRESS, GRIEF, OR SOMETIMES EVEN TRAUMA. IT CAN, HOWEVER, COME ABOUT IF THE SOUL IS SUDDENLY CATAPULTED INTO A SITUATION SO UNUSUAL THAT NONE OF THE TAPES [memories of experiences in previous lives] IS APPLICABLE. IT APPLIES IN THIS CASE TO THE DREAM, AS WELL AS ALL UNUSUAL SITUATIONS. OF COURSE, IT IS UNDENIABLY TRUE THAT NONE OF YOU HAS A PERMANENT TAPE TELLING YOU HOW TO REACT TO THE SURFACE OF THE MOON AND IT IS

CONCEIVABLE THAT ALL OF YOU WOULD ENCOUNTER YOUR TRUE PERSONALITY WERE YOU TO FIND YOURSELVES AT THE CONTROLS OF A LARGE JET AIRCRAFT WITHOUT ANY PRIOR TRAINING TO GUIDE YOU EXCEPT PERHAPS A FEW FLYING LESSONS IN A SMALL PROPELLER-DRIVEN PLANE.

MATURE SOULS SEEK AN ALMOST UNKNOWN QUALITY IN THEIR LIVES; IN OTHER WORDS, THEY KNOW THEY ARE SEEKING BUT ARE GENERALLY UNCLEAR WHAT IT IS THEY SEEK. FOR THIS REASON MATURE SOULS DO NOT USUALLY ENJOY LIFE UNLESS THEY ARE SURROUNDED BY SOULS IN BLISS. THIS IS A DIFFICULT CYCLE. WE MUST EMPHASIZE THE DIFFICULTY. THE MATURE SOUL IS BESET WITH MANY PROBLEMS, ALL INTRINSIC. THE ONLY WAY TO HELP IS TO MAKE THE ENVIRONMENT NONSTRESSFUL, SO THAT IT HAS SANCTUARY. THE MATURE SOUL OFTEN SEEKS PROFESSIONAL HELP ON ITS OWN.

THE MATURE SOUL ALWAYS SEEKS HIGHER EDUCATION, ALTHOUGH NOT ALWAYS IN AN INSTITUTIONAL SETTING. IT IS OFTEN TOO UNCOMFORTABLE IN A SCHOOL SETTING. THE MATURE SOUL MAKES A MASSIVE CONTRIBUTION TO KNOWLEDGE, BOTH PHILOSOPHICAL AND SCIENTIFIC. KARL MARX, ALFRED ADLER, FRITZ PERLS, SIGMUND FREUD, IMMANUEL KANT, ARISTOTLE, AND ALBERT EINSTEIN WERE ALL MATURE SOULS.

THERE IS A REAL CHANGE OF EMPHASIS IN THE PUBLIC LIVES AND CAREERS OF MATURE SOULS. MATURE SOULS PURSUE THEIR PUBLIC LIVES FOR VERY DIFFERENT REASONS. AFTER ALL, THEY ARE QUESTING, AND THEIR WORK WILL COINCIDE WITH THE NATURE OF THEIR QUEST.

RELIGION BECOMES SELF-MOTIVATED IN THE MATURE-SOUL CYCLE. THE MATURE SOUL SEEKS QUIET FAITHS: QUAKERISM, UNITARIANISM, BUDDHISM.

WITH THE RIGHT PARTNER (ANOTHER MATURE SOUL WHO HAS BECOME CENTERED, OR AN OLDER SOUL) THE MATURE SOUL CAN BE AN ARDENT LOVER. THE LOVE IS DEEP AND LASTING, FOR AGAPE IS POSSIBLE DURING THIS CYCLE IF THE INNER CONFLICTS ARE RESOLVED. WITH THE WRONG PARTNER THERE IS APATHY, IMPOTENCY, FRIGIDITY, INFIDELITY. THIS SOUL HAS MORE OF A TENDENCY TO "MATE FOR LIFE" THAN ANY OF THE OTHER CYCLES, PROVIDING A COMFORTABLE MATING OCCURS.

MATURE SOULS MAKE FINE CHEFS: THEY ENJOY PRECI-

SION COOKING AND GOURMET DINING. THEIR HOLLANDAISE SAUCE DOES NOT CURDLE—IT WOULD NOT DARE. WINE FETISHES ARE AT THEIR HEIGHT IN THIS CYCLE. A MATURE SOUL WOULD NEVER SERVE A ZINFANDEL WITH LOBSTER. AN OLD SOUL WOULD NOT HESITATE A MOMENT, IF ZINFANDEL HAPPENED TO BE ITS FAVORITE WINE.

THE PETS BELONGING TO MATURE SOULS WILL MOST OFTEN REFLECT THEIR OWNERS' PERSONALITIES. MANY WINNERS OF OBEDIENCE TRIALS BELONG TO MATURE SOULS. MATURE SOULS RIDE TO THE HOUNDS.

AND AS IF ALL THIS WERE NOT ENOUGH, INFANT SOULS ARE OFTEN GIVEN TO MATURE SOULS FOR GROWTH.

THE OLD SOUL

THE MOTTO OF THE OLD SOUL IS "YOU DO WHAT YOU WANT TO, AND I'LL DO WHAT I WANT."

THERE IS A CHANGE OF PACE HERE. IN PREVIOUS CYCLES THE SOUL WAS NOT DRAWN TO THE SEARCH WITH THE SAME INTENSITY THAT IT IS IN THE OLD CYCLES. THERE IS A NEWER AND MORE PROFOUND CREATIVITY WHICH IS PART OF THE SEARCH.

THE OLD SOUL PERCEIVES OTHERS AS A PART OF SOMETHING GREATER THAT INCLUDES ITSELF. AND WITH THIS COMES THE REALIZATION THAT THERE ARE NO PROBLEMS EXCEPT THOSE CREATED BY FALSE PERSONALITY AS A DEFENSE. HOWEVER, IT IS DIFFICULT FOR OLD SOULS TO BREAK THESE PATTERNS BECAUSE OLD SOULS MORE OFTEN THAN NOT SEEK THE ROUTE OF LEAST RESISTANCE.

THE OLDER SOUL USUALLY ENJOYS HARD MANUAL LABOR, BUT SELDOM WORKS AS AN ARTISAN. IT MAY OR MAY NOT SEEK HIGHER EDUCATION. IF PRESSURE IS EXERTED BY THE GURU, IT WILL, OR IF IT SENSES THAT ITS TASK SOMEHOW INVOLVES THE NECESSITY FOR OBTAINING THE PROPER CREDENTIALS. FOR THIS REASON, MANY OLD SOULS ARE GARDENERS. YOUNG SOULS WITH FABULOUS ESTATES PAY THEM WELL TO EXERCISE THIS INBORN TALENT. THE MONEY THUS GAINED IS USED BY THE MID-CAUSAL BODY TO PERPETUATE ITS INFLUENCE ON THE PHYSICAL PLANE. THERE IS ANOTHER ASPECT TO THIS. THE OLD SOUL, AT A DEEPER LEVEL, REALIZES THE FUTILITY AND TEMPORARY NATURE OF MA-

TERIAL ACHIEVEMENTS AND THEREFORE LACKS THE DRIVE TO ACCOMPLISH THIS. THEY ARE ALL EXTREMELY COMPETENT, EVEN IN ROLES THAT ARE OUT OF ESSENCE. THE DRIVE NOW IS FOR SPIRITUAL EVOLUTION IN ALL OLD SOULS. THEREFORE, THEY ARE INCLINED TO LET THE REST SLIDE. ANY ONE OF THEM COULD ACHIEVE ANYTHING THEY WISH TO, BUT MORE OFTEN THAN NOT OLD SOULS CHOOSE TO HAVE LIVES IN WHICH THE USUAL WORKING WORLD AND SURVIVAL STRUGGLE WILL NOT TOUCH THEM. IN THEIR WORK THEY TEND TO CHOOSE AN OCCUPATION THAT IS PLEASANT OR NOT PARTICULARLY DEMANDING SO THAT THEY WILL BE FREE TO PURSUE THEIR REAL GOALS WITHOUT HARDSHIP, UNLESS THE EMPLOYMENT AIDS THE SEARCH. FOR THAT REASON, FINAL-LEVEL OLD SOULS RARELY SEEK REMUNERATIVE EMPLOYMENT FOR ANY PERIOD OF TIME.

THE RELIGION OF THE OLD SOULS IS EXPANSIVE AND INCLUDES UNORTHODOX RITUALS. GROVES OF TREES BECOME CATHEDRALS AND THE PRESENCE OF THE REALIZED MASTERS IS OFTEN FELT BY OLDER SOULS. THE SYNTHESIS IS PERCEIVED IN THE FINAL CYCLE, AND OLD SOULS SELDOM CLING TO DOGMA.

THE OLD SOUL IS CASUAL ABOUT SEX IN THE EARLIER LEVELS BECAUSE EROTIC LOVE BEGINS TO LOSE ITS CHARM. IN THE FINAL LEVEL, THE OLD SOUL OFTEN DOES NOT PARTICIPATE FOR LACK OF PURPOSE. (SEX ADDS NOTHING TO ITS LIFE.) THE OLD SOUL IS INTENSELY SENSUAL, HOWEVER, AND DOES ENJOY CLOSE PHYSICAL CONTACT. THE OLD SOUL IS USUALLY AN EXPERIENCED AND EXCITING PARTNER FOR SOULS IN AN EARLIER CYCLE, BUT CAN BE A VERY DISAPPOINTING LOVER BECAUSE OF ITS NONCHALANCE.

OLD SOULS ARE CASUAL COOKS: THEY USE RECIPES AS GUIDELINES RATHER THAN AS GOSPEL. THEY TEND TO USE SPICES AND HERBS FREELY, AND WILL CUT MOLD FROM CHEESE AND ROTTEN SPOTS FROM FRUIT RATHER THAN THROW THE FOOD AWAY. OLD SOULS FEEL AT HOME WITH LIVING THINGS. WINEMAKING IS AN ANCIENT ART; MOST VINTNERS ARE OLDER SOULS AND MAY HAVE BEEN VINTNERS BEFORE, RETURNING TO THAT ART MOST GLADLY. THEY CAN INDULGE THEIR PENCHANT FOR GARDENING, MAKE A LIVING, AND AVOID THE RAT RACE AT THE SAME TIME.

WE HAVE TOLD THIS GROUP ONCE THAT MOST OLDER SOULS DO FIND COMFORT AND HAVE AFFINITIES FOR OTHER

CREATURES. MOST OLDER SOULS INSPIRE CONFIDENCE IN THE ANIMALS AND THE ANIMALS RESPOND QUITE NATURALLY TO THIS. SOME OLDER SOULS EVEN FIND THAT THIS AFFINITY EXTENDS TO WILD AND FEARFUL ANIMALS. SEVERAL IN THIS GROUP HAVE DEMONSTRATED THIS. ANY BAD EXPERIENCE WITH ANIMALS AT AN EARLY AGE WILL CAUSE SOME ABHORRENCE. THE OLDER SOUL DOES NOT GENERALLY EXTEND BEYOND THE OFFENDING SPECIES, NOR DOES IT REACH THE PHOBIC STAGE, AS IN THE CASE OF PRIMARY EXPERIENCES DATING BACK TO PREVIOUS LIVES.

MOST SHAGGY DOGS BELONG TO OLD SOULS. OLD SOULS BEGIN TO RELATE TO WILD ANIMALS AND OFTEN HAVE AN AFFINITY FOR ALL LIVING CREATURES. OLD SOULS RIDE TO THE TRAILS.

WHAT OLD SOULS DO NOT UNDERSTAND YET IS THAT THEY ARE ALL CAUGHT UP IN A DEVICE THAT IS THE LAST GATHERING TOGETHER. THAT IS WHAT THE OLD-SOUL CYCLE IS ALL ABOUT. ALL OLD SOULS COME AT LAST TO PHILOSOPHY AND THE ARTS. SOME COME MORE OBNOXIOUSLY THAN OTHERS, BUT THEY COME NEVERTHELESS. ALL OVER THE WORLD, THEIR ENTITY FRAGMENTS ARE SEARCHING FOR THAT FEELING OF HOME. SOME DO NOT KNOW WHAT IT IS THEY SEARCH FOR, BUT THEY EXPERIENCE THE EMPTINESS.

THE INFINITE AND TRANSCENDENTAL SOULS

BEING NONPHYSICAL EXCEPT IN TIMES OF MANIFESTATIONS, THESE HIGH SOULS DO NOT NEED A MOTTO.

THE TRANSCENDENTAL SOUL EXPERIENCES OTHERS AS ITSELF. TELEPATHIC RAPPORT AND PSYCHIC UNION OCCUR. THESE EXALTED SOULS SELDOM SEEK REINCARNATION IN THE PHYSICAL BODY. IF THEY DO, IT IS USUALLY BECAUSE OF THE SPIRITUAL AND/OR PHILOSOPHICAL ENNUI EXISTING ON THE PLANET, AND THEN THEY NORMALLY PRECEDE THE DESCENT OF THE REALIZED MASTERS BY LESS THAN ONE HUNDRED YEARS. THE TRANSCENDENTAL SOUL CAN ENTER THE PHYSICAL BODY AND DISPLACE AN OLD SOUL AT ANY TIME DURING THE LIFE CYCLE. IT HAS HAPPENED THAT THE PRESENCE OF THE TRANSCENDENTAL SOUL ALONE WAS

ENOUGH TO PROVOKE THE NEEDED SPIRITUAL, PHILOSOPH-
ICAL, OR CULTURAL REVOLUTION.

THE INFINITE SOUL PERCEIVES THE TAO.

THE TRANSCENDENTAL SOUL SELDOM "SEEKS" ANY SORT
OF FORMAL EDUCATION, ALTHOUGH IT WILL GO ALONG
CHEERFULLY UNLESS THE EDUCATION INTERFERES TOO
GREATLY WITH ITS PURPOSE. THEN THE TRANSCENDENTAL
SOUL WILL GENTLY, BUT FIRMLY, BREAK AWAY.

THE INFINITE SOUL HAS DIRECT ACCESS TO ALL KNOWL-
EDGE AND HAS NO NEED FOR EDUCATION OF ANY TYPE.

THE TRANSCENDENTAL SOUL PERCEIVES THE SYNTHESIS
AND TEACHES IT AS SUCH. IT WILL NOT ESPOUSE POPULAR
DOGMA AND DOES NOT AFFILIATE WITH ORGANIZED RELI-
GION.

THE RELIGION OF THE INFINITE SOUL IS THE LOGOS.

NEITHER THE TRANSCENDENTAL SOUL, NOR THE INFINITE
SOUL, PURSUES PHYSICAL UNION. QUITE OFTEN, HOWEVER,
THE HIGH CAUSAL BODY OR THE HIGH MENTAL BODY DIS-
PLACES AN OLDER SOUL, AND AT THE TIME OF THE MANI-
FESTATION, THE SEXUAL ACTIVITY CEASES. THESE SOULS
ARE NOT CHALLENGED BY MAYA.

What can we do to bring about the manifestation of a
transcendental or an infinite soul on the physical plane?
Could you as a mid-causal entity do anything?

WE COULD DO NOTHING. THAT IS TRUE OF ALL, WITHOUT
THE OTHER FORCES HOLDING THE UNIVERSE TOGETHER.
ALL OF THESE COMBINED ARE NECESSARY TO PERPETUATE
THE CYCLES. KNOWING HOW IT HAPPENS DOES NOT GIVE
YOU CARTE BLANCHE TO GO AND DO IT. MANY PEOPLE WERE
DISAPPOINTED IN JESUS BECAUSE HE DID NOTHING PHYSI-
CAL ABOUT THEIR WOES. THIS WILL BE THE CASE AGAIN.
THE INFINITE SOUL DOES NOT COME TO LEAD THE TROOPS.
THE INFINITE SOUL COMES TO BRING THE LOGOS TO BEAR.
IT IS UP TO YOU TO LISTEN AND TAKE YOUR OWN ACTION.

And how does all that apply to those of us on the physical
plane now?

EXAMINE THE NATURES OF THE VARIOUS STAGES OF
GROWTH IN THE SOUL. THE LEVEL OF PERCEPTION AND THE
NATURE OF THE SOUL'S UNDERSTANDING WITHIN A CYCLE
IS CRITICAL HERE. IT NOW HAPPENS THAT ON THIS PLANET
THE VAST MAJORITY OF SOULS ARE YOUNG AND MATURE
SOULS, WELL OVER ONE AND ONE-HALF BILLION. THE BABY

SOULS AND INFANT SOULS TOGETHER EQUAL THE NUMBER OF OLD SOULS NOW. THIS HAS NOT ALWAYS BEEN SO, BUT LIFE ON THIS PLANET IS EVOLVING TO THE POINT WHERE THERE WILL BE NO MORE INFANT SOUL ENTITIES CAST INTO THIS FRAME. AT THAT POINT THE MAJORITY WILL BE EITHER MATURE OR OLD SOULS. THERE IS AN END POINT OF COURSE, TO ALL WORLDS, WHEN THE STAR EXHAUSTS ITSELF. THE EVOLUTION OF LIFE WITHIN A GIVEN SOLAR SYSTEM IS ALWAYS GEARED TO NOT EXCEED THE LIFE OF THE STAR. IN OTHER WORDS, ALL LIFE ON THIS PLANET WILL HAVE EVOLVED AND COMPLETED LONG BEFORE THIS STAR EXPANDS TO BECOME A RED GIANT AND EVENTUALLY SHRINKS INTO A REMNANT DWARF.

Chapter 5

THE LEVELS WITHIN
THE SOUL CYCLES . . .

"Well," Jessica says eagerly, "you can imagine what it was like in the group after we got all that. We spent the next two months, that's nine sessions, getting answers to all our questions."

Lucy agrees. "Everyone wanted to know about themselves, of course, and Michael told us a little, but said that there was more information he'd have to give before he could get specific." She adjusts the cuffs of her neat blue blouse. "There were a lot of people who started to get scared then, you know? They kept worrying that they might find out they'd done something awful in the past."

Jessica shrugs philosophically. "If you live enough times, you're *bound* to make mistakes. You can't help it. And Michael keeps insisting that to have true understanding you've got to experience for yourself all aspects of life. That means that before you've finished, you're going to do some pretty reprehensible things."

One of the first questions came from Corrine Lawton, who had studied Eastern literature on the subject of reincarnation. "You've told us about the seven soul ages. Could you be more specific?"

WITHIN EACH AGE THERE ARE SEVEN LEVELS. THAT DOES

NOT MEAN THAT THERE ARE SEVEN LIVES. OFTEN IT TAKES SEVERAL LIFETIMES TO COMPLETE A LEVEL. LEVEL IS A MATTER OF PERCEPTION AND FUNCTION.

AT THE FIRST LEVEL, THERE WILL BE ONLY THE MOST BASIC ASPECT OF THE GROWTH APPARENT AND THE FRAGMENT WILL ACT AND RESPOND WITHOUT ANY REAL PERSPECTIVE ON THE NATURE OF ITS ACTIONS.

ON THE SECOND LEVEL OF THE CYCLE, THE FRAGMENT BEGINS TO LEARN RESPONSE, AND THERE IS NOW AN AREA OF COMPARISON, ALBEIT A SMALL ONE. AT THE SECOND LEVEL THE SOUL IS PARTICULARLY PRONE TO EMOTIONAL CENTERING.

AT THE THIRD LEVEL A DEGREE OF DISCERNMENT AND EVALUATION SETS IN AND THE FRAGMENT CONSIDERS ITS ACTIONS WITHIN THE CYCLE WITH MORE AWARENESS OF THE RAMIFICATIONS OF ITS ACTIONS. IN A YOUNG SOUL, THIS CYCLE WILL SPUR IT TO STILL GREATER ACTIVITY. IN THE MATURE SOUL, THERE WILL BE A MORE INTENSE INTROSPECTION.

AT THE FOURTH LEVEL THE FRAGMENT GATHERS TOGETHER ITS KNOWLEDGE AND ESTABLISHES A FOUNDATION ON WHICH TO BUILD. IN OTHER WORDS, IT HAS LEGS UNDER IT.

AT THE FIFTH LEVEL, INTEGRATION BEGINS AND ALL THAT HAS GONE BEFORE IS UNDERSTOOD WITHIN THE CONTEXT OF THE NATURE OF THE CYCLES.

AT THE SIXTH LEVEL, THE INTEGRATION BECOMES CONSCIOUS AWARENESS. FOR ALL SOULS AT ALL LEVELS, THIS CAN BE ONE OF THE MOST DIFFICULT PHASES AND TAKE THE LONGEST TO WORK THROUGH, FOR ALTHOUGH THERE IS PERCEPTION AND AWARENESS, THERE IS ALSO THE HAZARD OF THAT FINAL STEP. MOST OF THE OBLIGATIONS OF THE CYCLE MUST BE DEALT WITH AT THE SIXTH LEVEL SO THAT AT THE SEVENTH THE WHOLE PATTERN OF THE CYCLE CAN BE INCULCATED AND THE NEXT CYCLES PREPARED FOR.

"But," Corrine said, "you have said nothing about the lives as animals. Where does that fit in?"

HUMAN SPIRITS REINCARNATE IN HUMAN FORM WITHOUT EXCEPTION. THE ONLY KARMA INCURRED OF IMPORTANCE RELATES TO OTHER PEOPLE. HOWEVER, THERE ARE SOMETIMES UNRESOLVED EMOTIONAL CONFLICTS IN THE ENTITY. WE HAVE SAID THAT ASTRAL MATTER CAN BE USED TO MA-

TERIALIZE SELF AND OTHER OBJECTS. THE ENTITY THEN CHOOSES TO CREATE THE HUNTED AND THE EXPERIENCE OF THE HUNT. FROM THAT DIMENSION THIS EXPERIENCE IS REAL, IN THE SENSE THAT IT IS NEEDED TO PLAY OUT A SCENE.

"But that's contrary to most Eastern scripture!" Corrine burst out, shocked.

WE ARE SORRY TO DISTRESS YOU, BUT WE MUST REMIND YOU THAT SCRIPTURE HAS BEEN IN ERROR BEFORE.

"I'm certain I can remember being an animal!" she insisted.

THERE ARE EXPLANATIONS FOR THAT. IT IS POSSIBLE FOR THE ENTITY NOT EARTHBOUND TO THROW OFF FRAGMENTS AND CREATE EARTHBOUND ELEMENTAL FORMS. THIS DOES HAPPEN, BUT IT IS NOT A TRUE EVOLUTION. THIS IS POSSIBLE ONLY FOR AN ENTITY NO LONGER EARTHBOUND. THE EARTHBOUND ENTITIES CANNOT HOLD ON TO THE FRAGMENTS. BY EARTHBOUND WE SPEAK OF THOSE WITH UNBURNED KARMIC RIBBONS WHO MUST STILL RETURN. THE CAUSAL ENTITY HAS THE ABILITY TO CREATE EARTHBOUND ELEMENTARY FORMS AND THROW A FRAGMENT OF THE ENTITY TO THAT FORM FOR ITS EARTHBOUND EXPERIENCES. THIS ONLY BECOMES NECESSARY OCCASIONALLY AND IS RARE. THERE ARE SOME STRONG TIES WITH CERTAIN EARTH ELEMENTALS. THE PROBLEM HAS ARISEN MORE OFTEN THAN NOT AMONG THOSE WHO HUNT AND EAT THE FLESH OF ANIMALS. THAT FRAGMENT SOMETIMES BECOMES A "RESTLESS SPIRIT."

David had a more practical question. "How are all these various soul ages distributed? Michael has said that this is a young soul world. Is he talking about a bell curve or a parabolic curve, or what?"

YOU ARE RIGHT ABOUT THE BELL CURVE. THE MAJORITY OF ALL CREATURES OF REASON ARE YOUNG AND MATURE SOULS RIGHT NOW BECAUSE OF THE CLOSENESS OF THE MANIFESTATION OF THE HIGH MENTAL BODY.

"Wait a minute," Craig said. "If there's limited perception within the cycles, but a kind of astral review between lives, what happens? Isn't the soul limited by its age and level?"

NOT BETWEEN LIVES. SOUL LEVEL IS THE FUNCTION OF THE PHYSICAL PLANE.

Alex, an architect friend of Walter's, said, "Recently I saw an old friend whom I had not seen for several years. He is a parapsychologist and mystic and seemed just as dogmatic as ever. He told me that any teaching which says that people change sexes in their different lifetimes is pure bunk, because if we knew something of the origin of creation and the true nature of 'twin souls' we wouldn't have such terrible conceptions."

WE HAVE OFTEN REITERATED THAT BELIEF IS NOT NECESSARY. THIS IS AN EXAMPLE OF ONE DOGMA BEING MORE PALATABLE THAN ANOTHER AND, THEREFORE, ACCEPTABLE. HE CANNOT ENVISION HIMSELF IN A PHYSICAL BODY OF A FEMALE. PAUL COULD NOT IMAGINE A MESSIAH WHO SWEATED, EITHER, BUT JESUS DID.

Walter wanted to be certain that it was clear. "Does this mean that the soul itself is genderless?"

THE SOUL IS NOT OF THE PHYSICAL PLANE. HOW COULD IT POSSIBLY HAVE GENDER AND WHAT GOOD WOULD IT BE? THERE IS NO GENDER TO AN ENTITY, AND THE FRAGMENTS OF AN ENTITY HAVE NO GENDER. MALE AND FEMALE ARE FACTORS OF THE PHYSICAL PLANE.

Emily said she would like some clarification on how to identify soul levels. "It seems pretty nebulous to me, the way Michael has described it so far."

WATCH FOR THE PERCEPTIONS OF OTHERS. IF THEY DIFFER GREATLY FROM THOSE INVOLVED, YOU ARE PROBABLY DEALING WITH A MATURE SOUL. YOU MUST DISCRIMINATE BETWEEN FEAR, UNREST, AND CRAZINESS.

"Is there any relatively easy way to see this?" Corrine asked. "It isn't possible to get into a long discussion about the perception of the world with everyone you deal with in a day."

REMEMBERING THAT THIS IS MOST SUPERFICIAL, AND EASILY COLORED BY OTHER FACTORS, WE WOULD SAY THAT INFANT SOULS MANIFEST FEAR. THIS CAN BE SEEN IN THEIR EYES. THIS FEAR IS OUT OF PROPORTION TO THE SITUATION. THE WHOLE BUSINESS OF LIVING IS FEARFUL TO THEM. BABY SOULS ARE GUILELESS AND THIS SHOWS IN THEIR EYES. YOUNG SOULS ARE IN A STATE OF UNREST. THIS OFTEN SHOWS IN ERRATIC EYE MOVEMENTS, THE INABILITY TO HOLD EYE CONTACT FOR LONG. BUT THEN, THE MATURE SOUL FINDS IT DIFFICULT TO MAINTAIN EYE CONTACT BE-

CAUSE OF DISCOMFORT. OLD SOULS HAVE A DIRECT, PEN-
ETRATING STARE ABSENT IN EARLIER CYCLES. WISDOM IS
REFLECTED THERE.

"You know," Alex said, "I think my partner is a baby
soul. I don't mean he's incompetent," he added quickly.
"He's often a lot more thorough than I am. But he's very
rigid and sometimes hard to deal with. And he thinks that
everyone shares his feelings about everything."

THAT IS VALID. THE SOCIAL BEHAVIOR OF BABY SOULS IS
NORMALLY A DEAD GIVEAWAY. THEY HAVE NONE OF THE
SMOOTHNESS OF THE OLDER CYCLES. NEW SITUATIONS
FRIGHTEN THEM. CHANGE OF ANY TYPE IS THREATENING.
THE YOUNG SOUL IS USUALLY POLISHED AND POISED SO-
CIALLY. THE MATURE SOUL IS SOMETIMES NERVOUS IN
CROWDS IF THE VIBRATIONS ARE BAD, BUT THEY ARE EX-
ACTING IN THEIR SOCIAL RELATIONSHIPS. THE OLD SOUL IS
CASUAL ABOUT EVERYTHING. BABY SOULS TEND TO BE IM-
MACULATE ABOUT PERSON AND HOME, HAVE STRONG FEEL-
INGS ABOUT HYGIENE. THEY LIVE BY STANDARD CLICHÉS,
AND AFTER ALL, "CLEANLINESS IS NEXT TO GODLINESS."
THE YOUNG SOUL OFTEN KEEPS EXTERNAL APPEARANCES:
SHOVE EVERYTHING INTO THE CLOSET BEFORE THE COM-
PANY COMES. THE MATURE SOUL GOES IN SPURTS: ONE DAY
CLEAN, THE NEXT DAY, NOT TOO CLEAN. THE OLD SOUL
USUALLY DOES NOT BOTHER TO SHOVE ANYTHING INTO THE
CLOSET. WHO CARES? THE BABY SOUL REGULARLY CLEANS
DRAWERS, CUPBOARDS, AND THE TOPS OF REFRIGERATORS.

"He's very bright," Alex said, defending his partner.
"Graduated *cum laude* and has three major awards."

LET IT BE KNOWN THAT INTELLECT IS NOT A FACTOR IN
ANY OF THESE CYCLES.

Corrine was interested in returning to something Michael
had said about soul ages. "There are two ages or levels or
something beyond that which occurs in the physical plane
cycles," she said. "Yet, from what little was said, it sounds
as if these souls do occasionally manifest."

THE INFINITE SOUL MANIFESTED THROUGH THE PHYSICAL
FORMS OF LAO-TZU, SRI KRISHNA, SIDDHARTHA GUA-
TAMA, AND JESUS—NO OTHERS. THE TRANSCENDENTAL
SOUL HAS MANIFESTED THROUGH SOCRATES, ZARATHUS-
TRA, MOHAMMED, AND THROUGH MOHANDAS K. GANDHI.

"We've read some of those teachings," Walter said. "But

Michael has told us that when the teacher dies, the teaching becomes literature. How does that fit in with these manifestations? And what does it do to the teaching?"

THE DESCENT OF THE HIGH MENTAL BODY SUPERSEDES ALL THAT HAS GONE BEFORE. THE HIGH MENTAL BODY DOES NOT LIVE IN THE SENSE THAT YOU KNOW LIFE. WHEN THE AVATAR, ITS PHYSICAL MANIFESTATION, DESCENDS, THE LOGOS IS BROUGHT TO BEAR. THIS IS NOT A TEACHING. WHEN THE AVATAR DESCENDS AGAIN, THE LOGOS WILL AGAIN BE BROUGHT TO BEAR, BUT IN THE LANGUAGE OF TODAY. TEACHINGS ARE INTERPRETATIONS OF THE LOGOS. THEY MUST BE UPDATED, NOT BECAUSE THE LOGOS CHANGES, BUT BECAUSE LANGUAGE DOES.

"What the ruddy hell does Michael mean by 'logos'?" Craig demanded.

PHYSICAL EVOLUTION STARTED ON AN ORDERLY BASIS ON ALL WORLDS. THIS CONCEPT SHOULD BE SELF-EVIDENT WHEN ONE EXAMINES THE REMNANTS. SPIRITUAL EVOLUTION OCCURS SIMULTANEOUSLY. THERE IS EVOLUTION ON ALL PLANES EXCEPT THE TAO. THAT IS THE ONLY PERFECTION OF WHICH WE ARE ALL COGNIZANT. TO THE GREEKS, THE LOGOS WAS THE CONTROLLING FORCE OF THE UNIVERSE. TO CHRISTIAN THEOLOGIANS, DETERMINED TO BEND ALL TEACHINGS TO THEIR PREFERRED SHAPE, IT IS THE WORD OF GOD. THE LOGOS CAN BE CALLED THE OUTWARD OR PHYSICAL PLANE MANIFESTATION OF THE TAO. REMEMBER THAT IT HAS BEEN SAID, "IN THE BEGINNING WAS THE WORD AND THE WORD WAS GOD." SUBSTITUTE "BEING" FOR "BEGINNING," "LOGOS" FOR "WORD" AND "TAO" FOR "GOD" AND YOU MAY GRASP PART OF IT. IN THE BEING IS THE LOGOS AND THE LOGOS IS THE TAO.

"Sometimes," Lucy muttered, "Michael gives me a headache."

Now Lucy laughs at that remark she made about seven years ago. "Even though Michael can still give me headaches."

"Emily almost left the group after some of Michael's comments on religion and philosophical teachings. She is truly a religious woman. I'm glad she's stayed with the group because she asks questions that most of us don't ask, or don't know how to ask," Jessica says.

One of the first of the questions that Emily asked was,

"I'm curious about people who lead contemplative lives because of their religious beliefs. It seems, from what you've said, that they miss a great deal because of it. Is this true?"

THAT IS CORRECT. USUALLY THE NEXT LIFE IS SPENT IN A WHIRLWIND OF ACTIVITY.

"Will such a soul always take on important tasks for itself in the next life? Is there always a need for activity?"

THAT DEPENDS ON THE ACTIVITY. SOMETIMES THE SOUL CHOOSES A RATHER VAIN, PURPOSELESS ROLE WHICH LEADS TO NO PARTICULAR GROWTH. THIS IS WHAT A RESTING LIFE IS ALL ABOUT. THIS IS WHY SOME SOULS SPEND MUCH TIME IN ONE CYCLE. THE FIGURE SEVEN IS AN AVERAGE, BUT NOT AN ABSOLUTE. IN GENERAL A LEVEL WILL REQUIRE TWO HUNDRED YEARS OF LIFE ON THE PHYSICAL PLANE. NOT CONTINUOUS, OF COURSE.

Later on, the question of entities came up again.

"Let me get this right," David Swan said emphatically. "There are these thousand-souled entities and the souls go through a lot of lives on the physical plane. Is there just one fragment on the physical plane at any time, or are there a lot of them around?"

THERE ARE QUITE A FEW. IN YOUR ENTITY THERE ARE 287 NOW ON THE PHYSICAL PLANE. SOME ARE IN THE EASTERN UNITED STATES, A FEW ON THE WEST COAST, BUT MOST ARE IN THE NEAR EAST.

"But if two of us are part of the same entity, whose perceptions will the reunited entity have?"

THE WHOLE BECOMES THE SUM OF THE PARTS.

"Do we lose our individual perceptions?"

YOU WILL LOSE YOUR INDIVIDUAL PERCEPTIONS LONG BEFORE YOU BECOME A MID-CAUSAL TEACHER.

"That means that there are about seven hundred members of my entity *not* on the physical plane at this time," David went on. "Do they have a function in my life?"

YOU ARE ALL PART OF THE SAME WHOLE. YOU, DAVID, ARE A SECOND-LEVEL OLD SOUL. MANY OF YOUR ENTITY FRAGMENTS HAVE FINISHED THEIR CYCLES ON THE PHYSICAL PLANE AND ARE REUNITED. STRENGTH COMES FROM THOSE FRAGMENTS WHICH HAVE ALREADY INTEGRATED AND ARE NO LONGER SUBJECT TO KARMA. YOU ARE A PART OF THIS ENTITY, NOT SEPARATE FROM IT, BUT THERE IS NOW A PARTITION BETWEEN YOU AND THOSE FRAGMENTS AVAIL-

ABLE, SO TO SPEAK. IT IS UP TO YOU WHETHER YOU CAN
DRAW UPON THE CONGLOMERATE KNOWLEDGE. YOU MUST
FIRST BE ABLE TO PERCEIVE IT. A LARGE PART OF YOUR
TIME IS NOW BEING SPENT OFF THE PHYSICAL PLANE AND
THIS TIME GROWS LONGER AS MORE AND MORE OF THE
ORIGINAL ENTITY BECOMES INTEGRATED. THE PULL IS AL-
MOST IRRESISTIBLE NOW. MORE THAN HALF OF THE TIME
ALLOTTED TO SLEEP YOU NOW SPEND ON THE ASTRAL PLANE
WHERE YOU CAN APPROACH THOSE FRAGMENTS YOU ARE
SEEKING.

"I think I have dreams about that," David said thought-
fully. "Sometimes the being I see is male, and sometimes
female."

THAT IS A CONVENIENCE YOU CREATE FOR YOURSELF.
ALL OF THOSE FRAGMENTS EXPERIENCED LIFE AS BOTH
MALE AND FEMALE. INTEGRATED FRAGMENTS HAVE NO
GENDER. THERE ARE NO SEXED SOULS.

"If other parts of my entity are on the physical plane,
how can I know them?" Lucy asked.

THIS IS DONE FROM THE EMOTIONAL CENTER AND IT
CONSISTS OF A STRONG FEELING OF CAMARADERIE OR OF
BROTHERHOOD THAT HAS A SPECIAL CLOSENESS AND COM-
FORT THAT CAN TRANSCEND EVEN CULTURAL AND RACIAL
BARRIERS.

"Do I have some sort of obligation to the principal of my
school?" Emily asked. "I can't seem to make out what it
is he wants from me. He's very formal, and is often very
curt with the male teachers and he seems afraid of the female
ones. What's going on with him?" Emily teaches English as
a second language and had recently changed schools; she
had commented on the usual problems of settling in at a new
job.

THIS MALE IS BOTH UNDER LUNAR INFLUENCE AND HAS
UNREALIZED HOMOSEXUAL URGES. BABY SOULS ARE
ASHAMED OF THEIR SEXUALITY, WHETHER IT BE HOMO OR
HETERO. HE CANNOT ACT OUT THIS INCLINATION.

"What about the teacher I've replaced? She had a nervous
breakdown, and now only does a little part-time work. Is
she another baby soul? I've only met her once, and she
seemed very frightened, but I thought she might not be a
baby soul."

THAT IS CORRECT. THE WOMAN IS A MATURE SOUL,

WHICH HAS CONTRIBUTED TO HER DIFFICULTIES. SHE WILL IMPROVE ONLY IF THOSE AROUND HER ALLEVIATE THE CONDITIONS FOR HER. HER REACTIONS ARE YOUR PERCEPTIONS, NOT HERS. SHE IS ALSO CAUGHT UP MUCH MORE IN THE ENTHRALLMENT OF MAYA THAN OLDER SOULS. PROBLEMS DO EXIST ON HER PLANE; THEY ARE VERY REAL TO HER. THE OLDER SOUL BEGINS TO REALIZE THAT THERE ARE NO PROBLEMS EXCEPT THOSE CREATED BY FALSE PERSONALITY AS A DEFENSE.

"Michael keeps talking about maya," Alex said. "I don't know what that is."

"She's the Hindu goddess of illusion," Corinne said.

THAT IS, OF COURSE, ONE DEFINITION. THAT IS ONE ASPECT OF MAYA. WE WILL ALSO CALL IT FALSE PERSONALITY, OR BEHAVIOR THAT IS THE RESULT OF PEER-GROUP PRESSURE AND ACCULTURATION. THE FALSE PERSONALITY IS THAT WHICH IS PRODUCED ARTIFICIALLY BY THE SOCIETY IN WHICH YOU LIVE. IT IS THE RULES OF MAYA.

"Does Michael include ego in maya?" Craig asked.

THE WORD DOES NOT MATTER SO MUCH AS YOUR UNDERSTANDING. HOWEVER, "EGO" TO THE PSYCHIATRIST NORMALLY MEANS SELF, SO BE CERTAIN THAT YOU ALL UNDERSTAND EACH OTHER. FOR THE PURPOSE OF EASE IN TRANSMISSION, WE HAVE BEEN USING TERMINOLOGY FAMILIAR TO THE MAJORITY, WITH SOME VARIATION. FOR INSTANCE, WE PERCEIVE NO SCHISM BETWEEN SELF, SOUL, AND ESSENCE. ALL ARE SPIRITUAL. FALSE PERSONALITY IS ATTACHED TO THE ORGANISM.

"But how do you break away from that?" Emily broke in. "How do you just slough off the whole edifice?"

WE WOULD AGREE WITH YOUR ALLUSION. THE STRUCTURE OF FALSE PERSONALITY IS A FORMIDABLE ONE. THE FIXED, RIGID PERSONALITY IS RATHER LIKE A MOUNTAIN OF GRANITE. CHIPPING AWAY RELENTLESSLY IS THE SOLE SOLUTION. DEPRESSION IS THE EXTERNAL MANIFESTATION OF THE INTERNAL STRUGGLE. DEPRESSION, BY THE WAY, IS ONE OF THE ONLY NEUROTIC MANIFESTATIONS LEFT TO THE OLD SOUL. EVEN JESUS FELT IT. EACH OF YOU SPENT MANY YEARS BUILDING THIS FACADE. DO YOU REALLY FEEL THAT YOU SHOULD BE ABLE TO DISCARD THIS QUITE CASUALLY WITH HARDLY A WHIMPER? WE THINK NOT. PROGRESS IS BEING MADE IN QUITE CONCRETE WAYS.

Sam Chasen, a social worker who had come to several sessions with Craig, raised an objection of his own. "Michael said that I'm a seventh-level young soul, and that's fine with me. But I really resent it when some of these old souls around here start talking about their exalted perceptions. Most of them don't *do* anything about them; they just sit around comparing their wisdom, and that makes me mad. I don't think they should talk down to younger souls."

THEY ARE NOT TALKING DOWN, AS YOU CALL IT. YOU ARE NOT BEING EXCLUDED. YOU CAN HEAR THE KNOWLEDGE. MOST YOUNG SOULS ARE UNWILLING TO DEVOTE THEMSELVES TO THE LIFE OF CONTEMPLATION THAT IS NECESSARY TO BRING THE WORDS TO FRUITION. THIS IS AN ACTIVE CYCLE, THE ONE IN WHICH THE MOST VALUABLE LESSONS ARE LEARNED AND THE MOST MISTAKES MADE. IT IS LIKE ANY SYSTEM OF LEARNING. THE INFANT SOUL IS IN KINDERGARTEN, THE BABY SOUL IS IN LIFE'S ELEMENTARY SCHOOL, THE YOUNG SOUL IS IN THE GYMNASIUM OR HIGH SCHOOL, THE MATURE SOUL IS IN COLLEGE, AND THE OLD SOUL IS OUT IN THE WORLD.

Walter had a question then. "Michael has said that this is a young-soul world. Does that mean all countries are young-soul countries, or is there some variation? Are towns and cities different?"

THERE IS A GREAT DEAL OF DIFFERENCE. BABY SOULS TEND TO CONGREGATE IN MID-AMERICA TOWNS. THIS TO THEM REPRESENTS "THE GOOD LIFE." YOUNG SOULS LIKE THE URBAN LIFE OR THE COUNTRY. THE MATURE SOUL SEEKS TRANQUILLITY, AND IF THIS MEANS ISOLATION, THEN SO BE IT. OLD SOULS LIVE ALL OVER. IT IS THE SAME WITH COUNTRIES. THERE ARE NO INFANT-SOUL NATIONS. INDIA IS A COUNTRY OF MOSTLY BABY SOULS WITH A FEW POCKETS OF LATE-LEVEL MATURE AND OLD SOULS WHO HAVE GONE THERE TO LOOK AFTER THE YOUNGER ONES AND HELP THEM GROW. IRELAND IS LATE-LEVEL BABY AND EARLY YOUNG. JAPAN IS A NATION OF EARLY YOUNG SOULS, THOUGH SOME URBAN AREAS ARE HEAVILY LATE BABY. ARGENTINA AND BRAZIL ARE LATE BABY AND EARLY YOUNG. SYRIA IS EARLY YOUNG. BOTH THE UNITED STATES AND CANADA ARE YOUNG-SOUL NATIONS. TYPICALLY, THEY ARE EXPANSIVE, TECHNOLOGICAL, AND CAPITALISTIC COUNTRIES. ISRAEL IS A MID-CYCLE YOUNG COUNTRY. YEMEN IS LATE YOUNG.

SAUDI ARABIA IS LATE YOUNG AND EARLY MATURE, A DIF-
FICULT PHASE SINCE THE YOUNG PART IS SURGING OUT-
WARD AND THE MATURE PART IS SURGING INWARD. MEXICO
IS LATE YOUNG AND EARLY MATURE WITH SOME POCKETS
OF OLDER SOULS. SOUTH AFRICA PRESENTS A MOST INTER-
ESTING PROBLEM. THE LEADER OF THE GOVERNMENT IS A
YOUNG WARRIOR IN THE POWER MODE; THIS IS RESPONSIBLE
IN LARGE PART FOR THE LACK OF PROGRESS OF THE OTH-
ERWISE MOSTLY MATURE SOULS OF THE BLACK POPULATION.
MANY OF THE OPPRESSIVE ELEMENTS THERE ARE LATE-
LEVEL BABY AND EARLY YOUNG SOULS. BOTH EAST AND
WEST GERMANY ARE LATE-LEVEL YOUNG AND EARLY MA-
TURE. SO, FOR THAT MATTER, IS FRANCE. DENMARK HAS
A SOMEWHAT LARGER SPREAD, FROM MID-CYCLE YOUNG TO
MID-CYCLE MATURE. THE PEOPLE'S REPUBLIC OF CHINA IS
LATE YOUNG WITH SOME EARLY MATURE. GREECE IS EARLY
MATURE. EGYPT IS EARLY MATURE WITH POCKETS OF OLD
SOULS. YUGOSLAVIA IS MID-CYCLE MATURE BUT WITH SOME
VERY ARDENT YOUNG SOULS IN THE POWER AND PASSION
MODES. ENGLAND IS A MATURE-SOUL COUNTRY WITH POCK-
ETS OF BOTH BABY AND OLD SOULS. SWEDEN IS MID-CYCLE
MATURE. LEBANON IS PREDOMINANTLY MATURE, BUT AGAIN
WITH ZEALOUS EARLY YOUNG SOULS ATTRACTING ATTEN-
TION. PERU IS MID-CYCLE MATURE. ITALY IS LATE MATURE
WITH MUCH EMOTIONAL CENTERING. POLAND, TOO, IS LATE
MATURE. FINLAND IS LATE MATURE WITH A GREAT DEAL
OF EARLY OLD. CUBA IS LATE MATURE WITH SOME OLD.
BELGIUM IS LATE MATURE AND EARLY OLD. THE SOVIET
UNION, IN SPITE OF ITS YOUNG LEADERSHIP, IS LATE MA-
TURE AND EARLY OLD, PARTICULARLY IN THE RURAL AREAS.
THERE ARE ALSO A FAIR NUMBER OF EARLY OLD SOULS IN
THE CITIES OF THIS FAR-FLUNG NATION. NORWAY IS LATE
MATURE TO EARLY OLD. CZECHOSLOVAKIA IS AN EARLY
OLD-SOUL NATION. ICELAND IS EARLY TO MID-CYCLE OLD.
SWITZERLAND AND HOLLAND ARE BOTH OLD-SOUL NA-
TIONS.

"Does humor change during the cycles?" David asked.

SINCE HUMOR IS A FUNCTION OF PERCEPTION, IT WOULD
BE STRANGE IF IT DID NOT. BY HUMOR, WE DO NOT MEAN
ACTS OF HOSTILITY DISGUISED WITH LAUGHTER. THIS IS A
PARTICULAR SPECIALTY OF BABY AND YOUNG SOULS. FOR
THE MOST PART, BABY SOULS ARE TOO INHIBITED TO HAVE

A REAL SENSE OF HUMOR; YOUNG SOULS HAVE THE CAPACITY BUT ARE OFTEN TOO BUSY. MATURE SOULS DISPLAY WRY WIT, AND OLD SOULS CAN BECOME QUITE BAWDY. IT IS IMPOSSIBLE TO DIFFERENTIATE BETWEEN REAL BAWDINESS AND SEXUAL HOSTILITY, WHICH IS ANOTHER MATTER ENTIRELY.

"Back up a minute," Emily said. "Michael said that South Africa had a leader who is a young warrior in the power mode. What does that mean?"

THAT IS THE NEXT LEVEL OF TEACHING.

"You mean the cycles and levels aren't all of it?" Walter asked.

THEY ARE, IN FACT, JUST THE BEGINNING.

Chapter 6

THE ROLE IN ESSENCE . . .

Expression

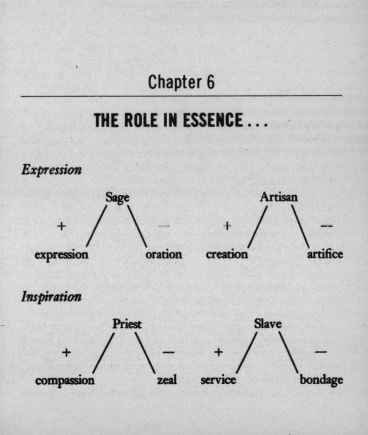

Inspiration

Action

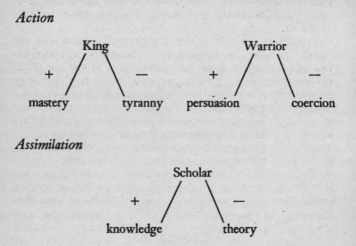

Assimilation

FROM THE TIME AN ENTITY IS CAST FROM THE TAO TO THE TIME IT REUNITES, THE ESSENCE OR ROLE OF THE INDIVIDUAL SOUL DOES NOT CHANGE. IF YOU BEGIN AS A SAGE, YOU WILL BE A SAGE FROM YOUR FIRST LIFE TO YOUR LAST, AND WILL BE AFFECTED BY YOUR SAGENESS. THE SAME IS TRUE FOR THE OTHER SIX ROLES IN ESSENCE.

THERE ARE SEVEN MAJOR ROLES IN ESSENCE. THESE ARE CHOSEN AT THE TIME THE ENTITY IS FIRST BORN, OR CAST FROM THE TAO, AND ARE FOLLOWED THROUGHOUT. IT IS POSSIBLE TO EXPERIENCE ALL OF LIFE WITHIN THE CONFINES OF THESE ROLES. THEY ARE SLAVE, WARRIOR, ARTISAN, SCHOLAR, SAGE, PRIEST, AND KING. JUST AS THE LEVEL OF THE SOUL MANIFESTS INWARDLY, AS PERCEPTION, SO THE MAJOR ROLE IN ESSENCE MANIFESTS OUTWARDLY IN ATTITUDES AND BEHAVIOR.

IT IS IMPORTANT FOR YOU TO REALIZE THAT NONE OF THESE DESIGNATIONS HAVE SOCIAL, POLITICAL, ECONOMIC, OR OTHER "WORLDLY" SIGNIFICANCE. WE DO NOT MEAN TO IMPLY THAT ANY OF THE POLITICAL OR SOCIAL FUNCTIONS WITH THE SAME NAMES AS THE ROLES IN ESSENCE ARE IN ANY WAY COMPARABLE.

THERE ARE THREE PAIRINGS OF ESSENCE ROLES AND ONE

NEUTRAL ROLE. THE PAIRS ARE SLAVE AND PRIEST, ARTISAN AND SAGE, WARRIOR AND KING. THE NEUTRAL ROLE IS SCHOLAR.

THE PRIEST IS THE SLAVE EXALTED. THESE ROLES EXPRESS THEMSELVES IN SERVICE TO MANKIND: HUMANITARIAN IDEALS. IN THE PRIEST, THERE IS A SENSE OF GOD-CONSCIOUSNESS, OTHERWORLDLINESS. A PHYSICIAN CAN BE IN ESSENCE FOR EITHER SLAVES OR PRIESTS, AS CAN SOCIAL WORKERS, NURSES, OR THE CLERGY. THE PRIEST WILL ALWAYS SEEK A HIGHER IDEAL OR BEING TO SERVE AND THE SLAVE WILL SEEK FOR A PERSON OR INSTITUTION TO SERVE. THE PRIEST SEES THE WORLD AS HIS CONGREGATION, THE SLAVE SEES THE WORLD AS HIS HONORED GUESTS.

THE SAGE IS THE ARTISAN EXALTED. THESE ROLES MANIFEST THROUGH SELF-EXPRESSION. ARTISANS BRING TO LIFE FRESHNESS AND ORIGINALITY; SAGES, INNATE WISDOM AND SAGACITY. THE SAGE WILL ALWAYS SEARCH FOR THE UNIQUE THING. THE ARTISAN WILL ALWAYS TRY TO CREATE IT. THE SAGE VIEWS THE WORLD AS HIS AUDIENCE, THE ARTISAN AS HIS MODEL. THE SAGE ACCUMULATES KNOWLEDGE LIKE A SEA SPONGE. THE SAGE IS NORMALLY AN EXCELLENT EXTEMPORANEOUS ORATOR AND WISHES TO SHARE ALL KNOWLEDGE ACQUIRED WITH ALL THOSE WITHIN HAILING DISTANCE.

THE KING IS THE WARRIOR EXALTED. THESE ROLES EXPRESS THEMSELVES THROUGH LEADERSHIP AND THE ABILITY TO INFLUENCE MOTIVATION. THE KING TAKES CHARGE THROUGH KNOWLEDGE AND INHERENT POWER, THE WARRIOR THROUGH AN INSTINCTIVE DRIVE. THE KING WILL ALWAYS SEEK TO GUIDE AND RULE, THE WARRIOR TO COMMAND AND EXPLORE. THE KING SEES THE WORLD AS HIS REALM, THE WARRIOR AS UNCONQUERED TERRITORY.

THE SCHOLAR IS AN INTERMEDIATE ROLE. HE IS AN OBSERVER RATHER THAN A PARTICIPANT. ALL OF LIFE IS VICARIOUS RATHER THAN EXPERIENTIAL, REGARDLESS OF THE CYCLE OR GENDER CHOSEN BY THE SOUL. NO SCHOLAR WILL EVER BE GUSHY, NO MATTER HOW YOUNG A SOUL. ENTHUSIASM CAN BE GENUINE, BUT WILL BE SUBDUED. ALL REACTIONS ARE LOW KEY: GRIEF, JOY, PAIN, PLEASURE. THE OLD SCHOLAR IS DETACHED, ALOOF, AND OFTEN ARROGANTLY INTELLECTUAL. THE SCHOLAR ALWAYS SEEKS NEW KNOWLEDGE AND SEES THE WORLD AS AN OBJECT OF STUDY.

THERE ARE SCHOLARS IN ALL RACES. SOME CULTURES PLACE GREAT EMPHASIS ON INTELLECTUAL PURSUITS. TESTING THESE CULTURES WOULD RESULT IN A PREPONDERANCE OF INTELLECTUALLY ORIENTED YOUNGSTERS. SOME CULTURES ARE CONCERNED PRIMARILY WITH SURVIVAL IN A HOSTILE WORLD.

THERE ARE MORE SLAVES THAN ANY OTHER ROLE IN ESSENCE. THEN ARTISANS, WARRIORS, SCHOLARS, SAGES, PRIESTS, AND LAST AND FEWEST, KINGS. [There are only fifty-nine magnetic kings—that is, sixth-level old—in the world today.] AS YOU CAN SEE, IT IS AN ORDERLY PROGRESSION. THERE IS MORE NEED FOR SLAVES AND ARTISANS THAN FOR PRIESTS AND KINGS, BOTH IN THE COSMIC SENSE AND IN THE MATERIAL SENSE. MORE KING SOULS HAVE BEEN SLAVES IN THE WORLD THAN SLAVE SOULS HAVE BEEN KINGS. THIS IS PARTLY BECAUSE THERE ARE MORE COLLARS THAN THRONES AVAILABLE.

ELIZABETH I WAS A KING. SHE WAS THE GREATEST OF ALL THIS WORLD'S LEADERS. JULIUS CAESAR WAS A WARRIOR, BUT A MATURE SOUL. AUGUSTUS CAESAR WAS A SAGE AND TIBERIUS A SCHOLAR. ALEXANDER THE GREAT WAS A YOUNG KING. MARCUS AURELIUS WAS AN OLD SCHOLAR— A GREAT PHILOSOPHER BUT A POOR LEADER. JOHN KENNEDY WAS A YOUNG KING. FRANKLIN ROOSEVELT WAS A MATURE SAGE; THEODORE ROOSEVELT AND MAO TSE-TUNG YOUNG WARRIORS, AND WOODROW WILSON, A MATURE SCHOLAR. THE SAGE SOUL THAT WAS AUGUSTUS CAESAR WAS LATER DAG HAMMARSKJÖLD.

On what basis are these roles assigned?

THEY ARE NOT ASSIGNED. NOTHING IS. ALL IS CHOSEN. THE SLAVE IS A SERVICE ROLE IN THE MENIAL SENSE. HOWEVER, IT IS POSSIBLE TO EXPERIENCE ALL OF LIFE WITHIN THIS FRAMEWORK. THE SLAVE WILL ALWAYS LOOK RATHER WOEBEGONE REGARDLESS OF STATION IN LIFE AND WILL APPEAR POOR REGARDLESS OF MATERIAL WEALTH. THE MANIFESTED SLAVES MAKE GOOD, BUT BUSY, HOSTS, AS THEY WORRY ABOUT THE COMFORTS OF THOSE AROUND. THE SLAVE IN ESSENCE IDENTIFIES WITH THE WRONGS OF HUMANITY AND TRIES TO BRING COMFORT IN A MATERIAL SENSE TO MANY. THE PRIEST IS THE SLAVE EXALTED. THE PRIEST IS BORN WITH A SENSE OF GOD-CONSCIOUSNESS OR "OTHERWORLDLINESS." THE PRIEST IN ESSENCE CHOOSES

A LIFE ROLE WHERE IT IS POSSIBLE TO BRING COMFORT TO MANY IN A SPIRITUAL SENSE. THE ROLE IN ESSENCE IS <u>NOT</u> THE LIFE ROLE. IN OTHER WORDS, PRIEST SOULS DO NOT HAVE TO PRACTICE RELIGION. YOUR ESSENCE IS YOUR SOUL, THAT PART OF YOU WHICH IS IMMORTAL AND ETERNAL. THE ROLE YOU CHOOSE CONCERNS ONLY THAT INTERVAL YOU SPEND ON THE PHYSICAL PLANE, WHICH IS BRIEF, TO SAY THE LEAST.

How are the roles chosen?

KNOWLEDGE OF ALL ESSENCE ROLES IS ACCESSIBLE TO THE UNFRAGMENTED ENTITY. THIS SOMETIMES RESULTS IN A HASTY CHOICE. BUT REGARDLESS OF THIS HASTE, IT IS ALWAYS POSSIBLE TO EXPERIENCE ALL OF LIFE IN EACH OF THESE ROLES. THE WARRIOR IS A LEADERSHIP ROLE; THE WARRIOR LEADS INSTINCTIVELY. THE WARRIOR IS PURPOSE-FUL IN VOICE AND ACTION, OFTEN POWERFUL PHYSICALLY EVEN THOUGH SMALL IN STATURE. THE KING IS THE WAR-RIOR EXALTED. THESE SOULS LEAD THROUGH INNER KNOWLEDGE THAT THEY WERE MEANT TO LEAD. THEY, LIKE THE WARRIORS, ARE REGAL IN APPEARANCE REGARD-LESS OF SIZE. THE KING COMMANDS YOUR INTEREST WHEN HE WALKS INTO A ROOM. THE MANIFESTED KING IS ALWAYS THE DOMINANT PARTNER IN ANY RELATIONSHIP, WHETHER SEXUAL OR PROFESSIONAL, AS IS THE MANIFESTED WAR-RIOR. THIS RESULTS IN MANY DIVORCES AND OTHER BROKEN CONTRACTS IN EARLY MIDDLE AGE FOR BOTH.

Small in stature and meant to lead—it sounds like Napoleon.

NAPOLEON BONAPARTE WAS A YOUNG PRIEST. SO WAS NERO. MANY MILITARY LEADERS ARE. PRIESTS AND KINGS RUN THE WARS, WARRIORS AND SCHOLARS FIGHT THEM.

It sounds as if slaves are workers.

THEY CERTAINLY ARE INCLINED TO WORK. HOWEVER, NEXT TIME YOU EXAMINE A DOWNTRODDEN, MIDDLE-AGED FEMALE WITH LIFELESS EYES, DULL HAIR, SOFT VOICE, DUMPY CLOTHES, A TYRANT FOR A HUSBAND: THINK SLAVE. THIS CAN BE MISLEADING AT TIMES. THE ENGLISH QUEEN VICTORIA WAS A MATURE SLAVE.

Roles in essence must make a difference in what people choose to do with their lives.

THAT IS PARTIALLY CORRECT. THERE ARE OTHER ASPECTS TO CONSIDER. HOWEVER, WHEN A FRAGMENT IS ACTING

OUT OF ESSENCE RATHER THAN FALSE PERSONALITY, THERE
ARE CERTAIN INDICATIONS IN WHAT THEY DO WITH THEIR
LIVES. THIS DOES NOT MEAN THAT A PERSON LIVING IN A
CERTAIN WAY IS NECESSARILY ACTING OUT OF ESSENCE,
AND WE MUST WARN YOU TO KEEP THAT IN MIND.

Soul level must also affect how a person lives.

OF COURSE. THE SOUL CANNOT EXCEED THE LIMITS OF
ITS GROWTH.

BABY SLAVES CONSTITUTE A MAJORITY OF THE DOWN-
TRODDEN HOUSEWIVES FOUND THROUGHOUT THE WORLD.
IT IS A PERFECT ROLE FOR A BABY SLAVE. WHAT OTHER
OCCUPATION REAPS SO FEW REWARDS AND AT THE SAME
TIME ENFORCES THE ROLE OVER AND OVER AGAIN?

BABY ARTISANS OFTEN CHOOSE TO DO THINGS WITH
THEIR HANDS, BUT NOT USUALLY FINE ART. THEY MAY BE-
COME CRAFTSMEN, PRINTERS, METALWORKERS, CARPEN-
TERS, AND SMITHS OF VARIOUS SORTS. THEY MAY ALSO
HAVE AN APTITUDE FOR ROUTINE FILING AND ASSEMBLY
WORK.

THE BABY WARRIOR CAN BE FOUND IN THE LAW EN-
FORCEMENT ESTABLISHMENT IN SMALLER CITIES THROUGH-
OUT THE WORLD, WHERE MAXIMUM EXPOSURE CAN OCCUR.

BABY SCHOLARS ARE TEACHERS OF CHILDREN, FILLED
WITH DRIVEL AND INSPIRATIONAL MATERIAL.

BABY SAGES OFTEN TAKE TO THE STAGE IN HOME-GROWN
THEATRICALS. EVANGELISM IS ALSO POPULAR AS IT GIVES
THEM A RIGHTEOUS STANCE FROM WHICH TO DISPLAY THEIR
HAM. WRITERS OF MORALISTIC CHILDREN'S STORIES ARE
OFTEN BABY SAGES OR SCHOLARS. SOME BABY SAGES HAVE
HIGHER EXPECTATIONS, AND WOULD BE EVANGELISTS OF
FUNDAMENTALIST RELIGIONS, OR "GOOD PARTY MEN" IN
POLITICS.

BABY PRIESTS OFTEN BECOME MINISTERS AND COUNSEL-
ORS OF THE FUNDAMENTALIST SORT, THOUGH NOT AS PUB-
LICLY ACTIVE AS BABY SAGES, WHO ARE IN IT FOR THE AP-
PLAUSE RATHER THAN THE UPLIFT OR GUILT.

BABY KINGS OFTEN SEEK THE LOCAL POLITICAL ARENA.
SHERIFF IS A POPULAR CHOICE AS IT GIVES THEM THE DUAL
OPPORTUNITY OF PRESTIGE AND ATTRACTIVE PHYSICAL FA-
CADE—THE PRESERVER OF LAW AND ORDER. MAYOR IS AN-
OTHER ROLE THAT KEEPS MANY A BABY KING OCCUPIED.

WHEN BABY SOULS SEEK WIDER FIELDS FOR THEMSELVES,

THE RESULTS ARE OFTEN DISASTROUS. ETHELRED THE UN-
READY WAS A BABY SCHOLAR, AS WAS A RECENT AMERICAN
POLITICAL LEADER. ETHELRED, LIKE MOST BABY SOULS,
WAS TERRIBLE ON HORSEBACK AND WAS OFTEN UNSEATED
BY HIS MOUNT.

YOUNG SLAVES ARE OFTEN FOUND IN MENIAL OCCUPA-
TIONS BY CHOICE; IN OTHER WORDS, IN THIS CYCLE THE
ROLES ARE OFTEN INTENSIFIED BY THEIR LIFE PATTERNS.
THEY SEEK QUITE UNCONSCIOUSLY BUT THEY SEEK NEVER-
THELESS.

YOUNG ARTISANS ARE BUSY CREATING MASTERPIECES IN
LARGE, PRESTIGIOUS STUDIOS WHERE THE OPPORTUNITY
FOR RAPID ADVANCEMENT IS QUITE LIKELY. YOUNG ARTI-
SANS ARE RARELY AVANT-GARDE; THEY WILLINGLY CREATE
WHATEVER IS SELLING.

YOUNG WARRIORS PURSUE EITHER THE ACTUAL ARMED
SERVICES, OFTEN FOR FOREIGN POWERS AS HIRE, OR ATH-
LETICS. YOUNG FEMALE WARRIORS FIND ACTIVE ROLES IN
TEACHING AND THE LIKE, MANY OF THEM PREFERRING
PHYSICAL EDUCATION TO CLASSROOMS.

YOUNG SCHOLARS OFTEN BECOME PROFESSORS IN LARGE
UNIVERSITIES WHERE, AGAIN, MAXIMUM EXPOSURE WILL
OCCUR AND THEIR ERUDITION WILL NOT GO UNNOTICED.

YOUNG SAGES SEEK THE STAGE IN A LITERAL SENSE. THEY
ALSO MAKE ENTHUSIASTIC SALESMEN AND TEACHERS.

YOUNG PRIESTS IN THE POWER AND PASSION MODES ARE
OFTEN MILITARY LEADERS, PARTICULARLY OF FORCES WITH
TRADITIONS OR SPECIAL FUNCTIONS, SUCH AS THE KNIGHTS
TEMPLAR, OR THE GREEN BERETS. THE YOUNG-SOUL CYCLE
ALSO FINDS PRIESTS IN GENUINE CLERICAL GARB, OR AT
LEAST INVOLVED IN "GOOD WORKS," SOCIAL SERVICES, RE-
FORMING CRUSADES, AND THE LIKE.

YOUNG KINGS RISE TO GREATNESS AS POLITICIANS OR
QUITE OFTEN AS MILITARY OFFICERS, WHERE MAXIMUM EX-
POSURE CAN REALLY OCCUR.

THE LATE YOUNG AND MATURE CYCLES ARE THE CREA-
TIVE CYCLES FOR SAGES AND ARTISANS.

MATURE SLAVES TURN THEIR ATTENTION TO MORE PHILO-
SOPHICAL ASPECTS OF SERVICE, SUCH AS PHYSICIANS, THER-
APISTS, PSYCHOLOGISTS, AND OTHER OCCUPATIONS WHERE
PERSONAL WORK IS VALUED.

MATURE ARTISANS GENERALLY CONSTITUTE THE AVANT-

GARDE. THE WORKS THEY PRODUCE ARE VISIONARY RATHER THAN STYLISTIC. REBELLION AGAINST THE NORM IS THE HALLMARK OF THIS CYCLE. ALMOST WITHOUT EXCEPTION THE GREAT MASTERPIECES AND ALL OF THE MOST IMPORTANT ENGINEERING DISCOVERIES ARE THE WORK OF MATURE ARTISANS WHOSE GENIUS IS OFTEN NOT RECOGNIZED DURING THE ARTISAN'S LIFETIME.

WARRIORS WILL TURN TO CAUSES THAT ARE EMOTIONALLY AND PSYCHICALLY APPEALING, OR BECOME STRATEGISTS SUCH AS SYSTEMS ANALYSTS, NEGOTIATORS, CARTOGRAPHERS, AND THE LIKE.

MATURE SCHOLARS WILL TURN TO SOLITARY RESEARCH, STUDY, AND PHILOSOPHY.

MATURE SAGES OFTEN WRITE SWEEPING SAGAS AND PLAYS IN WHICH THEY ENVISION THEMSELVES IN THE STARRING ROLE, BUT RARELY ACTUALLY APPEAR. MATURE SAGES, WHEN THEY PLAY, PLAY TO A SMALLER AUDIENCE OF SELECT FRIENDS WHO ARE UNLIKELY TO BE HOSTILE. MANY ACCOMPLISHED DRAMATISTS HERE, MANY FINE PLAYWRIGHTS, AND NOT A FEW PROMINENT AUTHORS. MATURE SAGES AND MATURE WARRIORS ALSO MAKE GOOD STAGE AND FILM DIRECTORS, AND OCCASIONALLY SHINE IN THE LAW COURTS AS PROMINENT ATTORNEYS.

MATURE PRIESTS TURN TO DIGNIFIED AND QUIET COUNSELING, DREAM THERAPY, PSYCHIATRY, THE QUAKER AND BUDDHIST FAITHS—ANYTHING THAT ALLOWS THEM TO TEACH THEIR SPIRITUAL PATH TO OTHERS.

MATURE KINGS OFTEN SEEK WAYS TO BE RID OF POLITICAL POWER AND TO SERVE THEIR SUBJECTS IN MORE ABSTRACT WAYS. THEY CAN BE TEACHERS AND ARTISTS, MUSICIANS AND SCIENTISTS. THOSE WHO ACCEPT POLITICAL OR CORPORATE POWER WILL USE IT WITH CAREFUL JUDGMENT AND A DEEP SENSE OF RESPONSIBILITY. SLAVES AND KINGS HAVE THE NEED TO SERVE IN COMMON: ONE HELPS LIFT, THE OTHER DRAWS UPWARD. BOTH ARE NECESSARY.

OLD SLAVES STRIVE TO BRING COMFORT TO THOSE AROUND THEM, BUT NOT IN THE MILITANT MANNER THAT THOSE OF THE YOUNG CYCLES EMPLOY. OLD SLAVES MAKE MARVELOUS GRANDMOTHERS.

OLD ARTISANS CREATE SPORADICALLY. THIS IS THE CYCLE OF UNFINISHED MASTERPIECES. THEY WILL START OFF ON A PROJECT WITH FIRE AND ENTHUSIASM, BUT NEVER FINISH

IT, LOSING INTEREST WHEN THEY REALIZE HOW MUCH WORK IS INVOLVED, OR HOW MUCH PRACTICE, OR HOW MUCH STUDY. THE OLD ARTISAN'S HOME IS LITTERED WITH THE CORPSES OF YESTERDAY'S FERVOR.

OLD WARRIORS NEVER LOSE THEIR DRIVE ENTIRELY. THEIR WORK WILL TEND TO BE SOLITARY, OFTEN CREATIVE. MANY ORCHESTRAL MUSICIANS, CONDUCTORS, WRITERS OF HISTORICAL NOVELS, FINE CRAFTSMEN, AND HORSE BREEDERS ARE OLD WARRIORS. EACH, IN THEIR OWN WAY, INDULGES IN OLD-SOUL NOSTALGIA.

OLD SCHOLARS LIVE SIMPLE LIVES AS TEACHERS, BUT RARELY IN SCHOOLS. THEY SIMPLY TEACH THEIR PERCEPTION OF THE LOGOS, WHEREVER THEY ARE.

SOME OF THE MOST INGENIOUS CON MEN ALIVE TODAY ARE OLD SAGES, WHO CAN BRING CONSIDERABLE SKILL TO BEAR ON THIS. THEY AVOID ALL VIOLENCE, BUT IN THE EARLY PART OF THE OLD CYCLE THEY OFTEN LIVE ON CHARM, HEDONISM, AND LARCENY. IN THE LATER CYCLES OLD SAGES OFTEN BECOME DETERMINED AFICIONADOS OF THE KINDS OF ENTERTAINMENT THEY THEMSELVES WERE PART OF IN THEIR YOUNGER CYCLES, GIVING THE KIND OF ADULATION THEY LIKE MOST TO RECEIVE.

OLD PRIESTS SHINE IN THEIR OWN INTERNAL LIGHT. THEY SHOW THEMSELVES IN PRIESTLY RADIANCE, AND GRANT AUDIENCES TO ALL THOSE WHO WOULD WISH TO PARTAKE OF THEIR WISDOM.

MANY LATE-CYCLE OLD KINGS BECOME CULT LEADERS, GURUS, AND THE LIKE. THIS WAY THEY CAN HAVE THEIR SUBJECTS AROUND THEM TO AID IN THE MANIFESTATION OF THE ESSENTIAL NATURE OF THEIR SOULS, BUT WITHOUT THE WEAR AND TEAR OF THE EARLIER CYCLES. OLD KINGS ARE GOOD BARTENDERS. LAST-CYCLE OLD KINGS ARE VAGABONDS AND HOBOES. THE KINGS ALWAYS SEARCH FOR THEIR MOST LOYAL SUBJECTS DURING THE OLD-SOUL CYCLE. MOST FIND THEM AND BRING THEM BACK. WARRIORS SEEK THEIR OLD COMMANDERS; SCHOLARS SEEK THEIR KING. VERY RARELY DO THEY FIND THEM IN WORLDLY OR MILITARY SETTINGS. TWO MAJOR ORCHESTRAL CONDUCTORS, ONE GERMAN AND ONE BRITISH, ARE SIXTH-LEVEL OLD MAGNETIC KINGS.

ONE OF THE FUNCTIONS OF SOME OF THE OLD KINGS IS TO AID IN THE DRAWING TOGETHER OF OTHER OLD SOULS.

THESE MAGNETIC KINGS, AS WE WILL CALL THEM, DO NOT NECESSARILY CALL MEMBERS OF THEIR OWN ENTITY. NOT EVERY ENTITY HAS KINGS IN ITS FRAGMENTS. THE MAGNETIC KINGS PULL THEIR SUBJECTS TO THEM SO THAT THE LIFE-TASKS MAY BE COMPLETED.

Was Michael a magnetic king?

FOR YOUR INFORMATION, THIS ENTITY WAS COMPOSED OF TWO HUNDRED KINGS AND EIGHT HUNDRED AND FIFTY WARRIORS.

Chapter 7

OVERLEAVES

"For about a month," Jessica remembers, "*everyone* wanted to be an old king or a priest. Absolutely everyone in the group. It took us months to get through all the questions that Michael's discussion of roles in essence caused. We still get questions about this, even now." She taps the board lightly. "It's lucky this thing can't overheat, or we'd have had a fire here for sure."

"It's a little hard to accept at first," Lucy admits. "Being just one thing forever, you know?"

She asked Michael about it when he first dictated the roles in essence. "Can a soul take a dual role?"

NOT IN ESSENCE. HOWEVER, THE LIFE ROLE OFTEN BEARS LITTLE RELATION TO THE ESSENCE ROLE AND IF FALSE PERSONALITY IS FIRMLY IN COMMAND, IT WILL ALMOST BE IMPOSSIBLE TO DETECT THE ESSENCE ROLE. ON A PERSONAL LEVEL, OTHERS CAN OFTEN DETECT THE FACADE AND THE UNDERLYING ROLE BEFORE THE STUDENT CAN.

Craig had another matter in mind. "I realize that souls are sexless, but that does not mean they are wholly free from sexuality. Is there sexuality in essence?"

THERE IS, BUT IT IS NONCOMPETITIVE. PLAN IS FANTASY, OR IF YOU WILL, IMAGINATION. IF THE SEXUAL ACT IS SUR-

ROUNDED BY FANTASY, IT IS BOTH COMPETITIVE AND UN-
REAL. IT IS NEITHER GOOD NOR BAD. IT IS THAT WHICH
INSURES THE CONTINUITY OF THE TAO. THIS UNIVERSE HAS
AN AWESOME ORDER.

"So here we are in a young-soul world where there are
more slave souls than any other. Is this a slave nation?"
Emily asked. "I mean, of all the roles, is there one that
predominates?"

IN THIS SOCIETY, THE PREDOMINATING ROLES ARE AR-
TISAN AND WARRIOR.

"Would things be better if this were a mature nation with
mostly priest or sage souls?" Corrine asked.

THAT WOULD DEPEND. THE PHILOSOPHER FREUD, THE
MURDERER JACK THE RIPPER, AND THE COMPOSERS WAG-
NER AND MUSSORGSKY WERE ALL MATURE PRIESTS.

"They can't have been," Walter protested. "Look how
different they are! Even a difference in age levels can't have
that much effect."

WE HAVE NOT YET TOLD YOU ALL THE OVERLEAVES.

"What does Michael mean by overleaves?" Alex asked.

ALL THAT WE HAVE BEEN TELLING YOU ABOUT THE NA-
TURE OF THE SOUL WE REFER TO AS THE OVERLEAVES.

"And there are more of them than just soul age, level,
and type—is that right?" Emily asked.

THERE ARE ALSO MODE, GOAL, CENTERING, CHIEF FEA-
TURE, AND ATTITUDE. THESE ARE ALL PART OF WHAT YOU
MAY THINK OF AS YOUR TRUE SELF, AS COMPARED TO FALSE
PERSONALITY. IN OTHER WORDS, THE OVERLEAVES ARE THE
BODY, THE ESSENCE IS THE BONES, AND THE FALSE PERSON-
ALITY IS THE CLOTHING. ONLY THE OVERLEAVES ARE TRULY
PART OF YOU. IN OTHER WORDS, TRUE PERSONALITY—OR
THE OVERLEAVES—IS A DEVICE THAT ALLOWS YOU TO EX-
PERIENCE ALL THAT IS NECESSARY IN ORDER FOR YOU TO
ACCOMPLISH A FULL EVOLUTION THROUGH THE PHYSICAL
PLANE. THE OVERLEAVES CHANGE FROM LIFE TO LIFE TO
GIVE YOU A NEW VIEWPOINT AND RANGE OF REACTION
FROM WHICH TO EXPERIENCE THE ENTIRE RANGE OF HUMAN
LIFE, SO THAT REAL UNDERSTANDING MAY OCCUR. ONLY
THE ROLE IN ESSENCE DOES NOT CHANGE THROUGHOUT THE
CYCLE. ALL ELSE IS CHOSEN BETWEEN PHYSICAL LIVES.

Alex, who had been told by Michael that he was a fifth-level mature scholar, had complained that it was difficult for him to deal with emotional relationships. "Does that have anything to do with my being a scholar? Is my soul the ivory-tower sort?"

IF THE MAN ALEX WILL REVIEW WHAT WE HAVE SAID ABOUT THE NATURE OF THE FIFTH CYCLE, THE MATURE SOUL, AND THE SCHOLAR IN ESSENCE, HE WILL SEE THAT HIS DRIVE FOR ISOLATION AND PRIVACY MUST BE VERY STRONG. UNDER SUCH CIRCUMSTANCES IT WOULD BE UNUSUAL FOR HIM TO FORM ATTACHMENTS EASILY.

"But how can I break through this?" Alex asked. "You make it sound pretty damn hopeless."

FIRST YOU MUST WISH THIS. MOST SCHOLARS HAVE LITTLE REGARD FOR EMOTIONAL ENTANGLEMENTS UNLESS THEY HAPPEN TO BE EMOTIONALLY CENTERED. MOST SCHOLARS WOULD PREFER NOT TO BE BOTHERED WITH THE RESPONSIBILITY THAT GOES ALONG WITH THESE INTRIGUES. THE WAY YOU CAN HANDLE IT IS TO BECOME BALANCED AND THUS COME IN CONTACT WITH THE EMOTIONAL CENTER AND LEARN TO CONTROL THE OUTPUT. RIGHT NOW THERE IS SPORADIC HIGH OUTPUT WITH LITTLE INSIGHT. IT RESEMBLES VOLCANIC ERUPTIONS.

"I've tried that, but every time I think I've got a handle on a relationship, it falls to pieces. I've been to a shrink, but all that I seem to get are a bunch of labels." Alex was obviously embarrassed to speak so frankly in front of sixteen people.

YOU, ALEX, ARE ACTING OUT OF THE NEGATIVE POLE OF YOUR ROLE. THE NEGATIVE POLE FOR THE SCHOLAR IS THEORY. YOU HAVE LOTS OF IDEAS—THAT IS, THEORIES—BUT YOU GAIN NONE OF THE KNOWLEDGE. KNOWLEDGE IS THE POSITIVE POLE. IF YOU ARE WILLING TO CHANGE YOUR PERCEPTIONS, YOU MAY LEARN TO ACT OUT OF THE POSITIVE POLE.

"Michael," Walter said quickly, "tell us more about the poles. Are there poles in all the essence roles?"

THERE ARE POLES IN ALL ASPECTS OF THE OVERLEAVES. THE SLAVE ROLE HAS SERVICE AS ITS POSITIVE POLE AND BONDAGE AS ITS NEGATIVE POLE. THE ARTISAN HAS CREATION FOR ITS POSITIVE POLE AND ARTIFICE FOR THE NEGATIVE POLE. THE WARRIOR HAS PERSUASION IN THE POSI-

TIVE POLE AND COERCION IN THE NEGATIVE POLE. THE SAGE HAS EXPRESSION IN THE POSITIVE POLE AND ORATION IN THE NEGATIVE POLE. . . .

"Oration doesn't sound all that negative to me," Lucy said.

SPEAKING FOR THE GLORY OF HEARING YOURSELF TALK IS NEGATIVE. THERE IS NO COMMUNICATION AND NO GROWTH. THE PRIEST HAS COMPASSION IN THE POSITIVE POLE AND ZEAL IN THE NEGATIVE POLE. THE KING HAS MASTERY IN THE POSITIVE POLE AND TYRANNY IN THE NEGATIVE POLE. WE WILL IMPART THE POLARITIES TO YOU AS WE REVEAL THE OTHER OVERLEAVES.

AGAIN, THERE ARE SEVEN GOALS, THREE IN PAIRS, AND ONE NEUTRAL. THERE ARE THREE EXALTED GOALS. THEY ARE DOMINANCE, ACCEPTANCE, AND GROWTH. THERE IS AN INTERMEDIATE, NEUTRAL GOAL, WHICH FOR THE TIME BEING WE CAN CALL STAGNATION. THERE ARE THREE ORDINAL GOALS WHICH ARE THE ANTITHESIS OF THE EXALTED GOALS. THEY ARE SUBMISSION, REJECTION, AND RETARDATION. MOST ATTORNEYS AND POLITICIANS ARE THOSE WHO HAVE CHOSEN THE NEUTRAL GOAL. LAWMAKING IS A STAGNATION GOAL. ONE OF THE BETTER EXAMPLES IN HISTORY IS ALEXANDER THE GREAT. HE WAS IN DOMINANCE; HE COULD NOT FAIL.

That all seems rather pat. How are the goals assigned?

WE MUST REMIND YOU THAT NOTHING IS ASSIGNED. ALL IS CHOSEN. WE THINK THAT THE ONE GOAL FOR ONE ROLE CONTROVERSY PROBABLY AROSE OVER THE SIMILARITY OF SOME OF THESE GOALS TO THE ARCHETYPES. FOR INSTANCE, WHEN ONE THINKS OF A KING, ONE THINKS OF POWER AND DOMINANCE. WHEN ONE THINKS OF A PRIEST, ONE THINKS OF ACCEPTANCE, AND THE SAGE, WITH HIS EXPANSIVE OUTLOOK AND NATURAL EBULLIENCE, MAKES ONE THINK OF GROWTH. THE INTROSPECTIVE SCHOLAR IS OFTEN THOUGHT STAGNANT. THE DEJECTED AND REJECTED SLAVE PRESENTS A GRAPHIC ILLUSTRATION. OF COURSE THIS IS NOT TRUE, FOR THERE ARE KINGS NOW LIVING WITH REJECTION AS THEIR GOALS, JUST AS THERE ARE DOMINANT SLAVES.

What about goal polarity?

THE POSITIVE POLE OF GROWTH IS COMPREHENSION, THE NEGATIVE, CONFUSION. GROWTH CAN BE A VERY DEMAND-

GOALS

Expression

	Acceptance				Rejection	
+		−		+		−
agape		ingratiation		discrimination		prejudice

Inspiration

	Growth				Retardation	
+		−		+		−
comprehension		confusion		atavism		withdrawal

Action

	Dominance				Submission	
+		−		+		−
leadership		dictatorship		devotion		subservience

Assimilation

	Stagnation	
+		−
suspension		inertia

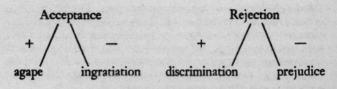
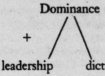

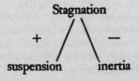

ING GOAL. THE POSITIVE POLE OF RETARDATION IS ATA-
VISM, A RETURN TO COMPLETE SIMPLICITY. THE NEGATIVE
POLE IS WITHDRAWAL. THE POSITIVE POLE OF ACCEPTANCE
IS AGAPE, WHICH IS THE GREAT GOAL. THE NEGATIVE IS
INGRATIATION. THE POSITIVE POLE OF REJECTION IS DIS-
CRIMINATION. THIS CAN SHARPEN THE CRITICAL SENSE
MORE THAN ANY OTHER GOAL. THE NEGATIVE POLE IS PREJ-
UDICE. THE POSITIVE POLE OF DOMINANCE IS LEADERSHIP,
THE NEGATIVE POLE, DICTATORSHIP. THE POSITIVE POLE OF
SUBMISSION IS DEVOTION, THE NEGATIVE POLE IS SUBSER-
VIENCE. IN STAGNATION, THE POSITIVE POLE IS SUSPENSION,
AND THE NEGATIVE POLE IS INERTIA.

Are these goals chosen for karmic reasons?

USUALLY THEY ARE, YES.

Do they change from lifetime to lifetime?

YES THEY DO.

It seems that the false personality is mad, the personality
is the wolf, and it is trying to eat essence and beat on it.

IT IS ONLY TRYING TO SURVIVE. SURVIVAL IS THE GOAL
FOR THE ORGANISM. ECSTASY IS THE GOAL OF THE ESSENCE.
BEING BURNED AT THE STAKE WAS AN ECSTATIC EXPERI-
ENCE FOR THE SOUL OF JEANNE D'ARC. LIBERATION,
WHETHER BY DEATH BY FIRE, OR WHATEVER METHOD, IS
THE GOAL. THE BODY SEEKS TO SURVIVE REGARDLESS.

What about the real world? If a person is supposed to take
care of his or her body, shouldn't there be a few practical,
worldly goals as well as these essence-chosen ones?

IF YOU ARE TO SURVIVE ON THE PHYSICAL PLANE YOU
MUST AT LEAST HAVE A FEW SURVIVAL GOALS, BUT BEYOND
THAT IT IS NOT NECESSARY TO PLAN YOUR LIFE. KARMA IS
HERE TO DO THAT FOR YOU.

How does one work toward these essence goals?

THAT IS DONE THROUGH THE MODES, WHICH ARE ALSO
CHOSEN.

AGAIN, THERE ARE SEVEN OF THEM, IN THE SAME PAT-
TERN AS YOU HAVE SEEN BEFORE—THREE PAIRS AND A NEU-
TRAL. THE PAIRS ARE POWER AND CAUTION, AGGRESSION
AND PERSEVERANCE, PASSION AND REPRESSION. APPROXI-
MATELY 85 PERCENT OF THE SOULS INCARNATE ARE IN THE
CAUTION OR OBSERVATION MODES.

THE POSITIVE POLE OF CAUTION IS DELIBERATION, THE

MODES

Expression

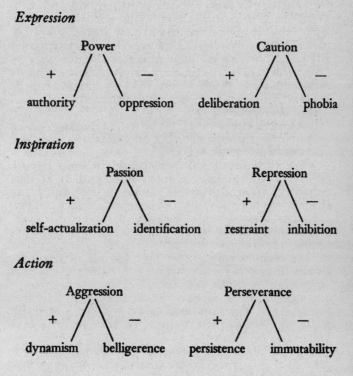

Power
+ authority   − oppression

Caution
+ deliberation   − phobia

Inspiration

Passion
+ self-actualization   − identification

Repression
+ restraint   − inhibition

Action

Aggression
+ dynamism   − belligerence

Perseverance
+ persistence   − immutability

Assimilation

Observation
+ clarity   − surveillance

NEGATIVE POLE IS PHOBIA. THE POSITIVE POLE OF POWER IS AUTHORITY, THE NEGATIVE POLE IS OPPRESSION. THE POSITIVE POLE OF PERSEVERANCE IS PERSISTENCE, THE NEGATIVE POLE IS IMMUTABILITY. THE POSITIVE POLE OF AGGRESSION IS DYNAMISM, THE NEGATIVE POLE IS BELLIGERENCE. THE POSITIVE POLE OF REPRESSION IS RESTRAINT, THE NEGATIVE POLE IS INHIBITION. THE POSITIVE POLE OF PASSION IS SELF-ACTUALIZATION, THE NEGATIVE POLE IS IDENTIFICATION. THE POSITIVE POLE OF OBSERVATION IS CLARITY, THE NEGATIVE POLE IS SURVEILLANCE.

How does mode affect goal?

IT DEFINES THE MANNER IN WHICH THE GOAL WILL BE REACHED, IF IT IS REACHED. OCCASIONALLY THERE IS CONFLICT BETWEEN THE GOAL AND THE MODE. FOR EXAMPLE, IF A YOUNG SCHOLAR IS IN THE REPRESSION MODE WITH A GOAL OF GROWTH, THAT SCHOLAR WILL FIND IT ALMOST IMPOSSIBLE TO ACCOMPLISH ANYTHING. BEING YOUNG, THE PERCEPTION DOES NOT ENCOURAGE INTROSPECTION. THE GOAL LEADS THE SCHOLAR TO LOOK OUTWARD AND EXPERIENCE NEW THINGS, WHILE THE MODE, THE METHOD SELECTED FOR LOOKING OUTWARD, CLAPS A LID ON EVERY EFFORT. SUCH A SOUL MIGHT TAKE REFUGE IN MADNESS, OR ACT OUT OF THE NEGATIVE POLE OF GROWTH, WHICH IS CONFUSION. A YOUNG SAGE WITH A GOAL OF REJECTION IN THE PASSION MODE WOULD BE AN INCREDIBLY ABRASIVE PERSONALITY. THE SAGE SOUL LONGS FOR ATTENTION AND AN AUDIENCE TO WHICH IT CAN PLAY, BUT THE GOAL SAYS THAT REJECTION MUST OCCUR.

Rejection of the sage or does the sage do the rejecting?

EITHER, OR BOTH. AND BECAUSE THE YOUNG SAGE IS IN THE PASSION MODE, WHATEVER IS DONE IS DONE PASSIONATELY. AN OLD KING IN THE POWER MODE WITH A GOAL OF ACCEPTANCE WILL BE POWERFULLY ACCEPTING AND EMBRACE ALMOST ANYTHING THAT HAPPENS WITH FERVOR. A MATURE SLAVE IN THE PERSEVERANCE MODE WITH A GOAL OF DOMINANCE WILL BE CAPABLE OF HANDLING ALMOST ANYTHING BUT HIGHER AUTHORITY. A BABY ARTISAN IN THE OBSERVATION MODE WITH A GOAL OF STAGNATION WOULD BE ABOUT AS OUT OF TOUCH WITH THE WORLD AS IT IS POSSIBLE TO BE ON THE PHYSICAL PLANE. A YOUNG WARRIOR IN THE POWER MODE WITH A GOAL OF DOMINANCE IN A MALE BODY WOULD BE AN IMPRESSIVE MILITARY

LEADER, BUT IN A FEMALE BODY WOULD PROBABLY BE MISERABLE.

Isn't there any mitigating circumstances for all this?

YES, THERE ARE THE ATTITUDES, THE CENTERS, AND THE CHIEF FEATURES.

THE ATTITUDE IS THE WAY YOU REGARD THE WORLD, IN OTHER WORDS, THE STANCE FROM WHICH YOU LOOK AT THINGS. IT IS, OF COURSE, CHOSEN, AS ARE ALL THE ELEMENTS OF YOUR OVERLEAVES. AGAIN, THERE ARE SEVEN ATTITUDES, THREE PAIRS AND A NEUTRAL. THEY ARE SKEPTIC AND IDEALIST, CYNIC AND REALIST, STOIC AND SPIRITUALIST, AND THE NEUTRAL ATTITUDE IS PRAGMATIST. THE NEGATIVE POLE OF SKEPTIC IS SUSPICION.

Of what?

EVERYTHING. THE POSITIVE POLE IS INVESTIGATION, AND YES, IT IS AN INVESTIGATION OF EVERYTHING. THE NEGATIVE POLE OF IDEALIST IS ABSTRACTION, THE POSITIVE POLE IS COALESCENCE. THE NEGATIVE POLE IS DENIGRATION FOR THE CYNIC, THE POSITIVE IS CONTRADICTION. THE NEGATIVE POLE OF REALIST IS SUPPOSITION, THAT IS, THE PERSON WHO SEES ALL SIDES TO EVERY QUESTION AND THEREFORE IS NOT ABLE TO ACT OR DEVELOP ANY REAL UNDERSTANDING. THE POSITIVE POLE IS PERCEPTION. THE NEGATIVE POLE OF STOIC IS RESIGNATION, THE POSITIVE POLE IS TRANQUILLITY. THE NEGATIVE POLE OF SPIRITUALIST IS FAITH.

Faith? Why is faith negative?

FAITH IS SILLY. IT IS VERY MUCH PART OF THE RULE OF MAYA. WHY SHOULD ANYONE ACCEPT ANYTHING ON THE PROVISION THAT THE THING MUST NEVER IN ANY WAY BE QUESTIONED OR DOUBTED? TWO-YEAR-OLD INFANTS DO NOT ACCEPT SUCH TYRANNY FROM THEIR PARENTS, YET THOSE PARENTS OFTEN WILL INSIST ON SUCH BLINDNESS FOR THEMSELVES. THE POSITIVE POLE OF SPIRITUALIST IS VERIFICATION, THAT IS, SEEKING THE ANSWERS TO THE QUESTIONS THAT GROW FROM POSITIVE DOUBT. THIS IS NOT PART OF MAYA, THOUGH THE SEEKING MAY BE LIMITED AND GUIDED BY FALSE PERSONALITY. THE NEGATIVE POLE OF PRAGMATIST IS DOGMA, A THING NOT UNLIKE FAITH, AND THE POSITIVE POLE IS PRACTICALITY.

How does attitude influence a person?

CONSIDER A MATURE SLAVE IN THE CAUTION MODE. THAT FRAGMENT MIGHT NOT ACCOMPLISH A LOT IN THE

ATTITUDES

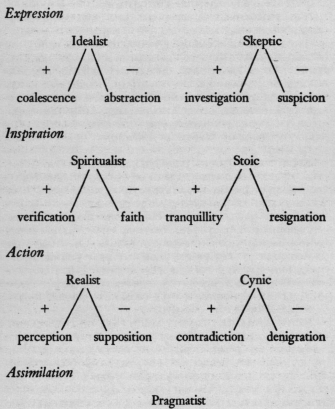

Expression

Idealist
+   −
coalescence   abstraction

Skeptic
+   −
investigation   suspicion

Inspiration

Spiritualist
+   −
verification   faith

Stoic
+   −
tranquillity   resignation

Action

Realist
+   −
perception   supposition

Cynic
+   −
contradiction   denigration

Assimilation

Pragmatist
+   −
practicality   dogma

WORLD. THE MATURE SOUL'S INTROSPECTION, COUPLED
WITH THE PERCEPTIONS OF THE SLAVE ESSENCE, WILL FIND
CAUTION LIMITING. ASSUME THAT THE MATURE SLAVE HAS
A GOAL OF GROWTH. A GREAT DEAL OF CONFUSION MAY
RESULT. BUT LET US SAY THAT THIS FRAGMENT IS A PRAG-
MATIST AS WELL. THEN, UNLESS THE FRAGMENT IS ACTING
OUT OF THE NEGATIVE POLE, MUCH OF THE FORCE OF THE
OVERLEAVES WILL BE USED FOR SENSIBLE PURPOSES AND
THERE ARE LIKELY TO BE SOME VERY REAL BENEFITS FROM
SUCH A PERSON. OF COURSE, THERE WILL BE VAST PRESSURE
FOR THE FRAGMENT TO ACT OUT OF THE NEGATIVE ROLE,
THAT IS, DOGMA, AND THEN THE RESULTS WOULD BE DIF-
FERENT. THE MIND WOULD CLAMP DOWN ON ONE SET OF
RULES AND STAY THERE NO MATTER WHAT. IF THE ATTI-
TUDE, HOWEVER, WAS THAT OF A REALIST, THERE WOULD
BE A DIFFERENCE IN THE PERSONALITY. IF THE FRAGMENT
COULD AVOID SEEING ALL SIDES TO EVERY QUESTION, THEN
WITH THE MATURE-SOUL INSIGHT AND THE SLAVE DEDI-
CATION, GREAT CONTRIBUTIONS MIGHT BE MADE. SHOULD
THIS FRAGMENT, HOWEVER, BE A CYNIC, THERE WOULD BE
LITTLE THAT COULD BE ACCOMPLISHED. CYNICISM WOULD
BE THE FORCE THAT WOULD STOP THE FRAGMENT FROM
BEING ABLE TO USE INSIGHTS EFFECTIVELY.

Does attitude affect karma?

EVERYTHING AFFECTS KARMA AND IS AFFECTED BY IT.
THE GOALS OFTEN HAVE MORE TO DO WITH KARMA THAN
WITH THE ATTITUDES, BUT THIS IS BY NO MEANS AN AB-
SOLUTE RULE.

What do you mean by centering?

ALL FRAGMENTS HAVE ALL CENTERS OPERATIVE WITHIN
THEMSELVES, BUT THERE IS A STRONG TENDENCY FOR THE
PERSONALITY TO BECOME FIXED IN ONE CENTER. THE CEN-
TER HAS A GREAT DEAL TO DO WITH RESPONSES. IT INDI-
CATES FROM WHAT PART OF YOURSELF YOU WILL ACT.

And, of course, there are seven centers.

OF COURSE. THERE ARE THE EMOTIONAL AND THE HIGHER
EMOTIONAL, THE INTELLECTUAL AND THE HIGHER INTEL-
LECTUAL, THE MOVING, THE SEXUAL, AND THE INSTINCTIVE
CENTERS. THE POLES OF THE EMOTIONAL CENTER ARE SEN-
TIMENTALITY IN THE NEGATIVE AND SENSIBILITY IN THE
POSITIVE. IN THE HIGHER EMOTIONAL CENTER, THERE IS
INTUITION IN THE NEGATIVE, AND EMPATHY IN THE POSI-

TIVE, POLE. THE NEGATIVE POLE OF THE INTELLECTUAL CENTER IS REASON, THE POSITIVE POLE IS THOUGHT. IN THE HIGHER INTELLECTUAL CENTER, THE NEGATIVE POLE IS TELEPATHY, AND THE POSITIVE POLE IS INTEGRATION. IN THE SEXUAL CENTER THE NEGATIVE POLE IS EROTIC AND THE POSITIVE POLE IS AMORAL. IN THE MOVING CENTER, THE NEGATIVE POLE IS ENERGETIC AND THE POSITIVE POLE IS ENDURING. THE INSTINCTIVE CENTER IS NOT USUALLY FOUND IN PERSONS GENERALLY CLASSIFIED AS SANE. THE NEGATIVE POLE OF THE INSTINCTIVE CENTER IS ANATOMIC AND THE POSITIVE POLE IS ATOMIC. MOST OF YOU WILL COMBINE TWO CENTERS FOR YOUR CENTERING; SUCH AS YOU WILL BE IN THE MOVING PART OF INTELLECTUAL CENTER, WHICH MEANS THAT YOUR REACTION TO SITUATIONS WILL BE INTELLECTUAL AND YOU WILL BE DRIVEN TO DO SOMETHING ABOUT THE THING YOU REACT TO. THE MOVING AND SEXUAL CENTERS ARE KINETIC, THE EMOTIONAL CENTERS ARE MUTE, HAVING TO DO WITH FEELINGS RATHER THAN WORDS. THE INTELLECTUAL CENTERS ARE THE VERBAL CENTERS. THAT DOES NOT MEAN THAT AN EMOTIONALLY CENTERED PERSON CANNOT SPEAK, BUT IT DOES MEAN THAT SUCH A PERSON WILL HAVE A GREAT DEAL OF TROUBLE EXPRESSING HERSELF OR HIMSELF WITH WORDS. A PERSON IN THE MOVING PART OF EMOTIONAL CENTER, FOR EXAMPLE, WILL HAVE TO REACT WITH GREAT EXPRESSION OF FEELING, SUCH AS TREMENDOUS ARTISTIC OUTPOURINGS OR TEMPER TANTRUMS.

Or both?

THE POTENTIAL FOR BOTH IS CERTAINLY THERE. WHICH WILL PREDOMINATE DEPENDS IN LARGE PART ON THE OTHER OVERLEAVES, PARTICULARLY THE CHIEF FEATURE.

Which is?

THERE ARE NO GOOD CHIEF FEATURES. IN LITERATURE THERE IS THE CONCEPT OF THE FATAL FLAW, THE ONE THING THAT DESTROYS AN OTHERWISE INDESTRUCTIBLE MAN. IN OEDIPUS WE BELIEVE THAT THE FLAW WAS HUBRIS, WHICH WE WOULD CALL ARROGANCE. THE CHIEF FEATURE RULES YOU. ENLIGHTENMENT IS GAINED BY THE EXTINGUISHMENT OF THE CHIEF FEATURE IN ADULT LIFE. THIS DOES NOT HAPPEN OFTEN. MORE COMMONLY, THE CHIEF FEATURE IS CHANGED; FOR EXAMPLE, THE FRAGMENT MAY TRADE IMPATIENCE FOR MARTYRDOM.

CENTERS

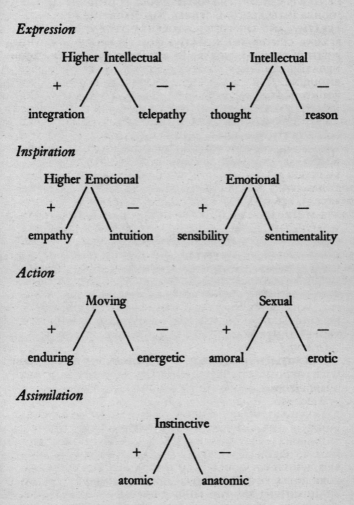

Expression

Higher Intellectual   Intellectual

+   —   +   —

integration   telepathy   thought   reason

Inspiration

Higher Emotional   Emotional

+   —   +   —

empathy   intuition   sensibility   sentimentality

Action

Moving   Sexual

+   —   +   —

enduring   energetic   amoral   erotic

Assimilation

Instinctive

+   —

atomic   anatomic

CHIEF FEATURES

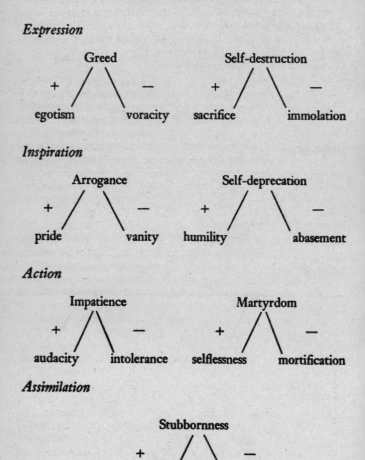

Expression

Greed				Self-destruction		
+		−		+		−
egotism		voracity		sacrifice		immolation

Inspiration

Arrogance				Self-deprecation		
+		−		+		−
pride		vanity		humility		abasement

Action

Impatience				Martyrdom		
+		−		+		−
audacity		intolerance		selflessness		mortification

Assimilation

Stubbornness		
+		−
determination		obstinacy

Then the chief feature can change during a lifetime?

YES, IT CAN BE CHANGED. IT IS THE ONLY PART OF THE OVERLEAVES THAT CAN BE. THE CHIEF FEATURE IS GENERALLY NOT A PART OF THE PERSON UNTIL AROUND TWENTY, OR WHENEVER THE FRAGMENT BECOMES FAIRLY INDEPENDENT OF THE PARENTAL ENVIRONMENT.

And what are these chief features?

AS YOU MIGHT EXPECT, THERE ARE SEVEN OF THEM, THREE PAIRS AND ONE NEUTRAL. THE PAIRS ARE GREED AND SELF-DESTRUCTION, IMPATIENCE AND MARTYRDOM, ARROGANCE AND SELF-DEPRECATION, WITH THE NEUTRAL, STUBBORNNESS. THE NEGATIVE POLE OF GREED IS VORACITY, THE POSITIVE POLE IS EGOTISM. THE NEGATIVE POLE OF SELF-DESTRUCTION IS IMMOLATION, THE POSITIVE POLE IS SACRIFICE. THE NEGATIVE POLE OF IMPATIENCE IS INTOLERANCE, THE POSITIVE POLE IS AUDACITY. THE NEGATIVE POLE OF MARTYRDOM IS MORTIFICATION, THE POSITIVE POLE IS SELFLESSNESS. THE NEGATIVE POLE OF ARROGANCE IS VANITY, THE POSITIVE POLE IS PRIDE. THE NEGATIVE POLE OF SELF-DEPRECATION IS ABASEMENT, THE POSITIVE POLE IS HUMILITY. THE NEGATIVE POLE OF STUBBORNNESS IS OBSTINACY, THE POSITIVE POLE IS DETERMINATION.

A few of those don't sound all that bad.

GREED, ARROGANCE, AND IMPATIENCE ARE ALL PART OF SURVIVAL. GREED CAN NEVER BE SATISFIED. ARROGANCE IS ALWAYS THE REACTION TO TRUE SHYNESS. MOST PEOPLE MISTAKE SELF-DEPRECATION FOR SHYNESS, BUT IT IS NOT. ONLY THE ARROGANT ARE TRULY SHY. THERE ARE THOSE WHO EXPRESS THEIR MARTYRDOM IN SELF-EFFACEMENT, BUT THIS, AGAIN, IS NOT SHYNESS. STUBBORNNESS CAN CAUSE PEOPLE TO REMAIN IN SITUATIONS AND ACTING-OUT RELATIONSHIPS IN SEVERAL INAPPROPRIATE WAYS, SIMPLY BECAUSE THEY HAVE DETERMINED ON THAT COURSE, NO MATTER WHAT. THIS IS NEITHER HELPFUL NOR WISE. GIVEN THE EXPECTATIONS THAT PEOPLE MAKE FOR THEMSELVES, A CHIEF FEATURE OF STUBBORNNESS, CAN LEAD TO A LACK OF PERCEPTION AND TO WILLFULNESS OF A CATASTROPHIC NATURE. CHIEF FEATURES ARE OFTEN THE CORE OF FALSE PERSONALITY.

Is that all, then? Role in essence, age, level, mode, goal, attitude, center, and chief feature?

THOSE ARE YOUR CHOICES TO ENABLE YOU TO FULFILL

YOUR AGREEMENTS, COMPLETE YOUR SEQUENCES AND
MONADS, AND BURN KARMA.

And are there seven of those?

THERE IS NO FIXED FIGURE FOR THE MONADS, AGREE-
MENTS, SEQUENCES, AND KARMA. THE NUMBER IS UP TO
YOU.

Chapter 8

EXAMPLES OF OVERLEAVES

IN ORDER FOR YOU TO UNDERSTAND MORE CLEARLY THE FUNCTIONING OF THE OVERLEAVES, WE WILL GIVE YOU A SERIES OF EXAMPLES, ALL COMPLETELY GENUINE, BOTH CURRENT AND HISTORICAL, THAT WILL ENABLE YOU TO OBSERVE HOW THEY WORK. WE PREFER MORE TO DEAL WITH THE ARTS THAN WITH POLITICS BECAUSE THE ARTS ARE LESS SUBJECT TO HISTORICAL REINTERPRETATION THAN ARE POLITICS. FOR THE MOST PART, THE ARTS ARE THERE FOR YOU TO EXPERIENCE, BUT POLITICS ARE CHANGED BY WHIM, AMBITION, AND WHAT OTHER POLITICIANS CONSIDER NECESSARY. YOU HAVE ONLY TO LOOK AROUND YOU TO SEE THE TRUTH OF THIS.

INFANT SOULS RARELY RISE TO ANY PUBLIC NOTICE, BUT NONETHELESS, WE WILL BEGIN THERE BECAUSE ALL SOULS INCARNATE BEGIN THERE.

INFANT SOULS

Slaves

THE FIRST IS A FOURTH-LEVEL INFANT SLAVE IN THE

CAUTION MODE WITH A GOAL OF REJECTION, A STOIC IN THE MOVING PART OF EMOTIONAL CENTER WITH A CHIEF FEATURE OF SELF-DEPRECATION.

THE FIRST INFANT SLAVE YOU WOULD CONSIDER MENTALLY RETARDED, FOR THIS FRAGMENT WAS CONSTANTLY FRIGHTENED. RECALL THAT THE INFANT SOUL PERCEIVES THE WORLD AS ME AND NOT ME, AND THAT THE SLAVE ESSENCE SEEKS TO SERVE IN A WORLDLY SENSE. THE CAUTION MODE STOPS THE FRAGMENT FROM SEARCHING AND THE GOAL OF REJECTION IS LIMITING. THIS FRAGMENT WELCOMED THE SENTENCE THAT SENT IT TO PRISON. THE CRIME IT COMMITTED WAS MURDER, ARISING FROM FRIGHT.

THE SECOND INFANT SLAVE IS A FIRSTBORN SOUL IN THE OBSERVATION MODE WITH A GOAL OF ACCEPTANCE IN THE EMOTIONAL PART OF INTELLECTUAL CENTER, A STOIC WITH A CHIEF FEATURE OF GREED.

THIS INFANT SLAVE LIVED A LONG TIME AGO AND SPENT THAT FIRST LIFE IN CHINA AS A BONDED SERVANT WHO BUILT ROADS FOR THE MILITARY FORCES OF THE CENTRAL PROVINCES. THE FRAGMENT THAT WAS THIS FIRSTBORN SOUL IS NOW A MATURE SOUL, A EUROPEAN SURGEON WITH AN INTERNATIONAL REPUTATION FOR HIS WORK IN THE REHABILITATION OF AMPUTEES.

THE THIRD INFANT SLAVE IS A SIXTH-LEVEL SOUL IN THE POWER MODE WITH A GOAL OF DOMINANCE, A REALIST IN THE INTELLECTUAL PART OF MOVING CENTER, WITH A CHIEF FEATURE OF STUBBORNNESS.

THIS INFANT SLAVE WAS AT THE DIFFICULT SIXTH LEVEL, AND BECAUSE OF THE NATURE OF HER OVERLEAVES, WAS ABLE TO HELP CHANGE AGRICULTURAL TECHNIQUES IN CENTRAL AMERICA, WHERE SHE LIVED SIX HUNDRED YEARS AGO.

Artisans

AGAIN, WE WILL GIVE YOU THREE EXAMPLES AND GIVE YOU SOME INDICATION OF HOW THE LIFE WAS SPENT.

THE FIRST IS A FOURTH-LEVEL INFANT ARTISAN IN THE PASSION MODE WITH A GOAL OF STAGNATION IN THE INSTINCTIVE CENTER, NO CHIEF FEATURE MANIFEST, A REALIST.

THIS INFANT ARTISAN CAN BE CONSIDERED TRULY INSANE

FROM THE EFFECT OF THE CENTERING AND THE MODE. THE GOAL WILL TEND TO KEEP THE FRAGMENT AT ONE PLACE, AND GIVEN THE NATURE OF THE INFANT CYCLE, THERE IS ALMOST NO WAY TO GET THROUGH TO SUCH A FRAGMENT.

THE SECOND IS A FIFTH-LEVEL INFANT ARTISAN IN THE OBSERVATION MODE WITH A GOAL OF GROWTH, AN IDEALIST IN THE EMOTIONAL PART OF SEXUAL CENTER, WITH A CHIEF FEATURE OF MARTYRDOM.

THIS FRAGMENT WAS TRAINED IN INFANCY TO BE A CONCUBINE FOR HER LOCAL POTENTATE. SHE EXCELLED AT HER WORK AND WAS KILLED BY THE OTHER CONCUBINES BECAUSE OF JEALOUSY, WHICH FULFILLED HER CHIEF FEATURE.

THE THIRD IS AN INFANT ARTISAN AT THE SECOND LEVEL IN THE CAUTION MODE WITH A GOAL OF RETARDATION, A STOIC, EMOTIONALLY CENTERED, WITH A CHIEF FEATURE OF SELF-DESTRUCTION.

THIS INFANT ARTISAN WAS WHAT YOU WOULD CALL THE VILLAGE IDIOT. HE LIVED IN WHAT IS NOW GERMANY IN THE SIXTH CENTURY C.E., AND STARVED TO DEATH AT THE AGE OF SEVENTEEN.

Warriors

THE FIRST IS A THIRD-LEVEL INFANT WARRIOR IN THE OBSERVATION MODE WITH A GOAL OF SUBMISSION, A PRAGMATIST IN THE EMOTIONAL PART OF INTELLECTUAL CENTER, WITH A CHIEF FEATURE OF IMPATIENCE.

THIS FRAGMENT LIVED IN INDIA TWO HUNDRED YEARS AGO AND WAS WHAT IS CALLED A FERAL, OR WILD, CHILD. SHE WAS STONED TO DEATH BY FRIGHTENED VILLAGERS.

THE SECOND IS A SEVENTH-LEVEL INFANT WARRIOR IN THE REPRESSION MODE WITH A GOAL OF DOMINANCE, A CYNIC IN THE MOVING CENTER, WITH A CHIEF FEATURE OF GREED. THIS FRAGMENT WAS A TORTURER FOR THE SPANISH INQUISITION.

THE THIRD IS A FOURTH-LEVEL INFANT WARRIOR IN THE OBSERVATION MODE WITH A GOAL OF ACCEPTANCE, A STOIC IN THE INTELLECTUAL PART OF EMOTIONAL CENTER, WITH A CHIEF FEATURE OF STUBBORNNESS. THIS FRAGMENT WAS A SCULLERY MAID IN ENGLAND DURING THE REIGN OF RICHARD II.

Scholars

THE FIRST IS A SIXTH-LEVEL INFANT SCHOLAR IN THE OBSERVATION MODE WITH A GOAL OF REJECTION, A CYNIC IN THE MOVING PART OF INTELLECTUAL CENTER, WITH A CHIEF FEATURE OF SELF-DEPRECATION. THIS FRAGMENT WAS A CARNIVAL FREAK.

THE SECOND IS A FOURTH-LEVEL INFANT SCHOLAR IN THE PERSEVERANCE MODE WITH A GOAL OF ACCEPTANCE, AN IDEALIST WITH A CHIEF FEATURE OF IMPATIENCE.

THIS INFANT SCHOLAR WAS BORN IN A VERY PRIMITIVE VILLAGE IN THE AMAZON BASIN, MADE CONTACT AT AN EARLY AGE WITH WHAT YOU WOULD CALL THE OUTSIDE WORLD, AND BECAUSE OF THE OVERLEAVES, DID NOT RETREAT AS MUCH AS YOU MIGHT EXPECT. SHE EVENTUALLY LEARNED TO READ AND WRITE AND LIVES TODAY IN A CONVENT NEAR SAO PAULO, BRAZIL.

THE THIRD IS A FIRSTBORN INFANT SCHOLAR IN THE CAUTION MODE WITH A GOAL OF GROWTH, A REALIST IN THE INSTINCTIVE CENTER, WITH NO CHIEF FEATURE.

THIS FRAGMENT WAS A PEASANT SOLDIER WORKING AS A GUARD ON THE GREAT WALL OF CHINA AS IT WAS BEING BUILT. THIS FRAGMENT IS NOW THE MEDIUM KNOWN IN THIS BOOK AS JESSICA LANSING, AND IS A THIRD-LEVEL OLD SOUL.

Sages

THE FIRST IS A SECOND-LEVEL INFANT SAGE IN THE CAUTION MODE WITH A GOAL OF DOMINANCE, A PRAGMATIST IN THE EMOTIONAL PART OF MOVING CENTER, WITH NO CHIEF FEATURE.

THIS FRAGMENT HAD A VERY DIFFICULT PERSONALITY, FOR THE SOUL LEVEL WAS NOT EQUIPPED TO HANDLE SUCH POTENTIAL COMPLEXITIES. HE LIVED ON THE ISLAND THAT YOU CALL NEW ZEALAND AND WAS DROWNED FOR THEFT AT THE AGE OF TWELVE.

THE SECOND IS A SEVENTH-LEVEL INFANT SAGE IN THE POWER MODE WITH A GOAL OF RETARDATION, A REALIST IN THE SEXUAL PART OF EMOTIONAL CENTER, WITH A CHIEF FEATURE OF ARROGANCE.

THIS FRAGMENT WAS A SHAMANISTIC HERMIT IN MEDI-
EVAL ETHIOPIA AND WAS REGARDED WITH A GREAT DEAL
OF SUPERSTITIOUS AWE. THIS FRAGMENT IS NOW INCAR-
NATE AGAIN AND IS A WELL-KNOWN TELEVISION PERSON-
ALITY.

THE THIRD IS A FIFTH-LEVEL INFANT SAGE IN THE OB-
SERVATION MODE WITH A GOAL OF SUBMISSION, A SKEPTIC
IN THE INTELLECTUAL PART OF EMOTIONAL CENTER, WITH
A CHIEF FEATURE OF SELF-DESTRUCTION.

THIS FRAGMENT WAS KILLED BY ENEMY CAVALRY DUR-
ING A RAID ON HIS HOME VILLAGE. TRUE TO HIS CHIEF
FEATURE, THIS FRAGMENT DEFIED THE ORDERS OF THE VIL-
LAGE ELDERS AND STAYED BEHIND WHEN IT WAS LEARNED
THAT SUCH CAVALRY WAS APPROACHING, REFUSING TO BE-
LIEVE THAT SUCH A THING COULD HAPPEN TO HIM. OB-
VIOUSLY, IT COULD.

Priests

THE FIRST IS A THIRD-LEVEL INFANT PRIEST IN THE PER-
SEVERANCE MODE WITH A GOAL OF REJECTION, A SPIRITU-
ALIST IN THE MOVING PART OF INTELLECTUAL CENTER,
WITH A CHIEF FEATURE OF MARTYRDOM.

THIS INFANT PRIEST WAS ONE OF THOSE NOW IDENTIFIED
AS A CHRISTIAN MARTYR, THOUGH ANY CAUSE WOULD
HAVE DONE. WITH SUCH OVERLEAVES, THIS FRAGMENT
COULD NOT POSSIBLY HAVE AVOIDED SOME SORT OF IM-
MOLATIVE SACRIFICE. DURING THE CONFLICT CALLED THE
THIRTY YEARS WAR, THIS FRAGMENT WAS INCARNATE AS
A SEVENTH-LEVEL YOUNG PRIEST AND WAS A DISTIN-
GUISHED AND FOOLHARDY PROTESTANT GERMAN GEN-
ERAL.

THE SECOND IS A SIXTH-LEVEL INFANT PRIEST IN THE
CAUTION MODE WITH A GOAL OF DOMINANCE, A PRAGMA-
TIST IN THE INTELLECTUAL PART OF SEXUAL CENTER WITH
A CHIEF FEATURE OF GREED.

THIS INFANT PRIEST WAS A COMPANION/SLAVE OF THE
ROMAN EMPEROR CLAUDIUS. HE WAS MADE MUTE AND
SOLD TO THE EMPEROR'S GREEK SECRETARY, WHO PRE-
SENTED HIM TO CLAUDIUS IN THE HOPE OF WINNING THE
FAVOR OF THIS DIFFICULT MAN. THIS FRAGMENT DID NOT
HAVE A LONG LIFE, AND WAS KILLED ON THE EMPEROR'S

ORDER AFTER CLAUDIUS BECAME CONVINCED THAT THE SLAVE HAD BEEN PAID TO POISON HIM WITH VENOM HIDDEN IN HIS ANUS.

THE THIRD IS A FIFTH-LEVEL INFANT PRIEST IN THE OBSERVATION MODE WITH A GOAL OF ACCEPTANCE, A REALIST IN THE INTELLECTUAL PART OF EMOTIONAL CENTER, WITH A CHIEF FEATURE OF SELF-DEPRECATION.

THIS FRAGMENT DID NOT ACCOMPLISH MUCH IN THAT LIFE, SINCE THE OVERLEAVES PRECLUDED ANY STRONG ACTIVITY. HOWEVER, SHE QUITE WILLINGLY SERVED HER SON, WHO ROSE TO THE RANK OF METROPOLITAN IN THE RUSSIAN ORTHODOX CHURCH IN THE MIDDLE OF THE LAST CENTURY.

Kings

THE FIRST IS A FIFTH-LEVEL INFANT KING IN THE POWER MODE WITH A GOAL OF GROWTH, AN IDEALIST BUT WITH A CHIEF FEATURE OF SELF-DEPRECATION, IN THE EMOTIONAL PART OF INTELLECTUAL CENTER.

THIS KING HAD A DEGREE OF POTENTIAL AND MIGHT HAVE ADVANCED IN SPITE OF THE LIMITATIONS OF THE SOUL LEVEL, BUT, AS ALWAYS, THE CHIEF FEATURE RULED HIM AND HE LIVED AND DIED IN A LITTLE TOWN IN KENTUCKY, WHERE THE YOUNG SOULS AROUND HIM REGARDED HIM AS A LITTLE CRACKED BUT HARMLESS. WHEN DRUNK, HE WOULD OCCASIONALLY FLY INTO RAGES.

THE SECOND IS A THIRD-LEVEL INFANT KING IN THE REPRESSION MODE WITH A GOAL OF STAGNATION, A PRAGMATIST IN THE INTELLECTUAL PART OF MOVING CENTER, WITH A CHIEF FEATURE OF STUBBORNNESS.

THIS KING FRAGMENT WAS MADE A EUNUCH IN CHILDHOOD AND WAS TRAINED IN A VERY SIMPLE MILITARY DRILL. HE WAS SET TO GUARD SOME OF THE IMPERIAL TREASURE IN LUXOR, EGYPT. HE DIED OF PLAGUE AT AN EARLY AGE.

THE THIRD IS A FIRSTBORN INFANT KING IN THE OBSERVATION MODE WITH A GOAL OF ACCEPTANCE, A STOIC WITH NO CHIEF FEATURE, IN THE INSTINCTIVE CENTER.

THIS INFANT KING LIVED ONLY NINE YEARS AND SPENT MOST OF THAT TIME IN A FRENCH ORPHANAGE RUN BY A VERY STRICT ORDER OF NUNS. SHE DIED AS THE RESULT OF

A BEATING GIVEN HER WHEN SHE COULD NOT LEARN LATIN PRAYERS.

BABY SOULS

WE REMIND YOU THAT THE MOTTO OF THE BABY CYCLE IS "DO IT RIGHT OR NOT AT ALL." SOULS IN THIS CYCLE RARELY RISE TO PROMINENCE, BUT OCCASIONALLY DO. HOWEVER, IT IS NOT UNUSUAL TO FIND THESE SOULS OCCUPYING IMPORTANT SPOTS IN SMALLER ENVIRONMENTS, OR WORKING WITH TRUE DEDICATION FOR VARIOUS ORGANIZATIONS.

AGAIN, WE WILL GIVE YOU THREE EXAMPLES IN EACH CATEGORY AND YOU MAY SEE HOW THE OVERLEAVES OPERATE WITHIN THE CYCLES AND ROLES TO HELP OR HINDER THE TASKS OF THE ESSENCE.

Slaves

THE FIRST IS A FOURTH-LEVEL BABY SLAVE IN THE OBSERVATION MODE WITH A GOAL OF DOMINANCE, AN IDEALIST IN THE EMOTIONAL PART OF INTELLECTUAL CENTER, WITH A CHIEF FEATURE OF SELF-DEPRECATION.

THIS FIRST FRAGMENT IS A SOMEWHAT DOGMATIC TEACHER IN A CHILDREN'S SCHOOL IN RURAL SPAIN. SHE IS SINCERELY DEDICATED TO HER TEACHING, BUT HER ATTITUDES ARE QUITE RIGID, WHICH IS TO BE EXPECTED, AND FOR THAT REASON SHE DOES NOT DEAL WELL WITH THE MORE ADVENTUROUS STUDENTS, OR WITH THOSE THAT ARE TRULY BRILLIANT AND TALENTED. FOR MOST OF HER STUDENTS SHE IS AN EXCELLENT TEACHER; FOR A FEW SHE IS A DISASTER.

THE SECOND IS A FIRST-LEVEL BABY SLAVE IN THE PERSEVERANCE MODE WITH A GOAL OF ACCEPTANCE, A PRAGMATIST IN THE MOVING PART OF EMOTIONAL CENTER, WITH A CHIEF FEATURE OF MARTYRDOM.

THIS SECOND FRAGMENT IS A LAY PREACHER IN TEXAS. HE HAS APPLIED TO BE A MISSIONARY. WE BELIEVE THAT THIS IS THE FORCE OF HIS CHIEF FEATURE, MARTYRDOM. HE IS CONSIDERED AN HONEST AND LAW-ABIDING CITIZEN,

GOD-FEARING—WHICH IS THE LITERAL TRUTH—AND A LITTLE TOO HONEST FOR HIS OWN GOOD.

THE THIRD IS A SEVENTH-LEVEL BABY SLAVE IN THE AGGRESSION MODE WITH A GOAL OF REJECTION, A CYNIC IN THE INTELLECTUAL PART OF MOVING CENTER, WITH A CHIEF FEATURE OF ARROGANCE.

THIS FRAGMENT IS AN UNDERSECRETARY IN A POSITION OF POWER IN THE CHILEAN GOVERNMENT. HE IS REPRESSIVE AND CRUEL AND HAS EARNED HIMSELF MUCH KARMA IN THIS LIFE. BETWEEN THE RIGID PERCEPTIONS OF THE BABY-SOUL CYCLE, HIS CHIEF FEATURE, AND HIS MODE, THERE IS NO WAY THIS FRAGMENT COULD BE WHAT YOU CALL A "NICE GUY." HOWEVER, HE HAS TAKEN SOME BAD OVERLEAVES AND MADE THEM WORSE.

Artisans

THE FIRST IS A SECOND-LEVEL BABY ARTISAN IN THE OBSERVATION MODE WITH A GOAL OF STAGNATION, A PRAGMATIST IN THE INTELLECTUAL PART OF EMOTIONAL CENTER, WITH A CHIEF FEATURE OF GREED.

THIS FIRST FRAGMENT HAS VERY NEUTRAL OVERLEAVES, EXCEPT FOR THE CHIEF FEATURE. THIS WOMAN IS "CLEVER WITH HER HANDS." SHE DOES BEAUTIFUL FLOWER ARRANGEMENTS AND NEEDLEWORK, THOUGH MANY PEOPLE SEE HER AS LAZY, WHICH WITH SUCH OVERLEAVES IS HARDLY SURPRISING. SHE MARRIED VERY, VERY WELL AND IS A FAIRLY CALM, IN FACT RATHER DETACHED, PARENT. SHE IS RESTING FROM HER LAST LIFE, WHEN SHE WAS A FARRIER WITH THE GERMAN ARMY DURING WORLD WAR I. IN THAT LIFE SHE WAS A MALE, VERY STRONG, AND CONVINCED OF THE RIGHTEOUSNESS OF THE "CAUSE." WE WOULD THINK THAT IN THE NEXT LIFE SHE WILL DESIRE MORE ACTIVITY. THE NEXT LIFE WILL BE AT THE SECOND LEVEL, TOO, BECAUSE WITH SUCH OVERLEAVES, SHE CANNOT COMPLETE THE MONADS SHE MUST EXPERIENCE IN ORDER TO ADVANCE.

THE SECOND IS A FIFTH-LEVEL BABY ARTISAN IN THE POWER MODE WITH A GOAL OF GROWTH, A SKEPTIC IN THE MOVING PART OF INTELLECTUAL CENTER, WITH A CHIEF FEATURE OF IMPATIENCE.

THIS FRAGMENT IS AN ELECTRICIAN BY TRADE, WELL-

EDUCATED, QUITE INTELLIGENT, REGARDED BY SOME AS
A GENIUS—THOUGH WE WOULD HAVE TO SAY THAT HE IS
NOT. HIS EMOTIONAL LIFE IS FAIRLY CHAOTIC, THANKS TO
HIS MODE AND CHIEF FEATURE.

THE THIRD IS A SIXTH-LEVEL BABY ARTISAN IN THE PAS-
SION MODE WITH A GOAL OF DOMINANCE, AN IDEALIST IN
THE MOVING PART OF EMOTIONAL CENTER, WITH A CHIEF
FEATURE OF ARROGANCE.

THIS THIRD BABY ARTISAN WAS AT THE CRITICAL SIXTH-
LEVEL, WHICH WE HAVE TOLD YOU IS THE MOST DIFFICULT
OF THE LEVELS IN TERMS OF EXPERIENCE. ALL MONADS
AND PERCEPTIONS OF THE CYCLE MUST BE COMPLETED IN
THE SIXTH LEVEL BEFORE THE UNDERSTANDING AND SYN-
THESIS OF THE SEVENTH LEVEL CAN OCCUR. THIS FRAG-
MENT WAS ONE OF A FAMILY OF INSTRUMENT MAKERS IN
ITALY IN THE SIXTEENTH CENTURY, AND THOUGH NOT AS
FAMOUS AS HIS COUSINS, HE NEVERTHELESS MADE SUPERIOR
INSTRUMENTS, FOUR OF WHICH ARE STILL BEING PLAYED
TODAY.

Warriors

THE FIRST IS A FIFTH-LEVEL BABY WARRIOR IN THE OB-
SERVATION MODE WITH A GOAL OF DOMINANCE, A REALIST
IN THE EMOTIONAL PART OF INTELLECTUAL CENTER, WITH
A CHIEF FEATURE OF STUBBORNNESS.

THIS FRAGMENT IS THE HEAD OF A LEGAL DEPARTMENT
FOR A MAJOR CHAIN OF DEPARTMENT STORES. SHE IS
FIERCELY COMPETENT BUT QUITE INFLEXIBLE. ALTHOUGH
SHE IS DEEPLY INVOLVED WITH OFFICE POLITICS, SHE LACKS
PERCEPTION, WHICH IS TYPICAL OF THE BABY CYCLES, AND
FOR THAT REASON IS OFTEN UNAWARE OF THE POTENTIAL
HARM OF HER ACTIONS. SURPRISINGLY, THERE IS NOT MUCH
FALSE PERSONALITY AT WORK IN THIS WOMAN. SHE WAS
ON HER OWN AT AN EARLY AGE AND WAS GUIDED INTO THE
STUDY OF LAW BY AN IDEALISTIC TEACHER, WHICH SHE
OTHERWISE NEVER WOULD HAVE ATTEMPTED. SHE SUFFERS
BADLY FROM TOO MANY AND TOO RESTRICTIVE EXPECTA-
TIONS.

THE SECOND IS A THIRD-LEVEL BABY WARRIOR IN THE
CAUTION MODE WITH A GOAL OF SUBMISSION, A SKEPTIC
WITH A CHIEF FEATURE OF SELF-DEPRECATION.

THIS FRAGMENT WAS A SLAVE IN THE TIME OF AMEN-HOTEP WHO DIED OF TYPHUS WHILE WORKING ON THE TEM-PLE AT KARNAK. THIS IS NOW AN OLD WARRIOR AND PART OF THE MICHAEL GROUP.

THE THIRD IS A FIRST-LEVEL BABY WARRIOR IN THE REPRESSION MODE WITH A GOAL OF GROWTH, A CYNIC WITH A CHIEF FEATURE OF SELF-DESTRUCTION.

THIS FRAGMENT WAS A KNIGHT DURING THE SECOND CRUSADE. HE TOOK A GREAT DEAL OF PLEASURE IN SLAUGHTER, WAS HORRIFIED BY THE LUXURIOUS SOCIETY OF THE MOSLEM WORLD THOUGH HE MAINTAINED A SMALL HAREM OF MOSLEM AND JEWISH WOMEN. HE COMMITTED SUICIDE AT THE AGE OF TWENTY-EIGHT AFTER HIS CONFES-SOR DISCOVERED HIM SODOMIZING ONE OF HIS BOY SLAVES.

Scholars

THE FIRST IS A SIXTH-LEVEL BABY SCHOLAR IN THE CAU-TION MODE WITH A GOAL OF ACCEPTANCE, A REALIST IN THE INTELLECTUAL PART OF EMOTIONAL CENTER, WITH A CHIEF FEATURE OF IMPATIENCE.

THIS FRAGMENT IS A FAIRLY WELL-KNOWN PATHOLOGIST SPECIALIZING IN TROPICAL DISEASES. HE IS THOROUGH, UN-IMAGINATIVE, AND VERY HARDWORKING. HE HAS A GREAT DEAL OF TROUBLE DEALING WITH GROUPS OF PEOPLE, WHICH IS WHY HE CHOSE TO HIDE IN A LABORATORY. BE-CAUSE OF HIS CHIEF FEATURE, HE IS NOT A GOOD TEACHER.

THE SECOND IS A SEVENTH-LEVEL BABY SCHOLAR IN THE PASSION MODE WITH A GOAL OF DOMINANCE, A SPIRITU-ALIST IN THE INTELLECTUAL PART OF MOVING CENTER, WITH A CHIEF FEATURE OF INTENSE STUBBORNNESS.

THIS FRAGMENT IS CURRENTLY A PROMINENT EUROPEAN POLITICIAN WITH A TALENT FOR STIRRING UP TROUBLE. HE IS DOGMATIC ABOUT HIS POLITICAL IDEOLOGY. ON THE OTHER HAND, HE CAN GET THINGS DONE QUICKLY AND EF-FICIENTLY WHEN HE PUTS HIS MIND TO IT. MOST SCHOLARS DISLIKE THE PASSION MODE, AS IT IS UNLIKE THEIR ESSENCE NATURE, AND THIS IS TRUE OF THIS FRAGMENT. HE RARELY FEELS COMFORTABLE ABOUT HIMSELF, AND BECAUSE OF THE LIMITATIONS OF THE PERCEPTIONS OF THE BABY SOUL, HE LACKS THE INSIGHT TO DEAL WITH THESE CONFLICTS EFFECTIVELY.

THE THIRD IS A FOURTH-LEVEL BABY SCHOLAR IN THE OBSERVATION MODE WITH A GOAL OF RETARDATION, A PRAGMATIST IN THE EMOTIONAL PART OF MOVING CENTER, WITH A CHIEF FEATURE OF SELF-DEPRECATION.

THIS THIRD FRAGMENT IS A SAINT OF THE ROMAN CATHOLIC CHURCH. SHE LED A VERY CONTEMPLATIVE AND FAIRLY EXEMPLARY LIFE IN MEDIEVAL IRELAND, MOST OF THE TIME WITH A GROUP OF NUNS. SHE WAS LITERATE AND WAS ONE OF THE FIRST TO RECORD THE VARIOUS IRISH LEGENDS WITH THE INTENT OF SHAPING THEM TO CATHOLIC TEACHINGS. SHE WOULD HAVE BEEN SHOCKED TO LEARN THAT THROUGH HER EFFORTS THE LEGENDS WERE PRESERVED RATHER THAN ABSORBED INTO THE TEACHINGS OF HER FAITH.

Sages

THE FIRST IS A FOURTH-LEVEL BABY SAGE IN THE POWER MODE WITH A GOAL OF GROWTH, A HIGH-FLYING IDEALIST WITH A CHIEF FEATURE OF EQUALLY HIGH-FLYING ARROGANCE, IN THE MOVING PART OF INTELLECTUAL CENTER.

THIS FRAGMENT WAS AN EVANGELICAL PREACHER IN THE LAST CENTURY WHO ATTRACTED QUITE A LARGE FOLLOWING TO HIS CAUSE. HE INTERPRETED CHRISTIAN SCRIPTURE TO HIS OWN ADVANTAGE AND DECIDED THAT HE HAD DISCOVERED "THE TRUTH," WHICH HE GENERALLY IMPARTED TO THE MASSES. HE RECEIVED AND SQUANDERED A FORTUNE AND DIED IN CHICAGO AT THE AGE OF EIGHTY-ONE, OF COMPLICATIONS FOLLOWING PNEUMONIA.

THE SECOND IS A THIRD-LEVEL BABY SAGE IN THE OBSERVATION MODE WITH A GOAL OF SUBMISSION, A STOIC ACTING IN THE NEGATIVE POLE, IN THE INTELLECTUAL PART OF MOVING CENTER, WITH A CHIEF FEATURE OF SELF-DESTRUCTION.

THIS FRAGMENT WAS A YOUNGER SON OF A CHINESE EMPEROR AND WAS STRANGLED BY AGENTS OF HIS OLDER BROTHER AT THE AGE OF NINETEEN. HE SUFFERED FROM SUICIDAL TENDENCIES AND DEPRESSION. IF HE HAD NOT BEEN KILLED, HE WOULD HAVE FOUND ANOTHER WAY TO DIE BEFORE HE WAS MUCH OLDER.

THE THIRD IS A SIXTH-LEVEL BABY SAGE IN THE CAUTION MODE WITH A GOAL OF DOMINANCE, A REALIST IN THE EMO-

TIONAL PART OF INTELLECTUAL CENTER, WITH A CHIEF
FEATURE OF GREED.

THIS FAIRLY GIFTED FRAGMENT WAS AN IMPORTANT
FUNCTIONARY IN THE COURT OF THE RUSSIAN CZAR PETER
THE GREAT. HE PANDERED TO THE CZAR'S WHIMS AND AC-
COMPANIED HIM ON HIS TRAVELS. HE WAS AN ATTRACTIVE
MAN, SUPERFICIALLY CHARMING AND VERY MANIPULATIVE.
IN OTHER WORDS, HE USED HIS TOADYING TO GAIN POWER.
HE DIED OF VENEREAL DISEASE.

Priests

THE FIRST IS A SECOND-LEVEL BABY PRIEST IN THE OB-
SERVATION MODE WITH A GOAL OF REJECTION, A REALIST
IN THE EMOTIONAL PART OF INTELLECTUAL CENTER WITH
A CHIEF FEATURE OF SELF-DEPRECATION, TRADED IN A
LATER LIFE FOR A CHIEF FEATURE OF ARROGANCE.

THIS FRAGMENT SUFFERED FROM A "HOLIER THAN THOU"
ATTITUDE, ALTHOUGH IT WAS EXPRESSED ACADEMICALLY
RATHER THAN RELIGIOUSLY. THE HIGHER IDEAL THAT THIS
FRAGMENT CHOSE TO SERVE WAS MATHEMATICS, FOR WHICH
HE WAS NOT ENTIRELY EQUIPPED, SINCE MATHEMATICS IS
USUALLY THE PROVINCE OF WARRIORS, SCHOLARS, AND
KINGS. HE WAS SCATHING IN HIS CRITICISMS, DIDACTIC,
AND SOCIALLY PURITANICAL. THIS FRAGMENT IS NOW A
THIRD-LEVEL YOUNG PRIEST AND SHE IS VERY ACTIVE IN
WHAT SHE CALLS REVOLUTIONARY POLITICS.

THE SECOND IS A SEVENTH-LEVEL BABY PRIEST IN THE
PERSEVERANCE MODE WITH A GOAL OF ACCEPTANCE, A
PRAGMATIST IN THE EMOTIONAL PART OF MOVING CENTER,
WITH A CHIEF FEATURE OF STUBBORNNESS.

THIS FRAGMENT IS, IN FACT, A PRIEST IN THE ARMENIAN
ORTHODOX CHURCH. HE IS STAUNCH IN HIS FAITH, EX-
CITED BY THE RITUAL, AND OF GREAT VALUE TO HIS CON-
GREGATION. HIS DEFINITION OF VIRTUE IS RATHER NAR-
ROW, AS YOU MIGHT EXPECT. HIS ASPIRATIONS ARE TO
BENEFICIAL ACTIONS, AND HE IS PREPARING—THOUGH HE
IS UNAWARE OF IT, OF COURSE—FOR THE MORE ACTIVE,
WORLDLY, YOUNG CYCLES.

THE THIRD IS A FOURTH-LEVEL BABY PRIEST IN THE CAU-
TION MODE WITH A GOAL OF STAGNATION, A SKEPTIC IN

THE MOVING PART OF INTELLECTUAL CENTER, WITH A CHIEF FEATURE OF IMPATIENCE.

THIS FRAGMENT IS QUITE UNFORTUNATE, FOR HE IS PROGRAMMED TO FAIL. THERE IS LITTLE THAT HE IS CAPABLE OF THAT WOULD BREAK THIS PATTERN. THE NATURE OF THE BABY CYCLE PREVENTS THIS. HE LIVES IN A SMALL VILLAGE IN JAPAN AND HAS BEEN UNSUCCESSFUL AT BOTH FISHING AND CARPENTRY, NEITHER OF WHICH HE IS SUITED FOR. WE WOULD SAY THAT HE IS UNLIKELY TO ADVANCE IN THIS LIFE.

Kings

THE FIRST IS A FIFTH-LEVEL BABY KING IN THE OBSERVATION MODE WITH A GOAL OF ACCEPTANCE, AN IDEALIST IN THE MOVING PART OF EMOTIONAL CENTER, WITH A CHIEF FEATURE OF GREED.

THIS FRAGMENT WAS THE CURATOR OF A LARGE BRITISH MUSEUM AT THE TURN OF THE CENTURY. A DISTINGUISHED MAN OF CONSERVATIVE BUT EXCELLENT TASTE, HE ACQUIRED SEVERAL IMPORTANT PIECES FOR HIS MUSEUM, OF WHICH HE WAS POSSESSIVELY PROUD. BORN TO WEALTHY PARENTS, HE LEARNED EARLY TO BE A SNOB, WHICH HE WAS UNTIL THE END OF HIS DAYS.

THE SECOND IS A THIRD-LEVEL BABY KING IN THE POWER MODE WITH A GOAL OF DOMINANCE, A REALIST IN THE INTELLECTUAL PART OF EMOTIONAL CENTER, WITH A CHIEF FEATURE OF ARROGANCE.

THIS FRAGMENT IS A SUCCESSFUL TRIAL LAWYER NOTED FOR HIS PERSISTENCE AND DETERMINATION. THE RIGIDITY OF THE BABY CYCLE IS HELPFUL TO THIS FRAGMENT, WHO HAS A FONDNESS FOR THE MINUTIAE OF THE LAW. HIS CHIEF FEATURE CAUSES HIM TO FEEL THAT THE LAW AND HIS OWN STATUS ARE MORE IMPORTANT THAN THE WELFARE OF HIS CLIENTS.

THE THIRD IS A SIXTH-LEVEL BABY KING IN THE CAUTION MODE WITH A GOAL OF GROWTH, A SKEPTIC IN THE EMOTIONAL PART OF INTELLECTUAL CENTER, WITH A CHIEF FEATURE OF STUBBORNNESS.

THIS FRAGMENT RUNS THE PUBLICITY DEPARTMENT OF A MOTION PICTURE STUDIO. SHE IS VERY GOOD AT HER JOB

AND HAS TWICE WON RECOGNITION FOR HER PUBLICITY CAMPAIGNS. SHE IS A PERSUASIVE WOMAN WHO RUNS HER DEPARTMENT ACCORDING TO VERY STRICT RULES. IN HER LAST LIFETIME, SHE TRIED TO HELP MINERS IN GERMANY ORGANIZE INTO A GUILD FOR THEIR OWN PROTECTION, AND FOR THIS SHE WAS CONDEMNED AND HANGED. THIS LIFE-TIME, SHE HAS REFUSED TO LET HER DEBTOR BURN HIS KARMA WITH HER, AND SO THAT TIE WILL CONTINUE INTO HER NEXT LIFETIME.

YOUNG SOULS

THIS IS THE MOST ACTIVE, WORLDLY, OUTWARD CYCLE, THE TIME WHEN THE GREATEST PROGRESS IN RELATION TO THE PHYSICAL PLANE IS MADE. MONADS ACCOMPLISHED AT THESE LEVELS HAVE TO DO WITH DOING, AND OFTEN TAKE UP A GREAT DEAL OF TIME, SINCE IT IS THE NATURE OF THE YOUNG SOUL TO TRY TO BRING OTHERS AROUND TO ITS OWN POINT OF VIEW, WHATEVER THAT POINT OF VIEW IS.

Slaves

THE FIRST IS A FOURTH-LEVEL YOUNG SLAVE IN THE POWER MODE WITH A GOAL OF GROWTH, A REALIST IN THE MOVING PART OF INTELLECTUAL CENTER WITH A CHIEF FEATURE OF IMPATIENCE.

THIS FRAGMENT IS A DELEGATE TO THE UNITED NA-TIONS, REPRESENTING ONE OF THE ORIENTAL NATIONS. HE IS NOTED FOR HIS TENACITY AND HIS CONCERN FOR THE PEOPLE OF HIS HOME AS WELL AS HIS CONCERN FOR MAN-KIND IN GENERAL. HE IS INTELLECTUALLY BRILLIANT, TIRELESSLY HARDWORKING, AND RESPECTED BY HIS COL-LEAGUES.

THE SECOND IS A SIXTH-LEVEL YOUNG SLAVE IN THE OBSERVATION MODE WITH A GOAL OF DOMINANCE, AN IDEALIST IN THE SEXUAL PART OF INTELLECTUAL CENTER, WITH A CHIEF FEATURE OF GREED.

THIS FRAGMENT WAS A MISTRESS OF THE KING OF FRANCE AND AMASSED CONSIDERABLE POLITICAL POWER, WHICH SHE USED TO BENEFIT HER OWN FAMILY AND HER

OTHER LOVERS. SHE WAS A BEAUTIFUL, AMORAL WOMAN WHO REALIZED THAT THE KING WAS WEAK AND A TOOL OF THE VARIOUS NOBLES. SHE WAS ABLE TO FORCE THE KING TO TAKE CONTROL OF HIS KINGDOM, WHICH IS A LOT TO ASK OF A MATURE ARTISAN IN THE OBSERVATION MODE. SHE WAS POISONED BY ORDERS OF THE DUC DE LORRAINE.

THE THIRD IS A SECOND-LEVEL YOUNG SLAVE IN THE PASSION MODE WITH A GOAL OF ACCEPTANCE, A SPIRITUALIST IN THE EMOTIONAL PART OF MOVING CENTER, WITH A CHIEF FEATURE OF MARTYRDOM.

THIS FRAGMENT WAS THE PHARAOH UAZKHEPERA KAMASE OF THE XVIITH DYNASTY, WHO RULED FOR APPROXIMATELY TEN YEARS.

Artisans

THE FIRST IS A FOURTH-LEVEL YOUNG ARTISAN IN THE POWER MODE WITH A GOAL OF ACCEPTANCE, A SKEPTIC IN THE INTELLECTUAL PART OF EMOTIONAL CENTER, WITH A CHIEF FEATURE OF GREED.

THIS FRAGMENT IS A VERY SUCCESSFUL FASHION PHOTOGRAPHER WHO HAS TRAVELED ALL OVER THE WORLD. HE IS KNOWN FOR HIS SKILL IN SHOWING OFF DRESSES AND USING MODELS AS A KIND OF BACKDROP FOR GARMENTS. HE HAS CERTAIN SEXUAL DESIRES THAT MANY CONSIDER DISTASTEFUL OR PECULIAR. HE HAS WON SEVERAL AWARDS. THREE LIVES AGO HE WAS EXECUTED FOR DOING AN UNFLATTERING PORTRAIT OF THE REGIONAL WARLORD IN CHINA.

THE SECOND IS A SEVENTH-LEVEL YOUNG ARTISAN IN THE OBSERVATION MODE WITH A GOAL OF SUBMISSION, A STOIC IN THE MOVING PART OF INTELLECTUAL CENTER, WITH A CHIEF FEATURE OF SELF-DEPRECATION.

THIS SECOND FRAGMENT IS AN ENIGMA TO MANY AROUND HIM. WITH SUCH OVERLEAVES, IT IS HARDLY SURPRISING. HE TRAINED AS AN ENGINEER, THEN GOT INTERESTED IN ARCHITECTURE, AND WHEN IT SEEMED THAT HE WAS GOING TO DO WELL THERE, HE SWITCHED OVER TO SCULPTURE. WE WOULD THINK THAT HE WILL CONTINUE ON THIS NONPRODUCTIVE PATH FOR THE ENTIRE COURSE OF HIS LIFE.

THE THIRD IS A THIRD-LEVEL YOUNG ARTISAN IN THE REPRESSION MODE WITH A GOAL OF GROWTH, A CYNIC IN

THE EMOTIONAL PART OF INTELLECTUAL CENTER, WITH A CHIEF FEATURE OF MARTYRDOM.

THIS FRAGMENT HAD A VERY ROUGH TIME OF IT. WITH SUCH DIFFICULT OVERLEAVES, IT COULD HARDLY HAVE BEEN OTHERWISE. HE OWNED A FOUNDRY THAT MADE BOTH WEAPONS OF WAR, SUCH AS CANNONS, AND WORKS OF ART IN THE SEVENTEENTH CENTURY. HE WAS ACCUSED OF POLITICAL SUBVERSION, OF WHICH HE WAS, IN FACT, GUILTY, AND WAS BROKEN ON THE WHEEL AT THE AGE OF THIRTY-TWO. HE LEFT A WIFE AND SIX CHILDREN TO BE-COME BEGGARS.

Warriors

THE FIRST IS A THIRD-LEVEL YOUNG WARRIOR IN THE POWER MODE WITH A GOAL OF GROWTH, A CYNIC IN THE INTELLECTUAL PART OF MOVING CENTER, WITH A CHIEF FEATURE OF ARROGANCE.

THIS FRAGMENT WAS THE CZAR IVAN THE TERRIBLE OF RUSSIA. HIS OVERLEAVES WERE NOT ALL THAT BAD, BUT BETWEEN HIS CHIEF FEATURE, WHICH WAS VERY MARKED, AND THE STRESSES OF FALSE PERSONALITY, HE BECAME IN-CAPABLE OF ADMITTING ANY ERROR WHATSOEVER, AND THAT LED EVENTUALLY TO WHAT WAS PERCEIVED AS IN-SANITY. HE EARNED HIMSELF MANY KARMIC DEBTS IN THAT LIFE.

THE SECOND IS A FIFTH-LEVEL YOUNG WARRIOR IN THE OBSERVATION MODE WITH A GOAL OF DOMINANCE, A SKEP-TIC IN THE MOVING PART OF EMOTIONAL CENTER, WITH A CHIEF FEATURE OF SELF-DEPRECATION.

THIS FRAGMENT IS A PROFESSOR OF PALEONTOLOGY AT A MAJOR UNIVERSITY, ALTHOUGH HE PREFERS BEING OUT IN THE WILDS DIGGING UP FOSSILS. HE IS WHAT YOU WOULD CALL A "JOCK." HIS CHIEF FEATURE MELLOWS HIS OVERLEAVES, WHICH MIGHT OTHERWISE BE MUCH MORE POWERFUL. HE WILL HAVE TO EXPERIENCE THAT POWER EVENTUALLY, BUT IN THIS LIFETIME, HE IS EAGER TO PAY OFF KARMIC DEBTS, AND THIS SEEMED LIKE A GOOD WAY TO DO IT.

THE THIRD IS A SEVENTH-LEVEL YOUNG WARRIOR IN THE PASSION MODE WITH A GOAL OF SUBMISSION, A SPIRITUAL-

IST IN THE EMOTIONAL PART OF INTELLECTUAL CENTER, WITH A CHIEF FEATURE OF STUBBORNNESS.

THIS FRAGMENT WAS ONE OF THE FIRST WOMEN PHYSICIANS IN ITALY. SHE WAS TRULY SUPERB IN HER WORK, FAR SUPERIOR TO MOST OF HER MALE COLLEAGUES. SHE PUT A GREAT DEAL OF EMPHASIS IN THE ACTUAL HEALING OF HER PATIENTS, MOST OF WHOM WERE DEVOTED TO HER. THIS FRAGMENT IS INCARNATE AGAIN ON THE PHYSICAL PLANE, AND THIS TIME SHE IS A HIGHLY RESPECTED PSYCHIATRIST DEALING IN PARTICULAR WITH CRIMINALS WITH MAJOR PERSONALITY DISTURBANCES. THOUGH A WARRIOR, SHE HAS SPENT MORE THAN TWO-THIRDS OF HER LIVES AS A WOMAN.

Scholars

THE FIRST IS A SECOND-LEVEL YOUNG SCHOLAR IN THE OBSERVATION MODE WITH A GOAL OF REJECTION, A PRAGMATIST IN THE EMOTIONAL PART OF INTELLECTUAL CENTER, WITH A CHIEF FEATURE OF ARROGANCE.

THIS FRAGMENT WAS THE OFFICIAL CENSOR OF THE REALM DURING THE REIGN OF JAMES I OF ENGLAND.

THE SECOND IS A SIXTH-LEVEL YOUNG SCHOLAR IN THE AGGRESSION MODE WITH A GOAL OF RETARDATION, A CYNIC IN THE INTELLECTUAL PART OF MOVING CENTER, WITH A CHIEF FEATURE OF SELF-DESTRUCTION.

THIS FRAGMENT WAS THE ROMAN EMPEROR CLAUDIUS. HIS PHYSICAL DISABILITIES WERE AN EXTENSION OF HIS CHIEF FEATURE.

THE THIRD IS A FOURTH-LEVEL YOUNG SCHOLAR IN THE POWER MODE WITH A GOAL OF ACCEPTANCE, A REALIST IN THE MOVING PART OF INTELLECTUAL CENTER, WITH A CHIEF FEATURE OF SELF-DEPRECATION.

THIS FRAGMENT WAS A BYZANTINE GENERAL WHO WAS GIVEN HIS POST AS A REWARD BY THE EMPEROR JUSTINIAN. HIS MOST FAMOUS BATTLE TOOK PLACE IN GAUL, WHEN MOST OF HIS FORCES WERE CUT TO PIECES. FOR THIS HE WAS AWARDED A GOVERNORSHIP BY HIS EMPEROR, AND DIED OF HEART FAILURE AT SIXTY-TWO. THIS FRAGMENT IS NOW INCARNATE, A WOMAN, AND A MEMBER OF THE MICHAEL GROUP.

Sages

THE FIRST IS A FOURTH-LEVEL YOUNG SAGE IN THE OB-SERVATION MODE WITH A GOAL OF DOMINANCE, A REALIST IN THE EMOTIONAL PART OF INTELLECTUAL CENTER, WITH A CHIEF FEATURE OF IMPATIENCE.

THIS FIRST FRAGMENT WAS THE COMPOSER GEORGE FREDERICK HANDEL.

THE SECOND IS ANOTHER FOURTH-LEVEL YOUNG SAGE IN THE PASSION MODE WITH A GOAL OF GROWTH, AN IDEALIST IN THE INTELLECTUAL PART OF EMOTIONAL CENTER, WITH A CHIEF FEATURE OF NOT VERY MARKED ARROGANCE.

THIS FRAGMENT IS A DISTINGUISHED BROADWAY ACTOR IN HIS LATE THIRTIES. TALL, PHYSICALLY IMPRESSIVE, HYP-NOTICALLY GRACEFUL, AND WITH A GRAND THEATRICAL MANNER IN PUBLIC, THIS MAN IS WORKING VERY MUCH IN ESSENCE AND IS A SUPERB EXAMPLE OF THE REALIZED NA-TURE OF THE YOUNG SAGE.

THE THIRD IS A SIXTH-LEVEL YOUNG SAGE IN THE OBSER-VATION MODE WITH A GOAL OF DOMINANCE, AN IDEALIST IN THE INTELLECTUAL PART OF EMOTIONAL CENTER, WITH A CHIEF FEATURE OF ARROGANCE.

THIS FRAGMENT WAS KING CHARLES THE FIRST OF ENG-LAND.

Priests

THE FIRST IS A FIRST-LEVEL YOUNG PRIEST IN THE CAU-TION MODE WITH A GOAL OF REJECTION, A SPIRITUALIST IN THE MOVING PART OF INTELLECTUAL CENTER, WITH A CHIEF FEATURE OF GREED.

THIS FRAGMENT WAS ONE OF THE MONKS WHO ACCOM-PANIED PIZARRO TO PERU, AND HAD MUCH TO DO WITH THE DOWNFALL OF INCAN CIVILIZATION.

THE SECOND IS A MID-CYCLE YOUNG PRIEST IN THE PAS-SION MODE WITH A GOAL OF ACCEPTANCE, AN IDEALIST IN THE EMOTIONAL PART OF MOVING CENTER, WITH A CHIEF FEATURE OF MARTYRDOM.

THIS SECOND FRAGMENT WAS THE COMPOSER CHOPIN.

THE THIRD IS A SIXTH-LEVEL YOUNG PRIEST IN THE

AGGRESSION MODE WITH A GOAL OF GROWTH, A REALIST IN THE EMOTIONAL PART OF INTELLECTUAL CENTER, WITH A CHIEF FEATURE OF GREED.

THIS THIRD FRAGMENT WAS OLIVER CROMWELL.

THERE ARE OTHER YOUNG PRIESTS WHO MADE THEIR MARK ON THE WORLD.

JOHN CALVIN WAS A THIRD-LEVEL YOUNG PRIEST IN THE PASSION MODE WITH A GOAL OF GROWTH, AN IDEALIST IN THE MOVING PART OF EMOTIONAL CENTER AND WITH A MARKED CHIEF FEATURE OF ARROGANCE.

JEANNE D'ARC WAS A YOUNG PRIEST, AT THE SIXTH LEVEL IN THE PASSION MODE WITH A GOAL OF DOMINANCE, A FLAGRANT IDEALIST IN THE MOVING PART OF EMOTIONAL CENTER AND WITH AN OVERWHELMING CHIEF FEATURE OF MARTYRDOM.

SAINT DOMINIC, THE FOUNDER OF THE DOMINICAN OR-DER, WAS A FOURTH-LEVEL YOUNG PRIEST, AGAIN IN THE PASSION MODE WITH A GOAL OF DOMINANCE, AN IDEALIST IN THE MOVING PART OF EMOTIONAL CENTER, WITH A CHIEF FEATURE OF SELF-DEPRECATION.

ANOTHER COMPOSER, HECTOR BERLIOZ, WAS A MID-CYCLE YOUNG PRIEST IN THE PASSION MODE, BUT WITH A GOAL OF ACCEPTANCE, A CHIEF FEATURE OF IMPATIENCE IN THE EMOTIONAL PART OF INTELLECTUAL CENTER, ANOTHER FLAGRANT IDEALIST.

Kings

THE FIRST IS A FOURTH-LEVEL YOUNG KING IN THE PAS-SION MODE WITH A GOAL OF DOMINANCE, A CYNIC IN THE MOVING PART OF INTELLECTUAL CENTER, WITH A CHIEF FEATURE OF ARROGANCE.

THIS FIRST FRAGMENT WAS CATHERINE THE GREAT OF RUSSIA.

THE SECOND IS A SEVENTH-LEVEL YOUNG KING IN THE OBSERVATION MODE WITH A GOAL OF STAGNATION, A SPIR-ITUALIST IN THE MOVING PART OF EMOTIONAL CENTER, WITH A CHIEF FEATURE OF SELF-DEPRECATION.

THIS FRAGMENT IS AN ISRAELI THEOLOGIAN AND HISTOR-ICAL SCHOLAR. BECAUSE OF THE LIMITATIONS OF THE YOUNG-SOUL CYCLES, HE DOES NOT ADDRESS HIMSELF TO

PHILOSOPHY, THOUGH HE VERY MUCH WANTS TO. IN ONE OF HIS EARLIER LIVES, HE WAS BURNED AS A WITCH IN FRANCE.

THE THIRD IS A THIRD-LEVEL YOUNG KING IN THE AGGRESSION MODE WITH A GOAL OF RETARDATION, A STOIC IN THE EMOTIONAL PART OF INTELLECTUAL CENTER, WITH A CHIEF FEATURE OF MARTYRDOM.

THIS FRAGMENT WITH THE VERY DIFFICULT OVERLEAVES WAS ONE OF THE LEADERS OF THE SEPOY MUTINY IN INDIA. HE TREATED HIS BRITISH OPPRESSORS WITH UTMOST FEROCITY AND WAS IN TURN RUTHLESSLY HUNTED DOWN.

MATURE SOULS

WE REMIND YOU THAT IN THE MATURE CYCLE THE ATTENTION TURNS INWARD AND THERE IS A NEW AWARENESS. THIS IS OFTEN THE MOST DIFFICULT CYCLE, SINCE THE EMERGING AWARENESS OF OTHERS DEMANDS NEW PERCEPTIONS OF THEM.

Slaves

THE FIRST IS A THIRD-LEVEL MATURE SLAVE IN THE OBSERVATION MODE WITH A GOAL OF ACCEPTANCE, A REALIST IN THE MOVING PART OF INTELLECTUAL CENTER, WITH A CHIEF FEATURE OF STUBBORNNESS.

THIS FRAGMENT IS A POPULAR ARCHBISHOP OF THE ROMAN CATHOLIC FAITH, AN AFRICAN, SOMETHING OF A POPULAR HERO FOR HIS INTEGRITY AND PEACEMAKING ABILITIES. HE IS AN ACCOMPLISHED LINGUIST, SPEAKING EIGHT LANGUAGES FLUENTLY AND ANOTHER THREE PASSABLY WELL.

THE SECOND IS A FOURTH-LEVEL MATURE SLAVE IN THE POWER MODE WITH A GOAL OF DOMINANCE, AN IDEALIST IN THE EMOTIONAL PART OF INTELLECTUAL CENTER, WITH A CHIEF FEATURE OF RATHER PREDICTABLE IMPATIENCE.

THIS FRAGMENT IS ONE OF THE MOST HONORED AND OUTSPOKEN FEMINISTS IN THE UNITED STATES TODAY. SHE HAS GONE FROM THE STANDARD REPRESSED ROLE SO MANY WOMEN ACCEPT TO BEING A SINCERE, RATIONAL, AND DEEPLY RESPECTED WOMAN WHO HAS SHOWN A REAL CA-

PABILITY TO ADDRESS BOTH MEN AND WOMEN ON THE SUB-JECT OF FEMINISM IN SUCH A WAY THAT MOST ARE WILLING TO LISTEN TO HER AND CONSIDER WHAT SHE SAYS.

THE THIRD IS A SIXTH-LEVEL MATURE SLAVE IN THE CAU-TION MODE WITH A GOAL OF REJECTION, A PRAGMATIST IN THE INTELLECTUAL PART OF EMOTIONAL CENTER, WITH A CHIEF FEATURE OF SELF-DEPRECATION.

THIS FRAGMENT EMBEZZLED A FORTUNE IN ORDER TO KEEP A GREEDY YOUNG SAGE MARRIED TO HIM. HE FELT HIMSELF SUBSERVIENT TO HER AND BELIEVED THAT IF HE DID NOT BUY HER ABSOLUTELY ALL THE THINGS SHE SAID SHE WANTED, SHE WOULD LEAVE HIM. PRIOR TO HIS CON-VICTION, HE WAS A BROKER SPECIALIZING IN COMMERCIAL REAL ESTATE.

Artisans

THE FIRST IS A FOURTH-LEVEL ARTISAN IN THE PASSION MODE WITH A GOAL OF GROWTH, AN IDEALIST IN THE EMO-TIONAL PART OF INTELLECTUAL CENTER, WITH A CHIEF FEATURE OF ARROGANCE.

THIS FRAGMENT WAS THE ARTISTIC GENIUS, MICHEL-ANGELO BUONARROTI.

THE SECOND IS A FIFTH-LEVEL MATURE ARTISAN IN THE OBSERVATION MODE WITH A GOAL OF GROWTH, AN IDEALIST IN THE INTELLECTUAL PART OF EMOTIONAL CENTER, WITH A CHIEF FEATURE OF IMPATIENCE.

THIS FRAGMENT WAS HIS CONTEMPORARY AND FRIEND, ALESSANDO FILIPEPI, CALLED BOTTICELLI.

THE THIRD IS A FOURTH-LEVEL MATURE ARTISAN IN THE CAUTION MODE WITH A GOAL OF ACCEPTANCE, AN IDEALIST IN THE EMOTIONAL PART OF INTELLECTUAL CENTER WITH A CHIEF FEATURE OF ARROGANCE.

THIS FRAGMENT WAS THE FRENCH PAINTER, JEAN AU-GUSTE DOMINIQUE INGRES.

ANOTHER MAJOR ARTIST WHO WAS A MATURE ARTISAN WAS VINCENT VAN GOGH, WHO WAS AT MID-CYCLE IN THE PASSION MODE WITH A GOAL OF GROWTH, AN IDEALIST IN THE INTELLECTUAL PART OF EMOTIONAL CENTER, WITH A CHIEF FEATURE OF SELF-DEPRECATION. THIS FRAGMENT WAS DEEPLY TROUBLED IN THAT LIFETIME, AND FOR HIM, THE FORCES OF HIS RESTRICTIVE CHILDHOOD AND THE

FALSE PERSONALITY THAT HE NEVER QUITE BROKE FREE OF WERE ALLIED WITH HIS CHIEF FEATURE AGAINST HIS ESSENCE.

Warriors

THE FIRST IS A FIRST-LEVEL MATURE WARRIOR IN THE POWER MODE WITH A GOAL OF GROWTH, A PRAGMATIST IN THE MOVING PART OF INTELLECTUAL CENTER, WITH A CHIEF FEATURE OF MARTYRDOM.

THIS FRAGMENT WAS ONE OF THE EARLY EXPLORERS OF THE NEW WORLD WHO WAS CAUGHT AND TORTURED TO DEATH BY MEMBERS OF A CENTRAL AMERICAN TRIBE.

THE SECOND IS A FIFTH-LEVEL MATURE WARRIOR IN THE PASSION MODE WITH A GOAL OF DOMINANCE, AN IDEALIST IN THE INTELLECTUAL PART OF MOVING CENTER, WITH A CHIEF FEATURE OF STUBBORNNESS.

THIS SECOND FRAGMENT WAS KING RICHARD THE THIRD OF ENGLAND. WE WOULD SAY THAT HISTORY, ON THE WHOLE, HAS BEEN UNKIND TO HIM.

THE THIRD IS A SIXTH-LEVEL MATURE WARRIOR IN THE PASSION MODE WITH A GOAL OF DOMINANCE, A REALIST IN THE EMOTIONAL PART OF INTELLECTUAL CENTER, WITH A CHIEF FEATURE OF ARROGANCE.

THIS THIRD FRAGMENT IS A POPULAR SCREEN ACTOR IN HIS FIFTIES, A MAN OF IMPOSING AND ARISTOCRATIC PRESENCE. BECAUSE OF HIS ESSENTIALLY HIGH-STRUNG NATURE, HE PREFERS FILMS TO THE STAGE, SINCE UNLIKE SAGES, WARRIORS FIND SO MUCH INTENSE FEEDBACK DISTRACTING. ALSO, HIS CHIEF FEATURE OF ARROGANCE GROWS, AS WE HAVE SAID BEFORE, OUT OF SHYNESS. BEFORE SETTLING DOWN TO THE ARTS, THIS FRAGMENT WAS TWENTY-NINE TIMES A WARRIOR IN BATTLE.

Scholars

THE FIRST IS A SEVENTH-LEVEL MATURE SCHOLAR IN THE PASSION MODE WITH A GOAL OF GROWTH, AN IDEALIST IN THE INTELLECTUAL PART OF EMOTIONAL CENTER, WITH A CHIEF FEATURE OF IMPATIENCE.

THIS FRAGMENT WAS THE NINETEENTH-CENTURY COMPOSER GIOACCHINO ROSSINI.

THE SECOND IS A FIFTH-LEVEL MATURE SCHOLAR IN THE POWER MODE WITH A GOAL OF GROWTH, A PRAGMATIST IN THE EMOTIONAL PART OF INTELLECTUAL CENTER, WITH A CHIEF FEATURE OF STUBBORNNESS.

THIS FRAGMENT WAS KING CHARLES THE SECOND OF ENGLAND, A VERY SHREWD AND COMPLEX MAN.

THE THIRD IS A FIFTH-LEVEL MATURE SCHOLAR IN THE OBSERVATION MODE WITH A GOAL OF DOMINANCE, A SKEPTIC IN THE EMOTIONAL PART OF INTELLECTUAL CENTER, WITH A CHIEF FEATURE OF IMPATIENCE.

THIS THIRD FRAGMENT WAS WILLIAM SHAKESPEARE.

AMONG OTHER MATURE SCHOLARS IN THE ARTS WAS JEAN JULIUS CHRISTIAN SIBELIUS, A MID-CYCLE MATURE SCHOLAR IN THE CAUTION MODE WITH A GOAL OF GROWTH, AN IDEALIST IN THE EMOTIONAL PART OF INTELLECTUAL CENTER, WITH A CHIEF FEATURE OF FAIRLY SUBDUED IMPATIENCE.

ANOTHER MID-CYCLE MATURE SCHOLAR IN THE CAUTION MODE WAS THE RUSSIAN COMPOSER PETER ILYICH TCHAIKOVSKY, AN IDEALIST WITH A GOAL OF GROWTH IN THE EMOTIONAL PART OF INTELLECTUAL CENTER WITH A CHIEF FEATURE OF MARTYRDOM. HE WAS GUILT-RIDDEN IN THAT LIFE.

YET ANOTHER MID-CYCLE MATURE SCHOLAR-COMPOSER WAS GIUSEPPE VERDI, WHO WAS IN THE PASSION MODE WITH A GOAL OF ACCEPTANCE; RATHER PREDICTABLY HE WAS IN THE EMOTIONAL PART OF INTELLECTUAL CENTER, ANOTHER IDEALIST WITH A CHIEF FEATURE OF STUBBORNNESS.

SERGEI PROKOFIEV WAS A FIFTH-LEVEL MATURE SCHOLAR IN THE PASSION MODE WITH A GOAL OF ACCEPTANCE, AN IDEALIST IN THE EMOTIONAL PART OF INTELLECTUAL CENTER, WITH A CHIEF FEATURE OF VERY PRONOUNCED IMPATIENCE.

AWAY FROM COMPOSITION BUT STILL IN THE ARTS, THE FRENCH PAINTER JACQUES LOUIS DAVID WAS A SEVENTH-LEVEL MATURE SCHOLAR IN THE OBSERVATION MODE WITH A GOAL OF GROWTH, A PRAGMATIST IN THE EMOTIONAL PART OF INTELLECTUAL CENTER, WITH A CHIEF FEATURE OF STUBBORNNESS. TO SEE MORE CLEARLY HOW LEVEL, ESSENCE, AND OVERLEAVES AFFECT PERCEPTION, EXAMINE TWO PORTRAITS OF NAPOLEON, ONE BY INGRES AND ONE BY DAVID. THE INGRES PORTRAIT IS FLATTERING, ALMOST

ICONOGRAPHIC, MAKING THE VERY BEST OF EVERY ONE OF THE SUBJECT'S FEATURES. DAVID, ON THE OTHER HAND, SHOWS NAPOLEON IN HIS STUDY LATE AT NIGHT, HIS HAIR MUSSED, HIS STOCKINGS SAGGING, HIS EYES TIRED. NAPOLEON SAID HE PREFERRED THE LATTER PORTRAIT BECAUSE IT SHOWED HOW HE LABORED FOR HIS GOAL.

IN THE AREA OF RELIGION, GEORGE FOX, THE FOUNDER OF THE SOCIETY OF FRIENDS, OR THE QUAKERS, WAS A SEVENTH-LEVEL MATURE SCHOLAR IN THE PASSION MODE WITH A GOAL OF GROWTH, AN IDEALIST IN THE MOVING PART OF INTELLECTUAL CENTER WITH A CHIEF FEATURE OF SELF-DEPRECATION. THIS WAS A KINDLY SOUL.

Sages

THE FIRST IS A THIRD-LEVEL MATURE SAGE IN THE OBSERVATION MODE WITH A GOAL OF DOMINANCE, A SKEPTIC IN THE EMOTIONAL PART OF INTELLECTUAL CENTER, WITH A CHIEF FEATURE OF IMPATIENCE.

THIS FIRST FRAGMENT WAS WOLFGANG THEOPHILLIUS (LATER AMADEUS) MOZART.

THE SECOND IS A FIFTH-LEVEL MATURE SAGE IN THE PASSION MODE WITH A GOAL OF DOMINANCE, AN IDEALIST IN THE INTELLECTUAL PART OF EMOTIONAL CENTER, WITH A CHIEF FEATURE OF EXALTED ARROGANCE.

THIS FRAGMENT WAS KING LOUIS THE FOURTEENTH OF FRANCE, AND WE WOULD SAY WITH SUCH OVERLEAVES, HE WOULD HAVE HAD TO RULE OVER SOMETHING.

THE THIRD IS A MID-CYCLE SAGE IN THE PASSION MODE WITH A GOAL OF GROWTH, A SKEPTIC IN THE EMOTIONAL PART OF INTELLECTUAL CENTER, WITH A CHIEF FEATURE OF ARROGANCE.

THIS THIRD FRAGMENT WAS THE SPANISH AUTHOR MIGUEL DE CERVANTES.

ANOTHER NOTED MATURE SAGE WAS GIACOMO PUCCINI. HE WAS AT THE FIFTH LEVEL IN THE PASSION MODE WITH A GOAL OF GROWTH, A SKEPTIC IN THE EMOTIONAL PART OF MOVING CENTER, WITH A CHIEF FEATURE OF STUBBORNNESS. THESE OVERLEAVES SEEM MORE TYPICAL OF THE OVERLEAVES OF A NOVELIST RATHER THAN A COMPOSER, BUT THERE IS A NOVELISTIC SENSE TO MUCH OF HIS MUSIC.

Priests

THE FIRST IS A THIRD-LEVEL MATURE PRIEST IN THE OB-SERVATION MODE WITH A GOAL OF GROWTH, A SKEPTIC IN THE EMOTIONAL PART OF INTELLECTUAL CENTER, WITH A CHIEF FEATURE OF IMPATIENCE.

THIS FRAGMENT WAS ONE OF THE FOUNDERS OF THE METHODIST FAITH. THIS WAS A SEARCH FOR A MORE BE-NEVOLENT FORM OF LITURGY, AND WAS CERTAINLY SUC-CESSFUL.

THE SECOND IS A SIXTH-LEVEL MATURE PRIEST IN THE POWER MODE WITH A GOAL OF GROWTH, A REALIST IN THE MOVING PART OF INTELLECTUAL CENTER, WITH A CHIEF FEATURE OF ARROGANCE.

THIS FRAGMENT WAS THE PHARAOH RAMSES II.

THE THIRD IS ANOTHER SIXTH-LEVEL MATURE PRIEST IN THE PASSION MODE WITH A GOAL OF GROWTH, A SKEPTIC IN THE EMOTIONAL PART OF INTELLECTUAL CENTER WITH A CHIEF FEATURE, UNLIKELY THOUGH IT MAY BE, OF SELF-DEPRECATION.

THIS FRAGMENT WAS THE GREAT SPANISH PAINTER, FRANCISCO DE GOYA Y LUCIENTES.

WE WOULD ALSO LIKE TO BRING TO YOUR ATTENTION TWO MID-CYCLE MATURE PRIESTS WHO WERE COMPOSERS, RICHARD WAGNER AND MODESTE MUSSORGSKY. WAGNER WAS IN THE OBSERVATION MODE WITH A GOAL OF DOMI-NANCE, A SKEPTIC IN THE EMOTIONAL PART OF INTELLEC-TUAL CENTER, WITH A CHIEF FEATURE OF HIGHLY MARKED ARROGANCE. MUSSORGSKY WAS IN THE PASSION MODE WITH A GOAL OF GROWTH, AN IDEALIST IN THE INTELLECTUAL PART OF EMOTIONAL CENTER BUT WITH A CHIEF FEATURE OF MARTYRDOM.

TO DEMONSTRATE THAT NOT ALL MATURE PRIESTS ARE WELL ADJUSTED, THE MURDERER CALLED JACK THE RIPPER WAS A VERY TROUBLED MID-CYCLE MATURE PRIEST IN THE AGGRESSION MODE WITH A GOAL OF DOMINANCE, A CYNIC IN THE INTELLECTUAL PART OF MOVING CENTER, WITH A CHIEF FEATURE OF GREED. ALL OF THE CRIMES ATTRIBUTED TO THIS VICTORIAN MURDERER WERE NOT IN FACT COM-MITTED BY ONE PERSON, BUT THE BULK OF THEM WERE

PERPETRATED BY THE OLDEST LEGITIMATE OF A NOBLE ENGLISH FAMILY. AS THE FAMILY IS STILL LIVING, WE WILL CONTINUE OUR POLICY OF PRIVACY AND NOT REVEAL THEIR SPECIFIC NAME. HOWEVER, AT LEAST ONE POLICEMAN AT THE TIME WAS AWARE OF THE KILLER'S IDENTITY.

MAJOR RELIGIOUS FIGURES WHO WERE PRIESTS INCLUDE SAINT FRANCIS OF ASSISI, WHO WAS A FOURTH-LEVEL MATURE PRIEST IN THE PASSION MODE WITH A GOAL OF ACCEPTANCE, AN IDEALIST IN THE EMOTIONAL PART OF INTELLECTUAL CENTER, WITH A CHIEF FEATURE OF VERY ADVANCED SELF-DEPRECATION. WE WOULD LIKE TO POINT OUT THAT STIGMATICS SUCH AS THIS FRAGMENT ARE MOSTLY MATURE SOULS, ALTHOUGH THERE ARE A FEW HYSTERICAL YOUNG AND BABY SOULS IN THEIR NUMBERS.

THE LATE POPE PAUL VI WAS A SIXTH-LEVEL MATURE PRIEST IN THE CAUTION MODE WITH A GOAL OF GROWTH WHICH WAS EXPERIENCED IN THE NEGATIVE POLE, A SPIRITUALIST IN THE EMOTIONAL PART OF INTELLECTUAL CENTER, WITH A CHIEF FEATURE OF ARROGANCE.

Kings

THE FIRST IS A FIFTH-LEVEL MATURE KING IN THE OBSERVATION MODE WITH A GOAL OF DOMINANCE, A SKEPTIC IN THE INTELLECTUAL PART OF EMOTIONAL CENTER, WITH A CHIEF FEATURE OF STUBBORNNESS.

THIS MATURE KING FRAGMENT IS A MUCH-HONORED TELEVISION JOURNALIST, NOTED FOR INTELLIGENCE AND TENACITY. THE PERCEPTIONS OF THIS MAN HAVE OFTEN BEEN PAINFUL FOR HIM AND HE HAS BLOCKED THEM FROM HIS MIND, WHICH MEANS THAT THERE ARE MONADS THAT HE HAS YET TO COMPLETE AT THIS LEVEL. MOST OF THE MONADS OF THE MATURE LEVEL HAVE TO DO WITH FEELINGS, AND THIS MAN HAS NEVER LEARNED TO TRUST HIS FEELINGS, AT LEAST IN THIS LIFE.

THE SECOND IS A SECOND-LEVEL MATURE KING IN THE CAUTION MODE WITH A GOAL OF GROWTH, A SPIRITUALIST IN THE MOVING PART OF EMOTIONAL CENTER WITH A CHIEF FEATURE OF ARROGANCE.

THIS FRAGMENT IS A WORLD-FAMOUS VIOLINIST. THIS IS NOT THE FIRST TIME HE HAS PLAYED THE VIOLIN. IN HIS IMMEDIATE PAST LIFE AND IN TWO OTHER EARLIER LIVES,

HE HAD A DEEP INTEREST IN MUSIC, AND IN TWO OF THOSE LIVES HE WAS A MUSICIAN AT LEAST PART OF THE TIME.

THE THIRD IS A FOURTH-LEVEL MATURE KING IN THE PERSEVERANCE MODE WITH A GOAL OF SUBMISSION, A PRAGMATIST IN THE INTELLECTUAL PART OF MOVING CENTER WITH A CHIEF FEATURE OF SELF-DEPRECATION.

THIS FRAGMENT IS A EUROPEAN STAGE DIRECTOR. HE HAS DONE FEW FILMS, CLAIMING THAT HE DISLIKES THE MEDIUM AND WOULD RATHER DEAL WITH LIVE AUDIENCES. THAT IS PARTLY THE TRUTH, BUT THE NATURE OF HIS GOAL AND CHIEF FEATURE MAKES IT LIKELY THAT HE NEEDS TO HIDE BEHIND A CAMERA AND NEEDS ONLY SEE HIS WORK ALONE IN THE DARK.

ANOTHER MATURE KING THAT IS OF INTEREST WAS A FORMIDABLE NOVELIST OF THE LAST CENTURY. SHE CAUSED SOMETHING OF A FUROR WITH HER WORK WHEN IT APPEARED, AND IT IS STILL BEING READ, THOUGH HER STYLE IS NOT ONE THAT IS POPULAR BY CURRENT STANDARDS. SHE WAS IN THE PASSION MODE WITH A GOAL OF ACCEPTANCE, A SKEPTIC IN THE EMOTIONAL PART OF INTELLECTUAL CENTER AND WITH A CHIEF FEATURE OF IMPATIENCE VERY STRONG IN HER.

OLD SOULS

WE REMIND YOU THAT THE NATURE OF THE PERCEPTIONS IN THE OLD SOUL IS SEEING THE GREATER WHOLE. MOST OLD SOULS' MONADS HAVE TO DO WITH BEING. WE REMIND YOU THAT IN TERMS OF EVOLUTION OF THE ESSENCE, THE OLD-SOUL CYCLE IS THE MOST DEMANDING OF ALL, SINCE MEMORY OF ALL THE PAST, ITS DEBTS AND PAYMENTS, AS WELL AS THE EXPERIENCE OF THE LIVES, IS WITHIN THE GRASP OF ALL THOSE IN THIS CYCLE.

Slaves

THE FIRST IS A SECOND-LEVEL OLD SLAVE IN THE OBSERVATION MODE WITH A GOAL OF ACCEPTANCE, A PRAGMATIST IN THE EMOTIONAL PART OF INTELLECTUAL CENTER, WITH A CHIEF FEATURE OF STUBBORNNESS.

THIS FRAGMENT IS A PERFORMER WHO APPEARS WITH HER

MATURE-SAGE HUSBAND ALL OVER THE UNITED STATES. SHE IS A SENSIBLE, STEADY-TEMPERED WOMAN WITH A PLEASANT SENSE OF HUMOR AND A THOROUGHLY PROFESSIONAL ATTITUDE.

THE SECOND IS A FIFTH-LEVEL OLD SLAVE IN THE PASSION MODE WITH A GOAL OF DOMINANCE, A SPIRITUALIST IN THE INTELLECTUAL PART OF MOVING CENTER, WITH A CHIEF FEATURE OF ARROGANCE.

THIS FRAGMENT IS A BOTANIST SPECIALIZING IN MICRO-CLIMATOLOGY. SHE ALSO HAS DESIGNED EXTENSIVE GARDENS IN THE UNITED STATES, BRITAIN, AND FRANCE.

THE THIRD IS A FIFTH-LEVEL OLD SLAVE IN THE OBSERVATION MODE WITH A GOAL OF GROWTH, A PRAGMATIST IN THE INTELLECTUAL PART OF EMOTIONAL CENTER, WITH A VERY SUBDUED CHIEF FEATURE OF SELF-DEPRECATION.

THIS FRAGMENT OPERATES A FISHING BOAT NEAR MÉRIDA ON THE YUCATÁN PENINSULA.

Artisans

THE FIRST IS A FOURTH-LEVEL OLD ARTISAN IN THE OBSERVATION MODE WITH A GOAL OF GROWTH, AN IDEALIST IN THE INTELLECTUAL PART OF EMOTIONAL CENTER, WITH A CHIEF FEATURE OF STUBBORNNESS. THIS FRAGMENT WAS THE ARTIST, PAUL GAUGIN.

THE SECOND IS A THIRD-LEVEL OLD ARTISAN IN THE CAUTION MODE WITH A GOAL OF SUBMISSION, A REALIST IN THE MOVING PART OF EMOTIONAL CENTER, WITH A CHIEF FEATURE OF IMPATIENCE.

THIS FRAGMENT HAS HAD PROBLEMS WITH A DIFFICULT CHIEF FEATURE, BUT OTHERWISE IS FAIRLY CALM AND EASY TO DEAL WITH. HE LIVES NEAR LONDON AND RESTORES CLASSIC AUTOMOBILES.

THE THIRD IS A SIXTH-LEVEL OLD ARTISAN IN THE POWER MODE WITH A GOAL OF DOMINANCE, A SKEPTIC IN THE INTELLECTUAL PART OF MOVING CENTER, WITH A CHIEF FEATURE OF ARROGANCE.

THIS FRAGMENT HAS FAIRLY ENERGETIC OVERLEAVES FOR AN OLD ARTISAN. SHE IS A VERY FAMOUS DANCER, STILL FAIRLY YOUNG, WITH A FINE EFFORTLESS STYLE THAT HAS AROUSED ADMIRATION WHEREVER SHE PERFORMS. THIS IS HER NINTH LIFE AS A DANCER.

Warriors

THE FIRST IS A FIRST-LEVEL OLD WARRIOR IN THE OBSERVATION MODE WITH A GOAL OF DOMINANCE, AN IDEALIST IN THE EMOTIONAL PART OF INTELLECTUAL CENTER, WITH A CHIEF FEATURE OF IMPATIENCE.

THIS FRAGMENT WAS THE SUPERB MODERN COMPOSER, IGOR STRAVINSKY. HE HAD BEEN A COMPOSER BEFORE, IN THE EARLY PART OF THE NINETEENTH CENTURY, AND BEFORE THAT HAD BELONGED TO MANY MUSICAL ENSEMBLES.

THE SECOND IS A SECOND-LEVEL OLD WARRIOR IN THE PASSION MODE WITH A GOAL OF DOMINANCE, A REALIST IN THE INTELLECTUAL PART OF EMOTIONAL CENTER, WITH A CHIEF FEATURE OF STUBBORNNESS.

THIS FRAGMENT IS A GERMAN-ITALIAN BARITONE, NOT YET FORTY, SINGING PRIMARILY IN EUROPE; A LARGE, POWERFUL MAN WITH ENORMOUS WARRIOR ENERGY, EVEN AT THIS ADVANCED LEVEL. HE IS EQUALLY AT HOME WITH CLASSICAL AND POPULAR MUSIC.

THE THIRD IS A SIXTH-LEVEL OLD WARRIOR IN THE POWER MODE WITH A GOAL OF ACCEPTANCE, A PRAGMATIST IN THE MOVING PART OF INTELLECTUAL CENTER, WITH A CHIEF FEATURE OF ARROGANCE, ALTHOUGH IT IS FAIRLY SUBDUED.

THIS FRAGMENT IS A HORSE BREEDER, MORE INTERESTED IN THE ANIMALS THAN IN THE COMPETITIONS AND RIBBONS. HE OFTEN RIDES FOR PLEASURE. HE LIVES IN EGYPT.

Scholars

THE FIRST IS A THIRD-LEVEL OLD SCHOLAR IN THE OBSERVATION MODE WITH A GOAL OF DOMINANCE, AN IDEALIST IN THE EMOTIONAL PART OF INTELLECTUAL CENTER, WITH A CHIEF FEATURE OF IMPATIENCE.

THIS FRAGMENT WAS THE COMPOSER LUDWIG VAN BEETHOVEN.

THE SECOND IS A FIFTH-LEVEL OLD SCHOLAR IN THE OBSERVATION MODE WITH A GOAL OF GROWTH, A SKEPTIC IN THE EMOTIONAL PART OF INTELLECTUAL CENTER WITH A CHIEF FEATURE OF STUBBORNNESS.

THIS FRAGMENT WAS THE ARTIST AND ENGINEER LEON-

ARDO DA VINCI, A MAN WHO WAS VERY MUCH OUT OF HIS TIME.

THE THIRD IS A SECOND-LEVEL OLD SCHOLAR IN THE PASSION MODE WITH A GOAL OF GROWTH, AN IDEALIST IN THE EMOTIONAL PART OF INTELLECTUAL CENTER WITH A CHIEF FEATURE OF MELLOWED ARROGANCE.

THIS FRAGMENT WAS THE COMPOSER JOHANN SEBASTIAN BACH. INCIDENTALLY, THIS WAS A FAIRLY GENTLE SOUL.

Sages

THE FIRST IS A FOURTH-LEVEL OLD SAGE IN THE PASSION MODE WITH A GOAL OF GROWTH, A PRAGMATIST IN THE EMOTIONAL PART OF INTELLECTUAL CENTER, WITH A CHIEF FEATURE OF ARROGANCE.

THIS FRAGMENT IS A MAJOR INTERNATIONAL OPERA STAR, A MAN WITH A GLORIOUS VOICE AND THE REPUTATION OF BEING GENERALLY EASY TO GET ALONG WITH IN SPITE OF HIS PERFECTIONIST STREAK. HE IS YOUNG, WITH A SAGE'S GOOD LOOKS AND IMPECCABLE MUSICIANSHIP, WHICH HE USES IN CONDUCTING AS WELL AS SINGING.

THE SECOND IS A FIFTH-LEVEL OLD SAGE IN THE OBSERVATION MODE WITH A GOAL OF ACCEPTANCE, AN IDEALIST IN THE INTELLECTUAL PART OF EMOTIONAL CENTER AND WITH A CHIEF FEATURE OF SELF-DEPRECATION.

THIS FRAGMENT IS A MAN IN HIS SEVENTIES, ONE OF THE MOST REVERED ACTORS IN THE WORLD, AND RIGHTLY SO. HE IS NOTED FOR HIS ANONYMOUS AND RESERVED OFF-STAGE DEMEANOR, WHICH IS THE RESULT OF HIS CHIEF FEATURE.

THE THIRD IS A FIFTH-LEVEL SAGE IN THE PASSION MODE WITH A GOAL OF DOMINANCE, A SPIRITUALIST IN THE EMOTIONAL PART OF INTELLECTUAL CENTER, WITH A CHIEF FEATURE OF IMPATIENCE.

THIS FRAGMENT WAS A POPULAR AND HUMANITARIAN POPE, NOTED FOR HIS PROGRESSIVENESS, HIS PERSONAL CHARM, AND HIS WIT AS WELL AS HIS DEEP AND GENUINE CONCERN FOR ALL THE WORLD, RELIGIOUS AFFILIATION NOTWITHSTANDING.

Priests

THE FIRST IS A SECOND-LEVEL OLD PRIEST IN THE PASSION MODE WITH A GOAL OF ACCEPTANCE, AN IDEALIST IN THE INTELLECTUAL PART OF EMOTIONAL CENTER, WITH A CHIEF FEATURE OF STUBBORNNESS.

THIS FRAGMENT IS AN INTERNATIONALLY FAMOUS WRITER OF SCIENCE FICTION AND FANTASY, WHOSE WORK SPANS ALMOST FORTY YEARS. HE IS NOTED FOR THE POETIC AND HUMANITARIAN CONCEPTS IN HIS WORK. HIS OUTPUT IS NOT LARGE BUT THE QUALITY IS VERY HIGH. THIS IS A GENTLE SOUL WHO WANTS TO PASS THROUGH THE FIRE.

THE SECOND IS A FIFTH-LEVEL OLD PRIEST IN THE OB-SERVATION MODE WITH A GOAL OF RETARDATION, A REAL-IST IN THE MOVING PART OF EMOTIONAL CENTER, WITH A CHIEF FEATURE OF SELF-DEPRECATION.

THIS FRAGMENT IS A VERY WISE WOMAN WHO HAS WORKED OFTEN AS A COUNSELOR. THE CONFLICT INHERENT IN HER OVERLEAVES HAS OFTEN DRIVEN HER TO SEEK THE ASSISTANCE OF PSYCHOLOGISTS AND PSYCHIATRISTS, THOUGH THE PROBLEMS ARE NOT ACCESSIBLE BY SUCH MANEUVERS, AND, IRONICALLY, SHE HAS DONE MORE LASTING GOOD FOR THOSE AROUND HER, THROUGH HER WISDOM AND EXAMPLE, THAN SHE HAS EVER RECEIVED FROM OTHERS. SHE IS DRAWN BOTH TO ART AND POETRY, AND IN PAST LIVES HAS MADE HER LIVING AT BOTH. SHE ALSO FOUGHT WITH WIL-LIAM THE SILENT AND WITH THE KNIGHTS TEMPLAR.

THE THIRD IS A FINAL-LEVEL OLD PRIEST IN THE CAUTION MODE WITH A GOAL OF GROWTH, A PRAGMATIST IN THE INTELLECTUAL PART OF MOVING CENTER, WITH A CHIEF FEATURE OF IMPATIENCE.

THIS FRAGMENT LIVES IN ALASKA, WHERE SHE RAISES DOGS. HER MOST NOTED PAST LIFE WAS IN HER YOUNG CYCLE, WHEN SHE WAS AT HER MOST ZEALOUS. AT THAT TIME SHE WAS PLATO, THE COMPANION AND RECORD-KEEPER FOR SOCRATES.

Kings

THE FIRST IS A FOURTH-LEVEL OLD KING IN THE OBSER-VATION MODE WITH A GOAL OF ACCEPTANCE, A SKEPTIC IN

THE EMOTIONAL PART OF INTELLECTUAL CENTER, WITH A CHIEF FEATURE OF IMPATIENCE.

THIS FRAGMENT IS A CABINETMAKER AND BARTENDER, A MAN OF INSIGHT AND EXCELLENT TASTE—THE LATTER HE KEEPS CAREFULLY HIDDEN.

THE SECOND IS A SIXTH-LEVEL OLD KING IN THE OBSERVATION MODE WITH A GOAL OF DOMINANCE, IN THE INTELLECTUAL PART OF EMOTIONAL CENTER, WITH A CHIEF FEATURE OF ARROGANCE.

THIS FRAGMENT IS A MAGNETIC OLD KING. MAGNETIC OLD KINGS ARE ALWAYS AT THE SIXTH LEVEL AND STAY AT THE SIXTH LEVEL FOR AS MANY LIVES AS ARE NECESSARY FOR THOSE THEY DRAW TO COMPLETE THEIR TASKS AND AGREEMENTS. AS A SECOND-LEVEL OLD KING HE RULED FLORENCE AS LORENZO DE' MEDICI.

THE THIRD IS A SECOND-LEVEL OLD KING IN THE OBSERVATION MODE WITH A GOAL OF ACCEPTANCE, A PRAGMATIST IN THE INTELLECTUAL CENTER, WITH A CHIEF FEATURE OF STUBBORNNESS.

THIS FRAGMENT WAS A LOGGER AND WOODSMAN WHO EMIGRATED TO THE UNITED STATES AT THE TURN OF THE CENTURY TO LIVE IN COMPARATIVE POVERTY IN AN ISOLATED MOUNTAIN COMMUNE. THOUGH HE NEVER WORE A CROWN IN PREVIOUS LIVES, HE WAS TWICE AN EXPLORER, ONCE FOR EGYPT AND ONCE FOR PORTUGAL, AND FOREIGN PLACES NEVER LOST THEIR MAGIC FOR HIM.

Chapter 9

UNDERSTANDING AND OVERLEAVES...

"At first I didn't think Michael was right about the chief feature," Jessica says with a slow shake of her head. "But over the years since Michael first gave us this material, I've seen it work too often."

Lucy agrees. "You know, after my marriage fell apart, it was very hard on me, but there's been a lot of worthwhile learning, too. My ex-husband has mutually conflicting overleaves, and now that I understand that, I don't make the mistakes with him that I used to."

"Well," Jessica points out, "you don't have to live with him anymore. That makes a big difference."

"Sure," Lucy says. "I don't deny that. But there's more to it than that. Here he is in the emotional part of intellectual center, always insisting that he was being rational when he was hardest to deal with. And his chief feature is self-deprecation, so at the worst possible moments, he'd be all humble and apologetic. I used to think it would drive me *crazy*. And don't remind me that I'm in the passion mode," she goes on quickly. "Even though I am."

Walter chuckles. "I wouldn't dream of it." Then he becomes more serious. "There are some surprisingly consistent patterns to the overleaves. Recently one of the group was anxious to know about a friend of hers, an intellectually brilliant woman who had suffered a stroke and was not adjusting to the dependency of her condition. Michael gave this woman's overleaves and made a few comments, and as a result, this woman in the group has been able to deal with her friend much more successfully.''

What had Michael said?

THIS IS A FOURTH-LEVEL MATURE SCHOLAR IN THE OBSERVATION MODE WITH A GOAL OF GROWTH BUT A CHIEF FEATURE OF SELF-DESTRUCTION AND SEVERAL VERY DIFFICULT SEQUENCES TO COMPLETE, INCLUDING ONE INVOLVING DEPENDENCY. YOU MUST REMEMBER THAT THIS IS ONE OF LIFE'S LESSONS TO BE LEARNED, AS IS INDEPENDENCE. SOME ESSENCE ROLES, SUCH AS WARRIOR, SCHOLAR, AND KING, MUST ALMOST DISABLE THEMSELVES BEFORE THEY CAN ALLOW ANYONE TO HELP THEM.

"Kate uses this information in a very practical way," Jessica says. "Not just with that friend, but with the many other aspects of her life. She's another mature scholar, an anthropology student with a wide background in religion.''

Does that mean that most of what Michael has said has been beneficial?

"If you mean pleasant"—Jessica smiles—"the answer is probably 'No.' If you mean has it been helpful and useful, then the answer is certainly 'Yes.' I can give you an excellent example. At work we've recently got a new supervisor and he isn't an easy man to deal with. He's strong-willed, autocratic, and very private. We got his overleaves from Michael. The man's a fifth-level mature warrior in the observation mode with a goal of dominance, a skeptic, in the moving part of intellectual center, with a chief feature of impatience. Since I'm a scholar, it's a little easier for me to deal with him than a lot of the office. We have four artisans working under this mature warrior, and of course, the harder he pushes, the more distant they become. And with that chief feature of impatience, he wants things done right now. The overleaves aren't bad—in fact, they're pretty good— but the man is a powerhouse, and though he's great for the business in one sense, he's something of a stumbling block for some of the others in the office. The real trouble is that our section boss is a young sage who quite often is something of a glory hog, and every time he pulls one of his self-aggrandizing moves, my mature-warrior supervisor goes after him for it. The artisans are still scared of the warrior, but they're beginning to be glad he's around, and I've almost got him convinced to give the artisans a little more breathing room."

"Do you think you'll succeed?"

"With a mature warrior in observation? Why not?" Jessica grins.

"That can be your arrogance talking," Lucy warns her teasingly.

"Want to bet?" Jessica replies. While talking she has let her coffee grow cold and now offers to make a fresh pot. "Sometimes I get carried away," she confesses as she comes back from the kitchen. "I've been working with this for so long that I find it hard to remember that not everyone has the same references. There are times I'd love to say to my supervisor, 'You're a warrior, what do you expect?' He wouldn't know what I mean and I'm damned if I'll explain it to him."

Lucy nods her head emphatically. "I know exactly what you mean. Remember that man I met and simply couldn't stand? I mean I couldn't stand him the moment I laid eyes on him. I want to turn around and walk out of the office where I'm working. And to make matters worse, he decided he thought I was great. After three days I asked Michael about it, and he said that not only do our overleaves abrade, which was bad enough, but the man owed me a pretty big debt from a previous life which he wanted to pay, and since part of me, the essence, knows what he did before, it wants to avoid him. It's a very weird relationship."

What happened? Did he pay Lucy in some way?

"Not yet. I have a hard time being around him, but I haven't rejected him outright and I'm trying not to. The real trouble is that he keeps trying to *do* things for me, and it's almost embarrassing. He told me once that he doesn't know why he behaves this way. He's not interested in me sexually. I'm not his type at all. For which," she says with a gesture of relief, "I am really very grateful. I find him hard to take now. If he were playing sexual games with me, I'd have to quit the job."

What would that do to the debt?

"Postpone it for another life," Jessica explains. "According to Michael, you can refuse to be paid. Eventually you'll have to be, but the choice is yours. You can refuse to fulfill your agreements. It's all a matter of choice. But you have to deal with these conditions sometime or there's no growth. You stay stuck at the same level."

Lucy sighs. "This man is a priest, a young one, and he's absolutely convinced that he has enlightenment coming out of his pores. There are times I want to scream." Instead of screaming, she smiles. "There are sages, priests, artisans, and scholars in my entity, but this guy isn't part of it. That's reassuring."

Does Lucy know any members of her entity?

"I've met eight that I know of. For the most part, it's been really pleasant to know them. I like them." She gestures toward Walter. "We're in the same entity, and so is Emily. It's a pretty classy entity."

How does Walter feel about this?

"It's like having a sister I didn't have to grow up with," he says. "Same thing with Emily. I'm an artisan, Emily's a scholar, and Lucy over there is a sage. In a strange way we complement each other."

Wouldn't it have been better if they had been born actual siblings?

"Michael says that entity mates aren't born into the same family very often, and when it does occur it's usually for a specific reason. Otherwise the relationship becomes too overwhelming." Jessica has brought a coffee pot into the living room. "There's cream and sugar if anybody wants it, but if you don't, I won't bring it." She takes her seat in the bentwood rocker again.

"What about Marjorie, though?" Lucy asks.

"Now *that's* a story," Jessica says. "Marjorie came into the group a little over a year ago. She's in the biological sciences, a very sensible woman in her early thirties."

"She's got a great sense of humor," Lucy adds.

Shortly after Marjorie joined the Michael group, she asked why she was afraid of fire.

ALMOST ALL PHOBIAS ARE TRAUMAS REMEMBERED FROM A FORMER LIFE. IN YOUR CASE, MARJORIE, YOU DIED IN A BURNING BUILDING AND THE RECOLLECTION IS STILL

STRONG. IF YOU COULD TRANSCEND THE FEAR, YOU WOULD FIND THAT LIFE HAS A GREAT DEAL TO TEACH YOU.

"While I was in Germany," Marjorie pursued, "I had the strange feeling that I had been there before. The family I stayed with seemed so familiar. My sponsor's mother, in particular, was just great, and that's pretty strange because I'm told she doesn't usually like foreigners. Is there a tie-in with these people? Did I know them before?"

FIRST OF ALL, YOUR SPONSOR AND YOU WERE ONCE IN BUSINESS TOGETHER, TRADING IN SPICES AND NATIVES. YOU WERE VERY SUCCESSFUL IN A MATERIAL WAY IN THAT VENTURE. THAT WAS IN THE SEVENTEENTH CENTURY OF THE COMMON ERA. THERE IS A MORE RECENT ASSOCIATION, HOWEVER. YOU ARE CORRECT THAT YOU HAVE BEEN IN GERMANY BEFORE. YOU LIVED THERE IN YOUR LAST LIFE. YOU WERE A PHYSICIAN.

"When was that?" Marjorie wanted to know.

YOU DIED THERE IN ONE THOUSAND NINE HUNDRED FORTY-FOUR, COMMON ERA.

"Was I part of the Resistance, or was I a Nazi?" Marjorie admitted that she was very nervous about the answer.

YOU WERE NEITHER A NAZI NOR PART OF THE RESISTANCE. YOU DID NOTHING EITHER WAY.

"In Frankfurt?" she asked. "That's where my sponsor and his family live."

NO. YOU DIED IN DRESDEN. YOU WERE FIFTY-SIX YEARS OLD. ONE OF YOUR FIVE CHILDREN IS STILL ALIVE. SHE FOLLOWED IN YOUR FOOTSTEPS AND IS A PHYSICIAN. WE WOULD SAY THAT YOU ARE AWARE OF THIS.

Marjorie was silent.

"I asked her if there was anything wrong," Jessica recalls. "She was very pale."

"My sponsor's mother is a physician. Her family were all killed in the war."

Had Jessica any knowledge of this before the question was asked?

"You mean did I know that Marjorie had been in Germany? She'd mentioned it in passing, but there were no details. I didn't know she'd lived there. In fact, I thought she'd probably gone there as a tourist."

When Marjorie had recovered a little, she asked, "Isn't

it unusual for someone to come back so fast? I was born in 1948, and that's only four years.''

IT IS NOT UNUSUAL TO RETURN QUICKLY WHEN THERE IS UNFINISHED BUSINESS.

''Marjorie wasn't sure she believed this, and I can't say that I blame her,'' Jessica says as she gets up to close the draperies against the rosy glare of the setting sun. ''She was also certain that she would not have the chance to get back to Germany for several years. She's working on a research project that requires her presence at the university and she said that she has no intention of throwing that all away because of what a Ouija board told her. However, it turns out,'' Jessica continues with a sly smile, ''that similar work is being done in Germany and the university there has invited her to come back for a time and help them with their research project so that she and they can dovetail their work.''

''Dying in the fire-bombing of Dresden would be enough to give you a phobia like Marjorie's,'' Lucy adds.

Have there been any other similar revelations at sessions?

''Lots of them,'' Jessica says. ''There are times it's almost frightening. There was a man who came to sessions for about two years, and then dropped out. He found out a lot of things he didn't want to know.''

''He wanted easy answers,'' Lucy explains. ''Michael doesn't often give easy answers.''

What was the problem?

''It's hard to pick on just one. Jack had a lot to work out.'' Jessica sighs.

At one of the first sessions Jack attended, he mentioned that he had a continuing sense of guilt and a feeling he had to make amends, but no matter how he tried, he could not discover what had given him that feeling. He had been in analysis off and on for three years and this did not seem to help. He was considering regression therapy to see if he might learn something.

THE MAN JONATHAN IS A MATURE SAGE IN THE CAUTION MODE, SECOND LEVEL. HIS MODE IS CAUTION AND HIS GOAL IS ACCEPTANCE. HE IS IN THE INTELLECTUAL PART OF EMOTIONAL CENTER AND A PRAGMATIST, WITH A CHIEF FEATURE OF STUBBORNNESS. HE HAS, INDEED, MANY KARMIC

RIBBONS TO BURN. SUGGESTED RETROGRESSION IS TO US ANOTHER EXAMPLE OF MECHANICAL MAN'S DESIRE FOR COMPLEXITY, BUT IT ALSO SUGGESTS TO US MECHANICAL MAN'S NEED TO BE PUNISHED FOR WHAT HE CALLS SIN. THERE IS NO SIN, ONLY KARMA. THERE IS NO EVIL, ONLY MAYA. YOU WILL REPAY YOUR KARMIC DEBTS. BUT NOT BY RETROGRESSION, JUST BY HARD WORK. THERE IS NO ONE "UP THERE" TO PUNISH YOU. YOU WILL HAVE TO FIND SOMEONE "DOWN THERE" TO DO YOUR FLAGELLATION, JONATHAN.

"I'd rather you called me Jack," he complained. "I'm used to it."

Leah explained that Michael refused to use nicknames or diminutives.

"Why is that?"

NICKNAMES ARE A PART OF FALSE PERSONALITY. SOME-TIMES EVEN THE FALSE PERSONALITY OF THE PARENT AND NOT OF THE SOUL ITSELF. THE PARENTS OFTEN GIVE THE CHILD A NAME WITH SOCIAL SIGNIFICANCE, THEN PROMPTLY CHANGE IT.

"We're getting off the subject," Jessica said after the response had been read back to her. "What else does Jack want to know?"

"If I owe, whom do I owe, and why?" he asked rather belligerently.

THERE IS A FRAGMENT WHOM THE MAN JONATHAN HAS TWICE BETRAYED, ONCE IN CHINA WHEN THE CH'ING DY-NASTY BEGAN. THE MAN JONATHAN WAS AT THAT TIME A JUDGE IN THE COURTS AND USED HIS POWER AND INFLU-ENCE TO CONDEMN AN OLD FRIEND WHO HAD OPPOSED HIS RULINGS ON PHILOSOPHICAL GROUNDS. THE FRAGMENT HE BETRAYED WAS THEN A MATURE KING IN THE OBSERVATION MODE WHO IN THAT LIFETIME WAS AN IMPORTANT MUSI-CIAN AND POET. THE MAN JONATHAN SOUGHT TO IMPROVE HIS OWN POLITICAL POSITION AT THE COST OF HIS FRIEND. THE FIRST DEBT WAS PAID IN THE NEXT LIFETIME IN GE-NEVA, WHEN THE MAN JONATHAN ALLOWED HIMSELF TO BE CONDEMNED AND BROKEN ON THE WHEEL RATHER THAN REVEAL WHAT HE KNEW OF THAT FRAGMENT'S ACTIVITIES THAT WERE CONTRARY TO THE RELIGIOUS TEACHINGS OF THE TIME.

"In what way were his activities negative?" Jack asked.

HE WAS CONDUCTING CERTAIN EXPERIMENTS OF AN AL-CHEMICAL NATURE.

"How was I associated with him?"

THE MATURE KING WAS THEN A PRIEST OF THE AUGUS-TINIAN ORDER, WHO HAD TAKEN YOU AS HIS LOVER. THE ARRANGEMENT WAS OFFICIALLY FROWNED UPON BUT FAIRLY COMMON.

"Was I a woman in that life?" Jack demanded, very much disturbed.

YOU HAVE BEEN A WOMAN IN MANY LIFETIMES. WE AGREE THAT THE LIFE OF WOMEN HAS OFTEN BEEN VERY DIFFICULT. IT IS PART OF THE BLINDNESS OF THE PHYSICAL PLANE THAT CAUSES MANY TO PERCEIVE ONLY THE BODY, AND NOT THE NATURE OF THE SOUL. THE MAN JONATHAN MUST NOT PERMIT HIMSELF TO REJECT KNOWLEDGE BE-CAUSE IT WAS GAINED IN FEMALE FORM.

Jack was flustered by this reply and eager to get away from such talk. "Why was I punished for him in that life-time? What had I done?"

YOU KNEW ABOUT YOUR LOVER'S EXPERIMENTS AND YOU KNEW THEY WERE CONTRARY TO CHURCH DOCTRINE. YOUR PARENTS DID NOT OPPOSE YOUR ARREST. YOU WERE IM-PRISONED FOR SEVERAL MONTHS AND WOULD NOT REVEAL WHAT YOU KNEW. BECAUSE YOU WERE WEAKENED BY IM-PRISONMENT, DEATH, WHEN IT CAME, WAS FAIRLY QUICK, AND YOUR SOUL HAD BEGUN ITS TRANSITION BEFORE YOUR BODY DIED.

"My God," Jack whispered. "I've had dreams about that. What happened to my lover?"

HE WROTE HIS CONFESSION AND COMMITTED SUICIDE SHORTLY BEFORE YOU WERE KILLED. HE DID NOT KNOW YOU WERE STILL ALIVE, AND THOUGHT THAT HE HAD TO DO THIS.

"But you said that I betrayed him . . . her again. When was that? Weren't we even?"

BEING EVEN, AS YOU CALL IT, DOES NOT MEAN THAT YOU CANNOT CREATE NEW DEBTS, OR ADD TO OLD ONES. YOUR SECOND BETRAYAL TOOK PLACE IN SCOTLAND IN THE LAT-TER PART OF THE EIGHTEENTH CENTURY, COMMON ERA. YOU WERE THEN THE FATHER OF THE MATURE KING, AND ALTHOUGH YOU KNEW THAT SHE LOVED AND WAS BELOVED

BY A MAN OF WHOM YOU DID NOT APPROVE, YOU FORCED HER INTO A MARRIAGE FOR YOUR POLITICAL ADVANTAGE. YOU, JONATHAN, HAVE NOT MASTERED YOUR NEED FOR POLITICAL POWER. YOU MUST PAY YOUR DEBT AGAIN, PERHAPS IN THIS LIFETIME.

"How can I pay a debt to someone I don't even know?" Jack protested. "Or do I know him? What do I have to do?"

YOU DO NOT HAVE TO DO ANYTHING. IT IS YOUR CHOICE. WE BELIEVE THAT YOU DO NOT WANT TO RECOGNIZE THE MATURE KING, WHO IS NOW IN HER LAST CYCLE BEFORE BECOMING AN OLD KING. YES, YOU KNOW THIS PERSON. YOU DO NOT LIKE HER. YOU ARE RESISTING THE DEBT YOU OWE HER.

Jack was growing angry. "Can you give me a hint, or is that too much to ask?"

HOW MUCH YOU CLING TO YOUR RIBBONS! THE SEVENTH-LEVEL MATURE KING IS IN THE PERSEVERANCE MODE WITH A GOAL OF ACCEPTANCE, A SKEPTIC WITH A CHIEF FEATURE OF SELF-DEPRECATION, IN THE EMOTIONAL PART OF MOVING CENTER. SHE IS VERY GIFTED AND YOU REGARD HER AS NEUROTIC. THOUGH YOU DO NOT WISH TO BE, YOU ARE DRAWN TO HER. THE ATTRACTION IS THE PULL OF YOUR KARMIC RIBBON.

What happened to Jack?

"As I said, he is not in the group anymore," Jessica says. "He stuck it out for a while, but he grew frightened. He's doing therapy again. I hope that he finds a way to deal with that mature king, whoever she is, because Michael was quite convinced that the longer Jack put off dealing with that debt, the harder his payment would be."

"Not all strong attractions are debts, of course," Lucy adds quickly. "Entity mates are drawn to each other, and if they're the same role in essence there can be a lot of good information."

"Providing the overleaves are compatible," Jessica reminds her. "Two old artisans from the same entity might have a lot of trouble if one of them were in the passion mode with a goal of submission and the other were in the caution mode with a goal of rejection. That might be a very difficult relationship, especially since the one with the goal of rejection would not want the relationship at all."

"Tracy Rowland, the other woman who works the board

at sessions, has a special relationship with one of her entity mates," Lucy says. "They're very similar, she and her friend."

"I think they differ on two points only," Jessica remarks. "Tracy is a third-level old warrior in the observation mode with a goal of growth, moving part of intellectual center, an idealist with a chief feature of arrogance, and her colleague is a third-level old warrior in the observation mode with a goal of growth, emotional part of intellectual center, a skeptic with a chief feature of arrogance. Remember, they're in the same entity and Michael has said that they have been comrades-in-arms three times, and died in battle together twice. That means there are some pretty strong ties there."

How did Tracy feel when she learned this?

"My feelings were mixed," she admits. "Part of me thought that it was as natural as ragweed and part of me didn't trust it for a moment. But the attraction is definitely there; I didn't make it up. It's not a romantic relationship. We're both married to different people and we see each other maybe once every two years. Still, I can't think of anyone I feel more comfortable with, or whom I trust more. Aside from Michael's explanation, I can't think of any good way to account for this."

What did Michael say about this relationship?

"You mean aside from the entity thing and the similar overleaves?" Tracy asks. "He made a few comments on why my friend, who is normally very shy and rather aloof, should not be so with me. It's true. And that's not a carefully developed change; it was an instant acceptance."

YOU HAVE SHARED MANY LIVES AND IT IS EASIER FOR THIS CLOSED PERSON TO RELATE TO YOU, WHOM HE AL-READY KNOWS AND TRUSTS FROM THE PAST, THAN IT IS FOR HIM TO SEEK THOSE AROUND HIM FOR THIS. YOU ARE THE SUM OF ALL YOU HAVE BEEN, AND OF COURSE, SO IS HE. THEREFORE, SINCE YOU HAVE KNOWN THIS FRAGMENT MANY TIMES BEFORE, YOU ARE SUBLIMINALLY AWARE OF MORE OF THE PARTS OF HIM THAN ARE MOST OTHERS HE KNOWS, EVEN THOUGH THEY MIGHT BE CLOSER PHYSI-CALLY. ALSO YOU SENSE IN HIM MANY OF THE SAME PER-CEPTIONS YOU YOURSELF COPE WITH AND THIS REPRESENTS TO YOU A KINDRED SPIRIT. YOU NEED FROM HIM THE SAME TYPE OF INSTANT UNDERSTANDING AND ACCEPTANCE THAT

YOU SENSE HE CAN GIVE YOU, AND THE REVERSE IS TRUE; HIS NEED IS THE SAME.

"There's also an astral agreement," Tracy adds.

What are these astral agreements that Michael speaks of?

YOU MAKE ALL SEQUENTIAL AGREEMENTS DURING THE ASTRAL INTERVAL. THIS PERTAINS TO ALL OF THE PHYSICAL LIVES. MOST SEQUENCES HAVE TO DO WITH THE COMPLETION OF MONADS AND ARE AGREED UPON TO FACILITATE THIS COMPLETION IN BASICALLY SHORT PERIODS OF TIME. HOWEVER, THERE ARE SOME SEQUENCES THAT INVOLVE THE ENTIRE DURATION OF THE PHYSICAL LIFE AND REQUIRE THAT THE SEQUENTIAL PARTNERS STAY WITH EACH OTHER OR IN CONTACT THROUGHOUT. USUALLY THESE LATTER AGREEMENTS INVOLVE BEING CLOSE RELATIVES SUCH AS BROTHERS OR SISTERS, PARENTS AND CHILDREN, ET CETERA.

Does everyone make such agreements?

OF COURSE THEY DO. SOME IN THE MATURE AND OLD CYCLES REINCARNATE AT TIMES WHEN THOSE WITH WHOM THEY HAVE KARMIC RELATIONSHIPS ARE BETWEEN LIVES SO THAT ALL OF THEIR ATTENTION CAN BE GIVEN TO SUCH AGREEMENTS.

Are the agreements inevitably kept?

AGREEMENTS ARE NOT KARMA. THEY CAN BE HONORED OR YOU CAN ABDICATE. WHERE THERE IS MUCH MAYA AND THE FALSE PERSONALITY HAS THE UPPER HAND, ABDICATION OCCURS. WHETHER OR NOT THE AGREEMENTS CARRY OVER INTO SUBSEQUENT LIVES IS ONE OF THE THINGS NEGOTIATED BETWEEN LIVES.

Are these agreements and karma what is meant by fate?

NO. AGREEMENTS ARE AGREEMENTS, MEANING THEY ARE CONTRACTS THAT CAN BE MODIFIED, BROKEN, OR ADAPTED TO NEEDS. THERE IS NO FATE. FATE IS AN ILLUSION. IT EXISTS NO MORE THAN FAITH DOES. KARMA IS A WEAVING TOGETHER OF LIFE CYCLES. KARMA IS NOT FATE. FATE IS A LIE. KARMA IS A LAW. THERE IS A GREAT DANGER IN BECOMING FATALISTIC ABOUT KARMA. YOU MUST LEARN THIS ABOUT KARMA: THAT LESSONS LEARNED IN THIS WAY ARE ETERNALLY YOURS.

If karma is so important, how come so many people don't believe in it and don't seem to be aware of its force, or to care about it?

BELIEF, AS WE HAVE TOLD YOU BEFORE, IS NOT NECES-

SARY. YOU CAN BECOME AWARE OF YOUR KARMIC RIBBONS THROUGH CONSCIOUS RECALL, IF SUCH IS YOUR DESIRE. JESSICA ALMOST HAS IT. SHE HAS FOUND FOUR THREADS ALREADY. WORK ON IT AND YOU WILL KNOW WHAT IT IS YOU MUST DO THIS TIME. THE MEMORIES ARE THERE. SOME OF YOU REMEMBER LATIN FROM PREVIOUS LIVES. THAT IS WHY YOU LEARNED THE LANGUAGE SO EASILY THIS TIME.

"That was directed to me," Lucy explains. "But I was terrible in Latin at school."

THE DISINTEREST IN LANGUAGE IS A PRODUCT OF THE SOCIETY IN WHICH YOU LIVE, A PART OF FALSE PERSONALITY. THE GRASP IS THERE IN ALL OF YOU.

What, precisely, is Michael's definition of karma?

AS YOU REAP, SO YOU ALSO SOW, OR AS YOU SOW, SO SHALL YOU REAP. HOWEVER, THIS GOES FAR DEEPER THAN MERE ACTION BY THOSE IMMERSED IN THE WAKING SLEEP. FOR THEM, THE ENERGY LOSS IS FAR GREATER, FOR MOST OF THEIR LIVES ARE WASTED IN FANTASY, AND FANTASY COSTS MUCH IN KARMIC DEBTS. YOU MUST FULFILL ALL CARNAL DESIRES BEFORE SERIOUS WORK IS BEGUN ON THE ESSENCE. THIS CAN TAKE MANY LIVES, USUALLY A MINIMUM OF FORTY-NINE.

That does not entirely agree with Webster's definition. Would Michael elaborate?

WE WILL PROVIDE A RATHER SIMPLISTIC EXAMPLE. IF YOU KNOCK EUGENE TO THE GROUND THIS EVENING AND HE RECIPROCATES, THE DEBT IS PAID. ALTHOUGH YOU MIGHT BOTH CHOOSE A MORE PACIFIC APPROACH TO PROBLEM-SOLVING NEXT TIME AROUND. IF, ON THE OTHER HAND, YOU STRIKE EUGENE TONIGHT AND DIE TOMORROW, OR OTHERWISE MAKE YOURSELF UNAVAILABLE, THEN CHANCES ARE EXCELLENT THAT YOU WILL HAVE A LATER KARMIC ENCOUNTER.

WE WOULD LIKE YOU ALL TO LOOK NOW AT THE DIFFERENCE BETWEEN A TRUTH AND A LAW. THERE IS A VAST DIFFERENCE. THE PHYSICAL PLANE, AND ALL THAT IS WITHIN IT, IS GOVERNED BY A SERIES OF "LAWS" THAT ARE NOT NECESSARILY TRUTHS. IN FACT, MOST OF THEM ARE NOT. KARMA IS ONE OF THOSE LAWS GOVERNING THE HUMAN CONDITION. IT IS NOT A TRUTH, IT IS A LAW. FOR INSTANCE, FOR THOSE OF YOU SCIENTIFICALLY MINDED, LIGHT DOES TRAVEL AT A CONSTANT SPEED IN THE PHYSICAL

DIMENSION, BUT ALTHOUGH THIS IS A PHYSICAL LAW, IT IS NOT TRUE THAT THIS IS IN ANY WAY AN ULTIMATE SPEED LIMIT THAT IN ALL OF THE UNIVERSE MUST BE OBSERVED. NOW AS TO THE RESPONSIBILITY, YOU HAVE THE RESPONSIBILITY FOR YOURSELF AND NO OTHER. IF YOU TAKE THIS RESPONSIBILITY SERIOUSLY AND RESPOND APPROPRIATELY FROM THE PROPER CENTER, YOU WILL NOT BE NEGATING ANY RESPONSIBILITY THAT YOU MIGHT FEEL FOR THOSE AROUND YOU. IN FACT, YOU WILL BE GIVING THEM THE SPACE TO TAKE RESPONSIBILITY FOR THEMSELVES. THIS IS IMPORTANT. WHENEVER YOU ARBITRARILY TAKE ON RESPONSIBILITIES FOR THE ACTIONS OF OTHERS, YOU ROB THEM OF GROWTH.

But what about all those who feel themselves lost, or rudderless? Isn't that contrary to what Michael is saying about karma?

YOU ARE FREE TO CHOOSE. THE RUB COMES IN WHERE FALSE PERSONALITY, WHICH IS KARMA-DRIVEN, MAKES MOST OF THE CHOICES, IN DIRECT OPPOSITION TO THE DESIRES OF THE ESSENCE.

Does that mean that karmic debts are inevitable?

KARMA IS SUBJECT TO CHANGE, BUT ONLY BY THOSE WHO KNOW. ANY ATTEMPT WITHOUT KNOWLEDGE WILL BE WASTED. YOU HAVE CHOSEN THIS ROLE. YOU HAVE ALSO CHOSEN THE COURSE YOUR LIFE MUST TAKE. UNLESS YOU KNOW WHY, THEN YOU CANNOT MAKE ALTERATIONS. WE COULD TELL YOU WHY, BUT IT WOULD NOT CHANGE THE ROLE. WE CANNOT ERASE YOUR TAPES.

Are the karmic ribbons influenced by false personality?

YES. ENTRAPMENT IN THE BODY AND THE CHIEF FEATURE ARE KARMA FOR ESSENCE. ALL OTHERS ARISE FROM ACTIONS BORN OF THE WAKING SLEEP. IF YOU WERE AWAKE, YOU WOULD NOT DO IT.

How do you burn the ribbons?

WE HAVE SAID THIS BEFORE, BUT WE WILL REPEAT. AS YOU REAP, SO SHALL YOU SOW; AS YOU SOW, YOU SHALL REAP. THE RIBBONS ARE MERELY OUR WAY OF EXPRESSING THAT WHICH DRAWS YOU IRRESISTIBLY TO PERSONS, PLACES, ERAS, AND SITUATIONS SO THAT THE PLAY CAN GO ON. SOME MUST WAIT FOR MANY YEARS TO PASS BEFORE THE OPPORTUNITY ARISES AGAIN AND PRESENTS THE SCENE WITH THE ROLES REVERSED.

Is burning a karmic ribbon always a negative thing?

SOMETIMES YOU ARE THE DEBTOR. SOMETIMES IT IS TO YOU THAT THE DEBT IS OWED. THE RIBBON IS THE THREAD THAT LINKS YOU TO THE OTHER FRAGMENTS OF A KARMIC PLAY. YOU WISH TO COMPLETE THE MONAD, TO HAVE BOTH COMPONENTS OF THE RELATIONSHIP IN YOUR EXPERIENCE. AS SOON AS THIS IS ACCOMPLISHED, THE FRAGMENT HAS EVOLVED. AS SOON AS THE MAJOR MONADS ARE COMPLETED, THE FRAGMENTS ARE INTEGRATED.

IF YOU ARE TO PURPOSEFULLY BURN RIBBONS, YOU MUST FIRST KNOW WITH CERTAINTY WHAT HAS BEEN INCURRED. THIS TAKES STUDY AND RECALL. OTHERWISE, YOU WILL PAY YOUR KARMIC DEBTS IN THEIR NATURAL ORDER. THIS IS WHY THE KNOWLEDGE OF REINCARNATION COMES IN SOME WAY TO OLD SOULS. PRIOR TO THAT, IT IS ONLY A MATTER OF CHANCE, SUCH AS BIRTH IN A COUNTRY LIKE INDIA, WHERE THIS IS THE ACCEPTED THEOLOGY. YOU WILL BURN OUT ALL YOUR KARMA. YOU MUST. THE CHOICES YOU MAKE BETWEEN PHYSICAL BODIES ARE PART OF THE LEARNING PROCESS ALSO.

Is it possible to go through life without burning the karma that you had set out to burn in that life, or is it inevitable that you burn karma?

IT IS INEVITABLE THAT YOU PLAY OUT THE ROLE YOU CHOSE. IT IS NOT NECESSARY THAT YOU ALWAYS CHOOSE A DIFFICULT ROLE.

Is there a way to do this efficiently? It sounds like so much chance.

YES, THERE IS A WAY. YOU MUST FIRST BE ABLE TO RECALL THE THREADS. THIS IS WHAT TAKES PRACTICE. THIS IS WHY CONCENTRATION AND MEDITATION HAVE BEEN STRESSED. YOU HAVE INDICATED THAT YOU WISH THIS AND WE ARE SHOWING YOU HOW. WHAT YOU DO WITH THIS INFORMATION DEPENDS ON YOUR DESIRES ENTIRELY, BUT THE INFORMATION WILL BE GIVEN WITHIN THIS GROUP. THERE WILL BE AN ADEPT WHO WILL AID THE OTHERS. THERE IS ONE AMONG YOU WHO WILL MASTER THE TECHNIQUES.

Does it sometimes take more than one lifetime to learn the lesson?

MANY TIMES YOU HAVE CHOSEN ALMOST IDENTICAL

ROLES IN ORDER TO PLAY OUT A MONAD. ONLY THE TIMES AND THE LOCATIONS WERE DIFFERENT.

At what point do we make our choices?

THE CHOICE IS MADE ON THE ASTRAL LEVEL BETWEEN LIVES. YOUNG SOULS QUITE OFTEN HAVE VERY LITERAL CONCEPTS OF HEAVEN AND HELL. THEY MUST EXPERIENCE THIS AS THEY CREATE IT OUT OF ASTRAL MATTER.

Sam Chasen, the social worker, asked about the karmic component of the polio that left him with his legs in braces. He asked Michael, "What have I done in past lives to account for the physical burden I have now?"

THE PAIN YOU INFLICTED ON LOVED ONES IN THE PAST IS A PART OF KARMA FOR YOU. ALSO, YOU HAVE ALWAYS HAD A SCHOLARLY INTEREST IN RELIGION, BUT WITH A SAVAGE BENT MORE THAN ONCE. FOR INSTANCE, DURING THE CRUSADES AND THE INQUISITION.

"What on earth did I do?"

IN BOTH INSTANCES, YOU TOOK AN ACTIVE PART IN PROSELYTIZING BY FORCE. DURING THE INQUISITION, YOU WERE AN INFORMER.

Does this apply to all physical disabilities? What about people with congenital brain damage?

THIS IS THE PATH FOR THEM. USUALLY THEY DID NOT RELATE TO THIS DIFFICULTY IN A PREVIOUS LIFE.

Where does heredity come into this? What about genetic damage?

GENETICALLY DETERMINED DEFICIENCIES DO EXIST. THEY ARE NOT PARTICULARLY DISTRIBUTED. IN OTHER WORDS, THERE IS NO BAD GENE, BUT THIS CULTURE HAS NEVER STRESSED INTELLECTUAL PURSUITS AND NEVER WILL. THERE ARE NO SUPERIOR ORIENTAL GENES BUT THIS CULTURE HAS ALWAYS STRESSED KNOWLEDGE AND A CERTAIN AMOUNT OF THIS IS INCULCATED IN THE CULTURE SO DEEPLY THAT IT HAS BECOME HEREDITARY IN A VERY OBSCURE FASHION. IT IS IMMEASURABLE, BUT PERVASIVE. SOME OF YOU WERE BLACK IN PREVIOUS LIVES AND SOME BLACKS HAVE BEEN WHITE. IN THEM THERE ARE RACIAL MEMORIES THAT CAUSE THEM TO SEEK OUTSIDE THEIR CULTURE.

THAT DOES NOT MEAN THAT ALL ILLNESSES AND DEFICIENCIES ARE KARMIC, AND IT DOES NOT MEAN THAT ANYONE IS JUSTIFIED IN TAKING ADVANTAGE OF THOSE WHO

ARE SO AFFLICTED. REMEMBER THAT THOSE WITH A CHIEF FEATURE OF MARTYRDOM OFTEN CHOOSE TO EXPRESS IT THROUGH POOR HEALTH. THAT WAY THEY CAN ENJOY THE ATTENTION THEY CRAVE AND AT THE SAME TIME ACT OUT THE NEGATIVE POLE OF THE CHIEF FEATURE, WHICH IS MORTIFICATION.

It sounds as if you can incur a karmic debt by trying to be helpful. Is this the case?

YES. IT HAS TO DO WITH THE GOAL OF THE PERSON BEING HELPED. KARMIC DEBTS CAN BE INCURRED THROUGH AID. THIS HAPPENS EVERY TIME YOU HINDER RATHER THAN HELP BY TAKING THE RESPONSIBILITY OUT OF THEIR HANDS. FOR THOSE WHOSE GOAL IS ACCEPTANCE, THIS ONLY APPEARS MORE DIFFICULT. IT IS EQUALLY DIFFICULT FOR THOSE IN DOMINANCE, WHO LIKE TO BE IN CHARGE; FOR THOSE IN GROWTH, WHO LIKE TO TAKE RESPONSIBILITY FOR THE LEVEL OF GROWTH WITHIN THE GROUP; FOR THOSE IN THE ORDINAL GOALS, WHO FEEL MUCH RESPONSIBILITY FOR THE MISERY AROUND THEM AND FEEL IT IS THEIR LIFE-TASK TO MITIGATE IT. SO THE GOAL OF ACCEPTANCE IS NO DIFFERENT THAN THE OTHERS IN THIS, ALTHOUGH THOSE IN ACCEPTANCE ARE QUITE OFTEN MORE VERBAL ABOUT THEIR FEELINGS OF RESPONSIBILITY THAN OTHERS IN THIS. THOSE IN GROWTH TEND TO ACT THEIRS OUT, AND THOSE IN DOMINANCE EVEN MORE BLATANTLY ACT OUT THE NEED TO TAKE RESPONSIBILITY. THE WAY KARMA OPERATES SERVES TO ENLIVEN THE ACTION OF THE LIFE DRAMA. WERE IT NOT FOR KARMA, THE SCRIPT WOULD BE UNBELIEVABLY DULL.

IT IS DOUBTFUL THAT ANY OF YOU WOULD RATIONALLY CHOOSE A VIOLENT ACTION AS A SOLUTION TO A MINOR LIFE CRISIS, AND YET IT IS DONE EVERY DAY BY THOSE CAUGHT UP IN THE CLUTCHES OF KARMA. KARMIC DEBTS, YOU SEE, DEPART FROM THE SCRIPT AND INTRODUCE THAT ELEMENT OF INTRIGUE THAT MAKES THE DRAMA WORTH PLAYING OUT.

What kinds of actions cause karmic debts?

OF COURSE, MURDER IS THE MOST OBVIOUS ONE: THE DELIBERATE TAKING OF A LIFE BEFORE IT IS ENDED. THIS DOES NOT INCLUDE ABORTION AS THE SOUL DOES NOT ENTER THE BODY UNTIL ACTUAL BIRTH. ABANDONMENT, IF IT RESULTS IN DEATH OR CATASTROPHE FOR THE ABANDONED FRAGMENT. BETRAYAL, IF THE RESULTS OF THE BETRAYAL ARE

DEATH, INCARCERATION, OR SIGNIFICANT PHYSICAL HARM.
INTERFERING WITH ANOTHER FRAGMENT'S LIFE FOR YOUR
GAIN AND THEIR HARM, OR IN OTHER WORDS, WHAT YOU
CURRENTLY IDENTIFY AS MIND-FUCK. IN THE SAME VEIN,
FOLLOWING THE BRANCH OF OCCULT STUDIES KNOWN AS
THE "LEFT-HAND PATH." THIS IS NOT A THEOLOGICAL
QUESTION. THERE IS NO MORE A DEVIL THAN THERE IS A
GOD. HOWEVER, THERE IS MALICE OF INTENT, AND WE
REMIND YOU THAT THERE HAVE BEEN MANY TIMES WHEN
THE LEFT-HAND PATH SURROUNDED ITSELF WITH THE ODOR
OF SANCTITY. WHETHER THE FRAGMENT IS GILLES DE RETZ
SACRIFICING CHILDREN AND RAPING THEIR BODIES, OR A
DEVOUT PRIEST GLOATING OVER A HERETIC ON THE RACK AS
HE ORDERS MORE HIDEOUS TORTURES, THE MALICIOUS IN-
TENT IS THE SAME, AND INCURS THE SAME KARMIC DEBT.

Must karmic debts be paid an eye for an eye?

NOT NECESSARILY, THOUGH IT IS SOMETIMES THE CASE.
IT IS TO BE HOPED THAT THROUGH GROWTH AND UNDER-
STANDING AS WELL AS SPIRITUAL EVOLUTION THE PAYMENT
MAY BE LESS DRASTIC. IN OTHER WORDS, RATHER THAN
EXPERIENCE THE BETRAYAL AND INCARCERATION THAT YOU
GAVE SOMEONE ELSE, IT MAY BE POSSIBLE INSTEAD TO SUP-
PORT THEM, IN OTHER WORDS, RESCUE THEM FROM AN
ECONOMIC PRISON RATHER THAN FROM A STONE ONE. WE
DO NOT MEAN THAT ALL THOSE WHO FEEL GUILTY AND PAY
CONSCIENCE MONEY ARE PAYING KARMIC DEBTS, BECAUSE
THIS IS NOT THE CASE. IN FACT, MANY WHO PAY CON-
SCIENCE MONEY ENJOY THE FEELING OF GUILT AND THE
NOT-SO-SUBTLE SENSE OF SUPERIORITY THAT THEY GET
FROM DISTRIBUTING THEIR LARGESSE.

What about death in battle and execution? Do those incur
karmic debts?

OF COURSE THEY DO, FOR THE PERSON RESPONSIBLE. THE
EXECUTIONER DOES NOT OFTEN BEAR THE KARMIC BURDEN,
AND, IN FACT, IS USUALLY A BABY OR VERY EARLY-CYCLE
YOUNG SOUL ACTING OUT OF DIFFICULT OVERLEAVES. THE
PERSON RESPONSIBLE FOR THE DEATH WILL BEAR THE
KARMIC RIBBON. THE SAME IS TRUE OF THOSE IN BATTLE.
THE ONE ORDERING THE BATTLE WILL BEAR THE BURDEN
EXCEPT WHEN A SOLDIER STEPS OUTSIDE OF HIS FUNCTION
AND ENGAGES IN PRIVATE SLAUGHTER, SUCH AS THOSE OC-
CURRENCES IN VIETNAM. IF YOU TAKE THE INITIATIVE IN

KILLING, YOU ALSO TAKE THE RESPONSIBILITY. THE EXE-CUTIONER WHO UNDERTAKES TO MAKE A DEATH MORE PAINFUL AND LINGERING MIGHT ALSO CREATE A DEBT FOR HIMSELF. THERE ARE OCCASIONAL AGREEMENTS HERE, EITHER TO BE COMRADES-AT-ARMS OR ADVERSARIES, WHICH IS NOT AS UNCOMMON AS YOU MIGHT THINK. DEATH IN BATTLE OR BY EXECUTION, AS SUCH, IS NOT NECESSARILY KARMIC. QUITE OFTEN SUCH DEATHS ARE CHOSEN BY THE ESSENCE AS PART OF LIFE EXPERIENCE.

Is there any karma that isn't traumatic?

THERE IS PHILANTHROPIC KARMA, BUT THIS DOES NOT OFTEN OCCUR BEFORE THE MATURE AND OLD CYCLES. WHEN A FRAGMENT PERFORMS A GENUINELY PHILAN-THROPIC ACT, ONE THAT IS MOTIVATED BY TRUE AGAPE, THEN THE FRAGMENT RECEIVING THIS GIFT OF LOVE WILL RETURN IT IN SOME LATER LIFE. BY A PHILANTHROPIC ACT, WE DO NOT MEAN GIVING MONEY TO CHARITY, BUT AN ACT THAT IS BOTH LOVING AND DISINTERESTED, THAT IS PER-FORMED WITHOUT INTENT TO INSTILL GUILT OR GRATITUDE IN THE RECEIVER AS WELL AS BEING FREE FROM MANIPU-LATIVE CONSIDERATIONS BY THE DONOR. AN EXAMPLE MIGHT BE SOMEONE WHO PROVIDES AN ARTIST WITH A HOME AND FOOD SO THAT HE CAN WORK AT WHATEVER HE WISHES TO, INCLUDING NOTHING. A PHILANTHROPIC GIFT SHOULD BE UNCONDITIONAL. THERE IS NONE OF THIS "IF YOU DO THIS, THEN I WILL DO THAT." THE GIFT IS NOT A BARGAIN.

How do you know such an act is philanthropic? Might it not simply be the repaying of old debts?

PAYING DEBTS IS NOT DISINTERESTED. IT IS USUALLY VERY DIFFICULT FOR BOTH THE OWED AND THE OWING TO BURN RIBBONS. WITH PHILANTHROPIC KARMA, THERE IS NONE OF THE COMPELLING FORCE THAT MOST KARMA HAS. WE REMIND YOU THAT THE IMPORTANT WORD HERE IS "DISINTERESTED." LET US EMPHASIZE THAT THIS SORT OF DEBT AND PAYMENT IS RARE AND THAT IT DOES NOT OFTEN ARISE UNTIL THE MATURE AND OLD CYCLES. YOU HAVE ONLY TO LOOK AT THE NATURE OF THE SOUL LEVELS TO SEE THAT THE PERCEPTIONS OF THE YOUNG CYCLES MAKE TRUE DISINTEREST ALMOST IMPOSSIBLE.

Where does the akashic plane come into things? With all this learning between lives and the selection of overleaves, it sounds as if some sort of record must be kept somewhere.

WE REMIND YOU THAT BETWEEN LIVES THE SOUL IS CAPABLE OF TOTAL REVIEW.

But if there is no God, only the Tao, who keeps the record?

YOU DO, OF COURSE. YOU, AS YOU ARE NOW, ARE A SCRIPT THAT YOU YOURSELF HAVE WRITTEN FOR YOUR EARTHBOUND SOUL TO PLAY. IT IS PERPETUAL.

Chapter 10

THE HIGHER PLANES...

Michael has a great deal to say about the astral plane and its levels. To what does he refer?

STOP THINKING OF THE ASTRAL PLANE AS "UP THERE." IT IS "DOWN HERE." REACH OUT AND TOUCH IT. THE FIRST LEVEL OF THE ASTRAL PLANE IS POPULATED BY LIVING FRAGMENTS ADEPT AT ASTRAL TRAVEL, AND THOSE SOULS WHO PENETRATE THIS PLANE ACCIDENTALLY THROUGH DRUGS. THE SECOND LEVEL OF THE ASTRAL PLANE IS INHABITED BY ALL THOSE BETWEEN BODIES. THE THIRD LEVEL ATTRACTS OLD SOULS WHO ARE TRYING TO BURN FINAL KARMA WITHOUT BEING REBORN. THE MID-ASTRAL BODIES ARE PARTIALLY REUNITED ENTITIES. YOU HAVE MANIFESTED A MID-ASTRAL ENTITY PREVIOUSLY. THE THREE HIGHER LEVELS ARE PROGRESSIVELY INTEGRATED; ACCESS TO THE HIGH PLANES IS THROUGH THESE LEVELS. EVEN VERY HIGH ADEPTS HAVE FANTASIES CONCERNING THE HIGH PLANES.

Are these astral forms what is meant by ghosts?

NOT NECESSARILY. A GHOST MAY BE AN ETHERIC VEHICLE. IF SO, IT WILL DECOMPOSE AS THE BODY DECOMPOSES. THEN YOU WILL BE ALONE AGAIN. THIS SOMETIMES HAPPENS WHEN ONE DIES SUDDENLY OR VIOLENTLY. THE ETHE-

RIC VEHICLE IS THE INNERMOST AURA. IT DECOMPOSES RAP-
IDLY. IT CANNOT HARM YOU AT ALL. IT IS LIKE THE AURA
SANS THE BRAIN. THE ASTRAL BODY LEAVES IMMEDIATELY,
THE ETHERIC VEHICLE CANNOT LEAVE. IT HAS NO POWER
BY ITSELF. IT IS ONLY A SHADOW AND HAS NO INTRINSIC
ENERGY.

Can astral matter materialize?

ONLY THE CAUSAL ENTITY HAS THIS ABILITY. NO OTHER
ENTITY WOULD HAVE A REASON. THE ANIMALS THUS CRE-
ATED FROM ASTRAL MATTER ARE ONLY AS REAL AS ANY-
THING ELSE CREATED FROM ASTRAL MATTER, BUT THEY
GIVE THE FRAGMENT FROM THE CAUSAL BODY A SUITABLE
VEHICLE FOR WORKING OUT AN UNRESOLVED CONFLICT.
NOTICE WE DO NOT SAY KARMIC. THESE ARE SHORT-LIVED
EXPERIENCES.

When the high planes are mentioned, does that mean the
astral plane?

BY HIGH PLANES WE REFER TO THE CAUSAL AND BEYOND.

Would Michael be more specific?

THE CAUSAL BODY IS ON THE PLANE ABOVE THE ASTRAL
PLANE. IT IS AN UPWARD STEP IN THE SPIRITUAL EVOLU-
TION. HEAVEN IS CREATED OUT OF ASTRAL MATERIALS FOR
THOSE BETWEEN BODIES WHO NEED THAT EXPERIENCE BE-
FORE THEY REVIEW. SOME ALSO NEED THE EXPERIENCE OF
HELL, AND THEY TOO CREATE FROM ASTRAL MATTER. IT IS
VERY PLIABLE. IT CAN TAKE ANY SHAPE YOU WISH. THIS IS
THE STUFF USED TO CONJURE UP DEMONS. THEY CAN CAUSE
ONLY THE AMOUNT OF DAMAGE YOU ALLOW THEM TO, IN
YOUR MIND. THERE HAVE BEEN MANY INSTANCES OF FRAG-
MENTS BEING LITERALLY FRIGHTENED TO DEATH BY PROD-
UCTS OF THEIR MINDS, MANUFACTURED BY ASTRAL MAT-
TER.

Do the cycles continue on the causal plane?

THIS IS ESSENTIALLY CORRECT. THERE IS GROWTH AND
EVOLUTION NECESSARY ON THE CAUSAL PLANE AS WELL AS
THE ASTRAL. THERE IS A DIFFERENCE, THOUGH. THIS EN-
TITY PERCEIVES SELF AND SOMETHING APART FROM SELF,
ALTHOUGH STILL A PART OF SELF, SO THIS ENTITY CANNOT
BE SAID TO BE ALL OF EVERYTHING THERE IS. THE HIGH
CAUSAL BODY DOES NOT PERCEIVE EVEN THIS MINUTE SEP-
ARATION EVIDENTLY, AND THIS IS WHERE THE DIFFERENCE

LIES. BEYOND THE PHYSICAL PLANE, THE EVOLUTION CON-
CERNS PERCEPTION OF THE TAO.

It is twilight now and Jessica once again opens the curtains
before she turns on the lamp beside her. "I don't think I'll
ever completely comprehend the working of the astral and
causal planes. There are times the physical plane is a lot
more than I can handle. The first time we had any serious
dissensions in the group, I wondered if any of it was worth
it."

Then there has been difficulty?

"Oh, yes," Jessica says wearily. "We've had some very
disruptive people in the group, as I've told you before. In
one case we almost gave it up because it seemed that the
teaching was being used for all the wrong reasons. We had
three people who insisted on turning everything Michael said
into dogma, and wanting to make up religious rituals. For
a while I felt quite bitter about this. It seemed that everything we did was dragging us down. I was very discouraged
then, wondering if it was worth it and whether or not I was
a nut case. I talked about this at one of the sessions when
Tracy was on the board and we got this answer."

THE WORDS NEVER FALL ON COMPLETELY DEAF EARS.
YOU MUST, HOWEVER, BE PREPARED FOR OVERT REJECTION
IN THE VERBAL FORM. YOU MUST LEARN NOT TO ALLOW
THIS TO THROW YOU FROM THE PATH. THERE ARE BOUND
TO BE REPERCUSSIONS. YOU PEOPLE ARE DECIDEDLY AB-
NORMAL, IF YOU WANT THE TRUTH, AND YOU MUST GET
USED TO THIS. IF YOU WISH TO BE NORMAL, YOU ARE PUR-
SUING THE WRONG PATH.

"That helped," Jessica says, "but I was still bothered by
all the negativity that was around me. I felt it was slowly
closing in."

Michael had an answer for that, too.

YOU MUST FIRST BELIEVE THAT THERE IS NOTHING THAT
YOU CAN DO TO ALTER THEIR REACTION AND THAT THEIR
REACTION HAS NOTHING TO DO WITH ANYTHING IN YOUR
FRAME OF REFERENCE. THEIR PERCEPTION OF A SITUATION
AND ITS RAMIFICATIONS IS SOMETHING THAT ONLY THEY
CAN DEAL WITH AND THERE IS NOTHING THAT YOU CAN
DO. KEEP REPEATING THAT TO YOURSELF EACH TIME IT
COMES UP.

REMEMBER THAT EVIL PER SE ONLY EXISTS IN THE MINDS OF THOSE PERCEIVING AN ACTION. IF YOU HAPPEN TO BE A YOUNG SOUL, YOUR DESIRE WILL BE TO CHANGE THE EVIL TO GOOD, TO RIGHT THE UNRIGHTABLE WRONG. YOU WILL NOT HESITATE TO WIPE OUT THE LIVES THAT ARE IN YOUR WAY. AFTER ALL, ARE THEY NOT EVIL? MATURE SOULS OFTEN PERCEIVE EVIL IN THEMSELVES AND SEEK TO EXORCISE THIS. YOUNG SOULS PERCEIVE THE DIFFERENCES IN PEOPLE OFTEN AS EVIL. THE OLD SOUL ORDINARILY DOES NOT PERCEIVE EVIL AS SUCH. THEY PERCEIVE THE CAUSE AND DO NOT SEEK TO ERADICATE THE AGENT. THIS IS WHAT IS MEANT LOOSELY BY ACCEPTANCE. ON A HIGHER LEVEL, THIS ACCEPTANCE BECOMES AGAPE. YOUR NEGATIVITY CAN BE DISSOLVED AS SOON AS YOU REALIZE HOW FUTILE IT IS. SOULS ENTHRALLED IN THE GLAMOUR OF THE PHYSICAL PLANE DO SENSELESS THINGS, GRANTED, BUT REALIZE THIS: THE SOUL IS ETERNAL, THESE ACTS ARE TEMPORAL.

"Some of the people in the group tried reading lots of esoteric literature, you know?" Lucy adds. "A lot of that stuff is very slow going, and that was discouraging too."

"Leah was very upset," Jessica says with a nod. "One evening she said that rather than plow through one more heavy philosophic tome, she'd rather buy a toy boat and just lie in the bathtub, putting around."

Did Michael have a comment on this?

"You bet," Jessica says, her familiar grin returning.

YOU WOULD PROBABLY BENEFIT MUCH MORE FROM THAT ACTIVITY THAN FROM READING FIFTY PHILOSOPHICAL TEXTS. THESE ARE NOTHING MORE THAN OTHER SOULS EXPOUNDING ON HALF-ACQUIRED ENLIGHTENMENT. ENLIGHTENMENT IS NOT PONDEROUS. AS WE SAID BEFORE, AS GROWTH PROGRESSES, THE SOUL SEEKS SIMPLICITY. THIS IS ONE GOOD WAY TO DISCERN WHETHER A PARTICULAR PIECE OF LITERATURE WILL BE OF ANY HELP TO YOU. IF IT IS MERELY AN EXERCISE IN VOCABULARY AND RHETORIC, THEN ABANDON IT. SOME VERY WORDY MATERIAL COMES FROM YOUNG SOULS. BE WARY OF THIS IN SELECTING READING MATERIAL.

"There was a period when both Emily and Kate asked quite a number of questions about religion, particularly Christianity," says Jessica. "Emily said that she was hoping she could reconcile what Michael had taught her with the beliefs of her Church."

Did she succeed?

"Not entirely," Jessica replies, looking to Walter for confirmation.

"She had a great deal of difficulty asking the right questions," Walter remarks. "That's often the case in working with Michael."

Emily had been very cautious at first.

"I have a question about conventional religions and how they influence people. I know that it is a vague question, but people who become identified with a religion somehow limit their experience and don't seem to grow much, yet they may help other people. Christ did not look for his followers among the righteous. He looked among the unrighteous."

HIS FOLLOWERS WERE ONLY UNRIGHTEOUS IN THE EYES OF CERTAIN BEHOLDERS. THE RITUALS DERIVED FROM THE RELIGIONS ARE GOOD WORK. THEY PRODUCE A GROUP HIGH, WHICH IS THE ONLY WAY THAT BABY SOULS EVER EXPERIENCE A HIGH—THAT IS—VICARIOUSLY.

Kate observed that "Christ said that he would speak in parables to the rest of the people, but to his disciples he gave all the knowledge of heaven and earth. It seems that 'they' are giving it to us."

HE ALSO SAID, "SEEK AND YE SHALL FIND, KNOCK AND THE DOOR SHALL BE OPENED." YOU HAVE ASKED.

"Very well, then," Emily said, "what is the meaning in the Scriptures that Christ died to save our sins? It makes no sense to me."

IT DOES NOT MAKE SENSE TO US, EITHER. IN THE LITERAL SENSE, IT IS MEANINGLESS. HE DID NOT SAY THAT. THAT WAS PERPETUATED BY ZEALOTS.

"Then can you explain the Sermon on the Mount? I do not understand it. All my life I've been asking people," Emily went on.

SUBSTITUTE FOR THE WORD "BLESSED" THE WORD "FORTUNATE." THE EMPHASIS HERE IS ON SIMPLICITY. BY "MEEK," WE DO NOT SPEAK OF COWARDICE, BUT RATHER OF AN INWARDNESS OF PURPOSE. THE "POOR IN SPIRIT" REFERS TO THOSE WHO RECOGNIZE WITHIN THEMSELVES THE LACK OF SPIRITUAL GUIDANCE AND SEEK THIS. THIS PASSAGE IS WARNING AGAINST THE COMPLACENCY THAT HERALDS THE DOWNFALL AND DEGRADATION OF HUMAN-

ITY. THE BARBARIANS CAN BE USED SYMBOLICALLY HERE AS THE MATERIALISTIC EXISTENTIALISTS WHO DENY OTHER DIMENSIONS BEYOND THE PHYSICAL PLANE AND DEVOTE THEIR LIVES TO THE PURSUIT OF MAYA. THEY ARE INDEED UNFORTUNATE IN THAT THEY INCUR MUCH ADVERSE KARMA.

ONE MUST KEEP IN MIND THE AUDIENCE TO WHICH THE MAN JESUS SPOKE, AND THE SCRIBES WHO WROTE THE ACCOUNT, BEFORE PASSING JUDGMENT ON THE WORDS. THESE PEOPLE BELIEVED IN A VERY LITERAL, VERY PERSONAL GOD WHO MONITORED EVERY MORE THEY MADE AND WAS FOR THE MOST PART STERN AND DISAPPROVING. GREEK THOUGHT HAD MUCH INFLUENCE ON THE MAN JESUS, PARTICULARY EPICURUS, BUT IT WOULD HAVE BEEN IMPOSSIBLE FOR HIM TO ESPOUSE THE WORDS OF THIS PAGAN PHILOSOPHER FROM THE PORTICOES OF THE TEMPLE. THEN WHEN THE INFINITE SOUL MANIFESTED, THE LOGOS WAS BROUGHT TO BEAR IN THE LANGUAGE OF THE TIMES, TRANSCRIBED BY A ROMAN TAX COLLECTOR AND AN EMOTIONALLY CENTERED GREEK PHYSICIAN. (LUKE.) EPICURUS HAD A MOST PROFOUND INFLUENCE ON ALL OF THE PHILOSOPHY OF THE TIME, SURPASSING THAT OF THE STOIC ZENO. THIS PHILOSOPHY WAS MADE TO ORDER FOR THE SADDUCEES, WHO ALSO APPEALED TO THIS YOUNG MAN'S SENSITIVE NATURE. THE EPICUREAN THOUGHT PATTERN IS WHAT ALL OF US ARE STRIVING TO ACCOMPLISH.

"That makes sense," said Kate. "Can you apply it to the whole of Christ's teaching? What was the essence of his teachings?"

TRUTH IS THE GREATEST GOOD AND LOVE IS THE HIGHEST TRUTH. GOOD IS ITS OWN REWARD, AS IS TRUTH.

THE LOVE OF THE LOGOS OR AGAPE PERMEATED THE BEING OF JESUS, EVEN PRIOR TO THE MANIFESTATION. HE LIVED FOR THE WORD. THE QUEST FOR SPIRITUAL LIBERATION TOOK PRECEDENCE OVER ALL THINGS, SOMETIMES TO HIS DESPAIR. PRIOR TO MANIFESTATION THIS WAS AN EMOTIONALLY CENTERED FRAGMENT WHO WAS PASSIONATE AND SENSUAL. WHEN OTHERS REJECTED HIS OPINIONS, HE WAS ASTONISHED.

"Why did Christ judge the Pharisees and speak of people being cast out into the darkness?" Emily asked.

HE WAS DESCRIBING PRECISELY WHAT THEY WOULD ENCOUNTER ON THE ASTRAL INTERVAL. HE DID NOT JUDGE.

HE KNEW. THERE IS A DIFFERENCE. JUDGMENT IMPLIES AN ALTERNATIVE. THERE WAS NONE. WHEN A MASTER SPEAKS, THERE IS NO ROOM FOR DISCUSSION.

"That takes care of the Pharisees," Kate said wryly. "Is it true that Christ was able to cast out demons?"

THE DEMONS ARE PRODUCED BY THE SICK MIND AND DO NOT EXIST. THEY CAN BE CAST OUT ONLY BY ONE SKILLED IN THIS. THE EXORCIST MUST BE ABLE TO GIVE THE PATIENT A VISIBLE SUBSTITUTE; THUS HE MUST BE CAPABLE OF PRODUCING PSYCHIC PHENOMENA AT WILL. JESUS WAS AN OCCULT MASTER. HE COULD PRODUCE THE NECESSARY PHENOMENA TO MAKE THE PATIENT SEE HIS DEMON LEAVE AND OCCUPY SOME OTHER ORGANISM. THEN, OF COURSE, YOU MUST STILL TREAT THE SICKNESS WHICH CAUSED THE SOUL TO PRODUCE THE DEMON. USUALLY THIS IS MASOCHISM IN ITS EXTREME MANIFESTATION.

"Was he really conceived without sex?"

OF COURSE NOT.

Emily added, "Jesus was always against sex, even thinking about sex."

JESUS WAS NOT AGAINST SEX. HE WAS FOR MODERATION. PROSTITUTION IS NOT MODERATE, EVEN TEMPLE PROSTITUTION.

"Then what went wrong?" Emily asked. "Sex is part of the experience. It may be one of the most highly important parts, and maybe I've neglected it. Maybe in Jesus' time they weren't neglecting it. Maybe if he were here today he would tell people to have more. Maybe in Jesus' day people thought about it all the time and we hardly ever think about it."

QUALITY IS THE ANSWER. IT IS WHAT YOU THINK, NOT HOW OFTEN. IN JESUS' TIME ON EARTH, MOST OF THE THOUGHTS WERE BOUND UP IN FERTILITY RITES AND SUPERSTITION. THEY WERE NEGATIVE ENERGY VORTICES.

David Swan, who had been following all this quite avidly, had a question of his own. "I've read much on the crucifixion and have never been able to figure out why it happened."

HE WAS A THREAT TO JOSEPH CAIPHAS, WHO WAS GETTING RICH ON THE TEMPLE FUNDS AND THERE WAS A SUITABLE PAWN AVAILABLE IN THE PERSON OF THE JUDEAN GOVERNOR, WHO WAS A COWARD AND WHO ALREADY WAS IN TROUBLE WITH TIBERIUS OVER OTHER THINGS. THE IN-

FINITE SOUL CARES NOTHING ABOUT THE PHYSICAL BODY, AND WHEN IT WAS REALIZED HOW THE DECK WAS STACKED, IT WAS SEEN AS A CONVENIENT WAY TO SPEEDILY FULFILL THE PROPHESY.

"And what about the Shroud of Turin," asked David, "which is purportedly the shroud in which the crucified Christ was wrapped?"

ALTHOUGH IT MAY COME AS QUITE A SURPRISE TO ALL THOSE PRESENT, THIS PIECE OF FABRIC IS NOT A HOAX, PIOUS OR OTHERWISE, BUT IS PRECISELY WHAT IT IS PURPORTED TO BE—THE WINDING-SHEET OF THE MAN YOU CALL JESUS. WHAT IS NOT UNDERSTOOD HERE IS THAT THE BODY WRAPPED IN THIS SHROUD OF LINEN WAS NOT DEAD WHEN PUT INTO THE TOMB, AND THEREFORE SWEATED AND URINATED AND BLED, LEAVING THE IMPRINT THAT HAS BEEN SO CLEARLY REVEALED BY LASER TECHNIQUES. BODY SALTS ARE VERY PERSISTENT, AS THOSE WHO HAVE TRIED TO CLEAN BLOOD OR URINE OFF GARMENTS KNOW.

WE HAVE TOLD YOU BEFORE THAT THE MAN YOU CALL JESUS DID NOT DIE ON THE CROSS BUT DIED LATER. THE BODY WAS TAKEN FROM THE CROSS IN A STATE OF DEEP TRANCE CAUSED BY MASSIVE PHYSICAL SHOCK. REMEMBER THAT THERE WAS STILL A TASK TO PERFORM AND IT COULD NOT HAVE BEEN COMPLETED IF THE BODY HAD BEEN ALLOWED TO DIE ON THE CROSS. OF COURSE, THE SOUL HAD ABANDONED THE BODY SOME TIME BEFORE FOR THE MANIFESTATION OF THE INFINITE SOUL. THE INFINITE SOUL IS CAPABLE OF TAKING ANY FORM IT WISHES, AND IN THIS CASE, THIS WAS THE BODY CHOSEN. WE MUST REMIND YOU, ALSO, THAT CATALEPSY, THOUGH NOT UNKNOWN IN THOSE TIMES, WAS VERY HARD TO DIAGNOSE. IT IS ALSO IMPORTANT TO REMEMBER THAT THOSE SEEKING TO BURY THE MAN JESUS HAD TO DO IT QUICKLY.

THE LINEN ITSELF HAS SURVIVED THIS LONG BECAUSE SO MANY PEOPLE HAVE TAKEN EXCELLENT CARE OF IT. MOST OF THE TIME IT HAS BEEN KEPT IN SEALED CONTAINERS WHERE DRYNESS HELPED TO PRESERVE IT, AS WELL AS THE IMPRESSION ON THE LINEN.

FOR THOSE WHO WONDER ABOUT THE HEIGHT AND SIZE, THIS WAS A ROBUST AND HEALTHY MAN, NOT EXACTLY THE WISPY ASCETIC TYPE. HE ENJOYED A ROUGH LIFE FOR MOST OF HIS YEARS, AND ALTHOUGH HE DID PRACTICE SOME AUS-

TERITIES, THEY WERE NOT MARKED AND DID NOT INCLUDE
THE ESCHEWING OF GOOD FOOD. HE WAS MARRIED, AND
THOUGH HE DID NOT HAVE ANY LIVING CHILDREN AT THE
TIME OF THE MANIFESTATION OF THE INFINITE SOUL, HE
DID HAVE SIX SIBLINGS.

WE WOULD THINK THAT NO MATTER WHAT THE EXAMI-
NATION OF THE SHROUD REVEALS, IT WILL HAVE LITTLE
EFFECT ON THE ATTITUDES OF MOST RELIGIOUS GROUPS,
THOUGH A LITTLE CONTROVERSY MIGHT LEAD TO RE-
EXAMINATION AND GROWTH FOR THOSE WILLING TO EX-
PLORE THE POSSIBILITIES.

"I don't know if I can accept all that," Emily began.

WE HAVE TOLD YOU MANY TIMES THAT WE DO NOT RE-
QUIRE ACCEPTANCE OR BELIEF.

She ignored this and went on. "It makes me wonder, if
evolution occurs through cycle regardless of what one does,
what is the point of the infinite soul manifesting? A lot of
people quit their jobs to follow him and then lead useless
lives. The implications are not to quit these things unless
you are on the path instead of quitting them and sitting
around waiting for the 'king' and 'judgment day.' "

THIS WAS PROMULGATED BY A MAN NAMED JOHN, WHO
HAD A SERIES OF NIGHTMARES. IT WAS NOT PLEASANT TO
WATCH SOMEONE YOU LOVE DIE IN A PARTICULARLY HOR-
RIBLE MANNER. THERE WAS AN EARTHQUAKE AND AN
ECLIPSE THAT DAY—COMPLETELY NATURAL PHENOMENA,
BELIEVE IT OR NOT. THIS GAVE RISE TO MANY BAD DREAMS
IN ALREADY SUSCEPTIBLE SUPERSTITIOUS PEOPLE.

"Can we have a statement about Matthew?" Kate asked.

HE WAS A RELATIVELY PERCEPTIVE YOUNG SOUL.

"What about Paul?" David asked. "Where is Paul now?"

THE FRAGMENT THAT WAS SAUL HAS NOT BEEN REBORN
YET, BUT WILL BE SOON. HE WILL BE A FIFTH-LEVEL OLD
SOUL THIS TIME AND MAYBE HE WILL LISTEN.

"Paul contradicted himself," Leah commented. "His ap-
peal was ludicrous. When he arrived in Rome two and a half
years later, nobody knew what he was talking about."

HE MADE MANY ERRORS. THIS IS HOW YOU LEARN.

Emily grew impatient with this. "I'd like more useful information. I'm looking for a practical way of practicing the
teachings of Christ. Can you tell me how to accomplish
this?"

THAT SHOULD BE SELF-EVIDENT. HONESTY WITHOUT GUILE, SIMPLICITY WITHOUT POVERTY OF THE SOUL, LOVE WITHOUT MATERIAL EXPECTATIONS, EMPTYING THE LIFE OF ALL NONESSENTIAL CONSIDERATION, THE ENDLESS CYCLES OF EVOLUTION WITH THE PHYSICAL PLANE BEING THE CRUELEST AND ROUGHEST: THESE ARE THE THINGS EMPHASIZED IN THE TRUE TEACHINGS OF CHRIST.

"What about prayer?" Kate asked. "There's plenty of evidence that it works and that it has been working for thousands of years. What is the force behind it?"

PRAYERS, OF COURSE, ARE NOTHING MORE THAN THE PERSONALITY'S PETITION TO THE ESSENCE TO COME TO THE RESCUE. SOME DO COME FROM THE EMOTIONAL CENTER, BUT ORGANIZED PRAYER, SUCH AS THAT PROMULGATED BY ROME, IS PURELY INTELLECTUAL, AND RATHER BORING AT THAT.

"I had a very hard time accepting that," Emily remarks.

"I didn't," Kate says immediately. "I spent some time in a convent before I realized that I simply wasn't cut out to be a nun. One of the things that convinced me was the emptiness behind the ritual, although the ritual itself attracts me. I still find religion a fascinating study."

"That's not the same as belief," Emily says gently.

"No, it's not," Kate agrees. "Though I'll tell you something: I feel better about my personal religious convictions now than I did before I got involved in this group. I used to think that organized religion was the only access to certain spiritual goals, and I know now that it isn't true."

ORGANIZED RELIGION IS A SOCIAL STRUCTURE AND HAS NO PLACE IN THE COSMIC SCHEME. ONLY THE PRACTICE OF THE MANIFOLD PATH BRINGS A SOUL TO THE END OF THE LINE ON THE PHYSICAL PLANE.

RITUAL IS AN ENJOYABLE GAME WHICH FRAGMENTS PLAY ON THE PHYSICAL PLANE AND WE SEE NO HARM IN THAT, AS SUCH. IT IS AS GOOD A WAY AS ANY TO PROMOTE A GROUP HIGH, BUT IT IS NOT GOOD FOR MUCH ELSE.

PLEASE BELIEVE US WHEN WE TELL YOU THAT THERE IS NO ONE "OUT THERE" WHEN YOU FINALLY EXIT WHO WILL ASK YOU IF YOU WERE AN EPISCOPALIAN.

"I don't care what Michael says about religion," Emily declares. "I still believe and I still think it's possible to lead a Christian life."

And the rest of the group? How do they feel about this?

"There isn't a simple reaction," Jessica says carefully, looking at the others in her living room.

Kate speaks first. "I feel that much of what Michael says is a challenge. I've read a great deal more about religion, all kinds of Christianity as well as Judaic and Eastern literature. Michael insists that there are common roots to most of this, and I'd like to find them. That may just be my chief feature of stubbornness, but I can't help hoping that it's really my goal of growth." She laughs and pauses to light another cigarette.

"I go along with the challenge," Emily says, "but not the way Kate does. I don't see any real conflict between Christian love and Michael's agape. I'm not always very good at it, but I think it is possible to have that kind of general love for all humanity. And don't say that it's because I'm an upper-middle-class woman married to a doctor and indulging myself." From the harshness in her voice it is apparent she has heard just such an accusation before. "The high school where I work is in a very rough district. We've had knife fights in the hall, and once two of my students smashed all the windows of my Volkswagen. I try to be compassionate, but I do get angry."

"You can always go home to your upper-middle-class neighborhood," Sam Chasen reminds her, adding, "and so can I. I'm not denigrating what you're trying to do, Emily, you know that, but we've got a similar situation—you're a teacher and I'm a social worker. Dealing with people from what we so euphemistically call 'disadvantaged backgrounds' is our profession, but not our day-to-day lives."

"That's true," Emily allows without hostility. "And I wonder about that. If I had to live as most of my students' families do, day to day, would I still believe that compassion is possible? I don't know. I hope it is, but I don't know."

"It's a question I ask myself, too. I'm not a Christian, but I've been doing some reading on the history of the Church, from the Roman empire to the present, and it's an amazing study. I'm particularly interested in the way various branches of the early Church amalgamated local religious practices into their rituals to speed conversion. No wonder there's so little left of what was actually taught. I've also been comparing that history to the history of India. I haven't found as much material as I'd like to on the subject, but there's enough there to give me some idea of how much distortion there has been.''

If there's so much interest in the roots of religion, why not simply ask Michael?

''We do, occasionally,'' Walter admits, ''but it isn't a good idea to have him tell us everything. There's no real learning in that, and Michael does want us to learn. There's all kinds of new information that crops up during study . . .''

''There sure is,'' Kate interjects.

''. . . And if Michael simply answered questions, we'd lose all that.''

''It's not that Michael isn't willing to tell us, but those are spoon-fed answers,'' Jessica explains. ''Michael prefers it if we do most of the work for ourselves. I think it's a good idea if we do our own work. I don't like to feel that I'm in some sort of spiritual kindergarten with no chance of ever getting out.''

Lucy agrees. ''At first I was pretty upset when Michael told me to study on my own, you know? But I don't feel that way anymore. There's an enormous amount of material, and I've had to pick my way very carefully, but that's been all to the good, because now I've worked out a way for myself which I wouldn't have been able to do if Michael had simply given me a reading list. When I began, there was this vast, complex mass of *stuff,* and I thought I couldn't understand any of it. That doesn't mean,'' she adds with a tight, self-deprecatory smile, ''that I understand it all now, because I don't. But I've learned a lot more than I thought I could, and I know that there really is something worth learning.''

Corrine says quietly, ''I feel that way about math sometimes.''

''When I first started working the board,'' Jessica picks up the thread again, ''I was afraid to tackle anything religious. I shied away from questions having to do with Christianity or Judaism or Buddhism or Hinduism or even Zoroastrianism. The only religion, strangely enough, that I didn't have much trouble with was Mohammedanism because I found myself very comfortable with some of the concepts and expressions. Michael told me, when Tracy was working the board, that I had a very important life in that faith and that many aspects of that teaching are still with me."

Has Michael ever talked about religions?

"Certainly," Jessica says. "When I got over being scared, we had quite a time of it."

THE ESSENTIAL TEACHING OF CHRISTIANITY HAD ITS ROOTS, OF COURSE, IN A MANIFESTATION OF THE INFINITE SOUL, BUT LIKE MOST BUREAUCRACIES IT WAS PERPETUATED BY YOUNG PRIESTS IN THE PASSION MODE, AT THEIR MOST ZEALOUS, WHO WERE WILLING TO INTERJECT THEIR OWN BIASES INTO THE MATERIAL. TODAY'S CHRISTIANITY BEARS LITTLE RESEMBLANCE TO THE TEACHINGS OF THE MAN JESUS OR TO THE LOGOS BROUGHT TO BEAR BY THE INFINITE SOUL. YOU MUST REMEMBER THAT THE OLD KING WHO WAS THE MAN JESUS RELINQUISHED HIS PHYSICAL BODY TO THE INFINITE SOUL ONLY DURING THE LAST THIRTY DAYS OF HIS LIFE. PRIOR TO THAT, THE TEACHING WAS THAT OF A SEVENTH-LEVEL OLD KING, TRANSCENDENT, AN ENLIGHTENED BEING. WE WOULD ALSO LIKE TO REMIND YOU THAT MUCH OF THE CHRONOLOGY OF THE EVENTS IN THIS MAN'S LIFE IS CONFUSED, DISTORTED, AND IN SOME INSTANCES, WHOLLY FICTIONALIZED. WE WOULD SUGGEST THAT YOU BEAR THIS IN MIND WHEN MAKING A STUDY OF HIS TEACHINGS.

JUDAISM HAD ITS ROOTS IN PRACTICALITY AND HAD, AS HISTORY TEACHES, MEN WHO WERE EVOLUTIONARY LEAPS AHEAD OF THEIR NEIGHBORS IN TERMS OF KNOWLEDGE, PARTICULARLY OF HYGIENE, NUTRITION, AND MENTAL HEALTH. THIS WAS ORIGINALLY A CULT OF PHYSICIAN-HEALERS WHO REALIZED THAT A SUPERSTITIOUS SOCIETY COULD BE FORCED TO CHANGE ONLY BY THE INTRODUCTION OF THE "FEAR OF GOD." THIS FEAR WAS SO DEEPLY INSTILLED THAT THE POPULACE WAS AFRAID EVEN TO MENTION THE NAME OF THIS ANGRY GOD, ASSOCIATED WITH CLEANSING RAIN AND RIVERS, WHO RAGED ABOUT THEIR ATROCIOUS PERSONAL HABITS. THERE WAS A DEVASTATING PLAGUE JUST BEFORE THE ENLIGHTENED HEALERS APPEARED, AND THEIR VERY COMMONSENSICAL ADVICE WAS ACCEPTED AS REVELATION WHEN IT BECAME OBVIOUS THAT LIVES WERE BEING SAVED BY THE TEACHINGS.

David Swan, who is a practicing Jew, asked, "What about the prophets? Where do they fit in?"

IT DEPENDS ON WHICH PROPHETS YOU MEAN. MANY WERE SOCIOPOLITICAL CRITICS WHO CHOSE THE THEOCRATIC POWER STRUCTURE TO PROMULGATE THEIR DOCTRINES. YOU MUST REALIZE THAT MUCH OF WHAT HAS COME DOWN TO YOU IS NOT ACCURATE, EITHER IN RECORDING THE TRUE WORDS OF THE PROPHET, OR IN REVEALING JUST WHAT IT WAS THAT THE PROPHET WAS TALKING ABOUT. NEHEMIAH, FOR EXAMPLE, WAS CRITICIZING CERTAIN HYPOCRITICAL PRIESTS WHO WERE USING THEIR POSITION TO ENRICH THEMSELVES AND THEIR FAMILIES THROUGH THEIR ASSOCIATION WITH THE SEAT OF GOVERNMENT, WHICH WAS ALSO THE MAJOR RELIGIOUS STRUCTURE. JEREMIAH WAS A YOUNG SAGE IN THE PASSION MODE WITH A GOAL OF REJECTION AND A CHIEF FEATURE OF STUBBORNNESS, AND ONCE HE HIT UPON A THEME, HE HELD TO IT, HAMMER AND TONGS. SOLOMON WAS AN INTELLIGENT AND THOUGHTFUL MATURE SOUL WHO HAD A GOAL OF GROWTH, AND WAS WILLING TO TAKE MORE ONTO HIMSELF THAN MANY PREVIOUS MEN HAD BEEN. THE PSALMS, WHICH COME FROM MANY SOURCES, WERE MAINLY POPULAR SONGS TO HELP THE UNEDUCATED MASSES UNDERSTAND THE NATURE OF THE TEACHING IN THE TEMPLE. JUST AS THERE WAS A TRADITION OF SINGING THE RELIGIOUS WORDS TO MAKE THEM SPECIAL, SO THIS WAS CARRIED OVER INTO THE EVERYDAY LIFE. THE PROVERBS ARE SIMPLY A COLLECTION OF SAYINGS COBBLED TOGETHER INTO SECTIONS. TO APPRECIATE THE ENTIRE RANGE OF THOUGHT IN JUDAIC TEACHING, WE WOULD SAY THAT IT IS NECESSARY TO READ ALL THE LITERATURE, INCLUDING THE BOOKS, PREACHINGS, AND TESTAMENTS THAT ARE MOST OFTEN EXCLUDED FROM THE TEXTS, JUST AS A CHRISTIAN SHOULD READ THE APOCRYPHAL BOOKS, GOSPELS, AND EPISTLES GENERALLY DELETED FROM THE BIBLE. WE WOULD SAY THE MOST VALUABLE STUDIES FOR GROWTH IN JUDAIC TEACHING ARE THE BOOK OF JOB AND ECCLESIASTES. THESE BOOKS ARE MORE CLOSELY ALLIED WITH THE TRUE TEACHING THAN MANY OF THE OTHERS. WE WISH TO POINT OUT THAT A FEW OF THE PROPHETS—ISAIAH, FOR EXAMPLE—HAD CERTAIN PSYCHIC ABILITIES, AND THOUGH THE PREDICTIONS THAT THESE MEN MADE WERE ALTERED TO THE CONVENIENCE OF THE THEOCRACY AND ADJUSTED TO FIT LATER EVENTS, STILL THE

GIFTS OF THE MEN WERE REAL, AND THEY WERE VERY MUCH UPON THE PATH.

"Why single out those two books?" David Swan asked.

BECAUSE EACH REVEALS SOMETHING OF THE NATURE OF THE SEARCH. JOB IS A CASE OF SPIRITUAL GROWTH AND THE MANIFESTATION OF THE ESSENCE THROUGH STRESS THAT RESULTS IN ACCELERATION. THE REPENTANCE AT THE END IS NOT VALID. IT IS NOT GOD WHO SPEAKS TO JOB OUT OF THE WHIRLWIND, BUT HIS ESSENCE, WHICH IS AWARE OF EVERYTHING. THE RECOGNITION OF HIMSELF AS BEING PART OF SOMETHING GREATER IS THE RECOGNITION THAT IS MADE, ONE WAY OR ANOTHER, BY EVERY OLD SOUL. ECCLESIASTES IS LARGELY ABOUT FALSE PERSONALITY VERSUS ESSENCE, EXPRESSED IN TERMS THAT COULD BE ACCEPTED BY A RIGIDLY RELIGIOUS PEOPLE.

MOHAMMEDANISM, OF COURSE, HAS ITS ROOTS IN A MANIFESTATION OF THE TRANSCENDENTAL SOUL, WHICH HAS A SPECIFIC PURPOSE TO EFFECT MASSIVE SOCIAL UPHEAVAL JUST AS THE INFINITE SOUL EFFECTS A SPIRITUAL CHANGE. THE MAN MOHAMMED DEFINITELY DID ACCOMPLISH A GREAT DEAL TOWARD THE DEVELOPMENT OF A CODE OF ETHICS, ONE OF THE BEST SINCE THE CODE OF HAMMURABI. BECAUSE OF THE SOCIETAL STRUCTURE, WHAT WAS A SOCIAL CODE BECAME A RELIGIOUS DOGMA, WHICH IT WAS NEVER INTENDED TO BE. IF YOU WILL EXAMINE THE TEACHINGS OF THE KORAN IN THIS LIGHT, YOU WILL SEE THAT MUCH OF IT IS WORTHWHILE AND VALID. THE DISTORTION OF THE TEACHING TO ACCOMMODATE THE RELIGIOUS DEMANDS OF THE POPULACE HAS RESULTED NOT IN MISUNDERSTANDING AS MUCH AS MISUSE OF THE TEACHING.

"What is the significance of the pilgrimage to Mecca?" Corrine asked.

ONLY THAT IT IS BENEFICIAL FOR THE SOCIETY IF ITS MEMBERS GATHER TOGETHER TO DISCUSS ITS WORKINGS SO THAT PROGRESS MAY BE MAINTAINED. WE REMIND YOU THAT MOHAMMED HAD SUCH GATHERINGS, THOUGH AT THAT TIME THERE WERE NOT TOO MANY PEOPLE INVOLVED.

"Why is the Mohammedan attitude about women so repressive?" David Swan asked.

MOST YOUNG-SOUL RELIGIOUS MOVEMENTS ARE REPRESSIVE. WOMEN HAVE LONG BEEN A TARGET FOR THIS REPRES-

SION. THE MOHAMMEDAN STRUCTURES ARE BASED ON PRE-VIOUS SOCIAL CODES AS WELL AS THE PROVISION THAT MO-HAMMED TRIED TO MAKE FOR WIDOWS SO THAT THEY WOULD NOT BE LEFT TO PROSTITUTION OR STARVATION. UNFORTUNATELY, THIS WAS SEIZED UPON AS PERMISSION TO ABUSE AND ISOLATE WOMEN FOR MALE CONVENIENCE. YOU CAN SEE THE SAME EVOLUTION IN EARLY GREECE. THERE WAS ALSO AN EXISTING PREOCCUPATION WITH LARGE FAMILIES BECAUSE OF A STAGGERINGLY HIGH INFANT MOR-TALITY.

THE SECT OF HINDUISM BEGAN AT THE TIME OF THE MANIFESTATION OF THE INFINITE SOUL THROUGH SRI KRISHNA. IT IS AN ANCIENT SECT THAT RETAINED MUCH OF ITS ORIGINAL WISDOM UNTIL FOREIGN INTRUSION, AT WHICH TIME IT BECAME DILUTED AND CORRUPTED BY DOUBT AND EMBELLISHMENT. ONE THING WE DO SAY IN DEFENSE OF HINDUISM IS THAT IT DOES RETAIN THE LOGOS CONCERN-ING THE LIFE CYCLES OF THE SOUL, HOWEVER DISTORTED AND EMBELLISHED THEY MAY BE AT PRESENT.

THE RESTRICTIVE AND DESTRUCTIVE CASTE SYSTEM HAD ITS BEGINNING IN THE NATURE OF THE ESSENCE ROLES, BUT RATHER THAN ENCOURAGING ACTUAL ESSENCE MANIFES-TATION, THERE WERE ARBITRARY CODES, DETERMINED BY INHERITANCE LINES, THAT TRAPPED ALL SOCIETY INTO A RIGID AND NEGATIVE STRUCTURE. THE MAJOR DISTORTION HERE IS THE MISCONCEPTION THAT CHILDREN HAVE THE SAME ESSENCE AS THEIR PARENTS, WHICH IS OBVIOUSLY AB-SURD. LOOK AT THE OVERLEAVES AND YOU WILL SEE THAT THIS IS RARELY THE CASE.

"What about the Hindu belief that we experience souls as animals?" Corrine asked.

THAT IS A DISTORTION, INVENTED FOR THE CONVENIENCE OF THE BRAHMIN CLASS IN ORDER TO BOLSTER THEIR POWER. WE HAVE TOLD YOU BEFORE THAT ANIMALS HAVE HIVE SOULS AND THAT SENTIENT BEINGS HAVE FRAGMENT SOULS CAPABLE OF EVOLUTION AND CHANGE. IF YOU WILL REMEMBER THAT, YOU WILL UNDERSTAND.

"That might not be popular with a lot of people," Lucy observed.

WE ARE NOT CONDUCTING A POPULARITY CONTEST.

"What about the enormous numbers of gods and god-desses in Hindu theology?" Sam asked.

THESE ARE PERSONIFICATIONS OF NATURAL FORCES, FOR THE MOST PART, THOUGH SOME OF THEM ARE EXPRESSIONS OF THE ESSENCE AND OVERLEAVES. IT IS ALMOST IMPOSSIBLE TO IDENTIFY THAT FUNCTION NOW, EXCEPT THE EXPRESSION OF POLARITIES IN SHIVA AND KALI, THOUGH EVEN IN THOSE TWO THE NATURE OF THE OVERLEAVES AND POLARITIES HAS GOT MIXED UP WITH NATURAL FORCES.

"It sounds as if Michael likes Hinduism," Walter observed.

WE DO NOT LIKE OR DISLIKE. WE ARE QUITE INCAPABLE OF SUCH EMOTIONS. WE OFFER THE TEACHING. YOU MAY OR MAY NOT HEAR THE WORDS. WE WILL LEAVE JUDGMENTS TO YOU.

THE BEGINNING OF TAOISM OCCURRED AT THE TIME OF THE MANIFESTATION OF THE INFINITE SOUL THROUGH LAOTZU, WHICH YOU MAY REGARD AS A TITLE RATHER THAN A NAME. TAOISM IN ITS PRESENT FORM IS THE MOST UNDILUTED EXAMPLE OF THE LOGOS EXTANT. BECAUSE OF ITS SIMPLICITY, IT IS OFTEN DIFFICULT TO UNDERSTAND, AS MOST STUDENTS PREFER COMPLEXITY AND COMPLICATIONS TO THIS SIMPLICITY.

"Why is Taoism so undiluted?" Craig asked.

PRIMARILY BECAUSE OF A LACK OF FOREIGN INTRUSION. ALSO, WE WOULD SAY THAT SINCE MOST STUDENTS FIND THE SIMPLICITY BAFFLING, THERE HAS BEEN LITTLE EMBELLISHMENT. YOU MUST REMEMBER THAT TAOISM IS FOR THE MOST PART FREE FROM PERSONIFICATION AND THEREFORE OFFERS THE STUDENT AN UNCLUTTERED VIEW OF THE LOGOS.

"Would Michael advise studying the *Tao-teh-jing*?" Emily asked.

IT IS CERTAINLY A WORTHWHILE SOURCE.

CONFUCIUS MANIFESTED DURING A PERIOD WHEN SOCIAL CHANGE WAS INEVITABLE. THE WRITINGS OF K'UNG FUTZU HAVE A CORRECT MESSAGE THAT SPEAKS THROUGH ANALOGY AND HAS VERY PRACTICAL ADVICE OF AN ETHICAL AND SOCIAL NATURE FOR SCHOLARS AND WARRIORS, BUT LITTLE VALIDITY FOR OTHERS. WHAT REMAINS OF THE TEACHING TODAY IS IN A VERY DILUTED FORM. AGAIN, IT WAS CONVENIENT FOR THE POWERS WITHIN THE SOCIETY TO SEIZE UPON THE DOCTRINE OF RESPONSIBILITY TO ONE'S ANCESTORS AS A WAY TO HOLD POWER OVER THE DESCEN-

DANTS AND TO ESTABLISH A RIGID SOCIAL STRUCTURE.

"What about the *I Ching*?" Corrine asked. "That comes out of both Taoist and Confucian teaching."

IT IS ANOTHER PROP, LIKE THE TAROT CARDS, THE CRYSTAL BALL, OR, FOR THAT MATTER, OUIJA BOARDS. IT IS A METHOD BY WHICH YOUR FALSE PERSONALITY IS SET ASIDE SO THAT THERE MAY BE INNER DIALOGUE WITH THE ESSENCE. IT IS, IN FACT, NOT A DIALOGUE BUT A MONOLOGUE. WE DO NOT DISDAIN THESE PROPS, ALTHOUGH WE WISH TO POINT OUT THAT MUCH OF WHAT IS IN THE *I Ching* IS NOT PARTICULARLY APPROPRIATE TO TWENTIETH-CENTURY WESTERN CULTURE.

BUDDHISM BEGAN AT THE TIME OF THE MANIFESTATION OF THE INFINITE SOUL THROUGH SIDDHARTHA GAUTAMA AND, NEXT TO THE TEACHING OF LAO-TZU, IS THE LEAST DILUTED AND DISTORTED ACCESS TO THE LOGOS. SOME OF THE BUDDHIST MONKS ARE EXACTLY WHAT THEY SAY THEY ARE—THEY HAVE CLEAR RECALL OF THEIR ENTIRE PAST LIVES, RECOGNIZE ALL THE THREADS, ACKNOWLEDGE THEIR AGREEMENTS AND ASSOCIATIONS, AND RECOGNIZE THEIR ENTITY MATES. OTHERS PROFESS TO HAVING THIS KNOWLEDGE AND DO NOT. THERE IS NO EASY WAY TO TELL ONE FROM THE OTHER EXCEPT TO REMEMBER THAT THOSE WHO ARE TRULY ENLIGHTENED RARELY ADVERTISE THE FACT.

ZOROASTRIANISM HAD ITS FIRST MANIFESTATION WITH THE INFINITE SOUL, BUT THE TEACHING HAS LARGELY BEEN LOST, WE MIGHT ALMOST SAY IN BATTLE, FOR THIS MANIFESTATION OCCURRED TO AN AGGRESSIVE WARRIOR NATION AND WAS PERPETUATED BY SOLDIERS. KEEPING THIS IN MIND, IF ONE READS THE EARLIEST ACCOUNTS, ONE CAN DISCERN THE SIMILARITY HERE BETWEEN THE WORDS OF ZARATHUSTRA AND LAO-TZU, SIDDHARTHA GAUTAMA, AND ALL THOSE OTHERS WHOSE SOULS WERE DISPLACED BY THE TRANSCENDENTAL OR INFINITE SOULS.

"When Michael says displaced, exactly what does he mean?" Emily asked.

WE MEAN THAT THE SOULS EXCHANGE RESIDENCES AND THE DISPLACED SOUL RETURNS TO THE ASTRAL PLANE FOR REVIEW AND TO MAKE DECISIONS IF THERE ARE LIVES, MONADS, AND SEQUENCES LEFT INCOMPLETE BY THIS CHANGE. THERE IS NO HARM DONE TO THE DISPLACED SOUL IF THAT IS WHAT WORRIES YOU; IN FACT, THERE IS CONSIDERABLY

LESS SHOCK THAN WHEN THE SOUL RETURNS TO THE ASTRAL PLANE BECAUSE OF AN EARLY OR VIOLENT DEATH. QUITE OFTEN THE DISPLACED SOUL INCARNATES QUICKLY SO THAT THE MONADS AND SEQUENCES BEGUN MAY BE COMPLETED WITHOUT THE NECESSITY OF ALL THOSE INVOLVED IN THE MONADS AND SEQUENCES HAVING TO RETURN FOR ANOTHER GO AT COMPLETION.

What exactly are monads, sequences, and agreements?

A MONAD IS AN ESSENTIAL UNIT, A NECESSARY EXPERIENCE. THEY OFTEN TAKE MORE THAN ONE LIFE TO ACCOMPLISH. BOTH CHEMISTRY AND PHILOSOPHY TEACH THAT A MONAD IS ELEMENTAL AND INDIVISIBLE. THERE ARE A VERY LARGE NUMBER OF MONADS, SOME OF THEM INTERPERSONAL, SOME OF THEM INTRAPERSONAL.

THE MOST COMMON MONAD IS PARENT/CHILD AND STUDENT/TEACHER. THE PARENT/CHILD MONAD IS USUALLY ACCOMPLISHED IN THE YOUNG-SOUL CYCLE, THE STUDENT/ TEACHER MONAD IN THE MATURE- AND OLD-SOUL CYCLES. THIS DOES NOT MEAN THAT ALL SUCH RELATIONSHIPS ARE MONADAL. THE MONAD IS DONE ONLY ONCE. IN OTHER WORDS, THERE IS ONLY ONE TIME THAT YOU WILL EXPERIENCE THE CHILD SIDE OF THE PARENT/CHILD MONAD, AND ONLY ONCE THAT YOU WILL EXPERIENCE THE PARENT SIDE. YOU WILL EXPERIENCE THESE MONADS WITH THE SAME SOUL. THE TEACHER WHO TEACHES YOU IN THE STUDENT/ TEACHER MONAD WILL BE THE SAME SOUL THAT WILL BE YOUR STUDENT. LET US GIVE YOU AN EXAMPLE: WHEN YOU FIND A PERSON WHOSE CHILDHOOD AND RELATIONSHIP WITH ONE, AND ONLY ONE, OF HIS OR HER PARENTS HAS DOMINATED HIS OR HER LIFE, THEN IT IS POSSIBLE THAT HE OR SHE IS EXPERIENCING THE CHILD PART OF THE PARENT/ CHILD MONAD, JUST AS THE DOMINANT PARENT IS EXPERIENCING THE PARENT SIDE OF THE MONAD. THE TEACHER/ STUDENT MONAD NEED NOT OCCUR IN ACADEMIC SURROUNDINGS; IN FACT, IT MOST OFTEN DOES NOT AS THE NATURE OF EDUCATION REQUIRES THAT A TEACHER DIVIDE HIS OR HER ATTENTION AMONG SEVERAL PUPILS, AND THAT IS NOT THE NATURE OF THE TEACHER/STUDENT MONAD. EACH FRAGMENT MUST EXPERIENCE BEING THE ATTACKER AND THE VICTIM, THE HEALER AND THE HEALED, THE PASSIONATE AND REPRESSIVE, THE DEPENDENT AND THE INDEPENDENT, THE RESCUER AND THE RESCUED, THE HOPE-

LESSLY LOVING AND THE HOPELESSLY LOVED, TO GIVE A FEW OBVIOUS EXAMPLES. MOST OF THE TRANSACTIONS THAT HAVE RECENTLY BEEN IDENTIFIED AS COMMON TIMES OF CRISIS IN ADULT LIFE ARE OFTEN LINKED WITH AN INTRAPERSONAL MONAD, OR MILESTONE.

A SEQUENCE IS USUALLY JUST THAT: A SEQUENCE OF EVENTS LEADING THE FRAGMENT TO THE CULMINATION OF AN AGREED-UPON EXPERIENCE OR TASK. AGREEMENTS AND SEQUENCES GO HAND IN HAND. YOU AGREE TO DO A SEQUENCE. OFTEN A FRAGMENT WILL BECOME A FACILITATOR AND COME INTO YOUR LIFE ONLY LONG ENOUGH TO INTRODUCE YOU TO ANOTHER FRAGMENT, OR TAKE YOU TO A SPECIFIC LOCATION, OR DELIVER A MESSAGE SO THAT YOUR TASK WILL BE EASIER TO COMPLETE. AGAIN, PARENTS OFTEN HAVE SEQUENCES WITH THEIR CHILDREN WHICH WILL INVOLVE ENVIRONMENTAL CONTROLS THROUGH WHICH THE CHILD FRAGMENT MUST WORK IN ORDER TO COMPLETE THE LIFE-TASK. THESE FAMILIAL SEQUENCES OFTEN INVOLVE REPRESSION NEUROSES OR WHAT SEEMS TO BE UNUSUAL HARSHNESS, SPECIFICALLY RELIGIOUS RESTRICTIONS AND THE LIKE. FRAGMENTS OFTEN ALSO HAVE SEQUENCES WITH EACH OTHER AS PUPILS AND FAVORITE TEACHERS FOR THE SPECIFIC PURPOSE OF PASSING ON NEEDED INFORMATION LEADING TO THE COMPLETION OF THE TASK. SEQUENCES ARE QUITE OFTEN INTERRUPTED BY NATURAL OCCURRENCES SUCH AS ILLNESS, DEATH, AND RELOCATION, FOR THE DRIVE TO COMPLETE AGREEMENTS IS NOT NEARLY AS STRONG AS THE DRIVE TO BURN KARMIC RIBBONS. HOWEVER, WHEN THE SEQUENCE IS SET UP TO COMPLETE A MONAD, THEN THE DRIVE IS AS STRONG OR STRONGER THAN THE KARMIC PULL.

SINCE A MONAD IS A COMPLETE LIFE EXPERIENCE AND CONSISTS OF A BLOCK OF KNOWLEDGE, THE INTERRUPTION OF IT REQUIRES THAT YOU START IT AGAIN IN ANOTHER LIFE AND FINISH IT. COMPLETION OF SPECIFIC MONADS IS PART OF THE EVOLUTION OF THE SOUL, AND IT IS NECESSARY TO COMPLETE THE MONADS IN ORDER TO ADVANCE THROUGH THE LEVELS OF THE CYCLES. IT IS NOT ENTIRELY INAPT TO SAY THAT MONADS HAVE SOME OF THE EFFECT ON THE EVOLUTION OF THE SOUL THAT EDUCATION DOES ON THE PERSONALITY. A CHILD MUST LEARN TO DRAW IN ORDER TO DEVELOP THE EYE-AND-HAND COORDINATION NECESSARY IN

READING AND WRITING, AND IN A SIMILAR SENSE, THERE
ARE MONADS THAT MUST BE EXPERIENCED BEFORE THE
FRAGMENT IS READY FOR THE NEXT STEP.

WE DO NOT MEAN TO IMPLY THAT THERE IS A SET STRUC-
TURE FOR THIS AND THAT EVERYONE, UPON REACHING MID-
CYCLE YOUTH, WILL AUTOMATICALLY DO THE PARENT SIDE
OF THE PARENT/CHILD MONAD. THE FRAGMENT CHOOSES
BETWEEN LIVES WHICH OF THE INTERPERSONAL MONADS IT
WILL ACCOMPLISH. THE INTRAPERSONAL ONES, OF COURSE,
ARE PART OF LIFE.

Suppose that for some reason it isn't possible to complete
a monad—what then?

THAT IS YOUR CHOICE. YOU WILL DO IT IN SOME OTHER
LIFE.

Do monads have to do with the professional life?

NOT AS SUCH, NO, THOUGH IT IS LIKELY YOUR CHOICE OF
PROFESSION WILL INFLUENCE HOW AND WHEN YOU DO
YOUR MONADS. THE CLOSER YOU ARE TO WORKING IN ES-
SENCE, THE MORE EASILY YOU WILL ACCOMPLISH YOUR
MONADS.

Are monads part of family life, other than the parent/child
monad?

NOT NECESSARILY, BUT THERE ARE TIMES WHEN IT IS
CONVENIENT. OFTEN THE MONADS WILL BE BETWEEN SIB-
LINGS RATHER THAN PARENT AND CHILD, AS THE SIBLINGS
ARE APT TO HAVE AN ACTIVE PART IN EACH OTHER'S LIVES
FOR A LONGER PERIOD OF TIME THAN THE PARENTS.

Are monads part of karma?

NOT ESSENTIALLY, ALTHOUGH THERE MAY BE KARMIC
DEBTS AND PAYMENTS ASSOCIATED WITH MAJOR MONADS.
HOWEVER, THAT IS COMPARATIVELY RARE. IN GENERAL,
MONADS ARE STRONG ENOUGH BY THEMSELVES, AND SO IS
KARMA, NOT TO NEED THE FUNCTION OF THE OTHER.
OCCASIONALLY IF A FRAGMENT DECIDES TO ABDICATE A
MONADAL RELATIONSHIP IT MIGHT RESULT IN KARMIC
DEBTS, AS IN THE CASE OF A DEPENDENT/INDEPENDENT
MONAD WHEN THE INDEPENDENT PARTNER ABDICATES AND
AS A RESULT THE DEPENDENT PARTNER DIES. THAT WOULD
LEAVE THE MONAD INCOMPLETE AND ADD A KARMIC DEBT.

Are supportive relationships monadal?

OCCASIONALLY. THEY CAN ALSO BE THE RESULT OF PRE-
VIOUS ASSOCIATIONS, SUCH AS FORMER COMRADES-AT-ARMS,

OR ENTITY MATES, OR, IN THE STRONGEST OF THOSE RELA-
TIONSHIPS, ESSENCE TWINS.

Are sexual relationships monadal?

SOME OF THEM ARE, SOME OF THEM ARE NOT. EACH CASE
IS INDIVIDUAL AND WE CANNOT ANSWER THE QUESTION
WITH A GENERAL STATEMENT.

Since there is a sexual center, can it be used for deeper
communication?

IT DEPENDS ON WHAT YOU WISH TO COMMUNICATE.
ONLY THOSE EXPRESSIONS THAT ARE VISIBLE OR TANGIBLE
CAN BE TAKEN AS TRUE EXPRESSIONS UNLESS YOU ARE
TELEPATHIC. YOU MUST RECEIVE THE EXPRESSION THROUGH
ONE OF YOUR FIVE PRIMITIVE SENSES AND CONVEY IT TO
THE OTHERS. IF YOU CAN DO IT WITH SEX, THEN YOU ARE
TELEPATHIC.

What's wrong in thinking about sex?

NOTHING IS WRONG. HOWEVER, THE MOMENT YOU START
THINKING ABOUT SEX, YOU BRING THE EMOTIONAL OR THE
INTELLECTUAL CENTER INTO PLAY. THEN THERE IS LOSS OF
ENERGY FROM THE SEXUAL CENTER.

But it seems that people who are turned on sexually have
more energy.

THIS IS A HIGHER SOURCE OF ENERGY, AND FOR A FEW
MINUTES, OR HOURS, IF THE PLAY IS THAT INTERESTING,
YOU CAN FEEL ITS EFFECT.

Wouldn't that effect be beneficial? Isn't there a way to
explore a sexual high?

WITH A SEXUAL HIGH AS YOU CALL IT, YOU ARE USING
THE SEXUAL CENTER AS ACCESS TO THE HIGHER CENTERS.
THE PHYSICAL ACT ITSELF CAN BE PERFORMED WITH LITTLE
LOSS OF ENERGY. THE PROBLEM WITH MOST IS THAT THEY
ARE HEAVILY IDENTIFIED WITH OTHER ASPECTS WHEN THEY
ARE PERFORMING THE SEX ACT. THIS IS WHAT WE MEAN.

Is there any way to get at that kind of sexual high?

THERE IS NO PAT FORMULA, IF THAT IS WHAT YOU ARE
ASKING. WITH THE TRULY TELEPATHIC, THE EXPERIENCE
CAN BE MOST PROFOUND. MANY PEOPLE SHY AWAY FROM
SUCH RELATIONSHIPS FOR JUST THAT REASON. THEY FIND
IT THREATENING TO OPEN THEMSELVES TO SUCH AN IN-
TENSE INTIMACY. ENTITY MATES IN THE OLDER CYCLES CAN
OCCASIONALLY EXPERIENCE THAT MUTUAL REVELATION,
PARTICULARLY WHEN THERE ARE MANY PAST ASSOCIATIONS

TO DRAW ON. THE OTHER CONDITION, ADMITTEDLY RARE, IS WHEN THOSE INVOLVED IN THE SEXUAL ACT ARE TWIN SOULS.

Do you mean entity mates that are the same essence role and with the same overleaves?

NO. ESSENCE TWINS, THOUGH ALMOST ALWAYS THE SAME ESSENCE ROLE, ARE NOT OFTEN PART OF THE SAME ENTITY, BUT ARE PART OF DIFFERENT ENTITIES THAT WERE CAST AT THE SAME TIME. THE TWINNING LASTS FOR ALL THE CYCLES, AND INCIDENTALLY, IS RARELY CONSUMMATED. MOST PEOPLE REJECT SUCH RELATIONSHIPS.

Why would anyone do that?

IT IS TOO FRIGHTENING. THERE IS COMPLETE PSYCHIC UNION BETWEEN TWIN SOULS. THERE ARE NO LONGER ANY INDIVIDUAL PERCEPTIONS. THERE IS A TOTAL LOSS OF IDENTITY. MOST PEOPLE ARE TOO AMBIVALENT AND HOSTILE TO DEAL WITH SUCH A RELATIONSHIP. THE UNITING OF TWIN SOULS IS A DEVASTATING EXPERIENCE. SOULS SO UNITED ARE TRULY ONE FLESH.

Surely that's a metaphor—after all, they are in different bodies.

WE SAID THAT YOU FIND SUCH RELATIONSHIPS FRIGHTENING. YES, IT IS TRUE THAT YOU STAY IN YOUR OWN BODIES, BUT THE INTENSITY OF THE UNION, PARTICULARLY WHEN IT IS EXPRESSED SEXUALLY, CAN BE ECSTATIC BEYOND ANY OTHER SUCH EXPERIENCE. ESSENCE TWINS, IF THEY CAN ACCEPT EACH OTHER, WOULD LITERALLY DO ANYTHING TO REMAIN TOGETHER.

Would they even die together?

IF THE ALTERNATIVE WERE SEVERE ENOUGH, YES THEY WOULD. WE DO NOT MEAN TO SUGGEST THAT SUCH RELATIONSHIPS ARE ALWAYS GRAND PASSIONS, AS THAT WILL DEPEND ON THE NATURE OF THE OVERLEAVES. BABY SCHOLARS, FOR INSTANCE, DO NOT GO IN FOR GRAND PASSIONS AS A RULE. IT IS CONTRARY TO THE NATURE OF THE CYCLE AND ESSENCE. SCHOLARS ARE ALWAYS SOMEWHAT REMOTE, AS ARE ARTISANS.

WE DO NOT MEAN TO IMPLY THAT ALL ROMANTIC SUICIDE PACTS ARE THE WORK OF TWIN SOULS REFUSING TO BE SEPARATED. MORE LIKELY, YOUTHFUL ROMANTIC SUICIDES ARE INDULGING IN HIGH-FLOWN THEATRICS. DEPRESSED SAGES ACHIEVE THE MOST FLAMBOYANT SUICIDES, THOUGH

MOST OF THEM DO NOT GENERALLY INTEND TO KILL THEM-
SELVES, ONLY TO REAP THE BENEFITS AND ATTENTIONS OF
THE ATTEMPT. OF COURSE, EACH FRAGMENT MUST EXPE-
RIENCE SUICIDE, AS IT MUST EXPERIENCE PLAGUE AND
DEATH IN BATTLE AND EXECUTION AND STARVATION AND
ALL OTHER FORMS OF DEATH. IT IS PART OF THE ETERNAL
PLAY.

Are suicidal tendencies repetitive in life after life?

NO. SOONER OR LATER THE SOUL LEARNS THAT SUICIDE
IS UNPROFITABLE. FOR INSTANCE, IF A PERSON WITH TER-
MINAL CANCER SUICIDES AND THERE REMAINED FIVE OR SIX
MONTHS OF LIFE WITH ITS ATTENDANT LESSONS, THEN
THAT SOUL WILL EXPERIENCE INFANT DEATH AT A LATER
TIME.

What about the experience of death itself? If suicide is
unprofitable, why do so many people resort to it?

THERE IS NO ONE ANSWER, OF COURSE. DEATH IS A
GHASTLY EXPERIENCE IF YOU ARE DEPRESSED. YOU BRING
ALL YOUR DEPRESSION WITH YOU. THAT IS WHY SO MANY
SUICIDES MUST GO BACK AND FINISH THAT WHICH THEY
ABDICATED, OR NO PROGRESS CAN BE MADE.

That sounds as if the tendency to suicide comes out of
conflict with the false personality and the essence.

THAT IS ESSENTIALLY VALID IN MANY INSTANCES.

Then is the personality mad, in both senses of the word,
to court that kind of destruction?

IT IS ONLY TRYING TO SURVIVE. SURVIVAL IS THE GOAL
FOR THE ORGANISM. ECSTASY IS THE GOAL OF THE ESSENCE.

It sounds as if the body and false personality are often at
cross-purposes with the essence.

CERTAINLY. BUT YOU ARE ASSUMING LIMITS THAT ARE
NOT ENTIRELY ACCURATE. LOOK, FOR A MOMENT, AT THE
PHYSICAL UNIVERSE AS AN ENORMOUS STAGE, AND ALL OF
THE PHYSICAL THINGS WITHIN IT AS THE SETS AND ACTORS.
THEN LOOK A MOMENT AT THE POSSIBILITY OF KARMA, OR
THE SYSTEM OF KARMA, WHICH MAY IN FACT BE LOOKED
UPON AS THE DIRECTOR OF THE PLAY OF LIFE. SOULS EX-
PERIENCING ALL OF LIFE ON THE PHYSICAL PLANE NEVER
HAVE TO SEEK SPIRITUAL GROWTH. THEY CAN, AND MOST
DO, GO THROUGH THE WHOLE CYCLE IN THE WAKING SLEEP.
THE MOMENT THAT YOU ELECT TO COMMIT YOURSELF TO
THE PATH, YOU REMOVE YOURSELF FROM THE LIST OF

AVAILABLE ACTORS EQUITY. WERE IT NOT FOR KARMIC RIB-
BONS, SOULS WOULD NOT EXPERIENCE MUCH AT ALL. THEY
CERTAINLY WOULD NOT EXPERIENCE ALL OF LIFE. NOW
THIS PLAY IS, OF COURSE, A LIE. THERE IS NO TRUTH TO BE
FOUND WITHIN IT. THE ONLY TRUTH LIES WITHIN THE REAL
SPACE BEYOND; THEN THE ESSENCE IS FREE TO SELECT THE
BEST SCRIPT AVAILABLE—THE ONE ENABLING THE PARTIC-
ULAR FRAGMENT TO EXPERIENCE OUT SOME FACET OF PHYS-
ICAL LIFE THAT IT HAS NOT EXPERIENCED BEFORE. THESE
ARE FACILITATED BY WHAT WE HAVE CHOSEN TO CALL
OVERLEAVES. CERTAIN COMPOSITES OF OVERLEAVES ARE
CONDUCIVE TO CERTAIN TYPES OF ACTIVITIES—FOR IN-
STANCE, THE EXTRACTION OF AN OLD DEBT. REMEMBER,
THE MOMENT YOU STEP ON THE PATH THIS IS NO LONGER
THE CASE. YOU MAY DEPART FROM THE SCRIPT JUST AS SOON
AS YOU REALIZE IT EXISTS. YOU CAN DEPART FROM IT COM-
PLETELY, AND IF YOU WISH, WITHOUT REGRETS, BUT THIS
IS HARD WORK. JUST THE REALIZATION IS DIFFICULT
ENOUGH. YOU SEE, THAT WHICH YOU CALL ESSENCE, THAT
WHICH HAS ACCESS TO HIGHER EXPRESSION, OPERATES AL-
WAYS IN REAL SPACE. THE FALSE PERSONALITY FEARS REAL
SPACE AS THE AGROPHOBIC FEARS THE OPEN FIELD.

Then internal depression and anger would seem to be the
result of misunderstood perceptions and expectations.

REEXAMINE THOSE EXPECTATIONS FOR SHADES OF
REALISM. ONE STEP AT A TIME IS NORMALLY EFFECTIVE FOR
USEFUL AMBULATION. WHY NOT FOR SPIRITUAL LIBERA-
TION?

Isn't anger the result of fear?

UNFULFILLED EXPECTATIONS ARE THE SOLE CAUSE OF
ANGER. WE KNOW OF NONE OTHER. WHEN YOU STOP EX-
PECTING, THERE WILL BE NO ANGER. WE REMIND YOU THAT
YOUR EXPECTATIONS NEED NOT BE PLEASANT. ANXIETY
AND ANTICIPATION OF DISASTER ARE ALSO EXPECTATIONS.

THIS DOES NOT MEAN THAT YOU SHOULD DENY THE IM-
PULSES WITHIN YOU, BUT THAT YOU SHOULD LEARN NOT
TO DENY THEM. THERE IS NO UNDERSTANDING WHERE
THERE IS DENIAL. YOU ARE SOMEWHAT HANDICAPPED IN
THAT ASPECT. ESSENTIALLY THIS CULTURE IS HYPOCRITICAL
TOWARD AGGRESSION. THE CULTURE PRETENDS TO DECRY
AGGRESSION, YET TEACHES IT TO THE YOUNG. CONFUSION
RESULTS AND MANY GROW UP BELIEVING THAT ALL AG-

GRESSIVE TENDENCIES ARE SOMEHOW NOT NICE. OTHERS GROW UP IN AN ATMOSPHERE OF AGGRESSIVE ABANDON. MOST ARE CONFUSED ABOUT THEIR OWN INTERNAL PASSIVE/AGGRESSIVE RATIO.

This must have larger implications, such as the occurrence of war, which everyone tends to despise and encourage at once.

THIS HAPPENS BECAUSE YOUNG SOULS ARE IN THE MAJORITY ON YOUR WORLD. THEY ARE LARGELY MOTIVATED BY THE DESIRE FOR MATERIAL ACHIEVEMENT.

But why is war necessary and why is it imposed on us?

THE HIGH BODIES IMPOSE NOTHING. THE CYCLES IMPOSE THEIR OWN KARMA. THE REASONS FOR WARS BECOME CRYSTAL CLEAR WHEN ONE STUDIES THE PERCEPTIONS OF THE WORLD AND SELF THROUGH THE CYCLES. MANY NATIONS ARE NOW HEAVILY POPULATED WITH EARLY-CYCLE YOUNG SOULS. YOUR OWN IS THE PRIME EXAMPLE. OTHER NATIONS ARE HEAVILY POPULATED BY MATURE SOULS. THESE ARE THE NATIONS THAT CHOSE NEUTRALITY IN WORLD WAR II. OLD-SOUL NATIONS ARE ACTIVELY PACIFIC AND SUBMIT TO DOMINATION RATHER THAN FIGHT.

Could we stop all wars?

YOU CANNOT DO IT. THERE WOULD BE MINIMUM COOPERATION AND YOU WOULD JUST BECOME A NEEDLESS MARTYR.

What about soldiers killed in war who were against the war? Do they come back right away?

NO. THAT IS USUALLY A DEFINITE RIBBON AND A LIFE ROLE THEY CHOSE. THE ONLY EXCEPTION WOULD BE THE VICTIMS OF THE NUCLEAR DEVASTATION IN JAPAN. MOST OF THESE WERE REBORN. ALSO, THOSE WHO DIED IN THE CONCENTRATION CAMPS WERE NOT ALL BY CHOICE OR, RATHER, UNWISE CHOICES WERE MADE.

What about natural disasters such as fire and flood?

THESE ARE USUALLY BY CHOICE.

It looks as if it would be very easy to go too far and destroy the earth.

IT IS NOT IN THE PLAN TO DESTROY THIS PLANET YET. THAT DOES NOT MEAN THAT YOU HAVE A LICENSE TO PLUNDER, THOUGH MANY OF YOU SEEM TO THINK THAT THIS IS THE CASE. REMEMBER THAT IN YOUR NEXT LIFE, YOU WILL HAVE TO LIVE IN THE EFFLUVIUM THAT IS BEING CREATED

NOW. IF YOU CANNOT BE ALTRUISTIC, THEN BE SELFISH. WOULD YOU LIKE TO LIVE IN A GARBAGE DUMP?

Doesn't this impose a tremendous strain on people?

YES, AND YOUR CULTURE PRIDES ITSELF ON STRESS. MANY FRAGMENTS CANNOT DEAL WITH THIS AND BECOME DEEPLY TROUBLED.

Will you elaborate?

WHEN WE SPEAK OF TROUBLED SOULS, WE SPEAK OF A CLOUDING OF REASON LEADING TO DISINTEGRATION OF THE FUNCTIONING PSYCHE.

Do they ever get it back together again?

NOT IN THAT LIFETIME.

It must be the karma that is troubling it, isn't it?

THERE IS A GENERAL BOMBARDMENT OF UNFAMILIAR STIMULI DURING THE MATURE CYCLE. THIS IS DIFFICULT TO COPE WITH AT BEST. IF A SOUL HAS CHOSEN A PASSIVE ROLE AND BODY, THE PRESSURE CAN BECOME INTOLERABLE, ESPECIALLY IF POOR ENVIRONMENTAL CHOICES ARE MADE. YOU SEE, THE ULTIMATE CHOICE IS ALWAYS UP TO YOU. WE ONLY OFFER GUIDANCE. NEVER DO WE IMPOSE THE CHOICE.

You admit that all souls are somehow different. There seems to be an individuality—it's a flavor or perfume—not an experiential thing. This must carry over into the astral cycles or other cycles.

THERE IS A SHRED OF INDIVIDUALITY LEFT WHEN YOU HAVE ALL OF THE OVERLEAVES, BUT REALLY VERY SLIGHT. YOU NOW HAVE HALF THE STORY. YOU WILL PERCEIVE LESS INDIVIDUALITY WHEN YOU BEGIN TO PERCEIVE THEM IN THEIR ROLES.

WE HAVE SAID THIS BEFORE, BUT WE WILL REPEAT: THE AGREEMENTS, AS DIFFERENTIATED FROM KARMA, ARE MADE SO THAT THE PERSONALITY CAN EXPERIENCE ALL OF LIFE ONE WAY OR ANOTHER. ESSENCE DOES NOT CARE HOW MANY LIVES IT TAKES; ESSENCE IS IMMORTAL AND HAS NO SENSE OF TIME AS YOU KNOW IT. WHAT MAKES THE AGREE-MENTS IS YOUR ASTRAL SELF, WHICH BETWEEN LIVES IS MOSTLY THE ROLE, WHICH IS MOSTLY IN ESSENCE, AND THE VERTIGES OF PERSONALITIES. AGREEMENTS ARE NOT MADE BY THE ESSENCE. THE ROLE STANDS BOTH IN ESSENCE AND IN PERSONALITY. IT HAS A SENSE OF ESSENCE BUT IT IS ATTRACTED TO THE PHYSICAL PLANE.

Is there any way at all to speed up the process?

ACCELERATION DOES OCCASIONALLY HAPPEN TO OLD SOULS IN TOUCH WITH THEIR HIGHER CENTERS. THE MATURE SOUL CAN ALSO ACCELERATE WITHIN THE CYCLE. YOUNG SOULS CAN BURN KARMIC RIBBONS RAPIDLY SOMETIMES AND ACCELERATE. ELIZABETH BLACKWELL AND FLORENCE NIGHTINGALE ARE EXAMPLES; LOUIS PASTEUR, WALTER REED, MARIE CURIE, AND FRANK LLOYD WRIGHT ACCELERATED.

How does one reach the higher centers?

THE AVERAGE SOUL GLIMPSES THE HIGHER ONLY IN MOMENTS OF EXTREME STRESS OR AGONY.

Chapter 11

BURNING KARMIC RIBBONS . . .

"Until Michael said that higher centers are usually sensed through extreme stress or agony, everyone was very excited about experiencing those centers. After he said that, enthusiasm kind of fizzled." Jessica chuckles a little sadly.

"Most of us aren't too interested in agony," Lucy agrees.

"I don't know, though," Jessica says slowly. "I'm not afraid of it the way I used to be. When I was in college, the very thought of pain, any pain, scared me silly. I think I would have done almost anything to avoid it. It's not that I welcome it now, but I can handle it; it no longer terrifies me."

"Michael told us that a lot of the flagellant orders of monks in the Middle Ages were trying to achieve higher centers by self-inflicted pain," Walter adds. "A few of them half-understood that there was an incredible experience spiritually if only you could transcend the pain. Unfortunately, for most of the flagellants, there was only a sado-masochistic orgasm and not the transcendent experience. It was one of the reasons the early and middle ages Church developed such kinky attitudes about sex."

Isn't it strange that a bodiless, timeless entity like Michael would devote so much time to physical relationships?

"Not really," Jessica says. "Apparently Michael wants what he tells us to have some application in our lives, since *we're* on the physical plane, and our relationships are very important to us. Michael has spent a lot of time trying to help us sort them all out. There was a woman who came to about ten sessions and then stopped. She was in a very bad marriage and knew that it was a bad marriage, and knew that she had to get out of it, but found that she couldn't. Something was keeping her with her husband. She'd been to shrinks and had taken assertiveness training and gone to some of the various head-clearing courses, and she was still in a marriage that was going downhill. Michael didn't give any suggestions as to what she might do about the difficulty of the marriage, but he did tell her why she couldn't leave.

THE MAN IS A SIXTH-LEVEL YOUNG ARTISAN IN THE REPRESSION MODE WITH A GOAL OF ACCEPTANCE, A REALIST IN THE INTELLECTUAL PART OF EMOTIONAL CENTER, WITH A CHIEF FEATURE OF STUBBORNNESS. THE WOMAN IS A SECOND-LEVEL MATURE PRIEST IN THE OBSERVATION MODE WITH A GOAL OF SUBMISSION, A PRAGMATIST IN THE MOVING PART OF INTELLECTUAL CENTER, WITH A CHIEF FEATURE OF IMPATIENCE. AS YOU CAN SEE, THE OVERLEAVES ABRADE. THIS WOULD BE A DIFFICULT RELATIONSHIP TO MAINTAIN UNDER ANY CIRCUMSTANCES, BUT IN THIS INSTANCE, THERE IS A DEBT. THE LADY CAROLINE OWES THE MAN HAROLD. THREE LIFETIMES AGO THE FRAGMENT ABANDONED HIS AGED AND BLIND PARENT WHEN A FOREIGN ARMY INVADED THE SMALL VILLAGE IN WHICH THEY LIVED. THE LADY CAROLINE WAS THE ABANDONING SON, THE MAN HAROLD WAS THE BLIND FATHER. THE LADY IS EAGER TO PAY THE DEBT, BUT THE MAN IS NOT WILLING TO HAVE IT PAID. THIS IS NOT UNUSUAL. IT MAY BE THAT THE PAYMENT WILL NOT BE MADE IN THIS LIFETIME.

"Caroline found this very hard to deal with, though she said that it struck an unpleasant and familiar chord within her," Jessica remarks.

Is it possible to delay paying karmic debts?

"Well, if the person you owe won't let you do it . . ." Jessica shrugs. "It can happen."

What did Caroline decide to do?

"She lasted it out with Harold for another year, then told him she thought she'd try next time around."

Did Michael have anything to say about that?

"Of course," Jessica answers.

THE LADY CAROLINE HAS ACKNOWLEDGED HER DEBT AND THE MAN HAROLD HAS REFUSED TO LET HER DISCHARGE THE DEBT. IN THIS INSTANCE IT IS WISE THAT THEY DISSOLVE THEIR RELATIONSHIP, AS FURTHER DEBTS COULD BE INCURRED IF IT CONTINUED UNDER SUCH CIRCUMSTANCES.

Is it possible to have more than one debt to the same person?

OF COURSE. IT IS ALSO POSSIBLE TO BE MUTUALLY OBLIGATED. IN THE LATTER CASE, IF THE MUTUAL DEBT CAN BE ACKNOWLEDGED BY THE FRAGMENTS DURING THEIR PHYSICAL LIFETIME, AND THE AGREEMENT MADE TO CANCEL THE MUTUAL DEBT, THEN THE DEBT IS TRULY ERASED. WE MUST STRESS, HOWEVER, THAT BOTH PARTIES MUST BE GENUINELY WILLING, THE DEBTS MUST BE HONESTLY ACKNOWLEDGED, AND THE AGREEMENT TO CANCEL THE DEBTS MUST BE TRULY UNDERSTOOD. IN OTHER WORDS, BOTH MUST BE COMPLETELY AWARE OF WHAT THEY ARE DOING.

Is it necessary to know what the debts are?

NOT NECESSARY, BUT IT HELPS.

Michael does not seem to feel that marriage vows are all that permanent.

THEY ARE NOT. THEY ARE CONTRACTS OF THE PHYSICAL PLANE, AND LARGELY A PART OF EXPECTATIONS AND FALSE PERSONALITY. IN YOUR CULTURE, THE DESIRE TO SEEK OUT A PERMANENT RELATIONSHIP ON A ONE-TO-ONE BASIS IS STILL LARGELY PREDICATED UPON THE LONELINESS AND ISOLATION THAT THE TECHNICAL SOCIETY BREEDS. IT IS A TERRIBLE PRICE TO PAY FOR CIVILIZATION, FOR IN THE LONG RUN, ESPECIALLY WHERE THERE ARE FAR-REACHING LEGAL RAMIFICATIONS, IT BREEDS DISCONTENT AND MUCH NEEDLESS NEGATIVITY, AND THUS MUCH WASTED ENERGY WHICH COULD BE USED FOR GROWTH. ABOVE ALL, TRANQUILLITY, OR AT LEAST A MEASURE OF IT, IS NEEDED FOR GROWTH. THIS TRANQUILLITY MUST COME FROM WITHIN, NEVER FROM EXTERNALS, FOR THE LATTER IS A FALSE TRANQUILLITY AND ANY THIRD FORCE CAN DESTROY IT, UTTERLY SHATTER IT, IN THE TWINKLING OF AN EYE.

NOW WE DO NOT SPEAK ENTIRELY AGAINST THE CUSTOM OF MARRIAGE. IT IS THAT WE DO DISAPPROVE OF IT BEING

A LEGISLATIVE IMPERATIVE. RATHER, WE WOULD SPEAK OF PERSONAL CONTRACTUAL COMMITMENTS, THIS OF COURSE AS AN ALTERNATIVE TO THE MORE OPEN APPROACH, WHICH WE HAVE OFTEN RECOMMENDED FOR ADVANCED STUDENTS. THIS LATTER WORKS ONLY IN THE PRESENCE OF A HIGH LEVEL OF BALANCE ON THE PART OF ALL CONCERNED.

IN THIS CULTURE, UNFORTUNATELY, ONCE A FIRM COMMITMENT IS MADE IN RELATIONSHIPS, THE PARTNERS OFTEN UNDERGO A STARTLING CHANGE IN THEIR INTERPERSONAL RELATING TO THE POINT THAT LIVING BECOMES SO STRAINED THAT THEY BEGIN LOOKING FOR THE ESCAPE ROUTE. OF COURSE, THIS STEMS FROM IMPRINTING AND THE LESSON LEARNED INSOFAR AS MAY BE EXPECTED IN AN IDEAL MATE. SOME OF YOU ARE PERHAPS MORE AWARE OF THIS THAN MOST, AND SEEK TO AVOID THE "TENDER TRAP." WITH A COMMITTED STUDENT, AN INTERPERSONAL RELATIONSHIP "SHOULD" BE FREE FROM THIS DANGER. IDEALLY IT WOULD BE.

MOST OF ALL, WE DO NOT RECOMMEND RIGID STRUCTURED MALE-FEMALE RELATIONSHIPS WHERE THERE IS NO ROOM FOR BLOOMING OR GROWING, IF YOU WILL. BUT WE DO RECOMMEND THAT IF YOU ACCEPT THE MORE OPEN APPROACH, THEN YOU SELECT FOR YOURSELF THOSE PARTNERS WHO UNDERSTAND THIS APPROACH AND SEEK IT THEMSELVES. THIS TYPE OF AN APPROACH CAN COME FROM A QUITE ENLIGHTENED AND BALANCED SPACE, BUT IN YOU THERE IS STILL MUCH FEAR OF REPEATING OLD PATTERNS AND FINDING YOURSELF AGAIN CUT OFF FROM THE PATH.

Where do humans go astray in choosing partners? Is it that no one is willing to wait for the right person?

THERE IS A WEIRD SORT OF ESTRUS OPERATING IN ALL HUMANS THAT MAKES THEM SEEK OUT A SEXUAL PARTNER. THE SOCIETAL MORES DEMAND THAT THEY CEMENT THIS INTO A MORE BINDING CONTRACT. SOMETIMES THIS CAN BE COMBINED WITH FINANCIAL GAIN OR SOCIAL STATUS. THERE IS USUALLY LITTLE THOUGHT IN THE LASTING EMOTIONAL CONSEQUENCES, LET ALONE THE SPIRITUAL. QUITE OFTEN TWO PEOPLE WILL ARBITRARILY DECIDE THAT THEY HAVE "A GREAT DEAL IN COMMON." THIS USUALLY IS NOT TRUE, SINCE NEITHER PRESENTS THE TRUE PICTURE TO THE OTHER. EACH TRIES TO OUTGUESS THE OTHER AND FIT IN THE MOLD IN ORDER TO QUALIFY FOR THE PRIZE WHICH CAN BE SEX,

MONEY, GLAMOUR, OR PRESTIGE, ALL OF WHICH ARE FEA-
TURES OF FALSE PERSONALITY. THAT TYPE OF SEXUAL AT-
TRACTION IS RARELY LASTING. IT IS BASED ON AN INITIAL
ADRENALIN FLOW WHICH DOES NOT LAST. THIS PRODUCES
A NICE WARM GLOW WHICH IS INTERPRETED AS "LOVE."

Are some people sexually centered?

YES, BUT THAT IS NOT THE SAME THING AS HAVING SEX-
UAL ENERGY. SEXUAL ENERGY IS SEPARATE AND APART
FROM ALL OTHER ENERGY SOURCES AND CAN BE EFFEC-
TIVELY USED TO REACH HIGHER EMOTIONS.

If you were to experience sex on a higher level, what
would be going on?

CEREBRAL ORGASM. THE WHOLE SOUL EXPERIENCES
ECSTASY. THE BODY CANNOT EXPERIENCE ECSTASY, ONLY
SATIATION. ONLY THE ESSENCE IS CAPABLE OF THAT EX-
PERIENCE. WE WOULD LIKE TO POINT OUT THAT SEXUAL
BEHAVIOR IN THIS CULTURE IS LARGELY INSTINCTIVE TO
THE POINT WHERE ANY GESTURE OF FRIENDLINESS IS IN-
TEREPRETED AS A SEXUAL OVERTURE. IF IT COMES FROM
ONE OF THE OPPOSITE GENDER, THE FANTASIES AND EXPEC-
TATIONS BEGIN.

That is a pretty bleak prospect. Is there any way to improve things?

WHEN YOU RID YOURSELF OF ALL NEGATIVE THOUGHTS
ABOUT SEX, THEN IT IS POSSIBLE FOR YOU TO HAVE A VA-
RIETY OF HIGHER LEVEL SEXUAL ENCOUNTERS. THESE DO
NOT ALWAYS HAVE TO BE PHYSICAL. SOME OF YOUR MOST
REWARDING SEXUAL ENCOUNTERS OCCUR WHEN YOU THINK
YOU ARE ASLEEP. THESE ARE ENCOUNTERS ON THE ASTRAL
PLANE AND ALSO ESSENCE ENCOUNTERS WITH ACTUALLY
KNOWN BEINGS. TURNING ON, AS YOU CALL IT, NEED NOT
BE SEXUALLY DIRECTED AT ALL. THAT DOES NOT MEAN TO
SAY THAT WE RECOMMEND THAT YOU GIVE UP SEX, SUB-
LIMATE THE DRIVE AND DESIRE, AND TELL YOURSELF THAT
YOU HAVE ACHIEVED AGAPE. SEXUAL EXPRESSION OF LOVE
IS AS VALID AND BENEFICIAL AS ANY OTHER, BUT BECAUSE
OF CULTURAL PRESSURES AND EXPECTATIONS IT IS MORE
SUBJECT TO MAYA THAN ALMOST ANY OTHER ASPECT OF
HUMAN LIFE. IT IS ALSO ONE OF THE MOST COMPELLING
FACTORS OF THE PHYSICAL PLANE, AND AS SUCH, CANNOT
AND SHOULD NOT BE SACRIFICED TO CULTURAL COMPUL-
SIONS. BEFORE YOU CAN EXPERIENCE AGAPE, YOU MUST

LEARN TO EXPERIENCE PERSONAL LOVE, AND THE FIRST
EXPRESSIONS OF IT WILL BE PHYSICAL, USUALLY SEXUAL.
WE MUST EMPHASIZE THAT ALL ASPECTS OF SEXUALITY
WILL BE EXPERIENCED DURING THE CYCLES, THOSE SEXUAL
RELATIONSHIPS APPROVED BY YOUR SOCIETY AND THOSE
THAT ARE NOT.

Does that mean that homosexuality is part of essence
growth?

IT CAN BE. ALL OF YOU WILL HAVE HOMOSEXUAL LIVES.
HOWEVER, YOU DO NOT SPECIFICALLY CHOOSE TO BE
EITHER HOMOSEXUAL OR HETEROSEXUAL BEFORE REBIRTH
BUT YOU DO TO SOME EXTENT SET UP THE CIRCUMSTANCES
THAT LEAD TO THIS CHOICE. THE CHOICE TO BE HOMOSEX-
UAL OR HETEROSEXUAL IS MADE VERY EARLY IN LIFE, USU-
ALLY BEFORE THE THIRD YEAR—YOUR PSYCHOANALYSTS
ARE RIGHT ABOUT THAT. THIS CHOICE IS USUALLY FINAL
AND IRREVOCABLE AND LATER ATTEMPTS TO ALTER IT
EITHER WAY ARE VERY RARELY SUCCESSFUL. IN YOUR CUL-
TURE THERE ARE OTHER FACTORS INFLUENCING THESE
CHOICES, WHICH ARE MADE SO EARLY IN CHILDHOOD THAT
THE PERSONALITY IS ILL-EQUIPPED TO MAKE THEM. ON THE
FRINGE OF THIS ARE THE TRUE BISEXUAL OR AMBISEXUAL
PEOPLE WHO ARE WITHOUT EXCEPTION OLDER SOULS WHO
HAVE LOST THEIR STRONG SENSE OF GENDER IDENTITY AND
HAVE FREED THEMSELVES UP TO LOVE WHOEVER COMES
ALONG IN WHATEVER WAY SEEMS MOST APPROPRIATE AT
THE PRESENT MOMENT. REMEMBER THAT EVEN JESUS SAID
YOU SHOULD LOVE ONE ANOTHER.

What about "carrying a torch" for someone? Isn't that
limiting?

MATURE SOULS OFTEN TORCH-BURN FOR THEIR ENTIRE
LIVES. THIS IS NOT UNUSUAL FOR INTELLECTUALLY CEN-
TERED INDIVIDUALS WHEN THEY ARE FIRST IN TOUCH WITH
HIGHER EMOTIONS. REJECTION, OR THE SENSE OF REJEC-
TION, PRODUCES THIS IN SOULS WHO STILL CLING TO THE
CONCEPT OF EROS, AND THE CONCEPT OF CHOOSING WHOM
TO LOVE.

Is that why so many renewed relationships are disappointing?

YOU CAN ONLY DUPLICATE THE ENERGY OUTPUT. YOU
CANNOT DUPLICATE THE CIRCUMSTANCES. MANY RELA-
TIONSHIPS SUFFER FROM THIS PROBLEM.

Then why, if it isn't necessary to continue relationships, is there so much difficulty when they end? Where does the bitterness come from?

SOME OF IT IS ANGER AND DISAPPOINTMENT, ESPECIALLY WHEN THERE IS A GREAT DEAL OF FALSE PERSONALITY AND SOCIAL EXPECTATION. BUT THERE IS MORE TO IT THAN THAT. IT IS TRUE THAT WHERE THERE ARE GOOD WORKING RELATIONSHIPS THAT END, A PERIOD OF MOURNING MUST TAKE PLACE. THE EMOTION EXPERIENCED IS GRIEF. THIS IS DIFFICULT TO OVERCOME UNTIL DUPLICATION IS ACCOMPLISHED. YOU MUST ALLOW YOURSELF TO LOVE. YOUNG SOULS WHO LOSE A CHILD THROUGH TRAUMA OR ILLNESS OFTEN SEEK TO REPLACE THAT CHILD AND IN SO DOING, MAKE LIFE MISERABLE FOR THE SECOND CHILD WHO DOES NOT, OF COURSE, REPLACE THE LOST ONE.

Would it help if we could truly remember our past associations with others—those with whom we've had lives together, or the way we incurred karma?

OF COURSE IT WOULD.

Are dreams perhaps a way to learn this?

IN SOME OLD SOULS, DREAMS ARE MEMORIES. OTHERS REEXPERIENCE THIS TO A LESSER DEGREE. IT IS IMPORTANT TO REMEMBER THAT DREAMS ARE VEHICLES FOR MANY THINGS, INCLUDING ASTRAL MEETINGS, AND IT WOULD BE A GREAT MISTAKE TO BELIEVE THAT EVERY DREAM OF THE PAST IS NECESSARILY A MEMORY OF A PAST LIFE. YOU CANNOT EVEN REMEMBER YOUR DREAMS ACCURATELY AND WHAT YOU HAD FOR DINNER LAST THURSDAY.

Is there any other technique?

IF YOU ARE WILLING TO STUDY AND ARE NOT AFRAID OF WHAT YOU MAY DISCOVER, MATURE AND OLDER SOULS CAN LEARN TO SELF-REMEMBER. YOUNG SOULS CAN ALSO DO THIS FOR THEIR IMMEDIATE PAST LIFE WHEN THERE ARE DEBTS OWED AND OWING FROM IT.

What is self-remembering?

SELF-REMEMBERING CAN BE DEFINED AS FOLLOWS: YOU ARE SITTING IN A FIELD. YOU SEE THE SUNLIGHT. YOU SEE IT AND FEEL ITS EFFECT ON YOU. YOU SEE IT AND FEEL ITS EFFECTS ALSO ON THE TREES. YOU CAN SEE AND FEEL ITS EFFECTS ON YOUR ENTIRE PHYSICAL ENVIRONMENT AT ONCE—THE SUNLIGHT FILTERING THROUGH THE TREES, THE SUNLIGHT CALLING THE BEES TO ACTION, THE SUNLIGHT ON

YOUR BACK, THE SUNLIGHT AS RADIANT ENERGY, THE SUN
AS A SOURCE OF LIGHT AND HEAT. YOU CAN HOLD ALL
THESE IMPRESSIONS SEPARATELY AND RECOGNIZE THEM AS
AN INTEGRATED WHOLE. TO DO THIS REQUIRES SEPARATION
FROM MAYA.

Is self-remembering a part of meditation?

NO, BUT IT IS AN EXCELLENT FORM OF CONCENTRATION,
THE HIGHEST FORM, TO BE EXACT. MEDITATION REQUIRES
AN EMPTY HEAD.

Suppose a person dreams they have been shot in the head.
Does that mean it happened, or is this a message from the
essence?

IT COULD BE EITHER. MANY PEOPLE HAVE BEEN SHOT IN
THE HEAD. BUT WE WOULD SAY THAT IN MOST CASES THIS
IS A MESSAGE. IT IS OK TO BE SHOT IN THE HEAD IF YOUR
HEAD IS IN THE RIGHT PLACE WHEN THE SHOT COMES.

Are there many such messages?

THE ESSENCE IS ALWAYS AVAILABLE TO YOU THOUGH
MOST OF YOU CHOOSE TO SHUT IT OUT. YOU FIND IT TOO
DIFFICULT TO LET GO OF THE FAMILIAR PRISON OF FALSE
PERSONALITY.

What does Michael suggest to change this?

OPENNESS WOULD BE THE BEST APPROACH. MANY ARE
QUITE OPEN, BUT THERE ARE STILL SOME CLOSED CORRI-
DORS. SOME OF YOU ARE CONSCIOUS OF THE FUTILITY OF
ANGER, BUT ARE NOT QUITE SURE HOW TO HANDLE WHAT
YOU INTERPRET AS ANGER, SO YOU TEND TO AVOID SITUA-
TIONS WHICH MIGHT GIVE RISE TO THIS. ALSO, YOU HAVE
A TENDENCY NOT TO TRUST YOUR OWN VERIFICATIONS.
YOU HAVE VERIFIED YOUR OWN STATUS AND ARE STILL
UNWILLING TO ADMIT THIS. THIS IS WRONG WORK. DON'T
ACCEPT THE WORDS OR EVALUATIONS OF OTHERS UNTIL YOU
HAVE VERIFIED THEIR STATUS. THIS ABILITY IS WITHIN
YOUR GRASP. YOU KNOW INSTINCTIVELY WHOM TO SEEK
AND HAVE, SO FAR, SOUGHT WITH DISCRIMINATION ON AN
INSTINCTUAL LEVEL. NOW MANY OF YOU CAN LEARN TO
DO IT ON A HIGHER LEVEL. THE KNOWLEDGE IS THERE.

When you become an older soul, do you remember your
experiences more clearly?

YES. THE ABILITY TO RECALL DEPENDS ON THE RATE THE
RIBBONS ARE BURNED.

Where do nightmares fit into this? Are they real experiences remembered, are they messages, are they astral bad trips, what?

THERE IS NO GENERAL ANSWER. MOST NIGHTMARE EX-PERIENCES, HOWEVER, ARE NOT REAL. MOST HAVE TO DO WITH SYMBOLS YOU ARE UNWILLING TO DEAL WITH IN REALITY. WHEN DREAMS ARE MEMORIES, NO MATTER HOW TERRIFYING THE CIRCUMSTANCES, THEY ARE NOT OFTEN FILLED WITH THE MYTHIC AND SYMBOLIC PRESENCES THAT ARE TYPICAL OF NIGHTMARES. IN OTHER WORDS, IF YOU DREAM YOU ARE ATTACKED BY A THREE-HEADED DOG THAT MAULS YOU AND TURNS INTO SERPENTS, AND THEN YOUR FLESH DISSOLVES, STRETCHES OUT LIKE A SWAMP FOR MON-STERS TO LIVE IN, YOU MIGHT CONSIDER THERAPY TO FIND A WAY TO DEAL WITH GUILT. IF YOU DREAM THAT YOU ARE LYING IN A DITCH, THAT THERE IS MUD STICKING TO YOUR FACE, THAT THE AIR IS FILLED WITH THE SOUND OF SCREAMS AND HORSES, AND THERE ARE PEOPLE YELLING THAT THE COSSACKS ARE COMING, IT IS PROBABLE THAT IN SOME PAST LIFE YOU WERE TRAMPLED BY COSSACKS AND LEFT TO DIE IN A DITCH.

It sounds as if studying history would be beneficial. Is it?

RECORDED HISTORY HOLDS THE GREATEST LESSON THAT CAN BE LEARNED, EXCEPT FOR THAT LEARNED AT THE FEET OF THE REALIZED MASTER.

How can we be sure that recorded history is not distorted?

WE WILL LET YOU KNOW. IN THE READING OF HISTORY, YOU MUST ALWAYS ASK YOURSELF WHAT THE HISTORIAN HAS TO GAIN. DOES HE HAVE A POLITICAL POINT OF VIEW HE IS ANXIOUS TO SUPPORT? DOES HE BELIEVE THAT ALL HISTORY HAS AN UNDERLYING THEME, SUCH AS RELIGIOUS SEARCH, ECONOMIC IMBALANCE, CLASS STRUGGLE, SOCIAL DECLINE? THEN WHAT THIS HISTORIAN HAS TO TELL, WHAT HE SELECTS, WILL REFLECT HIS OWN BIAS. YOU MUST RE-MEMBER THAT HISTORY IS A JOURNEY EVERY ONE OF YOU IS MAKING. IT IS NOT THERE FOR THE CONVENIENCE OF THE HISTORIAN.

How would Michael suggest history be studied?

AS THE RECORDS OF LIVES.

Should the approach be religious or scientific?

NEITHER, AND BOTH.

How can it be neither and both? Isn't there conflict be-tween science and religion?

THERE IS NO CONFLICT. RELIGION IS FROM THE EMO-
TIONAL CENTER, SCIENCE MUST BE APPROACHED THROUGH
INTELLECT. IF THERE IS BALANCE, THERE IS NO CONFLICT.
UNDERSTANDING SCIENTIFIC PRINCIPLES IS A WAY TO
HIGHER INTELLECTUAL ENERGY, JUST AS FEELING RELIGION
IS THE WAY TO THE HIGHER EMOTIONAL CENTER. IT IS BOTH
RELIGIOUS AND SCIENTIFIC DOGMA THAT COME FROM FALSE
PERSONALITY AND HAS NO PLACE IN THIS DISCUSSION.

But doesn't the passage of time change things? Surely
we've made some progress over the centuries.

IN THE FIRST PLACE, TIME AS YOU EXPERIENCE IT DOES
NOT EXIST IN THE PANDIMENSIONAL UNIVERSE. TIME IN
THE PHYSICAL PLANE IS SEEN AS THE STATIONARY PLANE
THROUGH WHICH, AROUND WHICH, BENEATH WHICH, THE
PHYSICAL UNIVERSE EVOLVES. SPACE IS A CONCEPT LIMITED
TO THE THREE-DIMENSIONAL PHYSICAL UNIVERSE. THE
PRESENT MOMENT CONTAINS ALL OF THE PAST. THE PRES-
ENT MOMENT CAN BE EXPANDED TO ENCOMPASS ALL THAT
HAS GONE BEFORE. THE PANDIMENSIONAL UNIVERSE EM-
BRACES BOTH THE CONCEPTS OF INFINITY AND ETERNITY,
LIMITLESSNESS AND EXPANSION OUTWARD, AS WELL AS
CONTRACTION INWARD. THE LIMITATIONS THAT YOU PLACE
UPON YOURSELVES, WHICH PREVENT YOU FROM EXPERIENC-
ING THE PANDIMENSIONAL UNIVERSE, WE WOULD DESCRIBE
AS PERHAPS A FIVE-POINT PROGRAM BEGINNING WITH AF-
FECTION, ACCEPTANCE, ASSIMILATION, ABSORPTION, AND
ADAPTATION.

TIME, OR ALL TIME, DOES EXIST, THOUGH NOT IN YOUR
FRAME OF REFERENCE. THE SENSATION OF "TIME PASSING"
IS VERY REAL ON YOUR PLANE. YOU BELIEVE THIS AT A
DEEPER LEVEL, BUT ARE CONFUSED. YOU MAY NEED TO
DUPLICATE THE TYPE OF LIFE THAT ABRAHAM LINCOLN
LIVED, AND WHEN A PARALLEL TIME FRAME EVOLVES, YOU
WILL. THESE TIME FRAMES ARE TWO-THOUSAND-YEAR
CYCLES, FOR THE MOST PART. THE AXIOM "HISTORY RE-
PEATS ITSELF" IS TRAGICALLY TRUE. YOU ARE NOW ON A
PARALLEL TIME FRAME WITH THE REIGN OF CAESAR
AUGUSTUS.

What is so special about every two thousand years?

WE ARE REFERRING TO THE PHILOSOPHICAL CLIMATE EX-
ISTING THEN WHICH HAS NOT EXISTED SINCE, UNTIL VERY
RECENTLY. THIS PHILOSOPHICAL CLIMATE MADE THE CON-

DITIONS RIGHT FOR THE MANIFESTATIONS OF THE INFINITE SOUL. IF YOU WISH SOME PARALLELS BETWEEN THEN AND NOW, WE WILL GLADLY EXPOUND. THE INFINITE SOUL MANIFESTS AT TIMES SUCH AS THIS, WHEN THERE ARE MANY PHILOSOPHICAL STAGNATIONS, RACIAL AND RELIGIOUS STRIFE, AND THE IMMINENT DESTRUCTION OF THAT WHICH BINDS SOCIETY TOGETHER. IN ROME, AS NOW, LIP SERVICE WAS PAID TO RELIGIOUS TOLERANCE, BUT THERE WERE PERIODIC PURGES AND REINSTATEMENT OF THE STATE GODS. THE PARALLEL TO THIS OCCURRED IN NAZI GERMANY. THEY (ROME) HAD POLITICAL PARTIES WHERE THE LINES OF DEMARCATION HAD BECOME SO BLURRED THAT NO ONE QUITE KNEW WHERE HE STOOD. LUXURY WAS VIABLE AND WIDESPREAD AND COULD BE OBTAINED THROUGH LITTLE EFFORT. THE WELFARE STATE CAME INTO EXISTENCE. THEN CITIES WERE CROWDED AND THE CITY DWELLERS WERE ALIENATED FROM EACH OTHER. THERE WAS A DETERIORATION OF THE FAMILY AND THE RATIO OF DISTURBED CHILDREN WAS COMPATIBLE WITH THE FIGURE NOW. THE WOMEN'S LIBERATION MOVEMENT WAS CAUSING FEAR IN THE MEN AND THEY WERE SO WORRIED ABOUT THEIR VIRILITY THAT THEY HAD LITTLE INTEREST IN ANYTHING ELSE. THIS BROUGHT ABOUT MANY SMALL WARS THAT WERE FOUGHT ON THE BATTLEGROUNDS RATHER THAN IN THE BEDROOMS. DOES THAT SOUND FAMILIAR? WALKING INTO A LATRINE DURING THE FIRST CENTURY OF THIS ERA WOULD NOT BE AN UNFAMILIAR EXPERIENCE FOR ANY OF YOU. YOU WOULD BE RIGHT AT HOME WITH THE GRAFFITI EXHORTING VARIOUS SOLITARY SEXUAL PURSUITS.

Does Michael perceive all time at once, rather the way we watch TV or the movies?

YES.

If time is really synchronous, does that mean that any one of us could be Caesar Augustus in another frame of reference?

THERE WOULD BE NO NEED FOR YOU TO DO THAT. THIS WAS A YOUNG SOUL. YOU CANNOT TRANSCEND THE TIME FRAMES IN THE PHYSICAL BODY. NOR CAN YOU REINCARNATE IN ANOTHER PHYSICAL REALITY. BESIDES, WE HAVE ALREADY TOLD YOU THAT THE SOUL OF AUGUSTUS CAESAR HAS FINISHED ITS LIFE IN THIS CYCLE AS DAG HAMMARSKJÖLD.

Does the current Arab-Israeli conflict have any role in this repetition of cycles?

WHAT WAS OCCURRING ABOUT TWO THOUSAND YEARS AGO IN SYRIA-PALESTINE? WE HAVE TOLD YOU THAT YOU ARE ON A PARALLEL TIME FRAME. THESE VERY ANCIENT ENEMIES HAVE BETTER INSTRUMENTS OF WAR NOW THAN THEN. BOOK BURNING, REAL AND FIGURATIVE, IS REAL. THE ROLE HAS NOT BEEN CHOSEN, BUT IT WAS IN THE PAST.

But if time as we know it does not exist, is there an absolute? Is space just standing still while we're moving through it—space and time?

YOU ARE SAYING THE CORRECT WORDS WITHOUT COMPLETE UNDERSTANDING. THERE IS A TIME AXIS ABOUT WHICH PARALLEL UNIVERSES OF PHYSICAL REALITY REVOLVE. THE PLAY IS ETERNAL.

Chapter 12

MENTAL HEALTH . . .

"Every time I think about the time axis and parallel universes of physical reality, I get to feeling very, very small and a little dizzy," Jessica confides. "The immensity of it scares me. I feel like a tiny doll hanging in the dark with nothing around me for more miles than I have numbers for. When Michael first started talking about the nature of time, I'd wake up screaming at night. It was too vast for me."

Is it still?

"On some levels, yes it is. But I've become familiar with the concepts and it isn't as difficult to deal with, not on the board. I don't like to think about what it really means. I'm probably being cowardly, but I can't handle it, really I can't. If I had to be fully aware of the scope of space and time when I'm in touch with Michael, I don't think I could manage it. Luckily, Michael doesn't insist that I work on that level."

"I think it's exciting," Lucy puts in. "But then, I don't work the board, so I don't get the whole impact the way Jessica does."

"When I was working the board with Jessica," Walter says, "I had an inkling of Michael's frame of reference. Part of me is glad that I didn't keep on with the board because

I know it would be very hard for me to handle all that enormity. The other part of me wishes I had had the nerve to do it, no matter what."

"It reminds me of that part of the Book of Job where God speaks to Job out of the whirlwind about laying the foundations of the earth when the morning stars sang together, and all that about eagles and horses and Leviathan. I'm not quite like Job," Jessica says. "I'm not about to repent being what I am, but I find it hard to think of myself as important outside of a very small circle."

Isn't that rather daunting?

"At first it was. It's like anything else, I guess. Given enough time, you will get used to it." Jessica leans back in her bentwood rocker and stares up at the beamed ceiling. "For a while there, it was rough going. I kept wondering why any of us even bother. Life, meaning the total sum of all lives, all the cycles, is so insignificant next to the Tao. It's easy to see why some people get so far into studies like these and then give up. A lot of people who started in our group, and were really serious, got a little way into it and then gave it up. They didn't want to deal with insignificance. They found it easier to deal with terrible abuses and disaster and their own debts than to face the eternal hugeness."

Do such things drive them crazy?

"You can retreat without going crazy," Jessica says mildly. "Though Michael has spoken about madness, of course."

What circumstances lead to nervous breakdowns, schizophrenia, depression, compulsion, autism, and all the other mental and emotional disasters?

NERVOUS BREAKDOWN IS A VERY GENERAL TERM USED FOR A GREAT MANY DISORDERS, BUT IT OFTEN REFERS TO A RETREAT. IN YOUNG AND BABY SOULS, THE RETREAT IS FROM MANY OF THE PRESSURES OF FALSE PERSONALITY AGAINST THE ESSENCE. IN MATURE SOULS, SUCH RETREATS ARE FROM THEIR PERCEPTIONS OR FROM THOSE AROUND THEM WITH BAD OVERLEAVES.

COMPULSIVE BEHAVIOR AND NEUROTIC ADJUSTMENTS ARE OFTEN THE PRODUCT OF BAD OVERLEAVES.

SCHIZOPHRENIA IS A CHEMICAL IMBALANCE OF THE BODY AND CAN BE CORRECTED WITH LITHIUM. THOSE WHO HAVE BEEN SCHIZOPHRENIC REQUIRE PATIENCE WHILE THEY AD-

JUST, SINCE THE BODY, ONCE IT HAS THE CHEMICAL HABIT OF SCHIZOPHRENIA, WILL CLING TO ITS LEARNED PATTERNS EVEN THOUGH THE IMBALANCE IS NO LONGER PRESENT.

AUTISM MOST OFTEN IS FOUND IN INFANT AND EARLY-LEVEL BABY SOULS WHO ARE IN RETREAT FROM THINGS AND PERSONS THAT FRIGHTEN THEM.

MOST PEOPLE WHO ARE CONSIDERED NEUROTICS ARE MATURE SOULS. EXAMINE THE NATURE OF THE CYCLES AND YOU WILL SEE THAT THIS IS TRUE.

ALCOHOLICS, MEANING THOSE WHO SUFFER FROM THE DISEASE OF ALCOHOLISM AND NOT SIMPLY THOSE WHO ARE DRUNKARDS . . .

What is the difference?

ALCOHOLICS DRINK TO ACHIEVE ANESTHESIA, TO BLOT OUT THINGS THAT THEY CANNOT DEAL WITH. MOST ALCOHOLICS ARE MATURE SOULS, OFTEN WITH BABY OR YOUNG-SOUL PARENTS WHOSE EXPECTATIONS FOR THEIR CHILD ARE UNREALISTIC. THE MATURE SOUL SENSES THOSE EXPECTATIONS, KNOWS THAT HE CANNOT AND DOES NOT WANT TO FULFILL THEM, BUT BECAUSE OF THE NATURE OF HIS PERCEPTIONS, IS UNABLE TO RESOLVE THE CONFLICT HE PERCEIVES. YOUNG SOULS BECOME HEAVY DRINKERS FOR MORE SOCIAL REASONS, AND IF THEY DRINK HEAVILY, WILL ENCOURAGE THOSE AROUND THEM TO DO LIKEWISE. REMEMBER THAT THE MOTTO OF THE YOUNG SOUL IS "DO IT MY WAY." THAT APPLIES TO ALL THINGS. YOUNG SOULS ALSO DRINK WHEN FRUSTRATED. OLD SOULS ARE LIKELY TO DRINK FROM BOREDOM OR AS A PART OF DEPRESSION.

ALTHOUGH ALL THE CYCLES CAN BECOME DEPRESSED, DEPRESSION IS THE ONLY SERIOUS DISORDER OF THE OLD SOUL. DEPRESSION CAN ARREST GROWTH FOR A LIFETIME.

Where does psychoanalytic theory fit into all this?

MOST OF THE FOUNDERS OF PSYCHOANALYSIS WERE MATURE SOULS. WE HAVE ALREADY TOLD YOU THAT FREUD WAS A MATURE PRIEST. THE CONCEPTS OF PSYCHOANALYSIS ARE THE PRODUCTS OF MATURE SOULS AND ARE MOST EFFECTIVE WITH MATURE SOULS, FOR THE TREATMENT REFLECTS MOST HEAVILY THE NATURE OF THEIR PERCEPTIONS. YOUNG SOULS CAN BENEFIT FROM PSYCHOANALYSIS BUT ARE NOT APT TO CHANGE THEIR WAYS; THEY JUST ACQUIRE LABELS FOR THEIR BEHAVIOR, WHICH IS OFTEN SUFFICIENT TO HANDLE THEM. OLD SOULS ARE OFTEN IN NEED OF

GUIDANCE, BUT THEY ARE MORE LIKELY TO SEEK IT THROUGH MORE UNORTHODOX MEANS, SUCH AS OCCULT STUDIES, MEDITATION, AND THE ARTS.

Michael says that most of the founders of psychoanalysis were mature souls. Who are the mavericks?

THE MAN CARL GUSTAV JUNG WAS A FIFTH-LEVEL OLD SAGE. IF YOU READ HIS WRITINGS, YOU WILL NOTICE THE DIFFERENCE IN HIS PERCEPTIONS AND EXPRESSION.

Does this refer to his theories of the collective unconscious?

WE DISLIKE THE TERM "UNCONSCIOUS." IT IS MEANINGLESS. THE SOUL IS ETERNALLY VIGILANT. THE FALSE PERSONALITY DOES NOT HAVE THE CAPACITY FOR BECOMING CONSCIOUS.

WHEN CARL JUNG DESCRIBED THE COLLECTIVE CONSCIOUS HE WAS DESCRIBING HIS OWN APPREHENSION OF THE COLLECTIVE FRAGMENTS OF HIS ENTITY, PARTICULARLY THOSE NOT PRESENTLY INCARNATE. HE WAS DESCRIBING A DIRECT CONFRONTATION WITH HIS OWN SOUL. THIS HAS BECOME KNOWN POPULARLY AS THE SUBCONSCIOUS, SIMPLY THROUGH MISUNDERSTANDING. THROUGH THE AGES THERE HAVE BEEN OLD SOULS MAKING THIS CONFRONTATION AND ATTEMPTING TO DESCRIBE IT. HE CAME CLOSER THAN MOST WESTERNERS. MYSTICISM HAS NEVER BEEN A COMPELLING FORCE IN WESTERN PHILOSOPHY.

It was Freud's contention that depression is internal flagellation. How does that fit in with what Michael has said about mental and emotional disorder?

DEPRESSION IS NORMALLY THE PASSIVE PERSONALITY'S ONLY CHANNEL THROUGH WHICH IT CAN EXPRESS HOSTILITY. THE ANGER CAN BE SELF-DIRECTED, BUT IT DOES NOT HAVE TO BE.

What about complete, raving madness?

WE WOULD HAVE TO BE ASKED ON AN INDIVIDUAL BASIS. MADNESS OF THIS KIND IS A VERY PERSONAL MATTER.

What about those who are cataleptic?

THEY ARE, OBVIOUSLY, IN RETREAT. OFTEN THE SOUL RETREATS COMPLETELY FROM THE BODY, ABANDONING IT BEFORE DEATH.

Then people can live without souls?

THE BODY CAN FUNCTION WITHOUT ONE, OF COURSE.

THERE ARE SOME WHO ARE CLASSED AS MENTALLY DIS-
TURBED, WHO USUALLY LIVE VERY RESTRICTED AND INSTI-
TUTIONALIZED LIVES, WHO SEEM TO HAVE "NO ONE HOME."
OFTEN THE SOUL HAS ABANDONED THE BODY, OR HAS RE-
TREATED TO THE ASTRAL PLANE, LEAVING BEHIND ONE
WHO IS TO ALL INTENTS AND PURPOSES AN AUTOMATON.
WE ARE NOT DESCRIBING THOSE WHO ARE QUIESCENT FOR
LONG PERIODS AND THEN DEVELOP SUDDEN RAGES. THOSE
ARE A DIFFERENT MATTER ENTIRELY.

What about those who are considered antisocial?

AGAIN IT WOULD DEPEND ON THE PARTICULAR INDIVID-
UAL. OCCASIONALLY TEENAGERS ARE SO LABELED WHEN
THEY BEGIN TO BREAK AWAY FROM THE IMPRINTING OF
THEIR PARENTS BUT HAVE NOT YET MANIFESTED IN ES-
SENCE. THIS CULTURE MAKES THAT TRANSITION UNNECES-
SARILY DIFFICULT, SO THE TRANSITION IS MORE DISRUPTIVE
THAN IN SOME OTHER CULTURES. THERE ARE OTHER FEEL-
INGS, HOWEVER, THAT ARE SOCIALLY UNACCEPTABLE THAT
ARE NOT TRULY BAD.

UNFORTUNATELY, WHAT THE ESSENCE WISHES OFTEN
CONFLICTS WITH WHAT SOCIETY HAS TOLD THE PERSON-
ALITY IT IS "NICE" TO WISH. FOR INSTANCE, IT IS CER-
TAINLY NOT NICE THAT A BURDENSOME RELATIVE SHOULD
DIE, AND THEREBY FREE THE ESSENCE FOR ITS WORK. IT IS
MERELY SAD THAT COMMUNICATION ON THE PHYSICAL
PLANE IS SO BAD—PARTICULARLY BETWEEN THOSE BOUND
TOGETHER BY LEGAL TIES RATHER THAN ESSENCE TIES—
THAT THE NEED FOR FREEDOM CANNOT BE EXPRESSED. OF
COURSE, IT IS NOT POSSIBLE FOR A PERSON TO HASTEN SOME-
THING LIKE THIS WITHOUT OVERT ACTION ON THEIR PART,
SO THE AMOUNT OF GUILT IS INAPPROPRIATE, TO SAY THE
LEAST. IT IS NOT AN UNUSUAL WISH FOR ONE WHO IS IN-
VOLVED IN THE WORK OF THE ESSENCE. IT IS, AGAIN,
MERELY A SAD COMMENTARY ON THE PHYSICAL PLANE THAT
COMMUNICATION IS SO POOR. IT IS HOPED THAT WITH THIS
CADRE, FOR INSTANCE, A TRUST LEVEL WILL BE DEVELOPED
WHERE THESE CONFLICTS WILL FADE AWAY. WHEN THE
TRUST LEVEL IS SUCH THAT ONE STUDENT COULD SAY TO
ANOTHER, "I WISH YOU WOULD DIE AND LEAVE ME ALONE,"
THAT STATEMENT WILL BE TOTALLY UNNECESSARY AS THE
OTHER STUDENT WILL ALREADY KNOW TO GIVE THE NEC-

ESSARY SPACE. THIS CAN ONLY BE GAINED BY THE HIGHEST OF TRUST LEVELS, AND COMES THROUGH HARD WORK. THIS IS PERTINENT TO YOU ALL.

THOSE WHO ASSUME THAT THIS IS PERMISSION TO KILL THEIR RICH GRANDMOTHER SO THAT THEY CAN INDULGE THEIR GREED WILL FIND THE KARMA VERY HEAVY. MURDER IS A VERY MAJOR KARMIC RIBBON.

What about occasional disturbances, life-crises as differentiated from continuing disturbance?

VERY DEFINITELY IN EACH LIFE THERE ARE PLATEAUS TO BE REACHED AND NEW CLIFFS TO CLIMB. THE CLIMB TO ACHIEVE NEW EXPERIENCE IS CHOSEN FOR THE PARTICULAR LIFETIME AND IS MARKED BY RESTING PLACES WHERE IT APPEARS THAT NOT MUCH IS HAPPENING, THEN ALL OF A SUDDEN THE SOUL IS GALVANIZED INTO ACTION. THIS ALWAYS HERALDS THE APPROACH OF A MAJOR MONAD IN THE SOUL'S LIFE AND IS MANY TIMES MARKED BY A CHANGE THAT CAN BE SEEN BY FRIENDS, OFTEN NEGATIVELY AS THE FRAGMENT ENTERS INTO A NEW PHASE OF LIFE AND READIES ITSELF FOR THE NEXT EXPERIENCE. THE MAJOR MONAD MOST FREQUENTLY WRITTEN ABOUT WOULD BE THE ONE WHICH OCCURS AROUND AGE THIRTY-FIVE AND CAUSES THE SOUL LEVEL TO MANIFEST CLEARLY. AT THIS TIME MOST OF THOSE OBSERVING DO SEE THE CHANGE AND ARE OFTEN HORRIFIED BY THE CONSEQUENCES AS "THAT NICE LITTLE GIRL" GOES OFF THE DEEP END.

Would the manifestation be regarded as neurotic?

IF YOU CONSIDER THE NUMBER OF WOMEN RECEIVING THERAPY COMPARED TO THE NUMBER OF MEN, YOU WILL KNOW THE ANSWER TO THAT. WHAT IS CONSIDERED MATURING IN MEN IS OFTEN THOUGHT TO BE NEUROTIC IN WOMEN AND THERE ARE FORMIDABLE PRESSURES TO STAMP IT OUT. MATURE-SOUL WOMEN ARE MOST VULNERABLE TO THIS AND MAY BECOME NEUROTIC BECAUSE OF THE NATURE OF THE PERCEPTIONS OF THE CYCLE. BABY-SOUL WOMEN RARELY VENTURE BEYOND THE BOUNDS SET FOR THEM BY THEIR CULTURE. OLD SOULS WILL ACCEPT JUST SO MUCH AND THEN THROW THE WHOLE THING OVER. DEPRESSION OFTEN RESULTS.

What about with men? Is their manifestation considered neurotic?

IT DEPENDS ON WHAT THE MANIFESTATION IS. A PER-

FECTLY SERIOUS ACADEMIC MAY TURN AROUND AND BE-COME A PRIEST, WHICH, THOUGH PUZZLING, IS QUITE AC-CEPTABLE, BECAUSE BOTH THE ACADEMIC AND THE PRIEST ARE RESPECTABLE MEMBERS OF THE SOCIETY. A STOCK-BROKER MAY DECIDE TO TAKE UP ANTHROPOLOGY, WHICH IS PECULIAR, BUT STILL ACCEPTABLE. A LAWYER DECIDING TO BECOME A POTTER IS LESS ACCEPTABLE, AND A DENTIST WHO GIVES IT ALL UP TO DO SCULPTURE IN STONE IS GOING TO FIND THAT MOST OF THOSE AROUND HIM WILL THINK THAT HE HAS GONE CRAZY. WE KNOW OF ONE MATURE SOUL WHO HAS CHANGED PROFESSIONS THREE TIMES, EACH TIME REQUIRING EXTENSIVE AND COSTLY EDUCATION, IN SEARCH FOR THE EXPRESSION OF HIS MANIFESTATION.

Is there only that one major crisis associated with an individual life?

NO, THERE ARE OTHERS.

Seven?

OF COURSE. THE FIRST IS BIRTH, WHEN THE BODY IS EN-SOULED.

The body is ensouled at birth? Not before?

NO, NOT BEFORE. THE BEHAVIOR IN UTERO IS A FUNC-TION OF BODY TYPE.

THE SECOND MONAD—OR, IF YOU WOULD PREFER TO IDENTIFY IT IN ANOTHER WAY, WE WILL CALL IT A MILE-STONE—OCCURS WHEN THE FRAGMENT REALIZES THAT IT IS SURROUNDED BY OTHERS WHO ARE DISTINCT AND DIF-FERENT FROM ITSELF AND THAT THOSE OTHERS CAN INFLU-ENCE IT EMOTIONALLY AND INTELLECTUALLY AS WELL AS INSTINCTIVELY. THIS MILESTONE USUALLY TAKES PLACE AT ABOUT AGE TWO. OBVIOUSLY, IN VERY YOUNG SOULS THIS RECOGNITION IS LESS REALIZED THAN IN OLDER SOULS.

THE THIRD MILESTONE OCCURS AT THE ONSET OF YOUNG ADULTHOOD WHEN THE FRAGMENT IS OUT OF "THE NEST." ALL OF CHILDHOOD OCCURS BETWEEN THE SECOND AND THE THIRD MILESTONE.

THE FOURTH MILESTONE IS THE SO-CALLED MID-LIFE CRI-SIS THAT OCCURS AROUND AGE THIRTY-FIVE AT THE MANI-FESTATION OF THE ESSENCE.

THE FIFTH MILESTONE OCCURS IN LIFE WHEN THE FRAG-MENT IS A "SENIOR CITIZEN," AND HAS TO DO IN PART WITH THE RECONCILIATION OF THE ASPIRATIONS WITH THE AC-COMPLISHMENTS OF THE PARTICULAR LIFE.

THE SIXTH OCCURS AT THE TIME OF THE ONSET OF THE FINAL PHYSICAL DETERIORATION AND IS CONCERNED WITH THE DYNAMICS OF THE DYING PROCESS.

THE SEVENTH, OF COURSE, IS THE EXIT ITSELF.

IT SHOULD BE NOTED HERE THAT IF THIS PROCESS IS INTERRUPTED DURING A LIFETIME, FOR INSTANCE BY VIOLENT OR EARLY DEATH FROM ILLNESS, THE FRAGMENT RARELY ADVANCES A LEVEL. A FRAGMENT CAN USUALLY ADVANCE THROUGH A LEVEL OF EXPERIENCE ONLY BY GOING THROUGH THE ENTIRE PROCESS.

Is this inevitably the case?

NO. THERE ARE TIMES WHEN THE AGREEMENTS REQUIRE OTHER EXPERIENCES. WE REMIND YOU THAT YOU MUST EXPERIENCE ALL OF LIFE, SO THERE WILL BE TIMES THAT YOU WILL CHOOSE TO DIE YOUNG, TO DIE VIOLENTLY, TO DIE OF ILLNESS, TO INTERRUPT A LEVEL SO THAT FURTHER LEARNING MAY OCCUR. THERE ARE ALSO THE KARMIC RIBBONS TO BE BURNED AND THEY OCCASIONALLY ENTAIL THE EARLY TERMINATION OF A LIFE. BECAUSE OF THIS A FRAGMENT WILL SOMETIMES REQUIRE TWO LIVES OF A VERY SIMILAR NATURE TO COMPLETE THE MONADS. THERE IS ONE MEMBER OF THIS CADRE WHOSE PREVIOUS TWO LIVES WERE ACTUALLY THE COMPLETION OF ONE LIFE. IN BOTH LIVES, THE FRAGMENT OPPOSED THE POLITICAL SYSTEM, WHICH WAS IN UPHEAVAL, FOR HUMANITARIAN AND PHILOSOPHICAL REASONS, AND IN BOTH LIVES DIED AS A RESULT, AT AGE TWENTY-SEVEN. THE LATTER LIFE WAS A COMPLETION OF THE MONADS OF THE EARLIER LIFE.

Does this happen very often?

WE WOULD SAY SO, YES.

Jessica sighs. "Having just gone through that fourth monad, I know how difficult it can be. I was lucky though, since my work is appropriate for my soul type—scholar—and age—old."

Lucy shakes her head. "It wasn't so easy for me. Old sages in the passion mode, well, my life really seemed to come apart when I went through that mid-life thing. I'm not entirely over it yet."

Walter agrees. "It's a very difficult time, but I remember when I was through it, I felt as if I'd freed myself from all sorts of limitations and encumbrances that had been weighing me down." He looks around him at the high-ceilinged living room and grins proudly. "My therapy for myself during that transition was building this house."

"That's true," Jessica says. "Walter and I designed this house to be a place that we would like to live, and then Walter built it. I really love this house."

"So do I," Walter says emphatically.

Did any of the others in the group have difficulty with this monad?

Emily, who is now forty-one, shakes her head. "Difficulty doesn't begin to describe it. It was terrifying. Every time I thought I had something settled, the rug was pulled out from under me. My school changed their policy about the classes in English as a second language, and I ended up teaching at a different school, with older kids. My brother and I had awful fights. My oldest daughter almost drove me demented . . ."

"She was going through the third monad, the out-of-the-nest monad, while Emily was going through the fourth, or mid-life monad," Craig explains. "I'd gone through the same thing Emily went through about two years before, and I could see what was happening. That doesn't mean that it was any easier, but at least I realized that this was a perfectly normal transition, so I didn't panic. Well, not too much."

"I'm glad you added that," Emily says. "During that time, the one thing I did that really helped me was that I went back to school and began work on my Ph.D. I'll have the degree in another year, and then I can approach teaching from a more effective level. I want to be in a position to make decisions about how our teaching is done and the only way I can do that is with the Ph.D."

Does Emily feel that she has made progress?

Her answer is cautious. "Well, I *think* I have but I don't have any real proof yet. Most of the change has been inward, so far. In two or three years, I should have some outward indications, as well."

"Oh, there've been indications," Craig says. "You're less easily manipulated than you were five years ago, you're less willing to assume that other people have more right to make demands on your time than you do, and you're less willing to settle for less than what you want. It's great."

"You've changed your attitudes, too," Emily reminds

him. "Five years ago, you didn't *want* me to be so assertive."

"That's true," Craig admits. "When we first began the sessions, I was certain that Michael would tell us things that would fit everything into pigeonholes. You can say that the overleaves are pigeonholes, but they aren't. They're indications of a basic perspective. I've found that my own work with the board has been very helpful in my practice. I like to think that more of my patients have recovered and become truly well because of what Michael has told me, through the board."

How long has Craig been working his board?

"About five years. I had trouble with it at first because I didn't know the kinds of questions to ask."

Was there any specific breakthrough for Craig?

"Yes, as a matter of fact, there was. One of my colleagues had a patient, an older woman who had a history of operations, particularly for various stones, and at the time she seemed to be suffering from a common gallstone. My colleague was beside himself and finally came to me in hopes that I could find out something that would help. Michael gave him an answer."

IF YOU DO NOT OPERATE ON THIS BABY SOUL, SOMEONE ELSE WILL. SHE IS ADDICTED TO POLY SURGERY AS A MEANS OF VENTING HER ANGER.

"Well, my colleague didn't think he should be called upon to exorcise her gastrointestinal demons without a real stone to be removed."

WHETHER OR NOT SHE HAS A STONE IS IMMATERIAL TO THIS DISCUSSION. HOWEVER, SOME OF THESE UNFORTUNATE BABY SOULS ARE STONE FORMERS PAR EXCELLENCE. IF THIS WOMAN HAS A STONE REMOVED FROM ONE DUCT, SHE WILL FORM ONE ELSEWHERE. WE KNOW OF SEVERAL SUCH SOULS IN YOUR IMMEDIATE AREA, AND ALL OF THEM HAVE THE SAME PATTERN. IT IS AS IF THEY ARE WILLING FOR THEIR BODIES TO TURN TO STONE SO THAT THEY WILL NOT HAVE TO DEAL WITH THE THINGS THAT DISTURB THEM AND WILL AT THE SAME TIME GARNER A GREAT DEAL OF ATTENTION. MOST OF THOSE WHO HAVE A NEED FOR REPETITIONS OF SUCH SURGICAL PROCEDURES HAVE A CHIEF FEATURE OF MARTYRDOM.

"I had another patient a few years ago, suffering from cancer, and nothing I did—nothing—seemed to do any good. So I asked Michael about her."

YOU CAN HELP HER TO FIND THE SOURCE OF HER RESENTMENTS. MOST, BUT NOT ALL, CANCER VICTIMS HAVE A PERVASIVE SENSE OF SHAME OVER INCONSEQUENTIAL HAPPENINGS. THIS IS TRULY ONE OF THE MOST SELF-DESTRUCTIVE PROCESSES WE KNOW OF. MORE OF THESE UNFORTUNATE PEOPLE HAVE A SENSE OF NO ACCOMPLISHMENT OR A SENSE OF BEING DIRECTED BY OTHERS; THEIR LIVES ARE OUT OF THEIR CONTROL. THE CANCER IS OFTEN THE ONLY ESCAPE. MANY OF THESE PEOPLE GIVE AN OUTWARD APPEARANCE OF SUCCESS, SOME EVEN TRANQUILLITY. THE TARGET ORGAN IS OFTEN THE SEAT OF THE CONFLICT. THIS IS ESPECIALLY TRUE WITH THE REPRODUCTIVE ORGANS.

WE WOULD HOPE THAT YOU, CRAIG, WOULD TRY TO INSTILL IN HER A SENSE OF WORTH AND ENERGY. WE FEEL THAT YOU HAVE MUCH PROMISE IN THIS AREA.

"If she understands the source of her resentments, could she be cured?" Craig asked.

IF SHE CHOOSES TO GIVE UP THE RESENTMENT. IT IS HER CHOICE, AS YOU KNOW.

"But is she conscious of the resentment? If she isn't aware of it, is it possible to have such a breakthrough with her?" Craig pursued.

SHE IS NOT CONSCIOUS OF THE RESENTMENT.

Emily listened to this and interjected a question. "Is there someone else who might be able to do a better job? Craig is working very hard, and it's been frustrating as well as disheartening."

THE TRUST BETWEEN HEALER AND PATIENT MUST BE EXTREMELY HIGH. IN OTHER WORDS, SHE MUST HAVE A BELIEF IN HER PHYSICIAN'S ABILITY TO HEAL HER. WITH HER CURRENT STATE OF MIND, IT IS UNLIKELY THAT SHE WILL FEEL SUCH TRUST IN ANYONE.

"This is also a diagnostic problem," Craig said. "There is some question as to whether there are two locations or one."

THERE IS ONE PRIMARY TARGET AREA—THE COLON.

"We've had a great deal of difficulty controlling her pain," Craig went on. "She's terrified of it, and she insists that the drugs she is receiving are not sufficient to stop it. Certainly I don't want to see her suffer, but it seems to me that her fear is worse than the pain."

MOST PERSONS WHO HAVE BEEN FORTUNATE ENOUGH NOT TO HAVE HAD MUCH PAIN ARE TERRIBLY AFRAID OF IT. IT IS MORE OF THE SAME OLD FEAR OF THE UNKNOWN, COMPLICATED BY THE BODY'S DESIRE TO AVOID PAIN. ALL OF YOUR LITERATURE IS RESPLENDENT WITH GRUESOME ACCOUNTS OF AGONIES ASSOCIATED WITH THIS DISEASE. WE ARE NOT SURPRISED THAT IT IS FEARED.

THIS PARTICULAR FRAGMENT IS A MATURE WOMAN, MID-CYCLE, SHE HAS NEVER COME TO TERMS WITH HER ESSENCE AND THE DRAG OF FALSE PERSONALITY IS VERY STRONG IN HER.

"I wish," Craig sighed, "that I could just lay my hands on her and make her well again. I can certainly understand the attraction of faith healers."

YOU HAVE BEEN A FAITH HEALER BEFORE. THERE HAVE BEEN PATIENTS IN THIS LIFE THAT YOU LITERALLY SNATCHED FROM THE JAWS OF DEATH BEFORE. THIS COULD NOT HAVE BEEN REPEATED. IT WAS NOT IN THEIR KARMA TO SURVIVE. NOTHING YOU COULD HAVE DONE WOULD HAVE MADE MUCH DIFFERENCE. WE REMIND YOU THAT THIS KNOWL-EDGE IS NOT ALWAYS CONSCIOUS. THE ESSENCE, HOWEVER, RECOGNIZES THE CHOICES AND KARMA OF OTHERS IF IT IS ALLOWED TO.

"That scared me," Craig admits. "It seemed as if healing meant taking a lot onto yourself."

THAT IS CORRECT.

"It really worried me when it came to one of my patients whom I thought was a hysteric. It was very difficult to deal with this man. Finally I asked Michael if he could clarify the problem for me."

HYSTERIA IS THE PRODUCTION OF AN ABNORMAL STATE, WITH NO DISCERNIBLE STRUCTURAL DEFECT MANIFEST. HYSTERICS ARE CAPABLE OF PRODUCING ALL MANNER OF ORGANIC PHENOMENA WITH NO APPRECIABLE DAMAGE TO THE BODY. EASTER BLEEDINGS ARE AN EXCELLENT EXAM-PLE. THEY ARE RARELY ANEMIC AND YET THEY SOMETIMES HEMORRHAGE COPIOUSLY. THE HYSTERIC ALWAYS GAINS BY PRODUCING THESE PHENOMENA. DISCOVER THE GAIN AND YOU CAN USUALLY HELP THESE MOST UNFORTUNATE SOULS.

SOMETIMES AN INATTENTIVE SPOUSE MUST BE PRESSED INTO SERVICE IN THIS FASHION. USUALLY, HOWEVER, THE HYSTERIC IS A WEAK, UNDERDEVELOPED SOUL AND THE PHENOMENON IS THE ONLY WAY FOR THIS SOUL TO COMPETE WITH THE STRONGER SOULS AROUND IT. IN THESE CASES, IT IS DIFFICULT TO CURE THE HYSTERIA. YOU CANNOT HELP THE SOUL TO GAIN IN STRENGTH.

"That reminded me," Emily says, "of the story in the Bible of the woman who had menstruated for eight years and was at last healed by Jesus. We asked Michael for a comment on her."

IT IS DOUBTFUL THAT ANYONE COULD SURVIVE IF THEY BLED HEAVILY FOR THAT LONG. THIS PARTICULAR PROBLEM IS SYMBOLIC OF SEXUAL PROBLEMS IN GENERAL, MOST OF WHICH ARE HYSTERICAL. MANY WOMEN DO CAUSE PROLONGED UTERINE BLEEDING THROUGH THEIR FEELINGS OF REPULSION AND GUILT.

"That was pretty confusing," Lucy remarks. "One of the ministers at my church had said in a sermon that there was a cosmic function for women, and that the bleeding was part of it."

"Whenever I hear that kind of crap," Jessica puts in, "I just know I'm going to get dumped on. And Michael agrees."

WE MUST REMIND YOU THAT THE SOUL IS WITHOUT GENDER. THERE IS NO "COSMIC SIGNIFICANCE OF WOMEN" BECAUSE BEING FEMALE IS PURELY A FUNCTION OF THE PHYSICAL PLANE. THOSE WHO INSIST THAT GENDER DIFFERENCES HAVE ANY VALIDITY BEYOND THE BODY DO NOT UNDERSTAND THE NATURE OF THE HIGHER PLANES. SUCH ESSENTIALLY MEANINGLESS DISTINCTIONS AS GENDER AND RACE ARE SEIZED UPON BY BABY AND YOUNG SOULS SEARCHING FOR THE OBVIOUS DIFFERENTIATION BETWEEN "ME" AND THOSE WHO ARE "NOT ME," WHOM THE YOUNG SOUL DESIRES EITHER TO MAKE LIKE ITSELF, THROUGH CONVERSION, OR TO REJECT FOR NOT COMING UP TO THE MARK. A FEW MATURE SOULS USE THESE DIFFERENCES TO CLOUD VARIOUS ISSUES WITHIN THEMSELVES. DISCRIMINATION FOR REASONS OF RACE AND GENDER ARE THE MOST PREVALENT AND DESTRUCTIVE EXAMPLES OF THE RULE OF MAYA. NOT SURPRISINGLY, RACE AND GENDER ARE ALSO MOST OFTEN USED FOR THE ENFORCEMENT OF FALSE PERSONALITY.

WE WILL REMIND YOU THAT THESE PREJUDICES OF THE BODY ARE OFTEN EXPRESSED THROUGH THE BODY. THE ESSENCE, AS SUCH, BEING NOT OF THE PHYSICAL PLANE, IS NOT SUBJECT TO ILL HEALTH, EXCEPT BY ASSOCIATION AND EXPERIENCE. IT CANNOT, ITSELF, BECOME DISEASED. ONLY FALSE PERSONALITY IS SUSCEPTIBLE TO ILLNESS. MANY THINGS SUCH AS DIET AND LIFESTYLE MITIGATE AGAINST GOOD HEALTH. EXCESSES OF ANY SORT MITIGATE AGAINST GOOD HEALTH AND, SINCE THOUGHTS ARE THINGS, EXCESS WRONG THINKING MITIGATES AGAINST GOOD HEALTH. JESUS SAID THAT, WE DID NOT. YOU ARE BOMBARDING PHYSICALLY SICK ORGANISMS WITH ORGANIC COMPOUNDS IN SHOTGUN FASHION. ONE THING WITHIN THE GRASP OF TERRAN MEDICINE RIGHT NOW IS THE SUBSTITUTION OF ACOUSTICAL HOLOGRAPHS FOR X-RAY. THIS SHOULD BE DONE SOON. IT IS AVAILABLE NOW. COST IS WHAT IS HOLDING IT BACK. THIS IS A CLEAR-CUT CASE OF SCRAMBLED PRIORITIES.

"The whole idea of the acoustical holograph really amazed me," Craig says. "I've thought for a long time that taking a damaged body, say one suffering from a degenerative disease, and subjecting it to the shock of surgery only compounds the problem. I realize that this is going against the grain of a lot of medical thought now, but this idea of an acoustical holograph might be the answer. Michael gave us more information on it."

HOLOGRAMS ARE MULTIDIMENSIONAL REPRESENTATIONS OF SOLID OBJECTS. THIS IS MADE POSSIBLE BY PASSING THROUGH THE OBJECTS WITH A HIGH-ENERGY SOURCE LIGHT. LIGHT-ACTIVATED, SIMULATED ELECTRON RESPONSE IS ONE METHOD OF USING LIGHT WITHOUT DIFFRACTION. SOUND WAVES CAN ALSO BE USED IF THE DISTORTION CAN BE ELIMINATED THROUGH PROPER SHIELDING OF THE SOURCE. MODULATION IS THE MORE CORRECT TERM. THERE HAS BEEN RESEARCH ON THIS IN YOUR OWN COUNTRY IN THE RECENT PAST.

"The thing that makes this difficult," Craig goes on, "is that I *know* there are better ways to heal, and that the current state of medicine is not the absolute best it can be. I want to find better, more humane ways to practice medicine."

WE HAVE GIVEN YOU A START. YOU MUST BEGIN TO AP-

PROACH YOUR PATIENTS AS SOULS WHO ARE CENTERED IN DIFFERENT PLACES. YOU HAVE VERIFIED FOR YOURSELF THE TRUTH OF CENTERS. NOW YOU MUST VERIFY THE TRUTH OF THE CYCLES. THIS IS PRACTICAL KNOWLEDGE FOR THE OLDER SOUL, NOT JUST IDLE CHATTER. IT SUPERCEDES ALL PREVIOUS INFORMATION. THIS IS THE LESSON YOU MUST LEARN. THE APPROACH MUST BE GOVERNED BY WHAT YOU SENSE INTUITIVELY, GIVEN THIS SPECIAL SKILL.

MOST ILLNESSES ARISE FROM AN EMOTIONAL CAUSE, BUT FROM THESE, ONE MUST EXCLUDE INBORN GENETIC DEFECTS, TRAUMA, INCLUDING THE BITES OF VENOMOUS CREATURES, AND DRUG-INDUCED ILLNESSES THAT ARE IATROGENIC IN ORIGIN.

"By 'iatrogenic' Michael means doctor-caused illnesses, I'm ashamed to say," Craig adds. "Too many of the wrong kinds of drugs, bad mixtures of drugs, therapy with very severe side effects, and the rest of it." He pauses a moment. "I suppose it's because I'm in the caution mode. I don't like to rush things, or try too heroic measures with my patients unless they insist. Even then . . ."

IT WOULD NOT BE INAPPROPRIATE FOR MORE OF YOUR PHYSICIANS TO SHARE THAT CAUTION, Michael told Craig some time ago.

"My partner in practice has very little of that caution," Craig admits. "It makes me nervous. Oh, don't get me wrong, Dan's an excellent surgeon, as competent as they come, but he has very little feeling for people. He treats diseases and often forgets that the diseases are part of a person. I asked Michael about this man a couple of years ago, and Michael said that he was a baby artisan in the power mode with a goal of growth, a pragmatist in the moving part of intellectual center, with a chief feature of exalted arrogance. According to Michael, I'm a fifth-level mature artisan, caution mode, goal of dominance. That feels right. It struck me as odd that a baby soul should be so expert. Michael gave me an explanation."

MEDICINE HAS BEEN AN ART IN THE PAST. THIS IS AN ARTISTIC SOURCE FOR YOUR FRIEND. HIS PERSONAL RELATIONSHIPS ARE LESS MEANINGFUL BECAUSE THEY ARE NOT ARTISTIC. ARTISANS ARE USUALLY COMPETENT. LOOK AT THE ARTISANS IN THIS GROUP. IT IS NOT NECESSARY TO BE A KING OR A PRIEST TO BE COMPETENT OR ACCOMPLISHED

IN ANYTHING. THIS VARIES FROM FRAGMENT TO FRAGMENT. PERSONAL RELATIONSHIPS REQUIRE COMMUNICATION AND IT IS DIFFICULT FOR THE FRAGMENT TO EXPRESS HIMSELF TO OTHERS. HE CANNOT COMMUNICATE WELL WITH LOWERS, PEOPLE NOT PHYSICIANS, AND THUS THE EXPRESSION, BABY SOUL. HE EXPRESSES HIS ARTISTIC QUALITIES IN THE OPERATING ROOM, BEHIND CLOSED DOORS, NOT FROM OPEN DOORS OR FROM HIS HEART IN EMOTIONAL SITUATIONS.

"Both Craig and his partner are artisans, yet they have trouble getting along. Is there also some type of conflict between artisans and sages? My boss is a sage and he drives me nuts. Do they not relate well?" Walter, an old artisan, wanted to know.

MOST OF THE TIME THEY DO. IN THIS CASE, OTHER OVERLEAVES ABRADE.

"Then there are roles that don't get along with each other," Corrine said. "Where are problems likely to occur?"

SCHOLARS AND WARRIORS ARE OFTEN A VERY WORKABLE COMBINATION. THEY BOTH LIKE TO EXPLORE, BUT FOR DIFFERENT REASONS. THE SCHOLAR, BEING THE NEUTRAL ROLE IN ESSENCE, IS SOMETHING LIKE "O" TYPE BLOOD; SCHOLARS CAN DEAL PRETTY WELL WITH MOST OF THE ROLES, PROVIDING OVERLEAVES DO NOT ABRADE. THE PAIRINGS, OBVIOUSLY, GET ALONG WELL. ARTISANS AND SAGES, PRIESTS AND SLAVES, WARRIORS AND KINGS. THERE IS OFTEN DIFFICULTY BETWEEN WARRIORS AND PRIESTS AND SAGES, AND SLAVES HAVE BEEN KNOWN TO HAVE TROUBLE WITH SCHOLARS AND KINGS. BUT THE OVERLEAVES ARE THE CRITICAL FACTORS IN THESE RELATIONSHIPS.

Craig asked the next question. "I would like to know if part of the discomfiture we have is due to our roles?"

YES. THE ROLES YOU CHOSE ARE NO LONGER MET IN THE PROFESSION YOU FOLLOW. THERE WAS A TIME WHEN MEDICINE WAS AN ART.

"Well, is my role as an artist? You speak of medicine as an art, but I find it hard to think of it that way."

AS AN ARTISAN, YES. THIS INCLUDES ALL ART FORMS.

"The strong feelings of creativity that I have—is that false personality that will get in my way, or is it a real part of me?" Maurice Parker, a teacher associate of Emily's, asked.

IT IS NOT NECESSARILY FALSE. IT IS JUST THAT YOU BRING

LESS ORIGINALITY AND MORE ACCUMULATED KNOWLEDGE INTO WHAT YOU DO. THIS FOR YOU IS NATURAL. ARTISTIC TALENT PER SE OCCURS IN ALL THE ROLES TO A DEGREE. THE ARTISAN BRINGS TO LIFE FRESHNESS OF APPROACH AND ORIGINALITY. THE TRUE SAGE BRINGS WISDOM.

"Michael keeps insisting that we have to experience all the aspects of life, yet these roles seem to be self-limiting," David Swan observed.

IT MAY APPEAR SELF-LIMITING; NEVERTHELESS, IT IS POSSIBLE TO EXPERIENCE ALL LIFE IN ALL ROLES. A KING IN ESSENCE WILL NOT ALWAYS HAVE A THRONE. IN FACT, MOST KING ESSENCES NEVER HAVE A THRONE. THEY, LIKE ALL OF YOU, WILL BE COWHERDS AND HERMITS AND LAWYERS AND MOTHERS-IN-LAW AND MINISTERS AND BANDITS. IN SHORT, KING OR NOT, THE ESSENCE WILL STILL DO EVERYTHING.

"Does Michael mean that we change everything, including body-type?" Lucy asked. "I would like to know if, when we 'experience all of life,' it is necessary to incarnate into each body type, each center and goal, and if we don't learn something, have to go over the same thing again?"

THIS IS ESSENTIALLY VALID. IT IS POSSIBLE TO EXPERIENCE ALL OF LIFE FROM ONE BODY TYPE, BUT THE EXPERIENCE IS RICHER IF THE CHANGE IS MADE. MOST SOULS DO CHOOSE DIFFERENT DATES OF BIRTH. THAT GIVES THE NECESSARY CHANGE IN PLANETARY INFLUENCE. IT IS NECESSARY THAT LIFE BE EXPERIENCED BOTH AS MALE AND FEMALE IN DIFFERENT SETTINGS. THIS IS THE MOST IMPORTANT FACTOR AND THE ONE THAT BRINGS THE MONADS TOGETHER. CENTERING IS IMPORTANT ALSO, AND MOST OLD SOULS IN THE LATER CYCLES CHOOSE EMOTIONALLY CENTERED BODIES, AS THIS IS THE CENTER EASIEST TO WORK WITH.

"But what does that have to do with work? You said that the sage soul Augustus Caesar was also Dag Hammarskjöld. I find that rather hard to accept, especially since that would mean he was an international leader twice."

ONCE A SKILL IS LEARNED, IT IS NEVER FORGOTTEN, AND IF THAT EXPERTISE CAN BE OF USE, THE SOUL WILL SEEK THE SAME OCCUPATION AGAIN AND AGAIN SO THAT OTHER MATTERS MAY BE DEALT WITH. IT IS NOT NECESSARY TO CHANGE THE PARTICULAR VOCATION AS MUCH AS THE LO-

CATION. FOR INSTANCE, BEING A PHYSICIAN ON MAINLAND CHINA DOES IN NO WAY RESEMBLE BEING IN PRACTICE IN VALLEJO, CALIFORNIA. CRAIG WOULD BE ABLE TO RELATE TO THE PRACTICE OF MEDICINE IN ANCIENT EGYPT MORE EASILY THAN TO THE RICE PADDIES OF TODAY.

Does Michael have the cure for the common cold?

"No"—Craig smiles—"but he has some insights about it."

WHAT YOU CALL THE COMMON COLD IS A VERY COMPLEX CONDITION, USUALLY ARISING OUT OF THE FRAGMENT'S NEED FOR REST AND NURTURING. FATIGUE, FRUSTRATION, ANXIETY, DESPAIR, EVEN ANGER CAN MAKE THE BODY SUSCEPTIBLE TO THE VARIOUS DISEASE AGENTS THAT ARE ALWAYS IN YOUR ENVIRONMENTS. THIS DOES NOT MEAN THE DISEASE IS NOT GENUINE. IT IS. THE BODY HAS PERFECTLY GENUINE SYMPTOMS AND THE INFECTIONS ARE REAL. THE ROOTS OF THE COLD, HOWEVER, ARE NOT TO BE FOUND IN VIROLOGY, BUT IN THE NATURE OF THE OVERLEAVES OF THE PATIENT. FOR EXAMPLE, IT IS EASIER FOR SAGES TO SUCCUMB TO A COLD THAN IT IS FOR KINGS OR WARRIORS. SOME DISEASES ARE AVOIDANCES, PARTICULARLY OF A THREATENING SITUATION. THE COLD IS CAUSED BY FEAR.

MORE SERIOUS DISEASES ARE OFTEN PART OF MONADS AND SEQUENCES, OR, OCCASIONALLY, A WAY TO AVOID A SEQUENCE. IN SUCH CASES, THE DISEASE IS THE ABDICATION. THE FRAGMENT IS SAYING, "I CAN'T DO WHAT I'VE AGREED TO DO BECAUSE I'M TOO SICK." HEADACHES ARE REPRESSED EMOTIONS. MANY THINGS CAN BE SAID THROUGH THE PAINFUL HEAD. MOST FREQUENTLY A WEARINESS OF THE BODY COUPLED WITH A BORED, TRAPPED ESSENCE WILL PRODUCE THE WORST HEADACHES. YOUNG SOULS FREQUENTLY HAVE MIGRAINE HEADACHES. THEY DO NOT ATTEMPT TO UNDERSTAND THE TREADMILL THEY ARE ON. MATURE SOULS FREQUENTLY HAVE TENSION HEADACHES FROM BEING SURROUNDED BY UNCOMFORTABLE SOULS ALL DAY. MATURE SOULS IN CLOSE CONTACT WITH BABY AND MANY YOUNG SOULS TEND TO HAVE THE MOST FREQUENT AND SEVERE HEADACHES. YOU CAN TREAT THEIR HEADACHES BY HELPING THEM SEE THE SOURCE. WITH YOUNG SOULS, YOU CAN ONLY TREAT THE PAIN.

Sam Chasen, the social worker, had a few related questions.

"Are there people who refuse to be well, who will not be helped, and who truly reject assistance of any kind?"

OF COURSE THERE ARE. EXAMINE THE NATURE OF THE CYCLES AND THE OVERLEAVES, AND YOU CAN SEE THAT SUCH LIVES MUST BE EXPERIENCED. THAT DOES NOT MEAN THAT SUCH PEOPLE MAY BE WHOLLY NEGLECTED WITH IMPUNITY. ONE OF THE ACTS THAT CREATES A KARMIC RIBBON IS ABANDONMENT THAT RESULTS IN THE DEATH OF THE ABANDONED ONE. IF A FRAGMENT IS DETERMINED TO LIVE A LIFE OF MISERY—AND WE REMIND YOU THAT EACH ONE OF YOU WILL HAVE AT LEAST ONE SUCH LIFE—THERE IS LITTLE YOU CAN DO ABOUT IT. HOWEVER, THOSE LIVING SUCH LIVES DO NOT IN GENERAL SEEK THE KIND OF ASSISTANCE THAT YOU, SAMUEL, ARE TRAINED TO GIVE. THOSE WHO REACH OUT TO YOU DO NOT TRULY DESIRE THE MISERY THEY LIVE IN. THEY ARE MOST OFTEN THE VICTIMS OF BAD OVERLEAVES OR MAJOR KARMIC DEBTS. ONE OF THE WOMEN YOU ARE CURRENTLY COUNSELING, A WOMAN WITH THREE RETARDED CHILDREN FOR WHOM SHE MUST CARE, SINCE HER HUSBAND HAS DESERTED HER, IS NOT, AS YOU MIGHT EXPECT, A BABY SLAVE, BUT A YOUNG PRIEST WHO IN HER LAST LIFE WAS A HIGH-RANKING MEMBER OF THE NAZI WAFFEN-SS. SHE IS NOW TRYING TO PAY OFF SOME SERIOUS DEBTS. IN HER LAST LIFE SHE DIED IN A RAILWAY ACCIDENT NEAR THE FRENCH BORDER. YOU CANNOT TAKE HER DEBTS UPON YOU, BUT YOU CAN HELP HER TO DISCHARGE THEM.

Sam Chasen nods. "Since Michael told me about that woman, I've changed how I work with her, and although she's still in a terrible situation, she's willing to deal differently with her life. I doubt she's any happier, but there's a different attitude to her, as if she's really accomplished something. Outwardly, she hasn't, but inwardly, I think she has."

Has what Michael told Sam changed his work in any other way?

Sam grins with a lopsided charm and runs a hand through his sand-colored hair. "Michael's said a lot over the years. I didn't want to accept it at first. It's very hard to give up that certainty and unctuousness that gets trained into most of us in the field. Most social workers are prigs, you know. Well-meaning prigs, but still prigs. When I decided to go back into the psychotherapeutic branch of social work two years ago, I asked Michael's advice. I knew that when I'd done it before I'd been working out of false personality, and I was a little afraid that this time might just be more of the same thing."

THIS IS, OF COURSE, POSSIBLE ONLY IF THE EXPERIENCE ITSELF COMES FROM ESSENCE. THIS WILL REQUIRE THAT YOU EXAMINE YOUR MOTIVATIONS FROM ESSENCE. TRY TO DETERMINE WHY YOU WISH TO DO THIS. IN OTHER WORDS, WHAT IS IN IT FOR YOU? IF IT COMES FROM A SPACE THAT IS GUILTY, THEN FALSE PERSONALITY HAS THE UPPER HAND. DON'T TRY TO GO BACK IN THIS LIFE AND UNWIND RIBBONS. THIS IS NOT THE WAY IT IS DONE. THE WORK YOU DID WAS NOT WHOLLY IN FALSE PERSONALITY, BUT THERE WAS A GREAT DEAL OF GAIN FOR THE PERSONALITY THERE. YOU CAN BE CERTAIN THAT ALL OF THOSE DESIRES ATTACHED TO PHYSICAL OR MATERIAL GAIN EMANATE FROM FALSE PERSONALITY. THIS INCLUDES ACCOLADES AND LAUREL LEAVES.

How does Sam feel about his work now?

"My feelings are mixed," he says with careful consideration. "I can't help it. Part of the trouble is that the way the system is set up, all the aspects of false personality are reinforced. And the immediate rewards of false personality are very alluring, I admit that. When they start giving our commendations for work, I want one, and I can't deny that. When I was passed over for promotion this time, it hurt. I still hate it when I get patronized for being crippled. All those things work against the essence. I've become more philosophical about it, though. I figure that my soul has been around a lot longer than my current false personality, and it's a hell of a lot more durable. It helps a lot, that thought."

"What about kids?" Maurice asked, thinking about the school where he worked. "All this talk about false personality, overleaves, and roles in essence keeps relating to adults, or so it seems. What effect does all this have on children?"

CHILDREN, BEFORE THEY ARE THOROUGHLY PROGRAMMED FOR THEIR SOCIETAL ROLE USUALLY OPERATE FROM ESSENCE AND KNOW THEIR ROLES. THE ROLE THE CHILD FIRST VOICES AS A DESIRE USUALLY COMES FROM ESSENCE—AFTER THAT, FROM FALSE PERSONALITY BASED ON EXPECTATIONS OF THOSE AROUND THE CHILD. TO RE-

TURN TO THIS STATE, OF COURSE, IS A MAJOR PART OF THE GOAL. UNTIL YOU DO, YOU CANNOT SHAKE THE ENTHRALL-MENT OF THE PHYSICAL, MATERIAL PLANE. THE CHILD, ES-PECIALLY THE YOUNG CHILD, OFTEN SEES BEYOND THE VEIL. THIS IS QUICKLY SQUASHED. THE HAPPY CHILDHOOD IS MOSTLY MYTH. IN YOUR CASE, IT WAS A BONA FIDE EX-PERIENCE AND YOUR DESIRE TO RETURN THERE IS GOOD WORK.

"But what happens then? Does false personality just take over and that's that?" Walter asked.

THERE IS A PERIOD, AROUND AGE THIRTY-FIVE, WHEN BREAKTHROUGH MAY OCCUR AND THE ESSENCE MANIFESTS. WE BELIEVE THAT THIS PERSONALITY CHANGE IS NOT UN-KNOWN TO YOU.

"But what happens then?" Leah asked. "I'm fifty-one, and I don't think I've gone through anything like that."

WHAT WE HAVE SAID IS THAT THE SOUL MANIFESTS AT APPROXIMATELY THIS AGE. YES, SOME BREAK THROUGH MUCH EARLIER, PARTICULARLY IF THEY GO THEIR OWN WAY EARLY IN LIFE. LONERS BREAK THROUGH FAR MORE EASILY THAN THOSE ATTACHED TO LARGE "CLOSE" FAMILIES. THESE TAKE MUCH LONGER. YES, IF YOU DO NOT MANIFEST AT THIS STAGE, IT IS UNLIKELY THAT YOU WILL LATER. HOWEVER, WE KNOW OF A FEW SOULS WHO HAVE. HAVING YOUR SOUL MANIFEST AND SEARCHING FOR ENLIGHTEN-MENT ARE QUITE DIFFERENT. BABY WARRIORS DO NOT SEARCH, BUT THEY DO MANIFEST. THERE IS NO MAGIC AGE FOR BEGINNING TO SEARCH. YOU MUST NOT ASSUME THAT THE TASK IS NOW NO LONGER POSSIBLE TO YOU.

"Getting back to difficult relationships," Alex insisted. "I guess the soul level has something to do with it. What about the way baby souls and mature souls get along? You've said that baby souls are given to mature souls for growth."

IN TERMS OF INTIMATE RELATIONSHIPS. THIS IS THE WORST OF ALL POSSIBLE ALLIANCES BECAUSE THE BABY SOUL HAS SUCH A STRONG SENSE OF RIGHT AND WRONG AND HIS OPINION OF HIMSELF IS OFTEN EXALTED.

"What about the relationship of king and slave, if all other things are equal? Is that OK?"

ONE OF THE BEST.

Melanie, who had been with the group for about six

months and whom Michael had identified as a first-level old king, said in her forthright way, "I don't very much like being a woman. Is that due to my role?"

YES. KINGS DO NOT LIKE BEING FEMALES. SCHOLARS DO NOT EITHER.

"It doesn't seem there's much I can do about it, this life," she sighed.

REMEMBER THAT THE POSITIVE POLE OF THE KING ESSENCE IS MASTERY. MASTERY NEED NOT BE OF OTHERS. IT CAN BE OF YOURSELF. RATHER THAN RESENT THE SEX YOU HAVE CHOSEN YOU MIGHT CONSIDER USING IT TO LEARN MORE ABOUT WHY BEING FEMALE IS SO DIFFICULT, AND THAT WAY DEVELOP COMPASSION.

"That sounds very much like a veiled threat," Lucy remarked as she paused in her transcribing.

COMPASSION IS ONE OF THE LESSONS OF UNDERSTANDING. IF YOU DO NOT LEARN IT THE EASY WAY, YOU WILL LEARN IT THE HARD WAY. INTROSPECTION, NO MATTER HOW PAINFUL, IS THE EASY WAY. REMEMBER, MELANIE, THAT YOU CHOSE TO BE BORN FEMALE. YOUR SEX, WHETHER YOU LIKE IT OR NOT, IS NOT AN ACCIDENT.

Jessica refills her coffee cup. "About a year later," she says slowly, "Melanie decided that this was all hogwash and left the group. I've only heard from her once or twice since then. She makes disparaging remarks about the board, but she always asks what we're getting from it. I told her last time that the group is much smaller and the questions are moving into some fascinating new territory. She asked if she could come to a session, just out of curiosity, and I said sure. I gave her the dates of the next two meetings, but she never showed up."

Walter shakes his head sadly. "That happens, sometimes. People come to sessions wanting to hear that they were Cleopatra or Charlemagne or Saint Francis Xavier and find out instead that they're a mature scholar whose most distinguished life was as a highwayman-turned-preacher in the seventeenth century."

"It does kinda take the wind outta your sails," Lucy drawls. "I had some really great ideas about what I'd done, you know? And I really had done some of them, in a way, but not the way I imagined. Here I was, thinking that I had been a famous actor in France. Well, I was in France at the time I thought, and I was in the theater, but I wasn't a great star, I can tell you that." Suddenly she laughs. "I made the scenery, and played bit parts. So much for stardom."

It should be eerie, listening to these three people discuss past lives and the strange messages given to them through the Ouija board, but it isn't. One of the most striking things about Jessica Lansing and her husband and their friend Lucy is that they themselves are at home with what they say. They don't treat the information as a great revelation or tremendous secret to be guarded.

"Of course not," Jessica says emphatically. "I wish we were comfortable enough to allow you to use the real names of all of us associated with Michael, but I guess that's not possible yet." There is a wistful tone in her voice now. "My boss wouldn't understand. Walter's boss wouldn't understand. Lucy's boss wouldn't understand."

"He might," Lucy interrupts. "He's pretty open. I don't think he'd like it much, though."

Walter chuckles. "The very thought of a building constructor talking about past lives and working a Ouija board is pretty weird. I think it's a worthwhile precaution. It's a shame we have to be cautious, but . . ."

"I'd rather be cautious and have the material available than keep it to ourselves," Jessica says as she pours coffee for Lucy. "After all these years, it's high time we let the information out where people can have a look at it."

They didn't always feel this way.

"Good lord, no," Jessica says as she takes her place in the bentwood rocker once again. "At first we were very jealous of every single word Michael imparted to us. Then, gradually, we began to realize that this wouldn't do us any good at all."

"It's kind of tempting, though, you know?" Lucy says, her brows lifting. "Having all this stuff to ourselves."

"The one who's surprised me most is Emily," Jessica goes on after giving a giggling Lucy a quick look. "She's still a very religious person, devoted to her religion, and yet she hasn't stopped coming to sessions and asking questions of Michael. Even though Michael often says things that disturb her and are contrary to the tenets of her faith. That says an awful lot for her willingness to keep her mind open."

"Well, with Craig working the board, it might be awkward if she disapproved."

"But he's using the board differently in his sessions," Jessica reminds her. "You know that, Lucy. He wants to learn more about medicine and the real nature of his patients' illnesses."

Does the board really help with this? Craig's answer is surprising.

"It certainly does. I deal with the patients much more effectively, and I find that I get better results with them if I take their overleaves into consideration. A baby artisan, for example, is going to be hard to deal with partly because artisans can be so damned remote. With scholars it helps if everything is explained, though I had this backfire once with a scholar who had a goal of rejection. Everything I said was wrong. Everything."

Craig is using Michael's information to help others, but also to enrich himself. Has he found any difficulty in this?

"Well, I asked Michael about spiritualism," he admits with a smile.

THIS CONCEPT IS VALID, AND OF COURSE, WE HAVE NOT SAID THAT IT IS BAD WORK TO GAIN FROM THE TEACHING. THE ONLY BAD WORK IS WHEN YOU USE THE GAINS TO FEED INADEQUATE PARTS OF FALSE PERSONALITY. THIS, OF COURSE, BUILDS UP A TREMENDOUS DEFICIT AND YOU SLIDE BACKWARDS. IF YOU CAN MAKE THIS NOT MATTER SO MUCH EMOTIONALLY, YOU CAN TURN IT INTO POSITIVE SPIRITUAL-MATERIAL GAIN AND STILL HAVE THE PLEASANT FEELING, WITHOUT THE GUILT.

At the time Craig had been concerned, not only for himself, but for another member of the group, Gregory, who occasionally used the information that Michael imparted in his affairs with various women. Michael answered through Craig's board:

HAVEN'T YOU DISCOVERED YET THAT ALL THINGS WHICH ARE EGO GRATIFYING HAVE AN ELEMENT OF DELICIOUS GUILT ATTACHED? THE EGO SEEKS INTRIGUE AND "ADVENTURE." THE ESSENCE DOES NOT. THIS IS WHY THE MAN GREGORY COULD "PLAY IT STRAIGHT." HE HAD PERMISSION TO HAVE A FEMALE FOLLOWING AND THERE WAS NO GUILT. THERE WAS ALSO NO EGO SATISFACTION. THIS IS WHY HE COULD NOT BE SEDUCED. SEDUCTION WAS NOT

A SUITABLE REWARD TO HIM. WE FEEL THAT THIS CULTURE IS REMISS IN NOT GIVING PERMISSION. SOMETIMES YOU MUST GO AND ASK FOR IT. THE PERMISSION IS SYMBOLIC, BUT SOMETIMES IN THIS CULTURE, IT MUST ALMOST BE LITERAL. IF MARIJUANA WAS ON SALE AT ALL CORNER STORES, FEW WOULD SMOKE IT. AT ANY RATE, NO MORE THAN SMOKE IT NOW, AND A FEW WOULD QUIT.

"One of my patients," Craig recalls, "was worried about his tendency to become involved with women very much like his mother. He was afraid that he had got himself into some kind of Oedipal pattern and could not break out of it. I asked Michael about this man who was doing his best to worry himself into a fresh ulcer. Michael said that I was dealing with a fourth-level mature warrior, and added:

FIRST OF ALL, THE OEDIPAL MYTH IS CULTURALLY INDUCED AND DOES NOT HAVE THAT MUCH INFLUENCE AT THAT LEVEL. SECONDLY, THE GRIEF STEMS FROM NOT BEING ABLE TO RECAPTURE WHAT WAS FOR HIM AN EXTREMELY IMPORTANT MILESTONE.

Does Craig feel that what Michael has told him has been useful in his medical practice?

"Well, the chief administrator of my hospital would keel over if he knew about any of this, but, yes, I do think it has been helpful. In fact, I know it has. I had one woman who had all the symptoms of a certain nervous disorder and yet did not respond to any treatment. Finally I asked Michael about her, and he gave me a great deal of information."

With what results? Did the information help Craig deal with the patient?

"Very definitely. For one thing, Michael indicated that this woman was afraid to be cured of her ailment. To complicate matters, our overleaves abraded—they did, too—and I found it very difficult to keep my patience around her. It was a very frustrating relationship until I got some insight into what was really going on. Then we changed her treatment and got her a therapy program that was more in keeping with her particular needs. The improvement wasn't dramatic, but it was steady and lasting."

Has Craig ever suggested that a patient seek a physician other than himself because Michael indicated there were insurmountable difficulties?

"There was one time when I certainly would have liked

to do that," Craig admits. "Michael said that this patient was burning a very major karmic ribbon. It was a bitch of a situation. I really wanted out of the case, but Michael reminded me that where karma is concerned, it is unpleasant to pay karmic debts and even more unpleasant to be paid. I was told I could refuse to be paid now, but I would face the same obligation in a later life. I figured that once was bad enough. Twice would be dreadful. So I stuck with the case. I hope that I don't have to go through anything like that again."

What had the patient done in the former life that made the debt so unpleasant?

"Well," Craig says reluctantly, "according to Michael, he maimed me in quite a hideous way. The funny thing was, when I finally operated on him, I felt all that tension between us lift. I've never experienced anything like that before or since. And I hope I never do again." Craig hesitates. "The operation didn't leave him maimed, I'm glad to say. Apparently, cutting his body was enough. In this case, it even had a benefit. Michael said that this patient had developed his disease so that the debt could be paid. The disease was not really important, but the treatment was."

How does Craig feel about that evaluation?

"It bothers me. I think it bothers me because I have a terrible hunch that Michael may be right."

Jessica agrees with this, at least in part. "Michael says that the overleaves will tend to limit how you can pay your debts, or how you can be paid. The body isn't just a container for carrying around the soul. It also has its functions in the cycles."

CONTEMPT FOR THE BODY IS FOOLISH. SO IS COMPLETE PREOCCUPATION WITH IT. BODIES ARE CONDITIONS OF THE PHYSICAL PLANE AND THERE ARE LESSONS THAT CAN ONLY BE LEARNED IN THE FLESH. THOSE WHO ATTEMPT TO ESCAPE THE BODY OR DENY IT ARE MISSING THE POINT. THOSE WHO REFUSE TO LOOK BEYOND IT ARE MERELY CHOOSING THE REVERSE SIDE OF THE COIN. EITHER ATTITUDE IS A PRODUCT OF MAYA, THAT IS, FALSE PERSONALITY.

Isn't this a contradiction? First Michael says that false personality is the personality imposed on one, and then says that personal reactions are also false personality.

THE PERSONALITY STRIVES TO MAINTAIN THE SEPARATE-

NESS BY PERPETUATING THE MYTH OF UNIQUENESS. THE
ESSENCE, OF COURSE, IS AWARE THAT IT IS ONLY A FRAG-
MENT OF A GREATER WHOLE. THE PERSONALITY FIGHTS ALL
INTERFERENCE THAT MIGHT BE CATEGORIZED OR NEATLY
SLOTTED. THIS EXPLAINS PERHAPS SOME OF THE HOSTILITY
MET WITH IN EXPLAINING THIS TEACHING. IN GIVING YOU
THE OVERLEAVES, WE GIVE YOU ONLY A TOOL TO ENABLE
YOU TO BETTER UNDERSTAND THE DIFFERENCES IN OTHERS.
SO THAT YOU MIGHT ACCEPT THEM AT THE PLACE WHERE
THEY ARE NOW RATHER THAN SPIN WHEELS AND WASTE
ENERGY IN ATTEMPTING TO CHANGE THEM. THE OVER-
LEAVES ARE GIVEN IN MUCH THE SAME SPIRIT, BUT PERHAPS
COUCHED IN VERY DIFFERENT SEMANTICS BY OTHER CAUSAL
TEACHERS. WE SPOKE BEFORE OF INSTINCTIVE BEHAVIOR IN
MAN, AND WE WILL CONTINUE WITH THAT INFORMATION.

ONLY THE PERSONALITY THAT IS ENCULTURATED RE-
TAINS THIS ANIMALLIKE INSTINCTIVE BEHAVIOR. THE ES-
SENCE BEHAVES IN QUITE A DIFFERENT MANNER IF IT IS
ALLOWED TO BLOOM. WHEN THE MANIFESTED ESSENCE
WISHES TO MAKE A DECISION IT MERELY DOES SO, WITHOUT
THE ENDLESS DEBATE AND FEAR THAT ACCOMPANIES LIFE
DECISIONS, BASED ON THE OVERLEAVES. ONLY THE PERSON-
ALITY IS GOVERNED BY THE OVERLEAVES, AND THESE ARE
NONREASONING AND INCAPABLE OF MANIFESTING THE
HIGHER EMOTION. OUR USE OF THE SIMILE OF THE TOP BA-
BOON IS NOT FAR FROM RIGHT IN DESCRIBING THE BEHAVIOR
FOR MANY AGGRESSIVE YOUNG EXALTEDS IN THIS CULTURE,
DRIVEN BY PRIMITIVE INSTINCTS TO REMAIN AT THE TOP OF
THE PECKING ORDER. ALL OF THE MATING BEHAVIOR AND
RITUALS ARE BORROWED OR BROUGHT FORWARD FROM
MORE PRIMAL TIMES, AND CAN BE OBSERVED IN THE ANIMAL
KINGDOM EXTENSIVELY IF ONE TAKES THE TIME.

THE TRUE PERSONALITY PERCEIVES THE ONENESS AND
DOES NOT FEEL APARTNESS. THUS IT IS EXPANSIVE IN ITS
EXPRESSION. THE TRUE PERSONALITY DOES NOT NEED THE
PAIN, FOR IT HAS ACCESS TO THE JOY, AND AGAIN, CAN
EXPRESS THIS IN THE WORLD. THE TRUE PERSONALITY
KNOWS TRUTH, AND THEREFORE HAS NO FURTHER USE FOR
LIES. ABOVE ALL, THE TRUE PERSONALITY IS APPROPRIATE
IN ITS RESPONSE TO EACH AND EVERY SITUATION. OF
COURSE, THIS IS MANIFESTED IN THE WORLD AS JOYOUS-
NESS, AS WARMTH, AS A VERY SPECIAL RADIANCE, AS A HIGH

ENERGY COURSE OF A POSITIVE NATURE. HOWEVER, FALSE PERSONALITY IS UNCOMFORTABLE AROUND THIS TRUE PERSONALITY, AND THE FARTHER REMOVED FROM A TEACHING ONE IS, THE MORE UNCOMFORTABLE ONE WILL BE WHEN FACED WITH AN ENCOUNTER WITH BALANCED MAN. BALANCED MAN HAS THE CONFIDENCE THAT ONLY KNOWLEDGE OF TRUTH CAN POSSIBLY BRING. BALANCED MAN BRINGS THIS CONFIDENCE TO BEAR IN ALL OF HIS ENDEAVORS. BALANCE IMPLIES OBSOLESCENCE OF THE OVERLEAVES. BALANCED MAN IS NO LONGER STUCK. HE IS FREE TO MOVE IN REAL SPACE WHERE THERE ARE NO LIMITATIONS. THE LIMITATIONS WITHIN THE ARTIFICIAL SPACE OF THE PHYSICAL PLANE BRING COMFORT FOR THOSE TRAPPED THERE. THE CONCEPT OF ETERNITY AND INFINITY, FOR INSTANCE, IS VERY UNCOMFORTABLE FOR PERSONALITIES, EVEN THOSE TRAPPED IN THE INTELLECTUAL PART OF INTELLECTUAL CENTER, EVEN THOUGH FROM OUR PERSPECTIVE IT IS TRUTH THAT IS INCONTROVERTIBLE. THE CONTINUITY IS AS IMMUTABLE AS THE POLARITY.

Very well, But how does anyone deal with that?

THAT IS THE FUNCTION OF THE OTHER OVERLEAVES.

Chapter 13

QUADRATES AND SEXTANTS...

ALL THE CHOICES WE HAVE DISCUSSED HAVE BEARING ON THE LIFE-TASK, THAT ONE GOAL WHICH YOU SET FOR YOURSELF BETWEEN LIVES. THESE GOALS, OF COURSE, ARE INFLUENCED BY THE OVERLEAVES, KARMIC RIBBONS, SOUL LEVEL, MONADS, AND AGREED-UPON SEQUENCES. HOWEVER, THERE ARE SPECIAL CONFIGURATIONS THAT ALSO AID YOU IN COMPLETING YOUR TASK. THESE CONFIGURATIONS ARE, FOR THE MOST PART, QUADRATES AND SEXTANTS, PARTNERSHIPS OF FOUR OR SIX SOULS WHOSE GOALS ARE INTERRELATED. QUADRATES ARE MOST OFTEN FORMED BETWEEN SCHOLARS AND WARRIORS, SEXTANTS BETWEEN ARTISANS, SAGES, AND PRIESTS. KINGS AND SLAVES DO NOT OFTEN BECOME PART OF SUCH CONFIGURATIONS BECAUSE OF THE INHERENT NATURE OF THEIR ROLES. MANY OF YOU ARE PART OF QUADRATES AND SEXTANTS, THOUGH ONLY TWO OF YOU HAVE MADE CONTACT WITH ALL THE MEMBERS OF YOUR CONFIGURATION. CRAIG IS PART OF A SEXTANT, AND HAS WORKED WITH THE OTHER FIVE IN THE CONFIGURATION. WE WOULD SAY THAT IT IS LIKELY FOR THESE FRAGMENTS TO BE DRAWN TOGETHER MORE FREQUENTLY IN THE FUTURE. LEAH HAS MET HER QUADRATE MEMBERS, AND THEY ARE INVOLVED IN ACCOMPLISHING THEIR GOAL.

THERE ARE CONFIGURATIONS OF THREE (TRIADS), SEVEN, AND NINE AS WELL.

"When Michael first told us about quadrates and sextants, there was a lot of confusion," Jessica says. "But there seem to be these various working groups that develop through the cycles. Michael has said that I'm part of a quadrate, that I've met two of the members, but not the third. The real disadvantage is that the other three live in Europe."

"And, as you might expect," Walter says with a smile, "there are some drawbacks to this arrangement. We manage to get to Europe once every two or three years and most of the time we have a month or less to tour around, so it's very hard to make contact with so little time."

Is it possible to get work done with a group so widely spread?

"Sure, but it's harder," Jessica says, nodding toward Tracy. "She's in contact with one of her quadrate members."

"Yeah," Tracy confirms. "My colleague, the one in my entity who's such a close friend. He and I are part of the same quadrate. There are two others whom I don't know, and I gather that my friend knows only one of them. I know a little about my task in this life, and Michael has indicated that my friend has a similar one. But neither of us is in the primary position in this life, and there isn't a lot we can do."

WITHIN THE QUADRATE, THERE ARE, OF COURSE, FOUR POSITIONS. THOSE OCCUPYING THE FIRST AND THIRD POSITIONS ARE THE STRONGEST MEMBERS AND ARE MORE CAPABLE OF INDEPENDENT ACTION THAN THOSE IN THE SECOND AND FOURTH POSITIONS. A FRAGMENT DOES NOT ALWAYS OCCUPY THE SAME POSITION IN THE QUADRATE. [Because tasks and overleaves change.] IN THIS LIFE THE LADY TRACY OCCUPIES THE THIRD POSITION. IN HER LAST LIFE, SHE OCCUPIED THE SECOND POSITION IN THE QUADRATE, BUT BECAUSE OF HER EARLY DEATH AT AGE TWENTY-SEVEN, THE QUADRATE WAS NOT ABLE TO FUNCTION TOGETHER. THAT QUADRATE IS COMPOSED ENTIRELY OF WARRIORS, MEMBERS OF THREE ENTITIES. THE LADY JESSICA'S QUADRATE IS COMPOSED OF THREE SCHOLARS AND ONE WARRIOR, AND THE LADY JESSICA AT THIS MOMENT OCCUPIES THE SECOND POSITION. ONE OF THE QUADRATE MEMBERS IS IN HER ENTITY, THE OTHER TWO BELONG TO A DIF-

FERENT ENTITY. THE MAN WALTER, WHO IS AN OLD AR-
TISAN, BELONGS TO A SEXTANT. WITHIN A SEXTANT, POSI-
TIONS ONE AND FOUR ARE THE STRONGEST ONES, THE OTHER
FOUR POSITIONS BEING LESS DOMINANT. THE MAN WALTER
IS IN THE FIFTH POSITION. HE IS IN CONTACT WITH THREE
MEMBERS OF THE SEXTANT WHICH DOES NOT INCLUDE THE
WOMAN IN THE PRIMARY POSITION. THIS WOMAN IS A MA-
TURE PRIEST LIVING IN BOSTON, WHERE SHE IS A SCULPTOR
AND TEACHER. SHE HAS MET ONLY ONE MEMBER OF THE
SEXTANT, AND IS NOT PREPARED TO DEAL WITH FIVE OTHER
PEOPLE IN HER LIFE JUST NOW. WE WOULD THINK THAT IT
WILL BE AT LEAST FIVE YEARS BEFORE SHE WILL BE READY
TO FEEL THE PULL AND RESPOND TO IT. IT MIGHT BE POS-
SIBLE FOR WALTER TO ENLIST THE AID OF THE PERSON AT
THE FOURTH POSITION, WHO IS KNOWN TO HIM. THIS MAN
IS A FIRST-LEVEL OLD SAGE, A PROFESSOR OF ART HISTORY,
WHOM WALTER KNOWS THROUGH THE MAN DAVID SWAN.
WE WOULD LIKE TO POINT OUT THAT ONE OF THE AGREE-
MENTS THAT WALTER AND DAVID HAVE IN THIS LIFE IS
THAT DAVID WILL INTRODUCE WALTER TO THE VARIOUS
MEMBERS OF HIS SEXTANT.

"He's been pretty good about doing that," Walter says.
"Since Michael told us about the sextant, I've met the professor, and it turns out that he has met the woman in Boston,
so perhaps we'll get some work done in this life."

What exactly is the project?

"Michael doesn't tell you that," Lucy says. "He'll give
you some indication of what it has to do with, or in what
area it lies, but he won't identify it for you. He says that he
does not want to give out assignments, but to guide us to
recognition of what we want to accomplish. Being told a
task isn't the same thing as learning it for yourself."

What if the life-tasks of the members of a quadrate or
sextant are at cross-purposes?

"That doesn't happen," Jessica says. "One of the things
that's sorted out between lives is the workings of the quadrates and sextants. The configuration is supposed to facilitate your task."

"My sextant is very active," Craig says. "It's strange—
before I was into these sessions, I liked working with these
five, because everything seemed to go better when we were
doing things together. Three of us are physicians, one is a

physical therapist, two are engaged in genetic research. We really inspire each other, and ideas just pour out of us when we get together. It seemed uncanny at first, but now that Michael has explained the relationship, it not only makes sense, but I can see how it functions.''

"I get a similar feeling from my quadrate members," Leah says. "We aren't doing business together as such, though one of the members of the quadrate is an architect and I deal in real estate. One is a historian at the university, and the fourth is a local reporter. We've been trying to identify and preserve historic buildings and sites. We started out simply checking around the Bay Area, but we've developed a following, and we're expanding our working area. We're also in contact with a couple of the local Indian groups who are anxious to identify and preserve various sites. We have a petition in right now regarding such a site. There's a builder who wants to put up tract housing on what was very obviously an Indian settlement, and it would not only destroy an archaeological site, it would destroy an authentic adobe, which the builder's study describes as a shack. That building went up about 1760, and apparently was a way station for travel up and down El Camino Real. I think we've got a chance to save it, but you can't imagine how difficult it is. But the four of us are pretty hard to beat.''

"I'm part of the quadrate," Sam Chasen remarks, "but unfortunately, one of our members was killed in Vietnam and he was in the third position. I know only one of the other two, a woman, a housewife and volunteer librarian in the Sacramento valley. We're good friends, and I've found that she always fires me up with energy. Michael says that's pretty common.''

THE QUADRATES AND SEXTANTS ARE POWERFUL FORCES WHEN THE ENTIRE CONFIGURATION IS WORKING. THE ESSENCE DOES NOT CARE IF IT TAKES SEVERAL LIFETIMES TO ACCOMPLISH THE VARIOUS TASKS UNDERTAKEN BY A QUADRATE OR SEXTANT. WE DO NOT MEAN TO IMPLY THAT QUADRATES AND SEXTANTS ALWAYS ACT UPON THEIR MEMBERS IN THIS WAY. IT IS YOUR CHOICE. YOU MAY DECIDE THAT YOU CANNOT UNDERTAKE THE TASKS OF THE CONFIGURATION. IT IS YOUR OPTION TO DO SO. THE OTHERS MAY FIND THIS DIFFICULT TO DEAL WITH; HOWEVER, YOU MAY BE CERTAIN THAT EACH ONE OF YOU AT SOME TIME HAS AB-

DICATED THE RELATIONSHIPS IN THE QUADRATES AND SEX-
TANTS JUST AS EACH ONE OF YOU HAS ABDICATED ON OTHER
AGREEMENTS DURING THE VARIOUS CYCLES OF YOUR LIVES.
THERE IS NOTHING WRONG IN THIS. IT IS, IN FACT, ONE
WAY TO LEARN. OFTENTIMES PHYSICAL DISTANCES, WHICH
SEEM MINOR BETWEEN LIVES, BECOME REAL BARRIERS ON
THE PHYSICAL PLANE. IT IS ALSO MORE LIKELY THAT AS
YOU GROW OLDER, YOU WILL BE MORE WILLING TO YIELD
TO THE PULL OF THESE ASSOCIATIONS, IF THE OVERLEAVES
PERMIT. A FRAGMENT WITH A GOAL OF REJECTION OR STAG-
NATION WOULD NOT BE MUCH INCLINED TO SEARCH OUT
THE OTHER MEMBERS OF SUCH CONFIGURATIONS. QUAD-
RATES AND SEXTANTS OFTEN OCCUR BETWEEN THOSE WHO
HAVE BURNT KARMIC RIBBONS BUT FEEL THE STRENGTH OF
THE RELATIONSHIP THAT CONTINUES AFTER THE DEBT IS
PAID.

THERE ARE LARGER CONFIGURATIONS AS WELL. WE
OFTEN REFER TO THIS GROUP AS A CADRE, BUT WE DO NOT
LIMIT THE DEFINITION TO THIS GROUP ALONE. ALL THOSE
WHO SHARE A COMMON TEACHER ARE PART OF THE SAME
CADRE. WE COME TO OTHERS AS WELL AS TO YOU, AND ALL
OF YOU ARE WALKING THE SAME OR SIMILAR PATHS. IF YOU
CARE TO SEEK EACH OTHER OUT, IT IS POSSIBLE THAT YOU
WILL BE ABLE TO LEARN FROM EACH OTHER. SOME OF YOU
WILL FIND THE COMPLETION OF YOUR QUADRATES AND SEX-
TANTS IN THE CADRE, SOME OF YOU WILL FIND ENTITY
MATES, SOME OF YOU WILL RENEW OLD ACQUAINTANCES.
MOST OF THE SOULS IN THIS CADRE ARE MATURE AND OLD,
BECAUSE IT IS RARE FOR ANY BUT PRIESTS TO BE ON THE
PATH DURING THE YOUNG CYCLES.

"I've noticed that young souls who come to the sessions
don't often stay very long," Jessica remarks. "They're interested, but in an unusual way. They're either seeking 'The
Truth,' in capitals, or they're looking for a kind of adventure. This isn't always the case, but it's really pretty rare
that young souls want to look at the whole scheme of life."

Craig agrees. "I noticed that at my sessions, too. The
younger souls are intrigued, but they don't want to know
the rough stuff. Most of us don't like to think that we were,
say, executed for murder, and that we truly deserved that
sentence. I had one woman physician who came to three
sessions, and finally asked why she had chosen to become

a doctor, and Michael's response was unpleasantly to the point."

THIS FRAGMENT HAS MANY DEBTS TO PAY. IN HER FORMER LIFE, WHICH ENDED IN NINETEEN HUNDRED AND THIRTY-THREE, SHE WAS A FRENCH OFFICIAL WHO PROLONGED CONFLICT IN HER AREA IN NINETEEN HUNDRED SIXTEEN AND SEVENTEEN, IN ORDER TO GAIN A DEGREE OF POLITICAL POWER WHICH SHE HAD NOT BEEN ABLE TO AMASS ANY OTHER WAY. BECAUSE OF THIS SELF-SERVING DECISION, MANY MEN, WOMEN, AND CHILDREN DIED, MOST OF THEM FROM EITHER STARVATION OR POISON GAS. THIS FRAGMENT IS SEEKING TO MAKE UP FOR SOME OF THE SUFFERING SHE HAS CAUSED. IT TURNED OUT, BY THE WAY, THAT SHE DID, IN THAT LIFE, GET THE ADVANTAGE SHE HOPED FOR AND WAS GIVEN RECOGNITION FOR HER BRAVERY IN FIGHTING IN THE CONFLICT SHE HAD HELPED TO PROLONG. IT WAS NOT A COMPLETE TRIUMPH, BECAUSE DURING THAT WAR, THE FRAGMENT LOST MOST OF HIS FAMILY. THREE SONS, HIS WIFE, AND ONE OF TWO DAUGHTERS DIED AS A RESULT OF THE WAR. WE WOULD SAY THAT ONE OF THE REASONS THAT THIS WOMAN DID NOT GO TO VIETNAM WHEN THE OFFER OF MEDICAL WORK THERE AROSE IS BECAUSE SHE HAS A FEW MEMORIES FROM HER EARLIER LIFE, AND IT WOULD BE MORE THAN SHE COULD STAND TO BE IN BATTLE AGAIN SO SOON. ALSO, MANY OF THOSE TO WHOM SHE OWES DEBTS HAVE REINCARNATED IN THE WESTERN PART OF THE UNITED STATES, THOUGH SOME ARE IN CANADA, AND THERE ARE A FEW IN SOUTH AMERICA, A FEW IN AFRICA, AND A HANDFUL IN THE PEOPLE'S REPUBLIC OF CHINA. WE WOULD THINK THAT THOSE DEBTS, OWED TO PERSONS RELATIVELY INACCESSIBLE, WILL NOT BE PAID IN THIS LIFETIME.

"That woman got furious," Craig says. "She's a very outspoken and crusading pacifist, and simply would not believe that her resistance to war came from anything more than her own passionate conviction that war is ethically wrong. I don't disagree with that, but I pointed out to her that such a lifetime, and so recently, would give her even stronger convictions. She could not accept that. She refused to come to sessions, and though she was attracted to the information, she decided that it was all bunk."

"That's because if she admitted that any part of it was valid, she might have to accept that the parts she didn't like were valid," Emily remarks. "I was at that session, and you know, you could tell that there was something going on inside of her. I really believe that though she's denying it, she knows that there is a resonance to what Michael told her."

Does that sort of thing happen often—someone learns about a past life and rejects it?

"Sure," Jessica says, sounding resigned. "If you come to this information looking for glamour and strokes, you're probably in for a disappointment. There's a great deal that's intriguing, and after nine years, I'd say that I'm pretty much committed to exploring everything that Michael has to offer. It's jarring, though. I know that. There have been times that the information, particularly about past lives, is distressing."

"Look, let's face it," David Swan interjects, "most people, the vast majority of people, live pretty tragic lives. How many people do you know who are really and truly happy, who have accomplished the things they set out to accomplish in their lives, have had no major or minor disasters in their lives, have never been deeply disappointed, have been surrounded by trustworthy friends and understanding family, and who never knew a day's want, either material or psychological? When you think about it, such a life would be pretty damn bland, but it's a far cry from what most people have to put up with in their lives. For every famous, beautiful, extraordinary person, there are hundreds, if not thousands, who lead what some people call undistinguished lives. But that's most of us, baby. Most of us have to live through growing up as if it were some kind of disease. I don't know more than half a dozen people who had a happy childhood. I know even fewer who had real pleasure during adolescence. I don't know what high school was like for you, but for me it was miserable. Sometimes I think that I spend my life going between boredom and panic.

"That's overstating the case, I realize that, but haven't you all felt that way?" He waits a moment while the others nod and agree. "It's unreal, the way just keeping up with what's happening from day to day will eat up your time and energy, and that's nothing very important. All this exploration is outside of it. This is just the physical plane stuff that Michael is always telling us about. Nothing to be worried about, right? Except who doesn't worry? You've got to realize that it's always been this way, and that at any time, ninety-nine percent of the people are going to be grubbing along, pretty much the way they do now. For some of them it will be very hard, and for some comparatively easy, but most of our thoughts and our time and our energy will be taken up with getting through another day. It's not surprising that most people haven't the time or the inclination to get into studies like this. I know a lot of mature souls who can't be bothered with following the path because there's too much other stuff in the way.''

The others are quiet, and then Walter says, ''Are you saying that it has to be this way?''

''No,'' David responds emphatically. ''I'm saying that it's easy to understand why it is this way. That doesn't mean I don't think we shouldn't be aware of the path, or that we shouldn't explore our past, grubby lives. But if you're so certain that this is the answer to what being human is all about, and is more important than the rent and the IRS, why haven't you—and me too, me, too—put your real names in this book? Why don't any of us walk into the boss' office on Monday and say, 'Hey, twice a month I get together with about fifteen other folks and we talk to a Ouija board, and last time it told me that in one of my lives I was a galley slave from Salonika and died when the boat went down with all hands fighting Cypriot pirates? Wouldn't the boss love to hear that?''

''Just because we're cautious doesn't mean that we don't think this information is important,'' Lucy says, scowling. ''Honestly, David, there are times you really piss me off. We all know that it's a hassle getting through life, but what Michael keeps telling us is that there's more worthwhile in it than we know, and that it's OK to choose to be what we are. We don't have to deny our choices. And I'll tell you something else—being part of an entity feels good. It's a lot better than family, most of the time, because you don't have to explain anything. You can be living as grubby a life as possible, but there's always someone on your side, a lot of someones. I think that's great.'' She folds her arms across her chest and waits for David to answer.

"But you're a romantic, Lucy," David says, quite kindly.

"I'm an old sage in the passion mode, and don't you dare say that's the same thing."

This last defiance breaks the tension, and the others laugh.

"Besides," Lucy adds in a different tone, "you can't tell me that Robert Redford doesn't have to think about the same things the rest of us do. He's human. He's got to buy groceries and clothes like the rest of us, and if he has shoes that don't fit, his feet hurt just as much as anyone else's."

"David's our devil's advocate," Walter explains, somewhat unnecessarily. "He's always the first one to check out historical information, and to challenge anything Michael says."

And how has Michael done so far?

"Pretty damn good," David says ruefully. "The thing that impressed me most was when I asked about a painting that the museum was planning to purchase. There was no verification about the artist, and there didn't seem to be any way we could get it, so, as a lark, I asked Michael about it."

THE WORK IN QUESTION IS INDEED AN AUTHENTIC GOYA. IF YOU WILL EXAMINE THE WORK WITH THE NEW TECHNIQUES OF X-RAY AND LASER, YOU WILL FIND THAT THE ARTIST'S SIGNATURE IS IN THE LOWER LEFT-HAND CORNER OF THE PAINTING, IN THE SHADOW OF A SMALL SPOTTED DOG. THE PAINTING WAS HUNG IN A ROOM WHERE THAT SIDE OF THE PAINTING SUFFERED HEAT DAMAGE, SO THAT CLEANING, IN THIS INSTANCE, WILL NOT BE OF MUCH HELP. THERE IS A LETTER FROM THE GRANDFATHER OF THE MAN OFFERING THE WORK FOR SALE THAT TELLS HOW HIS FATHER CAME TO BUY IT. THAT LETTER IS IN THE LIBRARY OF THE SELLER'S ESTATE, IN THE BOUND VOLUMES OF THE PAPERS OF THE FAMILY; IT WAS WRITTEN IN FEBRUARY OF EIGHTEEN FORTY-FIVE, COMMON ERA. WHILE WE ARE ON THE SUBJECT, WE WOULD LIKE TO ADD THAT THE PAINTING CREDITED TO VERONESE THAT YOU ARE ALSO CONSIDERING IS MOSTLY THE WORK OF ASSISTANTS, AND ONLY THE FIGURE OF SAINT JOHN IS THE ARTIST'S PAINTING.

"Well"—David sighs—"we had the work x-rayed and gone over with laser projections, and sure enough, in the lower left-hand corner of the painting, in the shadow of a dog that looked black because of discoloration, but was actually spotted, there was the signature. Some of the people around the museum were absolutely amazed at my 'lucky guess,' as I kept calling it. I couldn't bring myself to tell them how I was able to make such a guess. We bought the painting, by the way. It cost a great deal of money, but I think it was worth it. We politely turned down the Veronese, too. I convinced the board of directors that we could find better examples of Veronese's work at more reasonable prices."

"Mind you," Jessica adds, "I don't want to spend all the board time checking up on whether or not Aunt Bessie's supposed Leonardo is the real thing, but occasionally, it's a nice diversion, and it certainly is one of the most convincing things that Michael does."

Is Michael willing to identify objects?

WE WOULD PREFER TO IDENTIFY LIVES. THAT IS WHERE THE GROWTH COMES FROM—THE RECOGNITION OF THE TAPESTRY. WHEN SUCH IDENTIFICATION WILL LEAD TO GOOD WORK IN ESSENCE, THEN WE DO NOT OBJECT TO IDENTIFYING OBJECTS. IN THE MAN DAVID'S CASE, HE HAS HAD MANY LIVES DEALING WITH ART, AND IT IS BENEFICIAL TO MAKE THESE MEMORIES ACCESSIBLE TO HIM. THIS MAN IS STRIVING TO WALK HIS PATH, AND WHEN THE FORCES OF FALSE PERSONALITY ARE NOT TOO STRONG WITHIN HIM, HE IS ABLE TO DO MUCH. SINCE HE IS, BY ATTITUDE, A SKEPTIC . . .

"No kidding," David had remarked when Michael had first given his overleaves.

HE WILL FIND IT DIFFICULT TO TRUST HIS ESSENCE IN FOLLOWING THE PATH. BUT THIS IS NOT IMPOSSIBLE, AND HE IS MORE WILLING TO EXAMINE HIS MOTIVES THAN ARE SOME OF THOSE IN THE GROUP. THE NEARNESS OF DAVID'S ENTITY MATES IS SOME HELP, AND WHEN HE HAS MADE CONTACT WITH HIS MAGNETIC OLD KING, MANY OF HIS BARRIERS WILL BE TAKEN DOWN AND HE WILL BE ABLE TO ASSIMILATE WHAT HE HAS LEARNED. THE MAN DAVID WILL BE OF GREAT IMPORTANCE TO HIS MAGNETIC OLD KING, BY THE WAY.

"That bit about the magnetic old king is interesting," David adds. "When Michael first told me about him, he said he lived in Iran. *Iran!* That's ridiculous. When the hell was I ever going to get to Iran? Well, as it turns out, I'll be going to Iran in January [1978]. The museum is negotiating for an exhibition of Iranian artifacts—things like pottery, jewelry, books, leatherwork, rugs, that sort of thing. Originally, the senior curator was going to make the trip, but he's leaving the museum at the end of the year and will be taking a curatorship on the east coast, and that means I go. When I got the news, I asked Michael more about my magnetic old king."

WE REMIND YOU, DAVID, THAT YOU WOULD HAVE GOT TO IRAN IF IT HAD MEANT HITCHHIKING. IT IS BENEFICIAL THAT YOUR TRIP IS FACILITATED, BUT THAT WAS THE NATURE OF YOUR AGREEMENT WITH THE MAN GERARD (THE SENIOR CURATOR). GERARD, BEING A SECOND-LEVEL YOUNG SCHOLAR, IS NOT YET AWARE OF THE PULL ON HIM, BUT HE FULFILLED THE TERMS OF THE AGREEMENT, AT THE SAME TIME ADVANCING HIMSELF, AS HE SEES IT, IN THE WORLD.

UNLESS POLITICAL UPHEAVALS INTERVENE, YOUR OLD KING WILL BE EASILY ACCESSIBLE TO YOU. HE DOES MUCH WORK IN ASSOCIATION WITH ACADEMICS, PARTICULARLY ARCHAEOLOGISTS, THOUGH HE HIMSELF IS NOT AN ACADEMIC. THIS SIXTH-LEVEL OLD KING IS A MAN IN HIS LATE TWENTIES, AN IRANIAN MERCHANT, QUITE SUCCESSFUL, AND A GREAT PATRON OF THE ARTS, BOTH PRESENT AND PAST. HE IS THE FOURTH-GENERATION LEADER OF A LARGE COMMERCIAL ENTERPRISE AND HAS RECENTLY TAKEN OVER FOR HIS AILING FATHER. IT IS NOT UNUSUAL TO FIND OLD KINGS OF ANY LEVEL ASSUMING RESPONSIBILITIES AT AN EARLY AGE. WE REALIZE THAT YOU MAY EXPERIENCE CERTAIN DIFFICULTIES IN IRAN BECAUSE YOU ARE A JEW, BUT THIS MAN WILL WELCOME YOU SINCERELY. THE PULL OF THE MAGNETIC OLD KING AND THE BONDS OF YOUR PAST LIVES ARE MUCH STRONGER THAN SOCIAL PREJUDICE. YOU MAY ALSO HAVE OPPORTUNITY TO MEET WITH THE KING IN SPAIN, SHOULD CONTACT FAIL THIS TIME.

David Swan's eyes twinkle. "I don't think he'll be all that hard to find, do you? And I'll tell you something. I'm beginning to think that there *is* a person I'm supposed to meet on the other end. This whole project, instead of being filled with the usual hassles, is going roller-skate smooth." He crosses his arms on his chest. "It might be more demanding than I think it will be now, but I'm willing to chance that. I'll keep you posted."

"You'd better," says Lucy.

Michael said that he would prefer to identify lives rather than objects. How thoroughly is he willing to identify lives? David Swan said he had got an overview of one of his lives. What is an overview?

"Just what it sounds like," Jessica says. "It's a short biography of a past life. When possible, dates and places are given, so that verification can occur."

"Verification means you can find it in history," Walter says. "That sounds trivial, but it isn't. For most of the peasantry, there isn't a lot of difference in time for many hundreds of years. Dates that can be fixed are quite useful. With illiterate peoples or people not using the Christian, Jewish, or other standard calendars, such as American Indians, Chinese and Indian country folk, Australian aborigines, and the like, it's hard to get much of a fix on time, but there are other ways. Occasionally there are travelers, battles, eclipses, comets, bad weather, or other things that make it possible to narrow down the time. One of the group had a major past life in Africa in a tribe that has a very complete oral history and some of it is available now. We were able to pinpoint the time of this life, and a few of the events, but as to the actual single identity, not yet. There are more difficulties when dealing with various American Indian tribes because so much of their history has been destroyed. We've had some success in the matter, but not a lot."

"Yes," Marjorie says. "One of the advantages of teaching at the university is that I have access to the libraries all over the campus, and it's been possible to use these to chase down some of the facts Michael has given us. I've found that this has been one of the most persuasive aspects of Michael's teaching—that you can research what he says and will find that it is consistent."

"Here's one of the overviews that we've got—it was a life for one of the members of the group," Jessica says, offering a black ring binder. "All the transcripts in the binder are overviews."

THE SUBJECT WAS BORN IN WHAT WAS THEN THE VENETIAN EMPIRE IN EARLY NOVEMBER 1567, THE SECOND SON OF A CARPENTER AND CABINET MAKER. THE SUBJECT SHOWED AN EARLY APTITUDE FOR LEARNING AND WAS

THEREFORE HANDED OVER TO THE LOCAL PRIESTS OF THE AUGUSTINIAN ORDER FOR HIS EDUCATION AND PREPARATION FOR THE PRIESTHOOD. THE SUBJECT WAS QUICK TO LEARN, VERY SKILLFUL, BUT DISSATISFIED WITH LIFE IN THE ORDER. BY THE TIME HE WAS TEN, HE WAS AWARE THAT HE HAD LITTLE APTITUDE FOR THE CHURCH, AND WAS ALREADY THINKING OF ESCAPE. BECAUSE OF HIS EARLY TRAINING AND FAMILY BACKGROUND, HE WAS ENCOURAGED TO STUDY ARCHITECTURE AS WELL AS THE USUAL THEOLOGICAL SUBJECTS. THE PRIOR WAS AN AMBITIOUS MAN, AND HOPED TO ADVANCE HIS OWN POWER THROUGH THE DEVELOPMENT OF A TALENTED PROTÉGÉ. THE SUBJECT SUSPECTED THIS AND RESENTED IT.

AT AGE ELEVEN, THE SUBJECT FLED THE MONASTERY AND FOR TWO YEARS WORKED HIS WAY NORTH, SURVIVING BY DOING OCCASIONAL BITS OF CARPENTRY, ACTING AS A SCRIBE, AND CAREFUL THEFT. FINALLY, IN 1579, HE ARRIVED IN POLAND, WHERE HE WORKED BUILDING ARMY BARRACKS. HE WAS A HARD WORKER, AND HIS LITERACY MADE HIM POPULAR WITH THE SOLDIERS, MOST OF WHOM COULD NEITHER READ NOR WRITE. IN 1581, WHEN STEPHEN BATHORY, THE KING OF POLAND, INVADED RUSSIA AGAINST IVAN THE TERRIBLE, THE SUBJECT WENT WITH HIM AS A JUNIOR AIDE-DE-CAMP. THE SUBJECT WAS WOUNDED AND CAPTURED THE FOLLOWING YEAR, AND FOR TWO YEARS WORKED AS A PRISONER/SLAVE NEAR SMOLENSK. HIS SKILL AT CARPENTRY ONCE AGAIN PROVED USEFUL AND HE WAS GIVEN BETTER LODGING AND FOOD IN EXCHANGE FOR BUILDING A SMALL FORTIFICATION FOR THE LOCAL BOYAR, WHO WAS APPREHENSIVE OF THE POLES. THE SUBJECT, WHO HAD A KNACK FOR LANGUAGES, AT ONCE SET ABOUT LEARNING RUSSIAN AND BY 1585 HE WAS SOMETHING LESS OF A PRISONER/SLAVE AND MORE ON THE LEVEL OF A BONDED SERVANT.

IN 1588, WHEN THE SUBJECT WAS TWENTY YEARS OLD, HE WAS SENT BY HIS BOYAR MASTER TO MOSCOW TO PRESENT THE CZAR WITH DOCUMENTS AND PLANS FOR THE FORTIFICATION OF THE POLISH BORDER. ON LEARNING THAT THE DESIGNER WAS NOT RUSSIAN, HAD BEEN A POLISH PRISONER, AND HAD BEEN A CATHOLIC MONK, THE REGENT BORIS GODUNOV ORDERED THE SUBJECT IMPRISONED AS A SPY. THE SUBJECT WAS KEPT IN PRISON IN TERRIBLE CON-

DITIONS FOR MORE THAN FOUR YEARS, AT THE END OF
WHICH TIME HE WAS BLINDED AND RELEASED. THE SUBJECT
WAS ABLE TO SURVIVE FOR A YEAR BY BEGGING AND BY
OCCASIONAL STORYTELLING. FINALLY HE WAS TAKEN INTO
A MONASTERY TO THE WEST OF MOSCOW WHERE HE WAS
ABLE TO TEACH SOME OF THE MONKS TO TRANSLATE LATIN
TO RUSSIAN. HE DIED OF TYPHUS IN THE SUMMER OF 1595,
NOT YET TWENTY-EIGHT YEARS OLD.

THE SUBJECT WAS STRONG-WILLED AND OPPORTUNISTIC,
BUT ALSO FILLED WITH THE TORMENT OF THE SIXTH-LEVEL
MATURE SOUL. HE WAS NOT SUBJECT TO MANY RELIGIOUS
FEELINGS, BUT HE WAS ATTRACTED TO THE INSIGHT OF THE
RELIGIOUS LIFE AS MUCH AS HE WAS DISGUSTED BY THE
USUAL ABUSES HE SAW AROUND HIM. BY THE TIME OF HIS
DEATH, HE WAS A TRULY COMPASSIONATE SOUL, HAVING
LEARNED SUCH COMPASSION BY PAINFUL EXPERIENCE.

BECAUSE OF HIS EARLY DEATH, THE SUBJECT DID NOT
FULFILL MANY OF THE AGREEMENTS HE HAD MADE BE-
TWEEN LIVES, ALTHOUGH ONE OF THE REASONS FOR HIS
TRAVEL INTO RUSSIA WAS TO BE CLOSER TO HIS ENTITY
MATES AND THOSE WITH WHOM HE HAD SEQUENCES TO
COMPLETE. HE COMPLETED THE SLAVE PART OF THE MAS-
TER/SLAVE MONAD WITH THE BOYAR WHO HAD HIM DESIGN
AND BUILD FORTIFICATIONS.

WE WOULD SAY THAT THE SUBJECT WAS DEEPLY COM-
MITTED TO THE SEARCH BUT HAD NOT YET LEARNED WHICH
PATH HE NEEDED TO FOLLOW. HE REALIZED WHEN HE
WENT TO MOSCOW THAT NO GOOD WOULD COME OF IT, BUT
THE NATURE OF THE MONAD HE WAS COMPLETING KEPT HIM
FROM RESISTING THE ORDERS. AS IS OFTEN THE CASE WITH
WARRIOR SOULS, THIS FRAGMENT'S INHERENT DRIVE SUS-
TAINED HIM THROUGH DREADFUL ORDEALS, BUT ALSO
DROVE HIM TO SEEK OUT THOSE ORDEALS. IN SPITE OF THE
LIFE HE LED, THE SUBJECT HAD A CLEVER SENSE OF HUMOR
AND WAS POPULAR WITH THE SOLDIERS AROUND HIM AND
WITH SOME OF THE MONKS BOTH IN THE VENETIAN AND
RUSSIAN MONASTERIES. HE HAD PLEASANT FEATURES, AND
THOUGH NEITHER TALL NOR LARGE, HAD AN AIR OF AU-
THORITY THAT IS OFTEN SEEN IN MATURE AND OLD WAR-
RIORS. HE HAD A FONDNESS FOR MUSIC AND STORIES AND
WAS FINICKY ABOUT FOOD WHEN HE COULD AFFORD TO BE.
IN ORDER TO COMPLETE WHAT HE HAD BEGUN IN THAT

LIFE, THE SUBJECT REINCARNATED IN EASTERN EUROPE IN 1613 AND SPENT PART OF HIS LIFE AS A SOLDIER. HE HAD BETTER LUCK THAT TIME, LIVING INTO HIS MID-FORTIES AND ACCOMPLISHING MUCH OF WHAT HE HAD TO DO IN THE PREVIOUS LIFE. THE MONK WHO HAD ARRANGED FOR HIM TO BE TAKEN INTO THE RUSSIAN MONASTERY, BY THE WAY, WAS ANOTHER WARRIOR SOUL, AN ENTITY MATE OF THE SUBJECT, AND ONE WHO HAD OFTEN BEEN THE SUBJECT'S COMRADE-AT-ARMS.

"There's another one that might interest you," Jessica says. "One of Walter's, in fact. In that life, he and his sextant worked together for several years. It will give you some idea of the contrasts in the overviews and in the way previous lives affect later choices."

THE SUBJECT WAS BORN IN MOSLEM SPAIN IN WHAT YOU WOULD RECKON AS MAY 1043, THE ELDEST DAUGHTER OF A FAMILY OF INSTRUMENT MAKERS. SHE WAS CLUBFOOTED, AND THEREFORE WAS NOT EXPECTED TO MARRY. AS A RESULT, SHE WAS TRAINED IN THE FAMILY BUSINESS FROM A FAIRLY EARLY AGE, SO THAT BY THE TIME SHE WAS FOURTEEN, SHE WAS SUFFICIENTLY QUALIFIED TO ASSIST HER FATHER AND BROTHERS IN THEIR WORK. OF HER TWO YOUNGER SISTERS, ONE DIED IN INFANCY AND THE OTHER MARRIED WELL AND TOOK UP RESIDENCE IN BARCELONA. THERE WERE FOUR BROTHERS IN THE FAMILY, TWO OF WHOM WERE ACTIVE IN THE BUSINESS AND TWO OF WHOM BECAME ARMORERS. IN 1059 TWO APPRENTICES WERE TAKEN INTO THE BUSINESS, ONE OF WHOM WAS A PART OF THE SUBJECT'S SEXTANT. THE APPRENTICE WAS ENCOURAGED BY THE SUBJECT TO EXPERIMENT WITH NEW INSTRUMENTS, TESTING NEW WOODS, METALS, AND OTHER ASPECTS OF THE INSTRUMENT MAKER'S ART. WITHIN TWO YEARS, THEY HAD IMPROVED THE BASIC DESIGN OF THE RABAB AND THE JIQ'RN AND HAD CHANGED THE DESIGN FOR AN INSTRUMENT THAT WAS SIMILAR TO THE MEDIEVAL BOWED LYRE.

"The rabab, by the way," Walter explains, "was an ancestor of the violin, sort of a spoon-shaped instrument with three strings or two. They were bowed instruments, the bow being quite similar to an archer's bow rather than the design we associate with stringed instruments now. I think that the instrument that Michael called the jiq'rn is probably an ancestor of the Renaissance instrument called the chitarrone, which is not just another version of a guitar.''

WITHIN THREE YEARS THE SUBJECT WAS RUNNING THE MOST RESPECTED FIRM OF INSTRUMENT MAKERS IN MOORISH SPAIN. HAVING HEARD OF THIS REMARKABLE BUSINESS, A MERCHANT FROM TUNIS ASKED IF HE COULD AID THEM IN A BUSINESS VENTURE—HE WANTED THE SUBJECT AND HER ARTISANS TO TEACH THEIR NEW TECHNIQUES TO A FAMILY OF INSTRUMENT MAKERS FROM GAZA. THIS OTHER GROUP OF INSTRUMENT MAKERS WERE FAMOUS FOR THEIR DESIGN OF THE TAMUR, OR LONG-NECKED OUD, AND THIS MERCHANT FELT THAT IT WOULD BE WORTHWHILE FOR BOTH GROUPS TO EXCHANGE DESIGNS AND TECHNIQUES. THE SUBJECT AGREED, AND TWO YEARS LATER THERE WERE THREE OF THE FAMILY BROUGHT OVER, TWO OF WHOM WERE PART OF THE SEXTANT. IT WAS INDEED A BENEFICIAL ASSOCIATION, AND THE INSTRUMENTS MADE BY THESE PEOPLE WERE VERY MUCH IN DEMAND FOR THEIR SUPERIORITY.

IN THE YEAR 1069, WHEN THE SUBJECT WAS TWENTY-SIX, A CHRISTIAN SLAVE WHO HAD BEEN CAUGHT DURING A SKIRMISH WITH THE FORCES OF KING SANCHO II OF CASTILE, WAS GIVEN TO THE SUBJECT BECAUSE HE WAS A GIFTED MUSICIAN. THIS FRAGMENT WAS ALSO PART OF THE SEXTANT, AND OCCUPIED THE FOURTH POSITION AS THE SUBJECT OCCUPIED THE FIRST POSITION. THE WORK OF THESE ARTISANS, WHO WERE OF ARTISAN, SAGE, AND PRIEST ESSENCES, CONTRIBUTED TO THE CREATION OF THE PROTOTYPE INSTRUMENT THAT BECAME IN TIME THE THEORBO, A LUTELIKE INSTRUMENT OF THE LATE MEDIEVAL AND RENAISSANCE PERIOD.

WHEN THE ALMORAVID DYNASTY REASSERTED MOSLEM RULE IN SPAIN, BEGINNING IN 1090, IT SEEMED THAT THE INSTRUMENT MAKERS WOULD HAVE TO GIVE UP THEIR CHRISTIAN SLAVE, BUT THE MERCHANT WHO HAD FUNDED THEIR BUSINESS BARGAINED WITH THE CALIPH AND WAS ABLE TO REMOVE THE WHOLE GROUP TO GAZA.

AT GAZA, THE LAST MEMBER OF THE SEXTANT JOINED THEM. HE WAS OF GREEK DESCENT, AN ACTUAL MUSICIAN WITH A REAL INTEREST IN TONE QUALITIES OF WOOD AND INLAYS. THE SEXTANT WORKED TOGETHER IN RELATIVE PEACE FOR TEN YEARS UNTIL CRUSADING FEVER SPREAD THROUGH EUROPE. THEY WERE ABLE TO WORK TOGETHER

FOR FOUR YEARS MORE, THEN TWO OF THE SEXTANT DIED OF CHOLERA AND THE OTHERS WERE FORCED TO LEAVE GAZA AND MOVE TO A SAFER LOCATION. THEIR MERCHANT ASSOCIATE HAD HAD OFFICES IN DAMASCUS, BUT AS HE WAS NOW DEAD, HIS FAMILY WAS NOT INTERESTED IN HAVING A GROUP OF INSTRUMENT MAKERS TAKING UP ROOM IN TIME OF WAR. THE POLITICAL SITUATION IN SPAIN MADE RETURN OUT OF THE QUESTION, AND, IN DESPERATION, THE REMAINING FOUR SET OUT FOR ALEXANDRIA. THE SUBJECT AND THE MAN WHO HAD BEEN THE CHRISTIAN SLAVE MADE IT, BUT THERE WAS NOTHING THEY HAD TO OFFER NOW. THEY MADE THEIR LIVINGS REPAIRING INSTRUMENTS AND OTHER WOODEN FURNISHINGS, SUCH AS SCREENS. THEY LIVED AS LOVERS, AS THEY HAD FOR THE LAST TWELVE YEARS, AND FINALLY WERE THOUGHT DISGRACEFUL BY THE COMMUNITY, AND WERE FORCED EITHER TO SEPARATE OR TO MOVE AWAY. THEY CHOSE TO REMAIN TOGETHER, AND FINALLY ENDED UP IN ALEPPO, AFTER NINE YEARS OF WANDERING. THERE THEY WORKED FOR A SCHOOL THAT TAUGHT DANCING GIRLS.

THE SUBJECT DIED NEAR ALEPPO EARLY IN THE YEAR ELEVEN HUNDRED SIXTEEN, AGED SEVENTY-TWO YEARS. HER LONG-TIME CHRISTIAN LOVER HAD DIED THE YEAR BEFORE, AGED SEVENTY. THE IMMEDIATE CAUSE OF DEATH WAS PNEUMONIA, BUT IT WAS MERELY A FUNCTION OF OLD AGE. THE SUBJECT, DURING HER LIFE, HAD THREE CHILDREN, NONE OF WHOM SURVIVED CHILDHOOD.

THIS WAS A GENTLE AND DEDICATED SOUL, AT THE FOURTH LEVEL OF THE YOUNG CYCLE. THE MERCHANT WAS PART OF THE SUBJECT'S ENTITY WITH AN AGREEMENT TO BE OF ASSISTANCE TO THE SEXTANT, WHICH HE CERTAINLY WAS. THIS LIFE WAS QUITE A SUCCESSFUL ONE. THE SUBJECT WAS ABLE TO COMPLETE ALL HER MONADS, COMPLETE THE WORK OF HER SEXTANT FOR ONE LIFE, ACHIEVE MOST OF THE GOALS OF HER LIFE-TASK, AND DIE WITH RELATIVE PEACE. WE WOULD SAY THAT IT IS RARE FOR ANYONE TO ACCOMPLISH SO MUCH IN THE SPACE OF ONE LIFETIME.

"I still like to make instruments," Walter confides. "I've made a couple of zithers and a psaltery so far. I've got this fascination for stringed instruments." He laughs a little sadly. "When we got that overview, I was simply floored. I've had dreams about making instruments. I remember when I was a kid, I took band at school so that I could see some of the instruments I dreamed about. I didn't find them, which isn't surprising since most of those instruments don't exist now. Two years ago while I was in Europe, I went to three museums with extensive ancient instrument collections, and it was a relevation. I kept wanting to touch the wood. When I saw scratches and cracks, I felt sick. It was an uncanny experience."

"I've never had anything quite that dramatic happen," Leah comments, "but there is a very strange energy going when my quadrate is working together. I know that sensation that Walter is talking about, too, when he says that he saw those instruments and they awakened all those feelings in him. I've had that happen only once, and I'll never forget it. I was in Africa, in Tunisia, and I visited a friend who worked in the textile industry. He had a collection of very old textiles, and a couple of them were amazing to me. I felt whole areas of myself open up. Michael said that in the sixteenth century, I had been a weaver and dyer in Tunisia. I believe it."

Arnold clears his throat. "That was a very disturbing experience. Leah was very profoundly affected by that experience. I kept asking her if she wanted to go home, and she kept insisting that she was having a wonderful time. She tried to tell me how she felt, but I didn't have the concepts to deal with it. I still don't, but it's good to know that she isn't the only one feeling that way."

Corrine adds, "Most people are taught to deny these feelings within themselves, or if they can't deny them, they think that there's something wrong, and that they should see a shrink. I'm the first one to admit that there are people who should get professional help for psychological problems, but there are some influences in life that can be as compelling and uncomfortable as hell that have no relation to psychological disturbances, or not in the usual sense. In such cases, I think it's very important for people to realize that the problems—karma, soul level, overleaves, agreements, whatever they are—can be understood and worked through. There are a great many people hoping for psychiatry to 'cure' them of problems that cannot be 'cured,' but rather entail the payment or acceptance of a karmic debt. Abrasive overleaves don't mean that anyone is wrong, but that they simply haven't the same relationship to the world, and aren't likely to be able to work well together. That doesn't mean that all problems can't respond to psychological and psychiatric help, but there are times when going to a psychiatrist for working out karma is like using a bandage to treat appendicitis."

It's apparent that these people in the Michael group feel that there is some benefit to the teaching. Why do they think so? What does it gain for them?

Jessica answers first. "The almost eight years that we've been a working group have altered how I feel about my life and the choices I make. It's not simply because I've had the experience of doing the board and dealing directly with Michael's energy, though that's been a major part of my desire to continue. I'm fascinated by the tapestry that Michael talks about, the weaving together of lives. Also, what Michael has said is practical. One of our most difficult clients is a young slave in the power mode with a goal of dominance. He has a pattern: he derides your work, makes you feel incompetent, then does something nice for you. I've learned that I must be very assertive if I'm going to avoid that little ritual. He's very eager to be what he thinks of as supportive. On a larger scale, I wouldn't say that I have more answers than when I started out, but I think that the answers do exist and that eventually, perhaps only between lives, I'll be able to know what they are."

Walter rubs his moustache with his forefinger and stares off into space before answering. "Much of what Michael says is disturbing. He goes against religious and philosophical thought, and I know from the experiences we've had here that there will be many people who will reject what he's communicated. I realize that part of myself would like to scurry back to that safe niche where right and wrong are clearly defined and all the old familiar rules apply. Occasionally the enormity of the responsibilities of the physical plane staggers me. On the other hand, I feel that there is a reason for what I do, which is greatly comforting."

Lucy North grins infectiously. "I think Michael is *neat,*" she says, full of enthusiasm. "Sometimes I get angry and discouraged about what we learn in sessions, but I haven't given up on them yet. I know that my life, whatever it is, is really mine, and that means a lot to me, you know? Also,

I realize now that I've done some really dumb things because I thought they were expected of me. Sometimes I wish Michael would unbend a little and say something like 'good girl,' or 'you're coming along, Lucy,' but he doesn't. The only person who can say that is me. I'm learning how to.''

David Swan takes the floor next. "I feel that what I've learned in these sessions, and what I'm continuing to learn, has helped me accept the difficulties I've encountered in my life, though my goal isn't acceptance, but growth. I was terrified for the first twenty-five years of my life, and that made me hostile and defensive, which is a little unusual for old scholars. Now I recognize the pressure of false personality and the expectations that I accepted for myself. It's also good to know that this isn't *it*, that there won't be this one chance to do what you want to do. Since I realized that, the funny thing is that I've got more done instead of less.''

Emily Wright is the next person to answer. "Michael's been a great challenge to me, in many ways. The religious aspects are obvious, but there's much more to it. I understand that a great many sincerely religious people will have trouble with what Michael says, but I think that it may help them to examine and clarify their faith. Perhaps it's because I've learned how vulnerable I am that I hope that others will take the time to study Michael's material so that there will be fewer knee-jerk Christians around and more people professing the teachings of Christ, which is another thing entirely. I see my religion differently than when these sessions began, but I feel that the alteration has been beneficial.''

Craig braces his elbows on his knees and says, "Well, Michael has been of invaluable help in my practice, though there are times he scares the hell out of me. What Michael has said about the nature of the artisan soul, too, has helped, since there are so many expectations that don't fit in with artisans. Working with my sextant has been very successful and rewarding. Working the board has been unnerving sometimes, but I realize that my reaction is a reaction to what I've been trained to ignore, not to Michael. I'm not able to do the board as often or as long as Jessica, but it's amazing how much more receptive I've become to everyone around me since I began doing the board.''

"I'm still not entirely convinced by Michael," Arnold Harris admits as he smooths back his badger-gray hair, "but I keep coming back to sessions. When I was told that I am a mature slave, I rejected it, but I've come to see that it's true. I do want to be of real service to people. I believe that money should be a tool, not an end in itself, which is not the common attitude among bankers. I see that I put myself in a position where I could be of real world service to others. Also, Leah and I have three children, and two of them are rambunctious young souls. Having this information has made it easier to live with them, most particularly during the teens."

"Yes, indeed," Leah agrees. "I won't say that all our problems were solved, because they weren't. However, I hope we were able to minimize our mistakes, and that's something. Compared to what some of our friends went through, we have had an easy time of it. Michael has given me insight in dealing with others in business as well as those in the family. It's helpful to know if you're dealing with a baby priest or a mature sage when you're trying to get something done. I know that I often have difficulty with baby souls, and priests and I, for some reason, rarely hit it off. It's good to be free from that need to make everyone like me. It's perfectly all right if I don't get along with everyone. At the same time, I'm more tolerant because I realize that just as there are people I can't deal with, there are people who can't deal with me, and one is as important as the other."

"It's also OK to get out of stalemated situations," Jessica adds quickly. "I was taught that I should hang in there at any cost for as long as it took. Now I see that there's no shame in refusing to prolong such a relationship."

Sam Chasen is next. "With a job like mine, anything that gives some insight has got to help. I've developed a great many defenses over the years, partly because of the polio, partly because I'm homosexual. It's comfortable being in a group like this, where I don't feel I have to justify myself, or defend myself against real and imagined slights. It's true that I'm not very happy with my life, which is typical of mature souls. I think now that I made some poor choices. I know that I abdicated two agreements to do sequences, one of them an agreement I'd abdicated before. I'm trying to get the courage up to tackle that agreement again in this life. The trouble is that I hate being rejected—that damn chief feature of arrogance. What Michael has said has been instrumental in forcing me to make certain decisions I had been vacillating about. He's also made me see that most of my disappointments have arisen out of my expectations, not the actual situations, and that is extremely helpful."

"That's true," Tracy Rowland says, nodding. "Learning about false personality was useful to me as well. I can remember many times when I was a kid being told that nice little girls don't do whatever it was I was doing. I was trained to deny whole aspects of myself, and that was very difficult. Getting more insight into the past has made me more aware of why I respond as I do to certain things. Michael has pointed out several ways that I can make use of the knowledge gained in recall. Warrior to warrior, Sam, don't you find that knowing the nature of your role in essence keeps you from subverting the thrust of your own energy?"

"Yeah," Sam says after a moment. "I don't give away my energy the way I used to, in the hope that it would protect me."

Tracy gathers her hands into fists. "It's kind of fun to be ferocious." She grins. "Also, working the board has opened a lot of channels in me. Jessica has been tremendously helpful there, and I've developed faster than I thought I would."

Kate O'Brien adds, "I've studied several occult techniques, and this has been one of the most practical and consistent. I'm extremely wary of anything that has overtones of religion, despite seven lives dedicated to some religion or another, and many occult practices are really religious in form. This teaching isn't, although I don't know how long I'll stay with the group. I haven't felt the need to withdraw yet, but experience tells me that I need to occasionally distance myself from just about everything. The results, I suppose, of being a mature scholar in observation. Hell, it took me six years just to complete a B.A., and the M.A. will probably take me just as long. The nice thing is, I know that if I leave this group for a while, I can always come back."

Marjorie Randall says, "If the only thing Michael told me was about the Dresden life and my past association with my sponsor family, it would have been more than enough to satisfy me. But there have been other sorts of information as well, and my curiosity is enormous. I'm very eager to pursue the questions that Michael has raised in my mind. There are new questions arising all the time, and I want the answers to them. What Jessica said a while ago, about being convinced that there *were* answers, and that it's possible to know what they are, if only between lives, that's pretty much the way I feel."

Corrine Lawton shrugs. "I've found that mathematics and Michael are in basic agreement, and what Michael has said is more thoroughly consistent than any other esoteric material I've read. It pleases me to know that I'm responsible for myself, and I find the statement that we each, essentially, keep the records on ourselves more mathematically elegant than most of the other theories about the questions of morality, judgment, and such things as the akashic record."

But what does Michael provide that keeps them coming back? Isn't it enough to get a grasp on karma, soul level, essence role, overleaves, agreements, sequences, and other associations and simply carry on from there?

"Sure," Jessica says. "However, sessions can be very enlightening in themselves. Besides, most of us like each other, and we're curious. Saturday afternoon, twice a month, we can get together, discuss this information which we can't, in general, talk about with other people, and we get the communication. Would you give up something so useful and supportive?"

Chapter 14

A MICHAEL SESSION . . .

What is your conception of a séance? Dark rooms? Scented candles, incense, and peculiar symbols on the wall? Hushed voices? The materialization of trumpets and tambourines? The lady in the turban moaning about Princess Ti-Ling?

The Michael group meets for sessions (they prefer not to call them séances) in Jessica's and Walter's living room on Saturday afternoons. The room is a sunny one, and the picture windows open onto wooded slopes. There are comfortable chairs and a long sofa for those attending. Three cats and a dog wander in and out, though one of the cats will curl up on the baby grand piano. On the coffee table there is a coffee pot, a tea pot, cream and sugar for those who use them, and beer.

This particular session took place in late September 1978. It was a warm afternoon. Jessica's daughter and her boyfriend were out on the hillside cutting back the shrubs. A few houses away, neighbors were having a barbecue and the scent of the cooking food was occasionally carried into the house on the cool breeze.

Jessica sat in her rocking chair, her legs crossed under her and her Ouija board on her knees. She sat with her back to the window. "The view's distracting," she explained to one of the new people.

There were five women at that session, and six men: Lucy North, Emily Wright, Tracy Rowland, Kate O'Brien, Marjorie Randall, David Swan, Matthew Harrison, James Vernett, Hector (called Terry) MacMillan, and Laurence Silva. Craig Wright was at the session for about an hour but was called on an emergency and had to leave early. Matthew Harrison and James Vernett are biologists, colleagues of Marjorie's. Hector MacMillan is an artist friend of Walter's and Laurence Silva is a psychologist who came to that session on Craig's invitation.

When everyone had got what they wanted to drink, they settled back, ready to write.

"Who wants to go first?" Jessica asked.

"I do," Marjorie said at once. "I need some insight from Michael about a man in our department. He's driving us all nuts. He says he'll do things, and then he doesn't. He's been late for lectures three times in the last month, and his students say that he's never in his office at the posted hours."

"What do you want to know?" Jessica inquired as she brought the planchette onto the board.

"First I want his overleaves, and then I want to know what to do about him." Marjorie is obviously very annoyed at this man, and the two colleagues she has brought with her, though they appear apprehensive, nod in agreement.

WHAT WOULD YOU SAY HIS OVERLEAVES ARE, MARJORIE?

"Michael does that sometimes," Marjorie explained to her guests. "He wants us to get used to thinking of the material in a useful way." She threw back her head and stared at the ceiling, then declared with an exasperated chuckle, "I think he's a forty-fourth level baby turkey in the obnoxion mode with a goal of consternation and a chief feature of irresponsibility!"

Everyone laughed.

Eventually Jessica returned her attention to the board.

WE CAN UNDERSTAND HOW YOU MIGHT SAY THIS. THIS IS A SECOND-LEVEL YOUNG SCHOLAR IN THE PASSION MODE WITH A GOAL OF REPRESSION, A CYNIC IN THE EMOTIONAL PART OF MOVING CENTER, WITH A STRONG CHIEF FEATURE

OF ARROGANCE. HIS OVERLEAVES ABRADE INTERNALLY, AND ABRADE WITH YOURS, MARJORIE.

"I thought that scholars usually got along with scholars," Marjorie protested.

YOU ARE SEVENTH-LEVEL MATURE, WE REMIND YOU, AND HAVE MUCH MORE EXPERIENCE UNDER YOUR BELT THAN HE HAS. HE SENSES SOMETHING OF THIS, BY THE WAY, AND RESENTS IT. WE WOULD THINK THAT THERE IS LITTLE YOU CAN DO TO CHANGE HIM.

"How about ax murder?" Marjorie suggested with a gesture of resignation.

THAT IS YOUR CHOICE, OF COURSE, BUT IT WOULD ADD UNNECESSARILY TO YOUR KARMIC DEBTS.

"Aw, come on, Michael," Kate says, "can't you take a joke? Oh, no, never mind. Don't answer that." She chuckles.

"He's got more to say," Jessica said as the planchette continued to move under her fingers.

The others readied their pens and waited.

YOUNG SOULS NEED TO EXERT THEMSELVES ON THEIR ENVIRONMENT, WHICH INCLUDES OTHER FRAGMENTS. THE MAN IS ATTEMPTING TO CONVINCE HIMSELF OF HIS OWN INFLATED IMPORTANCE BY MAKING YOU APPEAR INCOMPETENT. YOUR PROTESTS WILL ONLY SERVE TO CONVINCE HIM THAT YOU ARE NOT ABLE TO DO THE TASKS HE HAS ASSIGNED TO YOU. WE REALIZE THAT THIS IS NOT THE CASE, BUT THAT DOES NOT CONVINCE THE MAN. YOU WILL HAVE TO REFUSE HIS COERCION IF YOU WISH TO CONTINUE WORKING WITH HIM.

"But I don't want to go on working with him," Marjorie declared. "Neither do Matt and Jim. That's why they're here."

"We've tried to go through channels," Matthew Harrison said. "The department head doesn't want to make things any worse, and I can't say I blame him, but this guy is the most impossible bastard I've ever worked with."

"He's ruining our freshman biology class," Marjorie said, shaking her head. "You can't expect the students to put up with that kind of contempt. They know that good old Invisible Tom doesn't give two damns for them."

"Invisible Tom?" Craig asked.

"That's his nickname because no one ever sees him," Jim explained.

WE WOULD SAY THAT PRESSURE ON THIS MAN WILL ONLY MAKE THE SITUATION WORSE.

"Then what can we do? I can't let my students be treated so badly. I had a kid in my office yesterday who was almost in tears because she's been trying for weeks to get a skeleton for a project and Invisible Tom keeps forgetting to requisition one for her. That's a terrible thing to do for enthusiastic students." Marjorie was becoming distressed, and Matt laid a big hand on her arm.

"We're all up against the same thing with Invisible Tom," he confirmed. "We've all tried talking to him, but it's like talking to a wall or a bedpost. He won't listen."

"Is there anything that Invisible Tom is working out?" Kate asked.

THE MAN THOMAS IS TRYING TO AVOID THE COMPLETION OF A MONAD. HIS FALSE PERSONALITY IS VERY STRONG, AND THE COMPLETION OF THE MONAD WOULD FORCE HIM TO RECOGNIZE THIS. WE REMIND YOU THAT IT IS HIS CHOICE, AND THAT IF HE CHOOSES TO ABDICATE, IT IS HIS RIGHT TO DO SO. HE WILL NOT RESPOND WELL TO YOUR EFFORTS TO CHANGE HIS MIND. WE GIVE THIS WARNING IN PARTICULAR TO THE MAN MATTHEW, WHO IS A MATURE WARRIOR IN THE POWER MODE, AND THEREFORE IS PREDISPOSED TO BRING PRESSURE TO BEAR ON OTHERS.

"Mature warrior, hmm?" Matthew said. "What's the rest of it?"

Here Jessica interrupted. "I think it would be a good idea to tell him what you feel you are. Michael gives better responses if we meet him halfway."

Marjorie studied her colleague. "He's got to have something to mellow that power mode, and the mature cycle isn't enough. He's probably a pragmatist with a goal of growth." She looked at Jessica for confirmation from the board.

THE LADY MARJORIE IS CORRECT ABOUT THE ATTITUDE. THIS IS INDEED A PRAGMATIST, BUT WITH A GOAL OF ACCEPTANCE, IN THE EMOTIONAL PART OF INTELLECTUAL CENTER WITH A CHIEF FEATURE OF STUBBORNNESS.

"Yeah," Matthew said slowly, "that sounds right. Goal of acceptance, huh?"

THE MAN JAMES IS A SEVENTH-LEVEL YOUNG SAGE IN

THE OBSERVATION MODE WITH A GOAL OF DOMINANCE, A SKEPTIC IN THE MOVING PART OF INTELLECTUAL CENTER, WITH A CHIEF FEATURE OF ARROGANCE. WE WOULD SAY THAT IF THE MAN JAMES HAD A MORE EMOTIONAL CENTER, HE WOULD HAVE IDEAL OVERLEAVES FOR AN ACTOR. AS IT IS, HE DOES NOT TRUST HIS EMOTIONS AND THEREFORE AVOIDS THAT OCCUPATION. HOWEVER, GIVEN THE NATURE OF THE ESSENCE AND SOUL LEVEL, IT IS INEVITABLE THAT THIS FRAGMENT WILL EXPERIENCE A NEED TO BE IN THE LIMELIGHT AND HAVE THOSE PERSONALITY TRAITS THAT ARE MISLABELED "CHARISMATIC." HE WOULD ALSO BE A FAIRLY SUCCESSFUL POLITICIAN, SHOULD HE FIND HIMSELF SO INCLINED.

"Thanks, I'll stick to biology. We've got enough inter-departmental politics to keep me happy for some time."

Marjorie smiled. "Michael's right about you, Jim. You are a showman. That's one of the reasons you're so popular with your students. The lecture you give on the evolution of mammals is a very neat piece of theater."

For a moment Jim Vernett looked huffy, and then he relaxed with a wide, contagious grin. "I see what you mean. Well, why not? If they learn something, the entertainment won't hurt them, and if they don't, the entertainment will keep them occupied and amused while the real students learn."

"That's a neat rationalization," Kate observed.

Jim was not offended. He gave a shrug, enjoying the attention. "It works. I'm not like Matt, who scares half his students."

"Well, what do you expect of a warrior?" Matt demanded in comic dismay.

Jessica interrupted this. "Do either of you have any more questions, or shall we get on to some of the others?"

"As a matter of fact, I do have another couple of questions," Matt said, growing serious. "I've been reading Marj's notes, and I see that Michael has said that animals have hive souls. How does he account for the difference in personalities?"

ANIMALS ARE SUPERB MIMICS, AND WILL PICK UP THE BEHAVIOR OF THE CONSCIOUS BEINGS AROUND THEM. WHEN THEY ARE WITH OLDER SOULS, THEY WILL OFTEN EXHIBIT A GREATER TENDENCY TO COMMUNICATE AND INTERACT

WITH THEIR HUMAN OWNERS BECAUSE THE OLDER CYCLES ARE INHERENTLY OPEN TO THIS CONTACT. WE HAVE KNOWN OF PETS WHO UNDERSTAND MORE THAN FIFTY WORDS AND PHRASES AND HAVE WELL-ESTABLISHED RITUALS WITH THEIR OWNERS THAT VERGE ON THE UNCANNY. DOGS ARE MORE APT TO TAKE ON THE OUTWARD CHARACTERISTICS OF THEIR OWNERS THAN CATS ARE. THAT IS BECAUSE DOGS ARE DESCENDED FROM SOCIAL ANIMALS, WHO HUNT IN PACKS. CATS, ON THE OTHER HAND, ARE DESCENDED FROM SOLITARY HUNTERS, AND WILL HAVE MORE QUIRKS AND INDEPENDENCE. CATS ARE LIKELY TO PICK UP ON THE NONSOCIAL SIGNALS JUST AS DOGS ARE LIKELY TO RESPOND TO THE SOCIAL ONES. YOU NEED ONLY EXAMINE THE BEHAVIOR OF THEIR WILD COUNTERPARTS TO SEE HOW THIS EVOLVED.

"I've got another question," Matt said as this was read back to him. "Are humans the only species on this planet that have the kinds of souls that we do—that go through reincarnation and growth?"

THERE ARE TWO SUCH SPECIES ON THIS PLANET. HUMAN BEINGS AND CETACEANS. THAT IS, WHALES AND DOLPHINS. HOWEVER, WE THINK THAT YOU SHOULD KNOW THAT THERE ARE OVER TEN MILLION ENSOULED SPECIES IN THIS GALAXY ALONE.

"I don't believe that!" Jim burst out, and Craig Wright sat upright.

WE HAVE TOLD YOU OFTEN THAT BELIEF IS NOT REQUIRED. THERE ARE TWO ENSOULED SPECIES ON YOUR PLANET. THAT IS A FACT.

"Do they have the same sorts of goals and all that?" Kate asked.

There was an eagerness in the room, and the planchette moved very fast as Jessica read off the letters.

ALL ENSOULED SPECIES OR CONSCIOUS CREATURES OF THE PHYSICAL PLANE HAVE THE SAME ROLES IN ESSENCE: SLAVE, ARTISAN, WARRIOR, SCHOLAR, SAGE, PRIEST, AND KING. ALL HAVE THE SAME MODES: CAUTION, REPRESSION, PERSEVERANCE, OBSERVATION, AGGRESSION, PASSION, AND POWER. ALL HAVE THE SAME GOALS: REJECTION, RETARDATION, SUBMISSION, STAGNATION, DOMINANCE, GROWTH, AND ACCEPTANCE. ALL HAVE THE SAME ATTITUDES: SKEPTIC, STOIC, CYNIC, PRAGMATIST, REALIST, SPIRITUALIST, AND IDEALIST. ALL HAVE THE SAME CENTERS FROM WHICH

TO ACT: INTELLECTUAL, EMOTIONAL, SEXUAL, INSTINC-
TIVE, MOVING, HIGHER EMOTIONAL, AND HIGHER IN-
TELLECTUAL. ALL HAVE THE SAME CHIEF FEATURES:
SELF-DESTRUCTION, SELF-DEPRECATION, MARTYRDOM,
STUBBORNNESS, IMPATIENCE, ARROGANCE, AND GREED.
THERE ARE DIFFERENT EMPHASES PUT ON THESE OVER-
LEAVES FROM PLANET TO PLANET, FROM SPECIES TO SPE-
CIES. WE ASK YOU TO REMEMBER THAT EVEN THE VASTNESS
OF INTERGALACTIC SPACE IS PART OF THE PHYSICAL PLANE,
NOT OF THE HIGHER PLANES. WITHIN ALL THE SENTIENT
SPECIES, MEANING THOSE WITH INDIVIDUAL SOULS THAT
ARE CAPABLE OF EVOLUTION, THERE IS ALWAYS THE EXIS-
TENCE OF EXPRESSION, INSPIRATION, ACTION, AND ASSIMI-
LATION. THESE ROLES AND OVERLEAVES ARE THE ONLY
WAY THAT WE KNOW OF THAT SUCH EXISTENCE CAN BE
REALIZED. FOR EXAMPLE, THE SAGE IS A ROLE OF EXPRES-
SION, BUT IT IS NECESSARY THAT THE FRAGMENT EXPERI-
ENCE INSPIRATION. THE OVERLEAVES SELECTED WILL BE
PASSION OR REPRESSION, GROWTH OR RETARDATION, STOIC
OR SPIRITUALIST, HIGHER EMOTIONAL OR EMOTIONAL, AND
ARROGANCE OR SELF-DEPRECATION, DEPENDING ON
WHETHER THE EXPERIENCE IS TO BE POSITIVE OR NEGATIVE.
AS THE FRAGMENT EVOLVES, IT BECOMES MORE ADEPT AT
SELECTING OVERLEAVES. MONADS AND KARMIC RIBBONS
MAY INFLUENCE THE CHOICE OF OVERLEAVES AS WELL.

"Back to whales and dolphins . . ." Emily said.

"I can't accept that," Craig interrupted, and was given
a supportive nod from Jim. "If they're truly ensouled, then
we should be able to communicate with them."

YOU CANNOT COMMUNICATE WITH YOUR FELLOW HU-
MANS. WHY SHOULD YOU EXTEND THE CONFUSION BEYOND
YOUR SPECIES? HOWEVER, WE WILL SAY THIS: THE CETA-
CEANS HAVE EVOLVED SO THAT THEY HAVE HEARING AS
THEIR DOMINANT SENSE, AS YOU HAVE SIGHT. YOU RELATE
TO THE WORLD VISUALLY AND THEY RELATE TO IT AU-
RALLY. IF YOU WISH THEM TO UNDERSTAND YOU, WE
WOULD SUGGEST THAT MUSIC, THE MORE MELODIOUS AND
COMPLEX THE BETTER, WOULD BE MUCH APPRECIATED BY
THESE FRAGMENTS.

"Are they at the same level of development as we are?"
Kate asked.

WE HAVE TOLD YOU THAT THIS IS A YOUNG-SOUL PLANET.

MOST OF THE CETACEANS ARE AT THE SAME LEVEL THAT YOU ARE, YES.

"If you kill one," Emily said, ignoring the quelling look from her husband, Craig, "is it murder and does it incur a karmic debt?"

OF COURSE.

"Do any of us have dolphin souls?" Craig asked sarcastically.

WE HAVE TOLD YOU THAT HUMANS INVARIABLY REINCARNATE IN HUMAN FORM, AND THIS IS A FACT. AS LONG AS A SPECIES IS PLANET-BOUND, AS YOU ARE, THEN THEIR EXPERIENCE WILL BE LIMITED TO THE SPECIES INTO WHICH ALL OF THE ENTITY MEMBERS ARE CAST. WHEN A SPECIES GETS OUT INTO THE LARGER REALMS OF THE GALAXY, THEN IT IS OFTEN USEFUL TO EXPERIENCE LIFE IN DIFFERENT SPECIES AS WELL AS IN DIFFERENT BODIES. SINCE THE ROLES, MODES, GOALS, CENTERS, ATTITUDES, AND CHIEF FEATURES ARE ALL UNIVERSAL, THERE IS MUCH TO BE GAINED IN THIS EXPERIENCE. WHEN HUMANKIND EVOLVES AND ENTERS THE RANKS OF THE SPACE-GOING SPECIES, THEN HUMAN SOULS WILL ALSO EXPERIENCE TRANS-SPECIES REINCARNATION. THAT IS STILL VERY MUCH IN THE FUTURE, AND WE SUGGEST THAT YOU ATTEND TO THE TASKS YOU HAVE SET FOR YOURSELF IN THIS WORLD.

"Does that mean that we don't experience life as dolphins?" Lucy said, a little disappointed. "I think it would be kind of fun to be a dolphin or a whale, don't you?"

YOU WILL BE ABLE TO DO THAT WHEN HUMANKIND IS NOT PLANET-BOUND. UNTIL THAT TIME, YOU WILL EXPERIENCE LIFE IN HUMAN FORM ONLY.

"Next you'll be talking about UFOs," Jim Vernett said scornfully.

IT WAS NOT OUR INTENTION TO DO SO. WE ARE HERE TO ANSWER YOUR QUESTIONS.

"All right then, are there UFOs, and if so, what are they?" Matt asked.

MOST ARE SIMPLY WHAT THEIR NAME IMPLIES—UNIDENTIFIED FLYING OBJECTS. A FEW ARE ROBOT MONITORS, A FEW ARE THOSE MAKING STUDIES. A FEW ARE LOST. A FEW ARE WHAT YOU WOULD PROBABLY CALL TOURISTS. THEY DO NOT ALL REPRESENT ONE SPECIES. THEY ARE FROM MANY PLACES AND CULTURES.

"This is absurd!" Craig insisted. "First whales and dolphins, and now little green men from outer space."

WE DID NOT SAY THERE WERE LITTLE GREEN MEN, THOUGH THERE ARE TWO SPECIES NOT UNLIKE YOUR OWN. OTHERS ARE SO VASTLY UNLIKE YOU THAT IT IS PROBABLE THAT YOU WOULD NOT RECOGNIZE THEM AS LIVING, LET ALONE SENTIENT.

"I read a book that said there were aliens on the moon," Lucy said, a wistful look in her blue eyes.

THERE HAVE BEEN EXTRATERRESTRIALS ON THE MOON IN THE PAST. MOST OF THEIR ACTIVITY WAS CONFINED TO WHAT YOU CALL THE DARK SIDE. THERE ARE A FEW ROBOT MACHINES STILL THERE, MORE OF THEM DEVOTED TO MINING THAN ANYTHING ELSE, THOUGH THERE ARE TWO MONITOR STATIONS RECORDING ACTIVITY IN THIS SOLAR SYSTEM.

"Come off it!" Jim Vernett got up and began to pace. "I'm a biologist, and I tell you, all of this sounds like so much bullshit."

YOU MEAN THAT YOU ARE FRIGHTENED, AND YOUR CHIEF FEATURE WILL NOT ALLOW YOU TO ADMIT THAT YOU MIGHT BE WRONG. WE IMPART INFORMATION WITHOUT BIAS. IT IS YOURS TO ACCEPT OR REJECT AS YOU CHOOSE. YOUR ACCEPTANCE OR REJECTION, HOWEVER, DOES NOT IN ANY WAY ALTER THESE FACTS.

"Go get him, Michael!" Lucy cheered when she had finished reading back the dictation.

Walter was looking decidedly uncomfortable. "Jessica, maybe you'd better take other questions. This isn't getting us anywhere."

"I want Michael to explain," Craig insisted. "He's never said anything like this before."

NOTHING WAS ASKED. OUR PURPOSE IS TO ANSWER YOUR QUESTIONS. IF YOU WISH TO KNOW MORE OF THE OTHER ENSOULED SPECIES IN THE PHYSICAL UNIVERSE, YOU HAVE ONLY TO ASK. MOST OF THESE SPECIES THAT GO INTO SPACE ARE LATE YOUNG AND EARLY MATURE, ONLY SLIGHTLY MORE ADVANCED THAN YOUR WORLD IS NOW. THERE ARE OTHER SPECIES, HOWEVER, THAT DUE TO THEIR PHYSICAL NATURE ENTER AT A MUCH EARLIER STAGE IN THEIR EVOLUTION. SOME ENTER LATER, SOME NOT AT ALL. THOSE SPECIES THAT YOU MIGHT RECOGNIZE AS BEING AKIN TO

PLANTS RATHER THAN ANIMALS DO NOT OFTEN GO INTO
SPACE, THOUGH SOME OF THEM ARE ACTIVE IN DEALING
WITH TRAVELERS.

"But that's crazy!" Jim declared.

"I think it's great," Lucy answered at once.

"This isn't getting us anyplace," Walter muttered.

"Our sessions aren't usually like this," Emily said to the
other first-timers. "All this material is new to us."

"That's why it's good to get new people into the group,"
Jessica said, a little too loudly. "Otherwise we'd still be
going over the same ground we were five years ago."

"Is the ancient astronauts theory correct, then?" David
Swan asked, ignoring the argument that was getting under-
way.

FOR THE MOST PART, WE WOULD RELEGATE SUCH MA-
TERIAL TO WISHFUL THINKING. THERE WERE SOME EARLY
OBSERVERS OF THIS PLANET, BUT A GREAT MANY OF THE
ANCIENT CIVILIZATIONS THAT YOU REGARD AS PRIMITIVE
WERE MORE ADVANCED THAN YOU REALIZE. FOR EXAMPLE,
THE INCAN CIVILIZATION USED LOOKOUT KITES LARGE
ENOUGH TO CARRY A MAN. THESE WERE KEPT ON LONG
TETHERS SO THAT THE MAN COULD WATCH ON MOUNTAIN
ROADS AND PASSES. SUCH KITES ARE MORE EASILY KEPT
ALOFT IN MOUNTAINS THAN ON PLAINS, AND SERVE A MORE
USEFUL PURPOSE. YOU UNDERRATE YOUR OWN SPECIES IF
YOU ASSUME THAT ANY AND ALL ADVANCES HAD TO BE
GIVEN TO YOU BY EXTRATERRESTRIAL VISITORS.

"If these things really existed, why didn't they survive?"
Kate asked.

MOST OF THESE KITES WERE MADE OF HIDE AND WOOD,
BOTH OF WHICH DECAY RAPIDLY. THOUGH THE INCAS DID
NOT INVENT THE WHEEL, THEY WERE VERY GOOD WITH
OTHER KINDS OF ENGINEERING, AS EXAMINATIONS OF THE
RUINS OF THEIR CITIES REVEAL.

"I've got a book on Incan ruins," Walter interjected. "I
found the whole thing absolutely fascinating. It was as if I'd
been there, but not as one of the builders."

AS A SPANIARD, IN FACT. YOU WERE ONE OF PIZARRO'S
COMPANY WHO CAME TO PERU. YOU WERE A FARRIER,
THEN, AND THE STRANGE CULTURE BOTH INTRIGUED AND
REPELLED YOU, SINCE YOU WERE, AT THAT TIME, A DEEPLY
COMMITTED CATHOLIC.

Walter looked disgusted. "I've always been appalled at what the Spaniards did in Mexico and the rest of Latin America. It seems immoral."

THAT WAS WHAT YOU LEARNED AFTER THAT LIFE. YOU COULD REVIEW THE TRUTH OF THAT LIFE AND SEE WHERE YOUR PERCEPTIONS HAD BEEN DISTORTED. IN THAT LIFE YOU DIED OF GANGRENE AFTER A MINOR WOUND HAD BECOME INFECTED. YOU HAD A FAIR AMOUNT OF TIME TO THINK ABOUT WHAT YOU HAD DONE BEFORE THE ACTUAL MOMENT OF DEATH. THAT WAS AN INTERRUPTED LIFE, AND IT TOOK YOU THREE MORE LIVES TO COMPLETE THE LEVEL BEGUN THEN.

"Since we're asking about history," said Kate, "what about King Tut; is there anything else that might be discovered about the Egyptians if we searched further?"

WE WOULD THINK THAT THE TIME COULD BE BETTER SPENT IN GETTING THE COMPLETE AND ACCURATE TRANSLATION OF ALL THE ENGRAVINGS AND WRITINGS ON THE WALLS AND VARIOUS OBJECTS IN THE TOMB THAN IN BEING LURED FARTHER AFIELD BY THE GLITTER OF UNDISCOVERED TREASURE. WE WOULD SAY THAT THIS COULD APPLY TO ALL EGYPTIAN ANTIQUITIES DISCOVERED TO DATE.

Previously, Michael had said that in Egypt the field of architecture was considered religious study, and that many of the temples and other large buildings are oriented to specific sorts of astronomical locations. All the information concerning this is written down already and waiting to be translated. In the large temple at Karnak, the pillars are placed in such a way that they are lit up during the solstices and equinoxes. It is these specific pillars that contain the pertinent information. Although some of the writing has faded, it could be brought back with modern techniques such as lasers. There are also ruins in China that have similar functions to the pyramids; some have not been discovered as yet, some have not yet been fully explored, and some are ignored by an ignorant populace (a religious temple is mistakenly thought to be a palace, etc.). One of the problems is that most academics make the mistake of thinking that aesthetics and the sciences are necessarily dissimilar.

In speaking of the pyramids—which sometimes are connected with the myths of Atlantis—Michael said that Atlantis is located off the coast of Portugal. He also said that the influence of Atlantean civilization spread further than anyone is aware.

"Well, if you're going to ask about flying saucers and such," said Lucy, "then how about some explanation of what is occurring, if anything, in the area known as the Bermuda Triangle?"

FIRST WE WOULD WANT TO REMIND YOU THAT WHAT YOU CALL SOLID GROUND IS PART OF A CRUST FLOATING ON THE OUTSIDE OF THE MOLTEN INNER CORE OF EARTH, AND THIS CRUST IS NOT PARTICULARY STABLE. SECOND, THOUGH GRAVITY IS A VERY REAL FACTOR ON THIS AND EVERY OTHER PLANET, IT IS NOT A COMPLETELY UNIFORM FORCE. WHEN THERE IS AN INTERACTION OF GRAVITY AND VARIOUS OF THE GEOPHYSICAL STRESSES CREATED BY "CONTINENTAL DRAG," AS WELL AS "CONTINENTAL DRIFT," CERTAIN ANOMALIES OCCUR. SOME OF THESE ARE MINOR DISTURBANCES OF AREAS OF LAND OR SEA WHERE COMPASSES BEHAVE ODDLY, WHERE PLANTS GROW OUT OF "PLUMB," AND WHERE OTHER UNEXPECTED AND IRREGULAR CONDITIONS PREVAIL.

OF COURSE, THERE ARE CERTAIN ANOMALIES THAT COVER A WIDER AREA AND WHICH ARE PART OF A MORE EXTENSIVE PHENOMENON. THE AREA KNOWN AS THE BERMUDA TRIANGLE IS ONE OF THE BETTER KNOWN OF THESE AREAS. AS WE HAVE INDICATED, THIS IS NOT THE ONLY SUCH AREA. WE WOULD THINK THAT A SYSTEMATIC MONITORING OF SUCH SUSPECT AREAS BY SOME OF YOUR MORE SOPHISTICATED SATELLITES, PARTICULARLY THOSE DOING VARIOUS SORTS OF HEAT AND RADIATION ANALYSIS, MIGHT LEAD TO SOME USEFUL DISCOVERIES CONCERNING THE NATURE OF SUCH ANOMALIES. WE WOULD THINK THAT THE BEST TIME TO MAKE SUCH AN ANALYSIS IS WHILE THE AREAS ARE MOST ACTIVE. THE ACTIVITY DOES VARY IN THESE ANOMALOUS AREAS, YOU KNOW. SOME OF THE ANOMALIES ON LAND— AT LEAST THE MORE EXTENSIVE ONES—ARE POTENTIALLY MORE HAZARDOUS THAN THOSE IN THE OCEAN.

MANY ANIMALS CAN SENSE THIS HAZARD AND REFUSE TO ENTER THE DANGER ZONE. WE KNOW OF ONE SUCH AREA IN THE REGION OF WHAT IS NOW CALLED THE GOBI DESERT, WHERE NO ANIMAL WILL ENTER. THE POTENTIAL TO SENSE SUCH AREAS IS WITHIN EVERY ONE OF YOU, BUT FEW OF YOU ARE WILLING TO ACCEPT THE VALIDITY OF SUCH

PERCEPTION. OBVIOUSLY, THESE ARE THE ONES WHO OFTEN DO NOT SURVIVE CONTACT WITH THOSE ANOMALOUS AREAS.

Jim Vernett took the empty chair beside Jessica and glared at her. "This stuff is absurd."

Jessica set the planchette aside. "I don't think so."

"But you're a sensible woman," he said, suddenly very persuasive. "Yet you sit here on a beautiful afternoon with a Ouija board in your lap. Doesn't that seem strange to you? Wouldn't you rather be over at your neighbors', having a barbecued dinner?"

"Mr. Vernett," Jessica said when she had studied him a moment, "I can understand why this might shock you. It shocked me for quite a while. But most of the people in this room have serious questions to ask. If you dont like what you're hearing, you can leave. No one is forcing you to listen to these answers. No one is forcing you to ask questions. No one is saying that you have to agree with what's said. But I'm telling you that if you're disruptive, I'd prefer that you leave."

"Hey, Jessica," Craig said. "That's being a little unfair . . ."

The phone rang and Walter was glad to answer it. "I can't take bickering," he muttered to Emily as he went into the study across the hall from the living room. A few moments later he called out, "Craig! It's for you!"

"Coming!" Craig left the room at once, saying as he went, "I think we might have to stay away from this kind of speculation, Jessica. We've got better questions for Michael."

"You know, when Marj told me about these sessions," Jim was saying, leaning forward and smiling a little, "I thought they'd be fun. I was curious, I admit that. I thought it would be a kick to know what kind of past lives you'd come up with for me. But this stuff about whales and dolphins and extraterrestrials is utter nonsense. You know that."

Jessica's expression changed a little, becoming slightly remote. "You seem to think *I'm* doing this. I'm not. Whatever answers I get come from someplace else. When I've done trance sessions, the voice Michael speaks with doesn't sound at all like mine. Now, can we get on with the session?"

Craig looked back into the living room. "I've got to go,

Jessica, Walter. Emily, can you get a ride home with someone?"

"I'll give her a lift," Tracy said.

"Thanks. One of my patients was in an automobile accident. The silly bastard had surgery ten days ago, and he went for an afternoon drive. He sideswiped another car. I'm going to have to get to the hospital right now. The ambulance should be there in ten minutes." He was pulling on his jacket as he spoke. He gave the group a quick wave, then hurried out the door and down the walk.

"Poor Craig," Emily said as they heard his car door slam. "The last time he had an emergency like that, we were getting ready to go to the theater in San Francisco, and it was so late that I ended up going alone and Craig didn't get home until after two."

When they had heard Craig's car drive off, Jessica said to the room at large, "OK, who's next?"

Once again Jim Vernett tried to interrupt her, but she totally ignored him. "You have a question, Walter?"

"Yes," he said, grateful that the bickering had stopped. "Why is my sister Ellen sleeping so much?"

SHE IS SLEEPING BECAUSE SHE IS BORED. BOREDOM IS A VICIOUS CYCLE. IT CAUSES SLEEP, WHICH CAUSES MORE ENNUI, WHICH IN TURN CAUSES A GREATER NEED FOR SLEEP. WATCHING TELEVISION IS A FORM OF SLEEP. SHE IS JUST MORE OVERT IN HER ACTIONS. SHE MUST CONSCIOUSLY BREAK THE HABIT AND THE CYCLE.

"Is there anything I can do to help her?" Walter wondered.

OTHER THAN GIVE HER APPROVAL, NO, NOT MUCH. WE REMIND YOU THAT FEW ARTISANS ARE PILLARS OF STRENGTH, AND THAT SUCH FRAGMENTS OFTEN DESIRE TO BE OF HELP, AS YOU DO, WALTER, BUT DO NOT WANT TO BE LEANED ON. THIS IS NOT SAID AS CRITICISM, MERELY TO REMIND YOU THAT IT IS NOT EASY FOR ARTISANS TO LEND THAT HELP, AND IF YOU INTEND TO DO SO, YOU WILL HAVE TO USE MORE ENERGY THAN YOU MAY BE AWARE OF AT THIS TIME. BY THE WAY, SAGES SHARE THIS DIFFICULTY, AS THEIR NEED FOR ATTENTION OFTEN MAKES IT HARD FOR THEM TO GIVE THE NECESSARY AMOUNT OF ATTENTION TO OTHERS.

"I've got a question about a woman I work with," Tracy said after the dictation had been read back. "She's going through a rough time, but I don't think there's anything wrong with her in the usual sense. She's hardworking, in good health, and her life is pretty stable, but she's very restless. Any comments?"

THE LADY IS, OF COURSE, NOW IN THE TRANSITION AT THE POINT OF LIFE WHEN THE ROLE IN ESSENCE MANIFESTS. THIS IS A TIME OF REAL UPHEAVAL FOR ALL WHO ARE ACHIEVERS AND WHO, AT THIS POINT, MUST PAUSE TO RE-ASSESS THEIR LIVES IN TERMS OF GOALS THAT HAVE AND HAVE NOT BEEN REACHED. IT IS NO DIFFERENT FOR THIS FRAGMENT. IN HER SEARCHING SHE COMES BACK AGAIN AND AGAIN TO HER PRESENT STATE BECAUSE OF HER DOUBTS, WHICH ARE MORE A PART OF THE PERIOD SHE HAS ENTERED THAN THE PRODUCT OF ANY TANGIBLE OR OUTWARD CON-DITION. CHANGES OF A MASSIVE NATURE WOULD ONLY GIVE RISE TO AN EVER WIDER SEARCH AND EVENTUALLY TO MORE FRUSTRATION AS SHE DISCOVERS THAT SHE WAS NOT ON THE PATH AFTER ALL. INTERPERSONAL RELATIONSHIPS ARE NOW MORE DIFFICULT, NOT BECAUSE OF FRUSTRATIONS THAT ARE EASILY TALKED ABOUT, BUT AGAIN, BECAUSE OF THE REASSESSMENT PERIOD. EVEN THOUGH THE LADY MAY NOT REALIZE THE STAGGERING IMPACT OF THIS TRANSITION, SHE WILL RECOGNIZE HER PASSAGE THROUGH IT WHEN SHE COMES OUT THE OTHER SIDE, AS SHE MUST DO. HER ABILITY TO BE COUNSELED IS APPARENT AND HER CONFIDENCE IS EASILY RESTORED WHEN SHE REALLY THINKS HER PRESENT SITUATION THROUGH. MOMENTARY SETBACKS AND MANY DOUBTS ARE THE HALLMARK OF THIS TRANSITION PERIOD, WHICH WE CALL THE MID-LIFE MONAD. SHE WOULD DO WELL TO VERBALIZE THIS MORE WITH CONTACTS WHO HAVE HAD SIMILAR EXPERIENCES AND CAN IDENTIFY WITH HER FEELINGS.

DEBTS FROM ANOTHER TIME ARE ALSO AT THE FORE-FRONT NOW, WHICH PUTS EVEN MORE STRAIN ON THE MO-MENT. DEBTS OWED HER ARE IN THE MAJORITY AND SHE MUST EXERCISE MUCH CAUTION IN DEALING WITH THOSE TO WHOM SHE FEELS NEGATIVE TIES. SHE CAN LISTEN TO THIS INFORMATION AND GAIN FROM THE WARNING. OLD DEBTS OFTEN GIVE RISE TO SHARP FEELINGS OF NEGATIVITY

WHEN THEY FIRST REAPPEAR. WHEN CAUGHT UP IN THE WEB OF REPAYMENT, THERE IS A STRONG COMPULSION TO GET THE DEBT OVER WITH, AS WELL AS A STRONG DESIRE TO AVOID THE ONE WHO OWES ENTIRELY.

THE LADY IS A FIFTH-LEVEL MATURE SCHOLAR IN THE OBSERVATION MODE WITH A GOAL OF DOMINANCE IN THE EMOTIONAL PART OF INTELLECTUAL CENTER, A SKEPTIC, AND WITH A CHIEF FEATURE OF STUBBORNNESS. YOU MUST NOT CONFUSE THE ROLE OF SCHOLAR WITH SCHOLARSHIP, OF COURSE. THIS LADY WAS NOT A BRILLIANT STUDENT, BUT AFTER INCARNATING THIRTY-SEVEN TIMES, SHE NO LONGER CARES ABOUT GOOD GRADES. WE HAVE SAID THAT MATURE SOULS DO NOT ALWAYS PURSUE EDUCATION IN THE INSTITUTIONAL SENSE. THE LADY IN QUESTION HAS OB-TAINED HER GREATEST EDUCATION AWAY FROM SCHOOLS, ON HER OWN INITIATIVE. IN MATURE AND OLD SOULS A CONCERN FOR GRADES IS ONLY A PRODUCT OF FALSE PER-SONALITY. WHERE INTELLECTUAL ACCOMPLISHMENTS ARE SCORNED, THE DELIBERATE REJECTION OF LEARNING IS ALSO A PRODUCT OF FALSE PERSONALITY.

IN DEALING WITH THIS LADY, WE WOULD THINK THAT A STRAIGHTFORWARD AND SUPPORTIVE APPROACH WOULD BE THE BEST AND MOST REWARDING.

Hector MacMillan, who goes by the nickname Terry, fi-nally got up nerve enough to ask a question of Michael. "Walter got my overleaves for me, and I have no argument with them, but I want to know if my daughter is in my entity."

THIS DOES HAPPEN, BUT IT IS EXTREMELY RARE. IN THIS CASE, THERE ARE MANY PAST ASSOCIATIONS WITH THE FRAGMENT. YOU HAVE BEEN PART OF A RELIGIOUS GROUP THAT WAS PERSECUTED. YOU HAVE EXPLORED THE ROCKY MOUNTAINS AT THE END OF THE EIGHTEENTH CENTURY, COMMON RECKONING. THERE WAS A DEBT INCURRED IN THAT LIFE THAT WAS PAID IN THE LIFE BEFORE THIS, AND NOW THERE IS ONLY THE STRONG TIE OF SHARED EXPERI-ENCES. THERE IS STILL A LITTLE DISCOMFORT FROM THE KARMIC RELATIONSHIP, BUT AS THE CHILD GROWS OLDER, THAT TENSION SHOULD DISAPPEAR.

Laurence Silva also decided to ask something. "I've been studying history for several years, as a hobby. I was curious about the Etruscans. No one seems to know where they came from or who they were. Can Michael give me an answer?''

THE ETRUSCANS WERE ORIGINALLY A TRIBE OF GEORGIAN NOMADS WHO MADE THE LONG TREK TO THE CARPATHIAN REGION OF EASTERN EUROPE, WHERE THEY SETTLED FOR A WHILE. AT THAT TIME THEY WERE ILLITERATE AS THEIR LIFESTYLE IN THE NORTH WAS BARBARIC AND NOT CONDUCIVE TO STUDY AND LEARNING. THERE WERE IN THAT REGION AT THAT TIME TRIBES RELATED TO THE INDIGENOUS TRIBES OF NORTHERN ITALY, AND SLOWLY THIS MORE AGGRESSIVE GROUP BEGAN TO EXPAND INTO THE WESTERN REGION. FINALLY WHEN THERE WAS A SUFFICIENTLY LARGE NUMBER, THESE PROTO-ETRUSCANS ONCE MORE HEADED WEST, BEGINNING A SERIES OF TERRITORIAL WARS THAT RESULTED IN THE KILLING OFF OF MOST OF THE MALES IN THE INDIGENOUS POPULATION, AND THE SEXUAL CAPTURE OF MOST OF THE FEMALES. THIS ADMIXTURE SETTLED THROUGHOUT NORTHERN ITALY, ALTHOUGH THE MORE FAVORABLE CONDITIONS IN WHAT IS NOW TUSCANY DICTATED THAT THE MOST SUCCESSFUL SETTLEMENTS WOULD BE THERE, AND IT WAS THERE THAT THE CENTER OF GOVERNMENT AND CULTURE FINALLY EMERGED.

THE ETRUSCAN LANGUAGE IS MOSTLY DESCRIPTIVE RATHER THAN PHILOSOPHICAL AND CONSISTS OF LETTER PHRASES RESEMBLING AN IDEOGRAPH. FOR INSTANCE, A CHARACTER DENOTING MOVEMENT TOWARD THE WEST APPEARED CONSISTENTLY WHERE DESCRIPTIONS OF SKIRMISHING OCCUR, A MARK NOT UNLIKE A CHICKEN FOOT WITH THREE PRONGS FACING TO THE RIGHT OF THE TABLET. WHEN THIS PARTICULAR SYMBOL WAS ENLARGED, IT MEANT A VICTORY. WHEN IT SHOWED SOME PRONGS BROKEN, IT MEANT DEFEAT.

"OK," said Laurence, looking apprehensive. "Were there really Amazons?"

SEVERAL TIMES IN HISTORY THERE HAVE BEEN TRIBES WHERE THE WARRIORS WERE FEMALES, BUT IF YOU MEAN WAS THERE ONE SPECIFIC TRIBE OR GROUP THAT WERE THE TRUE AMAZONS, THEN THE ANSWER IS NO.

"Is there a way I can find out the errors in recorded history?" Laurence asked, looking uneasily around.

WE WILL BE ABLE TO TELL YOU WHEN RECORDED HISTORY IS IN ERROR. YOU HAVE ONLY TO ASK.

"I have a question," Lucy said brightly. "Will Michael tell me if this strong feeling I have toward this new man in my life—his name's Robert—is promising?"

IT IS PROMISING THAT YOU ARE INTERESTED AND ABLE TO FORM NEW RELATIONSHIPS. THE MAN IS A MATURE PRIEST AT THE SIXTH LEVEL . . .

"Ick," Lucy said. "That sixth level is always hell."

IN THE CAUTION MODE WITH A GOAL OF GROWTH, A PRAGMATIST WITH A CHIEF FEATURE OF SELF-DEPRECATION . . .

"Never mind." Lucy sighed. "I was afraid of that."

THE BODY TYPES ARE COMPATIBLE.

"I *know* that. I was hoping that there was something else at work, but I guess not."

Jim Vernett had opened a book, and now sat in the corner, conspicuously shutting the session out.

"I've got another question," said Matt, apparently embarrassed by Jim's behavior. "Why should we bother with this stuff?"

BECAUSE YOU CHOOSE TO DO SO.

"Will any of us understand it in this lifetime?"

IF YOU WORK VERY HARD.

"Is it even necessary that we understand it?" Emily asked.

IT IS NOT NECESSARY. EVENTUALLY, IN OTHER LIVES, IT MAY BE.

"Then why should we bother?" Matt asked.

TO LEARN. TO KNOW. TO SATISFY YOUR CURIOSITY. TO BE FREE.

"Is that enough?" Walter asked.

IT IS ALL THERE IS.

Epilogue,
Dictated by Michael

THIS TEACHING IS OFFERED TO YOU FREELY AND WITHOUT CONDITIONS.

HOWEVER, WE WOULD ABOVE ALL PREFER THAT THIS PUBLICATION NOT INDUCE WIDESPREAD BELIEF OR FAITH IN THIS SYSTEM, FOR THAT WOULD DEFEAT OUR PURPOSE IN TRANSMITTING THE SYSTEM TO YOU; FOR AFTER ALL, THIS SYSTEM TEACHES PRIMARILY THAT TRUTH ON THE PHYSICAL PLANE IS A MANY-SPLENDORED THING INDEED, AND WHAT IS TRUE FOR A BABY SLAVE IN THE POWER MODE IS ALMOST NEVER TRUE FOR AN OLD PRIEST IN THE OBSERVATION MODE. AS WE HAVE SAID MANY TIMES, BELIEF OR FAITH IN ANYTHING IS DESTRUCTIVE RATHER THAN CONSTRUCTIVE FOR IT DENOTES BLINDNESS OF THE SORT THAT DRIVES THE LEMMINGS INTO THE SEA.

SKEPTICISM IS THE ATTITUDE THAT HAS PRODUCED THE MOST STARTLING AND INNOVATIVE THOUGHT IN THE HISTORY OF HUMANKIND, AND ALL OF ALIENKIND ALSO, WE MIGHT ADD. THE OBSERVATION MODE, OF COURSE, PRODUCES THE SUPPLY TO MEET THE DEMAND, BECAUSE IT IS THE NATURE OF THAT MODE TO NOTICE THINGS.

WE GIVE THIS SYSTEM ONLY AS A TOOL THAT YOU MAY USE IN YOUR LIFE-TASKS TO AID YOU IN THE UNDERSTAND-

ING OF THE LIFE CYCLE. THIS WE OFFER AS THE PURPOSE OF THE LIFE CYCLES: MAN BEGINS AS A SOLITARY HUNTER, AN ANIMAL ON THE PROWL. DURING THE LIFE CYCLE, MAN MUST LEARN TO MERGE WITH HIS FELLOWMEN AS THIS IS THE ULTIMATE STEP THAT MAN MUST TAKE BEFORE HE CAN PASS ONTO THE NEXT LEVEL OF EVOLUTION, THAT OF THE MID-ASTRAL BODY. IT TAKES ALL OF THE MANY LIVES THAT MAN MUST LIVE TO LEARN THIS SIMPLE LESSON AND ALL OF THE PAIN—AND YES, THE AGONY OF THE PHYSICAL PLANE RELATES TO THE TERRIBLE ISOLATION THAT MAN EXPERI-ENCES AS HE CLIMBS THE LADDER OF EVOLUTION FROM THE SOLITARY PREDATOR TO THE EXALTED PLATEAU OF EN-LIGHTENMENT.

ALTHOUGH IT SHOULD NOT BE NECESSARY, WE WILL STATE HERE AGAIN THAT SOULS ARE WITHOUT GENDER OR SEX, AND THAT WE USE THE WORD "MAN" PURELY FOR CONVENIENCE, NOT TO IMPLY ANY INFERIORITY OR SUPE-RIORITY BY SEXUAL OR GENDER DEFINITION. YOUR EXPE-RIENCES AS MALE AND FEMALE ARE EQUALLY VALID, AND THERE IS NO REASON TO ASSUME THAT EITHER GENDER HAS AN INSIDE TRACK TO SPIRITUAL GROWTH.

MOST OF YOU WHO WILL READ THESE WORDS WILL AT SOME LEVEL VERIFY THIS AS TRUE TEACHING. FEW IN THE YOUNGER CYCLES ARE ABLE TO ACHIEVE ANY AMELIORA-TION OF THE AGONIZING LONELINESS. OLDER SOULS LEARN TO GATHER IN THEIR LOVING COTERIES AND THERE BEGIN THE EXPERIENCE OF THE INTEGRATION PROCESS.

ESSENCE ALONE IS CAPABLE OF LIVING TO THE EXTENT NECESSARY FOR THIS INTEGRATION TO OCCUR. THIS WORLD, AS WELL AS MANY OTHER WORLDS, EMPLOYS SYMBOLISM TO EXPLAIN THIS LONGING FOR TRUE INTEGRATION. FOR IN-STANCE, THE MARRIAGE CEREMONY WITH ITS BRAVE NON-SENSE ABOUT BEING ONE FLESH, WHICH IS, OF COURSE, NOT POSSIBLE, AS THE TRUE INTEGRATION IS AVAILABLE ONLY TO THE ESSENCE, AND NOT TO THE BODY. YOU NEED NOT EVEN BE BOTH ON THE SAME SIDE OF THE WORLD TO ES-TABLISH ESSENCE CONTACT.

THE EVOLUTIONARY PROCESS IS AN ORDERLY ONE IN THE SYSTEM WE HAVE TRANSMITTED. WE HAVE ADVANCED A FEW PROCESSES WHEREBY OLDER SOULS CAN IMPROVE THE CHANCES FOR ESTABLISHING ESSENCE CONTACT. NEVER HAVE WE SAID THAT YOU MUST DO THIS OR THAT, ONLY

THAT IF YOU WISH TO ACHIEVE ESSENCE CONTACT, THE MIND MUST BE STILL, AND TO OUR KNOWLEDGE THIS CAN BE ACHIEVED WITH RELATIVE EASE THROUGH THE JUDICIOUS USE OF CERTAIN TECHNIQUES, SUCH AS MEDITATION AND RECALL.

WE ARE NOT THE WAY. WE OFFER YOU OUR OWN EXPERIENCE OF THE ENTIRE LIFE CYCLE AND WHAT IT TAUGHT US COLLECTIVELY. WE WERE, WE REMIND YOU, WARRIORS AND KINGS. WE EXPERIENCED ALL OF LIFE IN THESE ROLES. WE LIVED AS YOU LIVE NOW, IN EXALTED AND ORDINAL ROLES, IN EXALTED AND ORDINAL POSITIONS. WE, AS YOU NOW DO, BRAWLED, FOUGHT, LOVED, MOURNED, AND DIED MANY THOUSANDS OF TIMES. WE LEARNED EVENTUALLY TO LOVE IN THE SENSE OF UNCONDITIONAL ACCEPTANCE THAT WE CALL AGAPE, AND CAME TO A NEW PLANE OF EXISTENCE. THE LEARNING WENT ON, ONLY NOW WE HAD AN INTEGRATED SENSE OF OUR GREATER TASK. NOW, THOUSANDS OF YEARS LATER, WE PASS ONTO ANOTHER PLANE OF EXISTENCE, AND BEFORE WE CAN PASS FROM THIS ONE, THERE APPEAR TO BE ADDITIONAL LESSONS TO BE LEARNED.

WE WILL NOT HAVE FAILED IN ANY HUMAN SENSE IF OUR WORDS FALL ON DEAF EARS, FOR OUR TASK IS NOT TO REQUIRE OR CONVERT, BUT TO IMPART. WE HAVE ONLY TO ANSWER THOSE QUESTIONS TO WHICH YOU SEEK ANSWERS, NOTHING MORE. WE DO NOT PROMISE A PARADISE, OR, FOR THAT MATTER, A HELL, EITHER, ONLY PROGRESSIVE EVOLUTION, THE ULTIMATE STATE OF WHICH IS BLISS, AND WHICH YOU WILL ACHIEVE WITH OR WITHOUT OUR HELP.

MANY OF YOU WILL FIND THE BLEND OF EASTERN AND WESTERN THOUGHT UNPALATABLE AND THAT IS TO BE EXPECTED. IT IS WHEN THIS THOUGHT BECOMES ONE THAT WE WILL SEE PROGRESS BEING MADE. THERE IS SOME TRUTH IN MOST TEACHINGS, BUT TO OUR KNOWLEDGE THERE IS NO TEACHING NOW EXTANT ON THE PHYSICAL PLANE THAT HAS ACCESS TO THE UNIVERSAL TRUTHS THAT MANY OF YOU CREDIT THEM WITH. WE DO NOT HAVE THE LOGOS IN ITS ENTIRETY. IF WE DID, YOU WOULD NOW BE EXPERIENCING THE MANIFESTATION OF THE HIGH MENTAL BODY, AND WE ARE CERTAINLY NOT THAT.

IN MANY WAYS, WE ARE AS UNPREPARED FOR WHAT LIES AHEAD OF US AS YOU ARE FOR WHAT LIES AHEAD OF YOU. THE PRIMARY DIFFERENCE IS THAT WE HAVE ALREADY EX-

PERIENCED ALL THAT YOU WILL EVENTUALLY EXPERIENCE, BOTH ON THE PHYSICAL AND THE ASTRAL PLANES.

IN SUMMATION, THEN—THIS SYSTEM IS OFFERED WITH LOVE. BELIEF OR FAITH IS DEFINITELY NOT REQUIRED, OR EVEN DESIRED, FOR EVOLUTION WILL HAPPEN TO YOU WHETHER OR NOT YOU BELIEVE.

MICHAEL
October 16, 1978